American Writings on Popular Education

The Nineteenth Century

THE AMERICAN HERITAGE SERIES

The American Heritage Series

UNDER THE GENERAL EDITORSHIP OF
LEONARD W. LEVY AND ALFRED F. YOUNG

American Writings on Popular Education

The Nineteenth Century

RUSH WELTER

Bennington College

THE BOBBS-MERRILL COMPANY, INC.

INDIANAPOLIS · NEW YORK

In memory of M.E.W.,
who practiced what they preached

Foreword

The American Heritage Series was created to provide the essential primary sources of the American experience, especially of American thought. It constitutes a documentary library of American history, filling a need long felt among scholars, students, libraries, and general readers for authoritative collections of original materials. Some volumes illuminate the thought of significant individuals, such as James Madison or John Marshall; some deal with movements, such as the Antifederalist or the Populist; others are organized around special themes, such as Puritan political thought or American Catholic thought on social questions. Many volumes take up the large number of subjects traditionally studied in American history for which surprisingly there are no documentary anthologies; others pioneer in introducing new subjects of increasing importance to scholars and to the contemporary world. The series aspires to maintain the high standards demanded of contemporary editing, providing authentic texts, intelligently and unobtrusively edited. It also has the distinction of presenting pieces of substantial length which give the full character and flavor of the original. The series is, we believe, the most comprehensive and authoritative of its kind.

Leonard W. Levy
Alfred F. Young

Contents

Introduction

POPULAR EDUCATION AND DEMOCRACY
IN AMERICAN AND ENGLISH THOUGHT

The nineteenth century witnessed the development of public school systems intended to provide at least an elementary education for every child in the nation. This development was by no means peculiar to the United States—indeed, many seemingly American innovations were really imitations of European practice—but it was one of the striking facts about the young republic. For a variety of reasons, and in spite of the obstacles that regional differences and a federal form of government put in the way of any truly national system of schools, Americans succeeded in establishing public elementary education through the length and breadth of their country. They also went on to develop the public high school and the public university to the extent that by 1900 in many states an able graduate of the public schools could continue his education at public expense at least as far as the bachelor's degree, provided he could afford to feed, clothe, and support himself during the interval of his training.

During the twentieth century Americans have repeatedly discovered that the educational system they have inherited does not meet the standards of democracy that were imputed to the early common schools. Today's concern over the education of children in the black ghetto is only the most recent instance of such discoveries, which previously attached to women, to immigrants, to members of the working class, and to children who were culturally deprived by the circumstances of their families. Nevertheless, the vision of popular education Americans adopted during the nineteenth century was an important contribution to modern theories of education, for it stated the terms by which Americans would judge their failures as well as their successes. Without the precedent of nineteenth-century concepts of democracy and education, the very issues we debate today would have little meaning.

Stated in very general terms, the development of a characteristically American attitude toward popular education took the form of a gradual substitution of essentially democratic models of education for essentially republican ones. The distinction turns on the difference between a selective educational system geared to serving the needs of society by discovering, training, and elevating talented children to the positions for which they are most suited, and an egalitarian educational apparatus intended to equip every child with the necessary minimum of information and character to enable him to take his place as an autonomous being in a free society governed by popular suffrage. At most, this difference was only a difference in tendency and emphasis: democrats were not averse to rewarding talent, and their republican predecessors were often eager to extend primary education to everyone. But the difference did exist, and the history of American education is in large part a history of the insistent democratization of every level of schooling.

It is also a history of the increasing investment of public funds in the building, maintenance, administration, and improvement of formal educational systems. Bernard Bailyn has emphasized the extent to which education took place in the American colonies quite independently of schools, and Lawrence Cremin has pointed out the peculiar bias in the historiography of American education caused by Ellwood P. Cubberley's commitment to publicly administered and tax supported schools as vehicles of popular education during the educational awakening of the 1830s and 1840s. These recent admonitions are necessary correctives to histories of schooling that masquerade as histories of education, but they may distract us from the fact that during the nineteenth century (which was our first century of educational reform) Americans turned with ever greater enthusiasm to the extension and improvement of public educational institutions to achieve social ends they feared that established modes of education could not or would not reach. If Americans today identify education with their schools, it is not only because of their historians; it is also because of educational commitments made in the nineteenth century.

At the same time, while most Americans increasingly came to look upon public elementary schools, and subsequently upon public high schools and universities, as crucially important vehicles for the political and economic ends they had in view, they also came to define democracy itself in terms of informal educational processes. This was especially true of commentators of various shades of political opinion who were convinced that the American nation had somehow failed to achieve the full range of values they believed it stood for; in effect, they argued that democratic processes must educate public opinion in order to enable the democracy to refine its goals and to understand how to achieve them. Here as in the formal institutional sense Americans owed a good deal to the tenets of European liberalism, which held not only that every voter must be educated but also that the processes of politics should be deliberative rather than coercive. But they also introduced characteristic emphases of their own. On the radical side of political discourse, at least as radicalism was measured in the United States, they frequently maintained that substantial political and economic changes could be achieved by educational means. In other words, they very largely failed to consider whether education was an adequate cure for social evils because they were so sure that the development of additional educational devices would in fact enable the democracy to overcome them. On the conservative side, they continued to look to the influence of educated men and to the processes of public deliberation to combat public evils, meanwhile pressing reform of the schools to ensure that public deliberation would begin at a sufficiently high level to be instructive in practice as well as in theory. Radicals and conservatives alike looked to voluntary educational institutions—the lyceum and the library, the workingmen's association and the farm organization, even the labor union and the settlement house—to disseminate knowledge and enable every interested citizen to make his way in the world. The public schools were only the initial step in a life most educated Americans believed would be constantly devoted to education.

This volume is a documentary account of the evolution of the characteristic American faith. It opens with a number of typically republican discussions of education in which the problems the new republic faced have obviously caused men of widely differing temperaments to call for more systematic provision for the education of the people. Their opinions range from the liberal enthusiasm expressed by the young Nicholas Biddle for a system of schools that would eradicate class differences and enable every American citizen to enjoy the fruits of republican liberty, to the rather constrained vision of popular education expressed by Thomas Cooper, the friend of Thomas Jefferson, who obviously considered popular literacy a social necessity but contemplated an hierarchical apparatus of educational institutions devoted more clearly to the organic needs of society than to equality of opportunity. In his later years Jefferson himself hovered somewhere between Biddle and Cooper in his attitudes toward education, as his letter to Joseph Cabell indicates. Committed above all to the University of Virginia, he

also valued the preliminary education of the people and favored a system of schools that would offer an opportunity to
poor but talented children to rise to positions of eminence and
public trust. But he did not press public support for elementary
education with the same vigor as his fellow-Virginian, Charles
Fenton Mercer, a distinctly conservative advocate of public
schools for whom the power of the state and the legitimacy of
public expenditures did not cause the doubts they did for Jefferson. The most successful advocate among this early group
was probably Governor De Witt Clinton of New York, who
lived in a state in which a system of public education had been
initiated during the 1790s (as it had not been in the states to
the south), and whose often-reiterated support for popular education both reflected and influenced contemporary republican
sentiments.

At the same time, Clinton's messages indicated the
mixed and relatively hesitant nature of the provision for education that even advanced states were likely to make during the
1820s. So far as public funds were concerned, New York obviously hoped to meet its obligations by providing a common
school fund, the interest of which was to go toward the encouragement of public education. Otherwise, local school districts had to meet the costs of education, and it was customary
for them to make up the difference between public funds (their
own and the state's) with rate bills for tuition imposed on those
who could pay them. Hence New York State retained vestiges
of the pauper system of schooling, which was a major source of
complaint in Pennsylvania and elsewhere. Equally important,
Clinton looked to a private incorporated body, the Public
School Society, to help support and administer public education in New York City. The fact was important, not because
Clinton had long been active in the conduct of the Society, but
because it meant that the education of the urban poor would
be left to a combination of public and private enterprise.
Urgent as the needs of urban education may have been, its
best friends were either unwilling or unable to visualize it as a

predominantly public responsibility. They could be content with a mixed basis for education as long as their aspirations or their anxieties remained relatively modest.

Even new needs would be met in the first instance by public-spirited men rather than elected officials. The metamorphosis of the Free School Society of New York into a Public School Society exemplified the leadership that private agencies lent to educational reform; so did the multiplying efforts of pedagogical reformers, who undertook through institutes and publications to convey new methods of pedagogy to a teaching profession and a public who were largely unaware of them and often hostile when aware. Nor did these reformers confine themselves merely to pedagogical matters; the 1830s saw a proliferation of voluntary associations devoted to exploring and publicizing questions of school organization, curriculum, and equipment—all innovations that would become the responsibility and the focus of state boards and state superintendents of education when the states had assumed the full burden of public school systems. William C. Woodbridge's *American Annals of Instruction,* which William Ellery Channing reviewed in 1833, was an early effort of this sort; so was the Western Literary Institute and College of Professional Teachers at Cincinnati, whose annual *Transactions* served much the same purpose.

The lyceum was still another instance of private energies devoted to public purposes. On the one hand, as the statement by Josiah Holbrook indicates, it was intended to be an informal vehicle of individual self-improvement roughly comparable to the private academy and appealing to a literate and intellectually active population. The 1820s and 1830s saw the introduction of a number of such associations and institutes, usually geared to the dissemination of technical and scientific information (which the academies and colleges ignored) and premised upon the existence of elementary schools. On the other hand, the lyceum also foreshadowed the board of education and the normal institute: at least in the eyes of its founders and sponsors, who included many of the dignitaries of New England, it was intended to raise the level of primary instruction by encouraging pedagogical innovation and improving instructional equipment. In this sense it represented a dawning awareness that the educational establishment left by the founding fathers was inadequate or even seriously defective in reaching public needs.

Not everyone was willing to attend the schools and institutions that public and private enterprise together provided. The pamphlet *The Public Schools, Public Blessings* issued by the Public School Society in 1837 provides a good deal of insight into the paternalistic terms in which well-meaning advocates of schools sometimes visualized their establishments, as well as something of their sense that education must be used to combat pauperism and other social problems. Beyond this, it may suggest why even the friends of voluntary institutions turned increasingly to public agencies to secure universal education. At any rate, during the 1830s and 1840s educational reformers advocated systematic public provision for education, modeled as often as not on educational innovations in Prussia. The innovations they championed ranged across the whole practice of elementary instruction, taking account of such various needs as buildings, furnishings, and books as well as curriculum, methods of instruction, and methods of punishment, but their primary efforts were devoted to showing that only tax supported schools managed by public agencies could provide effectively for the children who most needed to be educated. By the same token, they more or less put aside questions of secondary and higher education until the elementary needs of the republic had been met; virtually the only interest they took in education beyond the elementary level was the interest they expressed in training teachers to make the primary schools more effective. The extracts from Henry Barnard's *Connecticut Common School Journal* and from Horace Mann's *Common School Journal* exemplify their range of interests and their generous if exaggerated hopes.

Even in New England there were several major obstacles to fully public school systems. One was the existence of private academies and other institutions to which prosperous parents were in the habit of sending their children; these parents sometimes resisted the improvement of public schools, partly because improvements at public expense meant increased taxes, and partly because they adhered to the belief (which had been relatively plausible during the early republic) that anyone who really wanted an education could already acquire it. (In addition, some diehards held that public elementary education would demoralize the lower classes by educating them above their station.) A closely related obstacle lay in the fact that a good many parents resisted common school education because it clearly implied education in a nondenominational setting, whereas the parents believed that to be moral education must be infused with religious principles. This was part of the context of the state legislature's quarrel with Horace Mann in Massachusetts. A Unitarian himself, Mann sought to promote a vaguely Protestant rather than a specifically Calvinist attitude toward life, and a number of legislators resented the attempt even though (or perhaps because) it had been an established objective of schooling in Massachusetts for over a decade.

The criticisms leveled at Mann in Massachusetts also had their roots in the antagonism that the Democratic party and a good many of its adherents felt toward the centralization and consolidation of political authority. Although the educational reformers generally complained that their various state school systems almost totally lacked direction, every step they took to establish a curriculum, to set minimum standards for teachers, and to secure improvements in buildings and equipment not only cost school districts money but also encroached on their autonomy. In effect, reformers asserted that unless their standards were met no education worth the name could take place, and rural democrats often responded—at least for a time—by asserting that what had been good enough for them would be good enough for their children, whether or not the secretary of the board of education agreed. The fact that many reformers drew their inspiration from Prussia and were at best rather reticent democrats lent weight to the opposition's charges.

Finally, the urban population that many reformers were most concerned to educate was often very largely Roman Catholic in religious persuasion. For this reason it resented even the nondenominational Protestantism the public schools sought to teach, and in New York City (where public funds were administered by the Public School Society as late as 1853) it had reason to demand that parochial schools share in the distribution of public funds. As the documents printed here show, the demand precipitated a violent controversy, which was intensified when Governor William H. Seward urged the state legislature to honor the proposal on the grounds that the children of immigrants must be educated for the sake of the republic as well as themselves. The controversy could be settled only by depriving the Public School Society of state funds and converting its schools into truly public schools administered by local school committees. Even this solution did not answer to the complaints of Roman Catholics, who rightly observed that the public school system that resulted was not Catholic, and whose leaders therefore renewed their efforts to establish a parochial school system paralleling the public system. But it generally satisfied Protestants, and may indeed have helped to reconcile them to a merely Protestant education, as Horace Bushnell's sermon on the common schools suggests.

Although changes sometimes took place in defiance of popular prejudices, the achievement of tax supported schools owing at least a shadowy allegiance to state-wide institutions of supervision also marked the fruition of various democratic efforts to convert the educational system established during the early years of the republic into an agency of democratic purposes. One force for educational reform was the repeated pro-

tests of "workingmen's" associations and parties, which spoke
for craftsmen and other small entrepreneurs during the late
1820s and early 1830s, that the established educational system
of the republican era favored the wealthy and demeaned aspiring men who worked with their hands. In Philadelphia committees of workingmen charged that their state's hierarchy
of educational institutions (extending from pauper schools to
colleges) and the curriculum of these same institutions (devoted to a predominantly literary training) were prejudicial to
equality. Similar groups made similar charges not only in Boston and New York but also in secondary urban centers like
Washington and Newark, and various spokesmen for labor reform continued their clamor during the 1840s. By this means
the workingmen gave an impetus to educational reforms that
other spokesmen for the producing classes more or less ignored,
and they also helped to spread the belief that universal elementary education would serve individual economic ends. The first
impulse of these democratic reformers was political, the wish to
protect their kind against the encroachments of "aristocracy"
and "monopoly," but the long-run impact may have been to
justify both so long as they were arrived at by equal competition.

Meanwhile many of the Democrats who bridled at
administrative centralization and called specific pedagogical
reforms into question gave evidence of their fundamental
attachment to popular education as a vehicle of democratic
liberties. Governor Morton's message to the Massachusetts
legislature expressed a devotion to common schools and common school districts as nurseries of democracy, and even the
legislative committee that seized upon his words as an occasion
for belaboring educational reform made a clear distinction between public education and its administration; in essence, both
identified democracy with the local administration of educational institutions that all parties conceded were indispensable
to freedom. Nor was it only in Massachusetts that the com-

mon school came to seem the palladium of American liberties. In most of the nation—West as well as East, South as well as North—democrats as well as reformers began to make systematic provision for public schooling even where none had been made before. Their accomplishments were epitomized in the deliberations of a whole host of state constitutional conventions, in which the advocates of education sought to incorporate basic provisions affecting the establishment, support, and supervision of public schools into the fundamental law of their states.

The deliberations of these conventions were especially significant because they reflected the triumph of Democratic dogmas of equality and of Democratic opposition to paternalism in government, which had been taken for granted by leaders of the National Republican party and by many of their Whig successors. On the traditional view of society, which these leaders inherited, state governments had the right and indeed the responsibility to encourage material prosperity, the diffusion of knowledge, and public happiness by a variety of means, most of which came down to lending the authority and sometimes the credit of the state to otherwise private economic enterprises. Hence republican legislatures had chartered banks and canal corporations, had assigned privileges like eminent domain and limited liability to the sponsors of internal improvements, and had granted funds to private colleges and academies as well as common schools. On the Democratic view, which owed something to the Jeffersonian Republicans but more to popular resentment of contemporary social changes associated with urban and industrial development, these legislative activities were both unequal and unwise: unequal in bestowing legal privileges on the favorites of the legislature, unwise in creating so-called artificial economic patterns in place of the so-called natural ones that had previously governed economic activity. Under these circumstances, the fact that most state conventions of the 1840s and 1850s provided in some small measure for a system of public schools was extraordinary testimony to the attachment Americans felt for education at public expense.

Some conventions also confronted a number of secondary issues that public education created. One was the role religion might play in the schools, which the Ohio convention "resolved" by denying state funds to "sectarian" institutions without examining the degree to which its public Protestant institutions might be thought sectarian. (In effect, it enacted into fundamental law the established American conviction that the only solution to religious differences was to remove them from the power of the state to influence for good or evil.) Another issue the Ohio convention dealt with was the rights Negroes might claim in a white society—not only suffrage, but education as the guarantee for all other rights. As the Ohio debates indicate, most white Americans were loathe to admit blacks to equal standing either at the polls or in their schools, and those who were most inclined to obliterate distinctions of race were often those who were least inclined to adopt the democratic dogmas of the age. Democrats who honored common schools usually gave short shrift to the claims of the nation's minorities because they did not define democracy so as to include those who were radically different from themselves.

Nevertheless, democratic resistance to schooling for free Negroes did not seriously undermine popular support for other egalitarian and liberal principles. Only dyspeptic conservatives like Francis Lieber and highly principled Democrats like James Fenimore Cooper followed Alexis de Tocqueville in assuming that equality and liberty were incompatible; other men were more likely to equate the one with the other and both with the diffusion of knowledge. This was true not only of commentators who spoke up for the common schools but also of those who appealed to a vision of free institutions as themselves educating and elevating mankind. Philosophically inclined democrats like George Camp and Frederick Grimke made much of this vision; so did rather more conservative figures like William Ellery

Channing and Nathan S. S. Beman. Channing extrapolated his extreme religious individualism into a theory that schools and life alike must be remodeled in order to elicit individual capabilities in spite of adventitious social distinctions. Beman argued that the whole of American life was educational in the sense of nurturing the fullest personal achievements and the greatest political wisdom individuals are capable of. Significantly, in 1823 a liberal republican writer, Charles Jared Ingersoll, had delivered an enthusiastic address before the American Philosophical Society on the influence of America on the mind; in 1846 Beman spoke to "The Influence of Freedom on Popular and National Education." In the eyes of such enthusiasts, democracy and education merged, and both were identical with liberty.

The only substantial challenge to the liberal democratic vision of education that evolved during the 1840s and 1850s came from southern apologists who made the fact of Negro slavery into grounds for denying that education and democracy were compatible. Southern spokesmen were by no means unanimous in making this charge; both the address Henry Wise sent his constituents in 1844 and the report the committee on education submitted to the constitutional convention of Louisiana in 1845 demonstrate the commitment southern leaders often expressed, while they also point to some of the circumstances that delayed development of systems of public education in the South. As the sectional controversy deepened, however, southern spokesmen became increasingly shrill in the defense of their peculiar institution, and by the 1850s it was a commonplace for southern magazines like the *Southern Quarterly Review* and even *De Bow's Review* to attack northern democracy as both unfree and illiterate. At worst, the apologists for slavery insisted that slavery was preferable to liberty for the producing classes; more typically, they took comfort from the fact that Negro slavery in the South made white slavery unnecessary. In either case the thrust of their argument was clear: they denied that men who worked with their hands could be sufficiently

well educated to govern themselves, and they ridiculed northern pretensions to ground democracy in education.

In doing so, they threw down a challenge to northern
democrats that was to haunt the South as sectional hostilities
deepened into civil war, for the ultimate outcome of southern
intransigence was to unite many shades of northern opinion in
a crusade to remake the South on the northern democratic
model. Here former conservatives and men who had only a
minimal sympathy with democratic dogmas like free trade and
popular sovereignty took the lead in shaping northern action,
but they did so in the light of liberal social aspirations that cul-
minated in popular education. Colonel Christopher C. Andrews
spoke for many northerners when he told the people of Little
Rock, recently occupied by Union forces, that the South had
seceded because its people were uneducated; it followed that
Henry Ward Beecher should greet the closing moments of the
war by urging his countrymen to trust to the education of the
freedmen to perfect their freedom. The terms in which he did
so demonstrated beyond any possibility of a doubt that he had
embraced democracy as well as education in his definition of
liberty.

Events after the war were to disappoint Beecher's hopes.
More generally, they should have called the American faith in
education into question, for the diffusion of knowledge did not
prevent a wide range of social evils that worsened as time
passed. Nevertheless, the war itself seems to have confirmed
American belief that the absence of education was a primary
cause of most of the nation's troubles and that the further provision of education would cure them. At any rate, Americans
turned with surprising energy to discovering or elaborating educational devices intended to make other devices unnecessary.
There were significant exceptions to this general rule: a good
many Roman Catholics joined in criticism of the public schools
because of their obviously Protestant and increasingly secular
orientation, while German-speaking Lutherans and other immi-

grant groups also found the American consensus in religion and education threatening to their cherished values. Even so, these dissidents were far from opposing education itself, as the argument of the *American Ecclesiastical Review* and of the opponents of Wisconsin's Bennett Law indicated late in the century. The issue between Catholic and Protestant or between immigrant and native involved the application and not the foundation of a common faith.

Certainly the Reconstruction of the South came to a focus in formal education. Granting northern explanations of the war, granting also the northern wish to initiate democratic institutions in the South, it followed that both white and black southerners who sympathized with Reconstruction should also accept the classic northern prescription for their society's problems. The debate in the constitutional convention of South Carolina illustrates both the deliberation with which the so-called radicals sought to change the structure of their society and the immense hopes they attached to public schooling. It also suggests the extent to which with the best of intentions the friends of the freedman left him substantially to his own devices, as if the public provision of an elementary education could make him overnight into a competent American democrat; but the testimony C. H. Johnson offered the Blair Committee in 1883 indicates that blacks as well as whites were likely to make this mistake long after Reconstruction had ended.

Meanwhile northern writers who had begun to sense the enormous problems that the nation as a whole confronted because of the war, because of industrial and urban concentration, and because of the growing gap between the rich and the poor, began to clamor for a more effective and a more extended system of public education to complete the work an earlier generation had begun. To some extent, they may have been influenced by nationalist sentiment engendered by the war itself; at any rate, William T. Harris, the nation's most prominent Hegelian philosopher, also became its most prominent educational administrator. They were most certainly influenced by a sense that the great emergency of their times warranted direct federal aid to elementary education in spite of constitutional scruples and historic precedents to the contrary. Initially the advocates of federal aid sought to devote it to schools in the South; before long, however, they had adopted the more general (and also politically more appealing) plan of allotting funds derived from sale of the public domain to the states according to their illiteracy rates as determined by the federal census. Former Senator James W. Patterson's address on the subject summarizes the case its advocates made in behalf of this unmistakably conservative measure.

Patterson's address also indicates that the idea of ensuring universal elementary education continued to involve liberal and democratic hopes. For one thing, it seemed to open the door to individual opportunities for advancement and self-culture; Patterson may have been naïve but he was not disingenuous in arguing that the common schools made further accomplishments possible. Senator Justin Morrill of Vermont assumed as much in sponsoring federal grants to agricultural and mechanical colleges; after his initial success in sponsoring the land-grant college act in 1862, he urged Congress to devote additional funds to college and elementary education alike, the better to serve both individual and national purposes. More important, perhaps, such spokesmen for middle-class values as Francis A. Walker attributed great promise to education and to the improvement of education as a means of overcoming industrial evils they could not ignore. Walker's testimony before the Blair Committee probably epitomized the attitudes held by educated men in his day: hostile to the power of government, committed in general to laissez-faire economics, he was ready to turn to legislation if he must but preferred to employ education to obviate economic evils. He also felt, as many of his kind apparently did, that the diffusion of knowledge would enable anyone who chose to rise above a menial position in life.

Walker was a professional economist and president of the Massachusetts Institute of Technology; perhaps it was inevitable that he should stress the improvement of public education and especially industrial education, which was a particular concern of professional educators during the 1880s and 1890s. If so, it is noteworthy that spokesmen for the early farmers' movement, the Patrons of Husbandry, stressed a comparable improvement of education for the agricultural classes. Obviously they held many of the same values and visualized employing much the same technique of social improvement as Walker. So did spokesmen for the later farmers' movements, especially the Northern and Southern Alliances that ultimately gravitated into the Populist party. Although the Grangers toyed with other kinds of reform (chiefly, the regulation of monopolies like grain elevators and railroads), and although the Populists were to advocate a whole series of quite unprecedented reforms ranging from a national subtreasury for farm produce to the eight-hour day in industrial employment, they did have in common the extension and improvement of formal schooling as one of their primary objectives.

Simultaneously they sought to develop an elaborate apparatus of informal education to enable the farmer to assume (as they saw it) his rightful place in society. The Grange was conceived as a school in which men and women might learn the principles of economic cooperation, the techniques of better management, and the principles of nonpartisan political reform. The Alliance followed very largely in its footsteps, and when it turned to partisan politics it did so (as the *National Economist* pointed out) in the belief that a process of popular education initiated by the victims of monopoly and great wealth must eventuate in a new Declaration of Independence, a new birth of freedom for the producing classes throughout the nation.

It is possible to read the expansive hopes and radical exhortations of Populist leaders as a call to action against the liberal economy of their times; a volume in this series has in fact made this case.[1] From the point of view of the attitudes they expressed toward education, however, it seems more plausible to suggest that the Populist leaders looked to a "revolution" that would restore most of the social conditions of the agrarian economy they remembered, by means that were at the same time pacific (grounded in persuasion) and middle-class (committed on the whole to a perfected liberal economy). At any rate, their devotion to education in both its formal and its informal aspects allied them more closely than they may have realized to the prevailing values of their society.

For one thing, it linked them to Terence Powderly of the Knights of Labor, who sought an end to the wages system, but who relied upon an almost mystical conception of "organization and education" to convert the whole of American society into a grand national cooperative. For another, it linked them to Edward Bellamy, whose frankly utopian *Looking Backward* portrayed a nationalized economy that had been arrived at by an undefined revolution in popular feeling. In his sequel to that novel Bellamy was to elaborate both his quarrel with the status quo and the operative mechanisms of the providential economy of the future without either abandoning his essentially middle-class perspective on the good life or his evangelical definition of revolution as conversion and conversion as the product of education. A more truly radical train of thought was exemplified by Laurence Gronlund, a domesticated Danish Marxian who shared many of Bellamy's social values but did not believe that they could be reached by social evangelism.

Even so, the radicalism that farmers and workers voiced caused dismay in the hearts of many men of goodwill. Some of them responded as did Andrew D. White, the former president of Cornell University, who appealed to the authority of educated men to suppress expressions of discontent by teaching

---

[1] *The Populist Mind,* ed. Norman Pollack (Indianapolis and New York: Bobbs-Merrill, 1967).

the public the error of the radicals' ways. In doing so he both built upon and undermined the theory George William Curtis had expressed at Union College in 1877, that college graduates might be the leaven of the democracy, working like the abolitionists before the Civil War to inspire it to its high duties. Curtis became increasingly hostile to the aberrations of party and populace before he died in 1892, but he never fully abandoned the antebellum faith that democracy would elevate itself through the discussion of public questions. By contrast, White represented popular education as a one-way process, an informal agency for disseminating the conclusions of experts in place of popular prejudice and popular ignorance.

Other men who shared many of White's fears sought none the less to meet radicalism part way by persuading the prosperous classes to interest themselves in the condition of labor and other economic developments they were all too likely to visualize in terms of classical political economy. Their orientation was religious and irenic rather than secular and class-conscious, but it eventuated in a deliberate effort—sponsored in different ways by Washington Gladden and the Chautauqua movement—to educate the middle classes to understand their social obligations.

In a different sense, this was also the function of a handful of secular commentators who shared middle-class prejudices but recognized that modern society required much more managing than traditional society had. They concluded that the social sciences were indispensable adjuncts of government and that experts must shape public policies. Francis A. Walker had adumbrated their position, as had Andrew D. White and E. L. Godkin before their emotions were stirred by the specter of populist socialism, but the most compelling spokesman for their cause was probably Charles W. Eliot, the president of Harvard University. Discussing the problems of municipal government in the *Forum*, Eliot not only took account of virtually every problem that beset the United States but also pointed the way to a time when they might be solved by intelligence as well as authority in government. In doing so, he also anticipated the major political developments of the twentieth century.

By 1900, in short, the Americans had achieved a distinctive vision of the ways in which education might serve a democratic society. Although they were far from agreeing among themselves, when allowance is made both for the normal range of opinion and the zeal with which partisans of different policies pressed their respective causes, the extent of their agreement is striking. It is even more striking when we consider the development of public attitudes toward popular education in England, by all odds the nation to which the American republic bore the closest ties. Obviously Great Britain was a constitutional monarchy, and equally obviously it was saddled with the remains of a feudal aristocracy as well as the mementos of its early and often appalling patterns of industrialization; it was to be expected that American attitudes toward education would be as different from English attitudes as American society was different from English society. Nevertheless, comparison may be instructive even if it only recognizes inevitable differences, and the patterns of English thought illuminate the patterns of American thought by their disparities.

We may best begin by calling to mind the circumstances in which public interest in popular education revived in England after the relative disinterest of the period between the Civil Wars and the French Revolution.[2] During the latter half of the eighteenth century, sweeping agricultural changes, an expanding commerce, the early stages of the industrial revolution, and the wars with France uprooted and also impoverished large segments of the laboring population, whom the English governments of that era generally surrendered to their fate

---

[2] The following sections of this introduction are a slightly revised version of an essay I originally drafted for presentation at the Symposium on the Role of Education in Nineteenth-Century America, sponsored by the Committee on the Role of Education in American History. It is used here with their permission.

when they did not actually legislate their dislocation. The chief remedy the authorities were willing to apply was the Poor Laws, and these were incapable either of dealing with the causes of poverty or of elevating the laboring classes to the point at which they might again be self-respecting members of society. Hence philanthropists who interested themselves seriously in the plight of the poor commonly hoped to find some means of improving them rather than merely subsidizing them, and they often turned to education to achieve their ends.

The objectives of that education were simultaneously religious and moral. One of the most distressing symptoms of social and economic dislocation was the appearance of a large population of religious illiterates, whose salvation demanded philanthropic effort. At the same time, the process of social and economic change had undermined traditional moral habits, in the countryside as well as in the towns; it seemed as important to teach the people to be good as it was to teach them the elements of religion. In addition, the thought of the times was inclined to attribute poverty to the moral decay of the poor and thus to suggest moral and religious training as a cure for economic evils. Hence philanthropic Englishmen set to work to create charitable day schools and Sunday schools, where poor children might learn to read the Bible and possibly to spell and to write, not to mention schools of industry and occasional factory schools, which had the advantage of connecting popular education with remunerative labor and thus helped to make charity less burdensome financially. Together with the traditional dame schools these various charitable endeavors provided such formal education as the poorer classes received, or were thought to need, before 1800.

It would be a mistake to minimize the importance or to belittle the motives of this educational philanthropy. Without charity schools of various kinds, a large proportion of the British working classes would have received no education at all, and the objectives of the philanthropists were truly generous. Nevertheless, the basis on which such education was available is significant. In the first place, it was intended solely for the poor. Not only was everyone else expected to pay for the education of his own children, but a stigma was attached to gratuitous instruction in spite of the philanthropy that supported it. Second, even pauper education was to be cheap and so far as possible self-supporting. There was little enough money to devote to the purpose, so long as the state provided none; but the effect of such innovations was to make economy a primary criterion in educating the people. Third, popular education undertaken in these terms was necessarily limited in scope. Not only did it extend only to the most elementary knowledge, which it was thought the worthy poor might enlarge through their own efforts, but it was intended to do no more than restore the religious and moral standing of the working classes. Generous as the early friends of popular education may have been, they did not propose to change the social structure or challenge existing social values.

Where it did not actually undermine educational philanthropy, the French Revolution and the radical agitation it stimulated in England simply reinforced the conservative bias of efforts to educate the people. A number of writers held that it was dangerous to educate the poor at all lest they learn to read Tom Paine. (Paine's proposal to establish compulsory education at public expense probably increased conservative fears.) Other writers concluded that the educated classes must combat French radicalism and infidelity by inculcating sound politics and morals. In pursuit of this aim they hastened to publish tracts and pamphlets designed (although not often well designed) to reach those who were already literate, and they also concerned themselves increasingly with the political orientation of such formal instruction as the poorer classes received. It goes without saying that their activity did not obliterate the stigma that attached to the education of the poor; neither did it challenge the belief that popular education could be accomplished economically and largely through voluntary efforts.

These general circumstances were the context in which

nineteenth-century reformers began to agitate for more systematic provision for popular education, even proposing government intervention to secure it. One mode of government activity was to be the Factory Acts, which were pressed for the most part by members of the Tory party and representatives of the landed interests, and which sought to make formal instruction a corollary or a condition of factory employment. (It was assumed that factory laborers were least likely to be educated and most likely to be dangerous, and in any event factories were a novel development that attracted widespread hostility.) Nevertheless, these Acts hardly challenged the terms on which education was to be provided. They assumed that only factory children required the assistance of the state; they left the conduct of their education to private agencies; and they proposed only the most limited kind of instruction. In addition, they were very largely ineffective because it was all too easy for a parent or an employer to evade the law, and because they extended only to children employed in factories, and in certain kinds of factories at that. Their failure was a comment on the intentions of the legislators as well as on the opposition the Acts aroused.

Most other attempts to educate the poor reflected the desire of essentially utilitarian reformers to remake English society on a competitive middle-class model. In 1803, for example, when Malthus proposed the abolition of the Poor Laws (which served only to encourage overpopulation and its attendant vices), he also urged the establishment of parish schools in which the people might be taught not only reading and writing but also the basic truths of political economy and such practical virtues as sobriety, industry, and frugality.[3] Four years later Samuel Whitbread introduced a general scheme of education along these same lines in Parliament, where he incorporated it into a plan for systematic revision of the Poor Laws intended to

---

[3] T. R. Malthus, *An Essay on the Principle of Population* (New edition) (London: J. Johnson, 1803), Book IV, chapter 8.

"exalt the character of the labouring classes" by encouraging thrift and the acquisition of property.[4]

Because Malthusian theory has been the target of so much abuse it is worth emphasizing that both Malthus and Whitbread visualized their reform as a constructive social innovation, one that would enable the working classes to rise out of the misery to which erroneous economic principles had condemned them. Malthus even held that until the people had been educated the upper classes had no reason to condemn their discontent. Nevertheless, the very fact that these reformers proposed to supplant the Poor Laws with education only reinforced the belief that popular education was a necessary form of charity, while the advocates of Whitbread's plan made clear that in addition to promoting a more prosperous laboring class the plan would serve to make the existing social hierarchy more secure. Their opponents followed precedent by predicting that the cost of educating the poor would be prohibitive; but Whitbread had anticipated their objection by suggesting that parish schools could easily teach a large number of children at minimum expense by following the scheme of monitorial instruction proposed by Joseph Lancaster on the example of Dr. Andrew Bell.[5]

Despite the growing urgency of the problems with which popular education was intended to deal, its advocates were slow to press it as a national responsibility. During the 1810s and 1820s they devoted themselves with increasing zeal to the establishment of monitorial schools supported by either the British and Foreign School Society or the National Society for Promoting the Education of the Poor in the Principles of the Established Church. Although these two groups expressed and

---

[4] Samuel Whitbread, Speech in the House of Commons, 19 February 1807, *Cobbett's Parliamentary Debates*, VIII, 865–918, 875. See also *Hansard's Parliamentary Debates*, IX, 538ff., for his bill.

[5] Debates in the House of Commons, 24 April and 13 July, 1807, *Hansard*, IX, 538–551 and 798–806.

intensified a distinction between Dissenters and Anglicans that was destined to haunt English education for another century, and although the British and Foreign Society was more inclined than its Anglican counterpart to teach practical disciplines and less inclined to teach dogmatic religion, the two were alike in assuming that the education of the poor should depend upon voluntary efforts and need not exceed what could comfortably be taught in a year or two of systematic instruction. Meanwhile Henry Brougham introduced a bill in Parliament in 1820 which would have permitted local authorities in areas that lacked adequate schooling to impose compulsory rates for the support of a schoolmaster. After reintroducing his bill in 1826, however, Brougham abandoned the compulsory principle in 1833, arguing that voluntary measures were fast overcoming the national deficiency and should not be discouraged. In subsequent years he sought to find ways in which the government might encourage popular education without either controlling it or requiring it.[6]

By the 1830s, indeed, the case for popular education was being made in more challenging terms, and it resulted in annual parliamentary grants to the two monitorial school societies to enable them to build additional schoolhouses. Still, the arguments for national education remained limited. In a classic account of the condition of the working classes in Manchester in 1832, James Kay, the physician who was to become the first secretary to the Committee of Council on Education, insisted that only a widespread and extensive education provided by the state would serve to combat the misery and degradation of the poor. Yet Kay also blamed most of the evils he described on paternalistic interferences with free trade, and he made plain

---

[6] See Brougham's speeches in the House of Commons, 8 May 1818, Hansard, XXXVIII, 585–611, and 28 June 1820, *ibid*, n. s., II, 49–66; and in the House of Lords: 14 March 1833, *ibid.*, 3d ser., XVI, 632–639; 21 May 1835, *ibid.*, XXVII, 1293–1333; and 1 December 1837, *ibid.*, 430–466.

that one of his chief objectives in urging the dissemination of virtue and intelligence was to safeguard property and inhibit popular tumult. Much the same motives influenced his wish to extend popular education beyond the level of minimum literacy. "The education afforded to the poor must be substantial," he wrote.

> The mere elementary rudiments of knowledge are chiefly useful, as a means to an end. The poor man will not be made a much better member of society, by being only taught to read and write. His education should comprise such branches of general knowledge as would prove sources of rational amusement, and would thus elevate his tastes above a companionship in licentious pleasures. Those portions of the exact sciences which are connected with his occupation, should be familiarly explained to him, by popular lectures, and *cheap treatises*. . . . The ascertained truths of political science should be early taught to the labouring classes, and *correct* political information should be constantly and industriously disseminated amongst them. . . . The poor might thus be also made to understand their political position in society, and the duties that belong to it—"that they are in a great measure the architects of their own fortune; that what others can do for them is trifling indeed, compared with what they can do for themselves; that they are infinitely more interested in the preservation of public tranquillity than any other class of society; that mechanical inventions and discoveries are always supremely advantageous to them; and that their real interests can only be effectually promoted, by displaying greater prudence and forethought."[7]

---

[7] James Kay-Shuttleworth, "The Condition of the Working Classes of Manchester in 1832," as found in his *Four Periods of Public Education* (London: Longman, Green, Longman, & Robert, 1862), pp. 3–75, 63–64. Kay changed his name to Kay-Shuttleworth on his marriage to Lady Janet Shuttleworth in 1842. His quotation is from John R. McCulloch, the disciple of David Ricardo.

If Kay expressed a generous hope that public education would solve most contemporary problems, he also looked upon it in more restrictive terms than Malthus, who had suggested that it might help to raise the laboring classes to the level of the middle class.

This is not to deny that Kay and his supporters sharply challenged a good many prevailing attitudes toward popular education in the years that followed.[8] They held that voluntary efforts were inadequate; they argued that cheap education was poor economy; they insisted on improving teaching and extending the curriculum; and they made war on critics who permitted religious bias or political inertia to stand in the way of educating the people. Some friends to popular education, among them Richard Cobden, went so far as to urge England to imitate the American republic and establish nondenominational common schools open equally to pupils of every social class and every religious persuasion, while Kay waxed sarcastic in a pamphlet of 1846 in which he castigated conservative clergymen and laymen who saw in popular education only a means to secure "quiet homage" on the part of a race which existed in their eyes "only to labour and to die."[9]

---

[8] Perhaps it should be said that I am deliberately focusing on the political and social perspectives of the educational reformers, ignoring the religious controversies that came to occupy an ever larger place in public discussions of popular education. Religious controversy obviously blocked practical implementation of various plans for public education, but it did not significantly affect the social perspective that shaped those plans. Except for doctrinaire Radicals, all advocates of public support for education seem to have assumed that some religious training was indispensable. In fact, widespread agreement on this proposition was what caused most of the controversy, inasmuch as England was divided religiously. Characteristically, the government resolved the religious issue during the 1840s by extending its grants to educational societies representing the Wesleyans and the Roman Catholics.

[9] Cobden, *England, Ireland, and America* (1835), as found in the *Political Writings of Richard Cobden* (2 vols.; London and New York: Appleton, 1867), I, 121–123, and *Speeches on Questions of Public Policy*, ed.

Nevertheless, the middle-class spokesmen who defined
the terms in which England's educational awakening took place
continued to represent it primarily as a philanthropic conces-
sion to necessity. A large part of their argument with conservative opponents took the form that there was more to fear from
the ignorance than from the education of the lower classes. To
some extent this argument reflected recurrent fears that England was on the verge of proletarian revolution. "It is astonishing to us," Kay wrote at the height of the Chartist agitation,
"that the party calling themselves Conservative should not lead
the van in promoting the diffusion of that knowledge among
the working classes which tends beyond any thing else to promote the security of property and the maintenance of public
order. To restore the working classes to their former state of
incurious and contented apathy is impossible, if it were desirable. If they are to have knowledge, surely it is the part of a
wise and virtuous Government to do all in its power to secure
to them useful knowledge, and to guard them against pernicious opinions."[10] But it also reflected a more general tendency
to urge public education as an investment the prosperous
classes must make in the national welfare. Whereas Brougham
expressed reservations that had to give way before the demonstrated failure of voluntary efforts to educate the whole people,
and whereas Cobden expressed radical and indeed utopian
hopes, Kay epitomized the uneasy combination of humanitarian
concern and political apprehension that gradually forced Brit-
ons to adopt a complex system of popular education based
upon state-supervised schools sponsored by both public and
private authorities and supported by a combination of local

John Bright and James E. Thorold Rogers (2 vols.; London: Macmillan,
1870), II, 567–607 *passim;* Kay-Shuttleworth, "The School, in its Relations to the State, the Church, and the Congregation," *Four Periods of
Public Education,* pp. 495–496.
[10] Kay-Shuttleworth, "Recent Measures for the Promotion of Education in
England" (1839), *Four Periods of Public Education,* p. 232.

rates, state grants, charitable contributions, parental fees, and pauper assistance.[11]

Although the sentiments summarized here gave a characteristic thrust to the development of educational institutions in England, another phenomenon played an ever larger part in determining the context in which Englishmen visualized them. This was the threatened democratization of the suffrage, which was only a distant prospect when Kay first championed public education, but which significantly influenced later developments. As might be expected, the prospect of universal suffrage intensified the anxiety with which many Englishmen committed themselves to popular education; the former Vice President of the Committee of Council on Education spoke for them when, in 1870, he burdened it with the aphorism that "We must educate our masters." But it is more appropriate for us to concern ourselves here with the light in which convinced advocates of democracy perceived it. Not only do they provide a better basis for comparison between English and American

---

[11] The first parliamentary grants, totaling £20,000, were made in 1833. The Committee of Council was established in 1839, when it initiated the inspection of aided schools but failed (for religious reasons) to secure funds for a normal school; in 1846 it introduced a system of apprentice teaching instead. In 1853 the Committee of Council made its first per capita grants to schools that met certain educational standards, and in 1855 Parliament authorized (but did not require) Poor Law Guardians to pay paupers' school fees. By 1857 parliamentary expenditures on education had risen from £30,000 in 1839 and £100,000 in 1846 to £541,233; they were to reach a peak of £813,441 in 1861, when the Revised Code stipulating "payment by results" went into effect. The Elementary Education Act of 1870 established a system of rate-supported public schools but also preserved the system of voluntary schools, which provided well over half of the school places available in 1897. Pauper children's attendance at school was required, and their fees paid, in 1873. Education was made compulsory in 1876; attendance, in 1880; and parents were authorized in 1891 to demand that their children's school fees be paid out of rates. The most convenient account of these developments is to be found in Charles Birchenough, *History of Elementary Education in England and Wales* (Third Edition) (London: University Tutorial Press, 1938).

thought because they shared democratic attitudes; they also constituted a peculiar influence on the terms in which English liberals came to adopt both democracy and education.

There were two main theories of democracy current in England during the nineteenth century. One may be described as the natural-rights theory, which held that every adult male has a right to participate in governing his society. The other developed out of Benthamite utilitarianism, which was hostile to all theories based upon natural rights, and which came to justify manhood suffrage by its presumed consequences. The first theory was discredited not only by Benthamite rationalism but also by the aberrations of working-class leaders like Feargus O'Connor, who identified the rights of man with violent radicalism. The second became the intellectual basis on which Parliament slowly extended the franchise, and as such it stood at the heart of English theories linking democracy and education.

In his early writings, Jeremy Bentham assumed that the legal and penal reforms he championed might be achieved through the voluntary action of King and Parliament as soon as they had grasped the greatest-happiness principle in all of its ramifications. But the English authorities frustrated Bentham's hopes, and by 1817 he had become an outright advocate of radical parliamentary reform including manhood suffrage, the secret ballot, and annual parliaments. In theory, at least, he was sure that popular participation in government would secure, not only the greatest happiness of the greatest number, but also the universal harmony of interests that his early reforms had always intended, by compelling those who were governors to observe the interests of the governed. According to Bentham's new belief, every voter in pursuing his own true interest would automatically contribute a proportionate share to the formation of public policy, which would thereby represent the true interest of all. At the same time, Bentham insisted that each voter must be qualified to know his own true interest, as distinguished from what he might erroneously judge to be his interest. Therefore he proposed to deny the suffrage to soldiers and sailors, mental incompetents, minors, and women, and also to deny it to illiterates. As he saw matters, there was no possibility that the first four categories of citizen (women excepted) might ever achieve the independence voters must have; but he felt that a literacy test offered only a temporary obstacle to manhood suffrage, inasmuch as anyone who wished to vote could master the art of reading in three months' time.[12]

Arguing in this fashion, Bentham made no signal contribution to popular education in England; in fact, he had expressed greater enthusiasm for it in *Principles of Penal Law* (1802?), in which he proposed to extend education to the poor both as a check to crime and as a preliminary step toward combating popular follies and errors through the press. Nevertheless, he succeeded in imposing two intimately related assumptions on the English idea of democracy. In the first place, he asserted that the common people are quite as capable as the aristocracy of recognizing their own true interests and those of society as a whole. In the second place he insisted that participants in government must always meet standards that he categorized under the heading of "appropriate intellectual aptitude."[13]

James Mill elaborated Bentham's occasional remarks into a systematic democratic theory. In 1813 he had already advocated public assistance to the education of the poor, both as a weapon against crime and poverty and as a safeguard of political stability. To this extent he simply identified himself with ordinary middle-class opinion, although his essay was ahead of its times in anticipating that national education would

---

[12] Jeremy Bentham, Plan of Parliamentary Reform, *The Works of Jeremy Bentham,* ed. John Bowring (11 vols.; Edinburgh: William Tait, 1843), III, 462–465.

[13] *Ibid.,* I, 567–570; *ibid.,* III, 462. Bentham extended the criterion of intellectual aptitude to office-holding as well as voting; he proposed to restrict office to men who had attained a certain level of education. See his Constitutional Code, *ibid.,* IX, 59–60.

be impossible so long as the voluntary religious societies continued to dominate it. However, in his essay on government,
prepared for the Supplement to the *Encyclopaedia Britannica,*
Mill systematically grounded expansion of the suffrage in the
education of the people. As he put it, those who govern may
be mistaken in one of two ways. If they are members of an
aristocracy, they will have a personal interest in misgovern-
ment and so persevere in their mistaken view of the general
interest. On the other hand, if they are part of the body of the
people, they may make mistakes in judgment, but they will
have an interest in good government and so be amenable to
correction through education. In addition, Mill argued, disseminating a high degree of knowledge among the people is
entirely feasible, and he equated those who claimed power on
the grounds of superior competence with the priesthood of
former times who had monopolized knowledge.[14]

Here was the theoretical basis for much of the agitation
in behalf of popular education at public expense that went on
in Parliament: according to the developed Benthamite theory,
an educated popular electorate would secure all of the ends
that the aristocratic classes had thus far denied. In 1833, for
example, J. A. Roebuck proposed a far more comprehensive
plan of elementary education than any member of Parliament
had yet sponsored. It called for compulsory attendance of children between six and twelve at schools their parents might
choose, together with the establishment of popularly controlled
and publicly assisted infant schools and schools of industry in
every parish. Pupils of every social class were to be encouraged
to attend these parish schools, which would not only teach
them the usual elementary subjects but also instruct them in
the main laws of political economy and acquaint them with the

---

[14] Mill, "Education of the Poor," *Edinburgh Review,* XXI, 41 (February
1813), 207–219; "Government," *Essays . . . Reprinted, by Permission,
from the Supplement to the Encyclopaedia Britannica* (London: J. Innes,
n.d.), chapter 10.

nature and rewards of pure "scholarship." The grounds on which Roebuck urged parish schools were as significant as the scope of his plan. He conceded that popular ignorance was a powerful obstacle to extension of the suffrage, but he insisted that its extension was inevitable, and he made no secret of his belief that "the people will never be well governed until they govern themselves." By the same token, although he echoed the concern of middle-class reformers like Kay that the laboring classes must be taught the principles of political economy, Roebuck also turned the tables on the educated classes by suggesting that the universal diffusion of knowledge was as necessary to combat their economic fallacies as to combat those of the working classes.[15]

More generally, whereas middle-class reformers sought to educate the political opinions of the working classes chiefly in order to rectify them, the parliamentary radicals visualized popular education as a way of equipping the people to take an active part in shaping government policies. It was a commonplace of their thought that further extensions of the suffrage would compel the nation to educate. They treated this necessity as one evidence of the virtues of democracy, and George Grote went so far as to suggest in 1831 that popular pressure on Parliament to elevate the laboring classes through education might well serve as a precedent for compelling even a reformed Parliament to respond to other popular needs.[16] In short, England's philosophical radicals followed Mill in identifying democracy with the intelligence of the electorate, and the intelligence of the electorate with popular education. Although

---

[15] Roebuck, Speech in the House of Commons, 30 July 1833, *Hansard*, 3d ser., XX, 139–166, 160, 145. Roebuck's plan also called for instruction in a trade, an element common to proposals of the era.

[16] Grote, "Essentials of Parliamentary Reform" (1831), *The Minor Works of George Grote*, ed. Alexander Bain (London: John Murray, 1873), pp. 25–26. See also Roebuck, *Hansard*, 3d ser., XX, 145, 146, 159; Thomas Wyse, *ibid.* (19 May 1835), XXVII, Appendix, pp. xiii–xiv; and Charles Buller, *ibid.* (19 June 1839), XLVIII, 557.

Bentham had made intellectual aptitude a criterion of participation in government, most radicals simply assumed that the
criterion would be met by instructing the people.

At the same time, Bentham's followers also subscribed to
a definition of the political process that, while it helped to
assure them that democracy would be effective, added another
dimension to their belief in cultivating the intelligence of the
people. James Mill's essay on liberty of the press stated their
belief in fairly systematic form: "When various conclusions are,
with their evidence, presented with equal care and with equal
skill, there is a moral certainty, though some few may be mis-
guided, that the greater number will judge right, and that the
greatest force of evidence, wherever it is, will produce the
greatest impression." In other words, he suggested that democratic politics would consist of an illuminating discussion of
public issues, conducted by authoritative commentators, and
followed attentively by responsive voters.[17]

Bentham had adumbrated this doctrine, as he had the
doctrine of intellectual aptitude; but he had visualized informal
education largely as a process of keeping the electorate informed about the actions of its governors. (Hence the importance of a free press, of removing the taxes on knowledge, and
of reporting the debates in Parliament.) Mill enlarged it to include a much more comprehensive process of informal learning
that would supplement the formal schooling he proposed; he
equated popular government with thoughtful consideration of
contemporary issues. The parliamentary radicals went further
still, holding out the hope and indeed the expectation that an
educated people would voluntarily pursue every sort of knowledge. Partly, they looked upon informal education of this sort
to counteract popular fallacies; partly, they thought that it
would open public deliberations to the influence of informed

---

[17] Mill, "Liberty of the Press," *Essays Reprinted from the Britannica*,
p. 22.

commentators; partly, they anticipated that formal education would beget a continuous quest for pure knowledge.[18] In this fashion they attached intellectual excellence to intellectual aptitude as a criterion of popular government and suggested that popular education conveyed through the schools was important primarily because it would ensure a continuing process of popular education outside them. Nevertheless, they seem to have felt no real doubts that popular education along informal lines would flourish as soon as schools were universally available and the press was completely free. If they tended to make the level of public discussion a second criterion of democratic government, they also believed that an educated democratic electorate was more likely than any less numerous body of men to seek knowledge as a basis for action.

The philosophical radicals adopted democracy long before the First Reform Bill, which neither satisfied their belief in manhood suffrage nor confronted them with the need to choose between popular rights and intellectual excellence. Hence it remained to their most eminent successor to erect their criteria into criticisms of democratic politics. We can well afford to examine the political theory of John Stuart Mill in some detail, for it explored most of the difficulties liberal democrats confronted as England extended the suffrage. By the time the younger Mill had completed his political ruminations, he had repudiated virtually all of the Benthamite radicals' proposals for parliamentary reform because he was afraid that democracy as they understood it would be incapable of securing a truly harmonious ordering of the nation's interests.

In *Considerations on Representative Government* (1861), Mill explained that the very mechanisms which make representative government responsible to the electorate also undermine its capacity to rule well. In part, he feared that popular

---

[18] See particularly Roebuck, *Hansard*, 3d ser., XX, 142, 143, and 160.

rule would mean class legislation in behalf of the most numerous class, just as aristocratic rule had meant class legislation in
behalf of the aristocracy; it was a plausible extension of Bentham's principles. But his fears were more intellectual than the
class vocabulary in which he often expressed them. Rather, he
was afraid that any modern government would threaten human
liberty and progress unless both the policies it adopted and its
administration of those policies were held to the standard of
intelligence.[19] Hence he proposed such innovations as a suffrage dependent upon minimal standards of education, additional votes on an ascending scale for those who could prove
higher degrees of education, an educated civil service, the use
of experts in preparing legislation for Parliament to accept or
reject, and (above all) proportional representation on Hare's
plan, which would serve to introduce members of the "instructed minority"—"the very *élite* of the country"—into Parliament. Measures of this nature, intended to secure intelligence
in government, would counteract not only the agitation of class
interests but other democratic shortcomings as well.[20]

Questioning the intellectual aptitude of the people, Mill
also radically altered the concept of public deliberation Bentham had associated with democracy. When he reviewed the

---

[19] Mill, *Considerations on Representative Government* (New York: Liberal Arts Press, 1958), chapters 2 and 6.
[20] *Ibid.*, chapters 5, 7, and 8; pp. 117, 113. It is worth noting that Mill
urged greater intelligence partly on the grounds that contemporary governments must undertake new tasks; he did not propose to limit their
scope, but to elevate their standards of performance. Yet his proposition
involved him in a paradox. In effect, he accepted the public judgment
that contemporary social and economic evils must be remedied, but
denied that majority opinion should define a government's responsibility
for dealing with them. There is a striking passage in his *Autobiography*
in which he explains that he and Harriet Taylor had lost faith in democracy but gone beyond it to a belief in socialism. See Mill, *Autobiography of John Stuart Mill* (New York: Columbia University Press,
1924), p. 162.

second part of *Democracy in America*, for example, Mill dis-
avowed many of Tocqueville's pessimistic inferences and insisted, on Tocqueville's own evidence, that popular institutions
are an outstanding agency of informal political education. But
he also suggested that only national authorities (rather than
local democratic institutions) could shape popular deliberations
on a sufficiently elevated model, and he was to turn again and
again to the ideal of an elite educational influence operating to
check the vagaries of public opinion. As he explained in his
essay on liberty, "No government by a democracy or a numerous aristocracy, either in its political acts or in the opinions,
qualities, and tone of mind which it fosters, ever did or could
rise above mediocrity except in so far as the sovereign Many
have let themselves be guided (which in their best times they
always have done) by the counsels and influence of a more
highly gifted and instructed *one* or *few*." The essay on representative government ended by measuring public deliberation
in terms of its "deference to mental superiority."[21]

Many of the devices *Representative Government* proposed were intended to encourage such deference. They included not only plural voting, expert administration, and
proportional representation (which Mill advocated for their
salutary effect on popular concepts of democracy as well as
for their practical value in elevating the conduct of affairs), but
also public voting in place of the secret ballot, longer terms of
elective office, and the consolidation of local government,
which he expected to produce the same effect. More than this,
he held that parliamentary representatives must maintain their
independence of the electorate in all but the ultimate sense of
having to stand for election, and he argued that the electorate

---

[21] Mill, *Dissertations and Discussions* (3 vols.; Boston: Spencer, 1865),
II, 100–104; *On Liberty* (New York: Liberal Arts Press, 1956), pp. 80–
81; *Representative Government*, p. 179. See also Mill's review of Tocqueville's first volume (*London Review*, II, 3 [July 1835], 85–129), which
expresses most of the same views but does not carry them to a conclusion.

should respect even an undistinguished representative for the superior political competence he acquires by participating in parliamentary deliberations. In other words, although Mill continued to hold that discussion was the basis of true democracy, discussion now had only an indirect connection with the popular participation in the governing process that his theory had once assumed. Even when he spoke enthusiastically in Parliament about the educational effects of extending the suffrage, he suggested that one of its chief values would be the "tranquillising" effect parliamentary discussion of public issues would have on popular agitation.[22]

Mill's conception of true democracy as a vehicle for intelligence not only distorted the Benthamite equation between democracy and education; it also distorted Mill's own educational principles, which he himself had applied to politics. In his essay on Tocqueville, for example, he advocated extensive popular participation "in the business of government in detail," partly on the grounds that "It has often been said, and requires to be repeated still oftener, that books and discourses alone are not education; that life is a problem, not a theorem; that action can only be learnt in action." His words suggested, not only that a people must learn their own lessons from experience, but also that they must be free to reshape their policies in the light of that experience. The same doctrine reappeared in *Representative Government*, where Mill repeatedly invoked the images of education and of the school as a model of politics. The essay made much of the argument that the process of government must cultivate popular intelligence and initiative as well as secure efficient management of public affairs, and it reiterated Mill's belief that if politics is to be educational the choices the electorate makes must represent bona fide choices of policy. Even in his anxiety Mill never repudiated what R. P. Anschutz

---

[22] Mill, *Representative Government*, chapters 10, 11, and 15; pp. 142–143, 182–185; Speech in the House of Commons, 13 April 1866, *Hansard*, CLXXXII, 1253–1263, 1261.

has described as his belief in the "homeopathic" theory of democracy, which rested on the belief that democracy itself is educational.[23]

Yet Mill also described a school of politics that very largely transcended the experience of the electorate. Significantly, he employed his educational metaphor in discussing the uses of a bicameral legislature, which he praised chiefly because two houses have an educational effect *on each other*. More important, in the very act of hailing American politics as "a most valuable school" he complained that it was also "a school from which the ablest teachers are excluded; the first minds in the country being as effectually shut out from the national representation, and from public functions generally, as if they were under a formal disqualification." Under these circumstances, the metaphors of education were suspiciously limited, suggesting that Mill wished primarily to lecture the public, not to elicit their own best judgment through the processes of politics. Recognizing that centralized control of local administration would curtail local political functions and hence restrict local political education, he advocated it on the grounds that "It is but a poor education that associates ignorance with ignorance and leaves them, if they care for knowledge, to grope their way to it without help, and to do without it if they do not. What is wanted is the means of making ignorance aware of itself and able to profit by knowledge, accustoming minds which know only routine to act upon and feel the value of principles, teaching them to compare different modes of action and learn by the use of their reason to distinguish the best. When we desire to have a good school, we do not eliminate the teacher."[24] In short, Mill continued to employ

---

[23] Mill, *Dissertations and Discussions*, II, 103, 102; *Representative Government*, chapters 2 and 3; pp. 128–130, 148, 219–220; R. P. Anschutz, *The Philosophy of J. S. Mill* (Oxford: Oxford University Press, 1953), chapter 3.

[24] Mill, *Representative Government*, pp. 187–188, 129, 228.

educational criteria of politics, but in such a fashion as to encourage didactic instruction by the people's intellectual superiors.

Nevertheless, Mill's views were logically consistent with
the Benthamite premise that democracy depends upon intellectual aptitude reinforced by the informal diffusion of knowledge.
His reservations arose simply because he developed a qualita-
tive evaluation of the role education should play in politics,
itself a reflection of his broadening sense of the needs government must meet. Where Bentham and the elder Mill had contented themselves with popular literacy, the younger man
insisted upon discriminating intelligence. Where the older men
had contented themselves with seeking an untrammeled diffusion of knowledge, the younger man insisted that politics
consists of much more than an informed choice between alternative policies, that good government depends upon high-
minded discussion of fundamental issues. In a quite genuine
sense, Stuart Mill challenged the rule of the people precisely
because he equated representative government with the highest standards of popular education.

Mill's views were not simply logically consistent with
Benthamite assumptions; they also represented the natural outcome of a long process of development. James Mill had made
over Bentham's rather unsophisticated vision of democratic
politics as the weighing of literate opinion into a weighing that
had been informed by educated men. The parliamentary radicals carried the process of refinement further, treating democratic education not only as a vehicle for informed political
leadership but also as a stimulus to the acquisition of pure
knowledge. Stuart Mill insisted that the intellectual commitments of aptitude and knowledge be fully met; and because
he knew that popular politics could not meet them unaided,
he turned to government by discussion and a deferential
electorate to achieve the general interest.

Nor was Mill alone in challenging most of the democratic doctrines that Bentham had originated. Even the so-

called liberal realists who advocated democratization of the suffrage during the 1860s shared many of Mill's hesitations. One of them was John Morley, who championed both extension of the suffrage and a full-fledged national education. According to Morley, the working classes had displayed far greater wisdom than their social superiors in dealing with major questions of public policy like recognition of the American Confederacy, disestablishment of the Anglican Church in Ireland, and the Irish Land Act. Yet Morley also criticized the working classes for valuing political power before they had acquired education, and the severest criticism he leveled against the governing classes was the charge that in their complacency they had neglected the education of the "ignorant multitudes" who were becoming "the political masters of the realm."[25] Even more strikingly, Lord Houghton, another powerful advocate of suffrage reform, exhorted the ruling classes to "admit the Working-men into the great school of Public Life" and at the same time expressed the belief that wealth, intellect, and experience would continue to prevail over them. Lord Houghton also held, in *Essays on Reform*, that popular discussion would almost surely divide rather than unite the working classes, and Leslie Stephen took similar comfort from the same prospect.[26] Their views may indeed have been realistic; but they came perilously close to adopting as a virtue the constitutional balance of interests that Bentham and James Mill had excoriated because it substituted equilibrium and the status quo for justice as the basis of government. If they were confident that England

---

[25] Morley, "Public Affairs," *Fortnightly Review*, n.s., I, 1 (January 1867), 104; "The Struggle for National Education," *ibid.*, XIV, 81 (September 1873), 420.

[26] Lord Houghton, "On the Admission of the Working Classes as Part of Our Social System; and On their Recognition for All Purposes as Part of the Nation," *Essays on Reform* (London: Macmillan, 1867), pp. 66, 63; Stephen, "On the Choice of Representatives by Popular Constituencies," *ibid.*, p. 122; and see William Molesworth, "History of the Reform Question from 1848 to 1866," *Fortnightly Review*, n.s., I, 6 (June 1867), 747.

had little to fear from her new masters it was because they were
confident that the suffrage would not bring democracy.

Perhaps this outcome was inevitable in a society as
complex and as tradition bound as England. The English commitment to popular education had arisen in the first instance as
a negation of democratic politics when it involved political
opinions at all, and the radicals who challenged it were compelled to demand democratic politics and education on terms
which suggested that each must be justified by its consequences
for the other. In addition, the Benthamite argument for universal education, like the argument for manhood suffrage, originated in theory rather than experience. So long as the evils of
aristocratic government were apparent on every hand, democratic theory seemed sufficient both to account for them and to
point the way to their eradication; but as a reformed Parliament began to deal with many of them, the reformers had second thoughts about how necessary further political innovations
were, about how much popular education could be expected to
accomplish. Other plausible reasons might be adduced, were
we compelled to explain what we are committed only to recognize here: inevitable or not and explicable or not, John Stuart
Mill's liberalism and the political theory of the liberal realists
brought half a century of democratic agitation to a close. Radical theories of politics and radical theories of education eventuated in a liberal theory of politics that was geared to a theory of
liberal education.

American political thought—the middle-class theory of
democracy in the United States—followed a different path.
That path is already familiar to us, so familiar that it would be
possible to let the contrasts and comparisons that are already
implicit in this account stand as its conclusions. However, the
argument would then remain formally incomplete, and at the
risk of laboring the obvious I propose to comment briefly on
characteristic American attitudes toward democracy and edu-

cation that I think this survey of English thought has thrown into high relief.[27]

The differences between English and American thought are made more striking by the fact that at the beginning of the nineteenth century American attitudes toward education closely paralleled English views. It is true that the Americans were more widely educated than the English, largely as a result of the schools established during the colonial era as well as a relatively stable and reasonably democratic society. Yet many of the educational institutions and most of the educational ideas Americans cherished would have been familiar to an English advocate of popular education. Outside of New York and New England our educational "system" was almost wholly voluntary; generally, it was free only to paupers; and it was as economical as its sponsors could make it. Americans also made feeble gestures toward requiring the education of child laborers, and the Lancasterian system of instruction was popular in New York City as well as London, where it was often advocated for the same political and social reasons.

Nevertheless, even during the early years of the century Americans tended to see popular education in a perspective that only English radicals could share. Advocates of educational reform like Thomas Jefferson, Nicholas Biddle, and De Witt Clinton pressed for the wider diffusion of knowledge because republican institutions depended upon it, and they

---

[27] Obviously I have not sought to cover the whole range of English social thought during the nineteenth century, which saw the development of Tory radicalism as well as Christian socialism, secular socialism, and a powerful labor movement. My purpose has not been to make all possible comparisons, but to examine the attachment to liberal democracy and to education its handmaiden that was expressed in the two nations. Much the same considerations help to explain my neglect of Matthew Arnold, who—though at bottom a democrat and by profession an educator— played so idiosyncratic a role in English life as to defy being treated as a representative liberal.

assumed that education should be available to the people as citizens and voters, not as paupers and potential revolutionaries. Within a generation, moreover, most Americans came to insist that education must be available on equal terms to all if it were to be truly effective in serving their political and social values; hence they moved with a surprising degree of consensus to supplant voluntary efforts with publicly controlled and publicly supported school systems. We should honor the philanthropy of those who provided free schools for the poor in the United States as well as England, and we should recognize the errors into which historians like Cubberley have led us by holding all education to the public model; but Cubberley's prejudices point to values that increasingly affected educational practice as well as educational theory in this country. By mid-century the United States had adopted a system of public education that was far more widespread and accessible than England's schools for the people—as agitators like Richard Cobden recognized in holding the complex and unsatisfactory English arrangements to the test of American precedents.

Moreover, spokesmen for American democracy related it to popular education in ways that exempted democracy from the anomalous second thoughts to which Benthamite premises led John Stuart Mill. Taking utilitarian reason as their guide, the Benthamites developed a highly intellectualized conception of politics. Utility was to be the object of specific reforms; reason was to be the vehicle; public education was to elevate popular deliberation to the point at which reason would always be effective. The outcome was an idealized view of public deliberation that ultimately employed the criteria of intellectual competence and rational discussion as counterbalances to democratic politics. By contrast, the Americans began by assuming popular suffrage. On the one hand, it existed as a historic precedent; by English standards, at any rate, the United States was democratic at least fifty years before the Second Reform Bill. On the other hand, the Americans also hastened to adopt democracy as a political principle. When the English radicals pressed for an extension of the suffrage on strictly utilitarian grounds, Americans already assumed it as a natural right. Hence they were not likely to question the intellectual competence of the people, nor to look with favor on theories of politics that made democracy conditional on learning.

Americans refused to make democracy conditional upon learning, but they were quick to insist upon the education of the people; this fact is as important as their faith in manhood suffrage. In part, they visualized education as an indispensable instrument of popular sovereignty, an intellectual resource against tyranny and the machinations of "aristocracy." In this sense they were quite willing to concede that knowledge gives men political advantages, but they denied that those advantages should belong to the few. In part, they visualized education as a necessary moral influence, preventing the evils their society feared and encouraging the values it cherished. Here their outlook was obviously conservative; but the institutions they wished to preserve were their own, and education was a way of reinforcing democratic mores. Finally, they thought of education as an economic asset—not primarily an asset to society, however, nor a cure for the degrading effects of poverty, but a vehicle for individual prosperity and a prop to individual success.

It goes without saying that American opinion about both democracy and education ranged more widely than these very general remarks suggest. Some few men opposed both, but their opposition has been exaggerated; by comparison with Englishmen, at any rate, the Americans adopted both with open arms. Others, among them many of the educational reformers, expressed great anxiety lest the sovereign people be left uneducated and dangerous; they may therefore remind us of their transatlantic contemporaries. Still, the differences in assumption and emphasis are at least as striking as the similarities, as even a superficial comparison between the writings of Kay and those of Horace Mann will suggest. The closest parallel may lie between the post-Malthusian liberals in England who advocated educating the lower orders against vice and tumult and misery, and American missionaries and nativists who sought to redeem westerners and Roman Catholics and immigrants from their sins. But even here there was a difference of emphasis between suppression and redemption, and in general educational reformers and nativists seem to have shared with other Americans a belief that popular education properly undertaken would raise everyone to the level at which he would be a good American.

Before the Civil War the Americans generally assumed that the distribution of virtue and intelligence through the schools would serve most of their political purposes; in this sense they shared Bentham's views rather than those of James Mill, for they believed that a literate people would already know how to vote when confronted with questions affecting the public interest. Like Bentham, however, they also counted upon a free press and other informal agencies of education to augment popular intelligence; without hinging democracy on it, they assumed that informal education would take place. After the war, moreover, they revised their estimates of the kind and degree of education that were necessary to sustain democratic institutions. On the one hand, they gradually raised the standards and broadened the scope of formal education. On the other hand, they enlarged the role of informal education to the point at which some of them equated democratic politics with a process of informal popular education. In this sense they followed in the footsteps of the second generation of Benthamite radicals; but they turned to informal education without adopting the increasingly restrictive definitions of democracy the later Benthamites adopted.

Indeed, the leading American proponents of democracy understood as an educational process were also leading spokesmen for movements of radical protest. Agitators as different as Edward Bellamy, Wendell Phillips, and Henry Demarest Lloyd appealed to an already educated electorate to inform itself more fully for the necessary tasks of reform. The leaders of organized movements of protest expressed the same idea. In both the Grange and the Knights of Labor they committed their followers to "organization and education," while the leaders of the People's party sought to treat their whole movement as a vehicle of massive popular education. The word "populist" has become a term of reproach in recent years, partly because it has been taken to include all of the faults of the American democracy: its fundamentalism, its majoritarian outlook, its insensitivity to the scruples that highly educated men assert. Yet Populist party leaders, not to mention the social critics who sympathized with them, are better criticized for the naïveté of their belief in education as a way of dealing with pressing economic evils than they are for subverting liberal definitions of democracy. Undoubtedly they expressed an unsophisticated faith in democracy defined as popular participation in government. But they also represented democratic politics as an educational process in which the combat of opinion would secure the national interest.

While reformers and populists equated democracy with informal political education, a small band of liberal unrealists erected the criteria of intellectual aptitude and "government by discussion" into obstacles to popular rule. These were the mugwumps and civil service reformers like George William Curtis and E. L. Godkin, disciples of John Stuart Mill in a literal as well as a figurative sense, whose political careers reduced to one long lament that the electorate refused to defer to intelligence. Indeed, many of their particular criticisms of contemporary politics were well taken. Political campaigns were admittedly a travesty on reason; the two political parties were undoubtedly interested primarily in spoils; neither elective nor appointive officials seem to have been capable of dealing with contemporary social problems even if they had been so inclined. Thanks to their roots in classical liberalism, however, the mugwumps usually felt that the government should not attempt to deal with most of the problems popular sentiment had defined, and they tended to visualize a political elite that would not interfere with society, to propose greater intelligence in government as a way of curtailing popular reforms.[28] Andrew D. White's diatribe against free silver was a fitting climax to their agitation.

It was also largely irrelevant. The ideas of liberal reform did not dominate American politics as they did English developments; the best the reformers could hope to do was play an independent and in some sense mediating role in American politics, which the American democracy tended to ignore rather than defer to. (The chief reason the self-proclaimed Independents were able to exercise political influence was that in a few key states they held the balance of power between the two major parties—just as some of them complained that illiterate immigrants might hold the balance of power in national elections.) In other respects they were right-wing critics of democracy whose insistence on popular intelligence betrayed the narrowness of their vision. The one genuine contribution they made to democratic politics was to insist that even democracy required expert knowledge, but they could not make that case plausible on their terms. Instead, it was left to men like Charles W. Eliot, the sponsor of the "five-foot shelf" as well as a major influence for reform in American higher education, to argue that democracy could and must meet new demands upon its intelligence as effectively as it had met earlier demands. It was Eliot rather than White who pointed the way to the developments of the twentieth century, and Eliot rather than Mill who spoke for the American liberal tradition.

---

[28] This evaluation of their attitudes becomes even more persuasive when we recognize how bitterly they fought the urban political bosses, who dealt with social problems the mugwumps often ignored, or when we recall the schemes for negative constitutional reform that proliferated at the end of the century.

Selected Bibliography

GENERAL HISTORIES OF EDUCATION

Lawrence Cremin is at work on a definitive history of American education for our time. Meanwhile the following works will serve as a useful introduction to the subject.

BAILYN, BERNARD. *Education in the Forming of American Society: Needs and Opportunities for Study.* Chapel Hill: University of North Carolina Press, 1960. (Bailyn's book is devoted to colonial developments, but it is of central importance in understanding popular education as a social phenomenon.)

BUTTS, R. FREEMAN, and LAWRENCE A. CREMIN. *A History of Education in American Culture.* New York: Holt, 1953.

CREMIN, LAWRENCE A. *The Wonderful World of Ellwood Patterson Cubberley: An Essay on the Historiography of American Education.* New York: Teachers College, 1965.

DABNEY, CHARLES W. *Universal Education in the South.* 2 vols. Chapel Hill: University of North Carolina Press, 1936.

EDWARDS, NEWTON, and HERMAN G. RICHEY. *The School in the American Social Order: The Dynamics of American Education.* 2d ed. Boston: Houghton Mifflin, 1963.

MONROE, PAUL. *Founding of the American Public School System: A History of Education in the United States, from the Early Settlements to the Close of the Civil War Period.* New York: Macmillan, 1940.

TREATMENTS OF SPECIAL TOPICS

ADAMSON, JOHN W. *English Education 1789–1902.* Cambridge: Cambridge University Press, 1930.

BEALE, HOWARD K. *A History of Freedom of Teaching in American Schools.* New York: Scribner's, 1941.

BODE, CARL. *The American Lyceum: Town Meeting of the Mind.* New York: Oxford University Press, 1956.

BOND, HORACE M. *The Education of the Negro in the American Social Order.* Englewood Cliffs, N. J.: Prentice-Hall, 1934.

CREMIN, LAWRENCE A. *The American Common School: An Historic Conception.* New York: Teachers College, 1951.

————. *The Transformation of the School: Progressivism in American Education, 1876–1956.* New York: Knopf, 1961.

CULVER, RAYMOND B. *Horace Mann and Religion in the Massachusetts Schools.* New Haven: Yale University Press, 1929.

CUROE, PHILIP R. V. *Educational Attitudes and Policies of Organized Labor in the United States.* New York: Teachers College, 1926.

CURTI, MERLE. *The Social Ideas of American Educators.* New York: Scribner's, 1935.

DITZION, SIDNEY. *Arsenals of a Democratic Culture: A Social History of the American Public Library Movement in New England and the Middle States from 1850 to 1900.* Chicago: American Library Association, 1947.

ELSON, RUTH MILLER. *Guardians of Tradition: American Schoolbooks of the Nineteenth Century.* Lincoln: University of Nebraska Press, 1964.

FITZPATRICK, EDWARD A. *The Educational Views and Influence of De Witt Clinton.* New York: Teachers College, 1911.

GOULD, JOSEPH E. *The Chautauqua Movement.* Albany: The State University of New York Press, 1961.

HANSEN, ALLEN O. *Early Educational Leadership in the Ohio Valley: A Study of Educational Reconstruction through the Western Literary Institute and College of Professional Teachers.* Journal of Educational Research Monographs, Number 5 (1923). Bloomington, Ill.: Public School Publishing Company, 1923.

HONEYWELL, ROY J. *The Educational Work of Thomas Jefferson.* Cambridge: Harvard University Press, 1931.

JACKSON, SIDNEY L. *America's Struggle for Free Schools: Social Tension and Education in New England and New York, 1827–1842.* Washington, D.C.: American Council on Public Affairs, 1941..

KATZ, MICHAEL B. *The Irony of Early School Reform: Educational Innovation in Mid-Nineteenth Century Massachusetts.* Cambridge: Harvard University Press, 1968.

KIMBALL, ELSA P. *Sociology and Education: An Analysis of the Theories of Spencer and Ward.* Columbia University Studies in History, Economics and Public Law, Number 369. New York: Columbia University Press, 1932.

KRUG, EDWARD A. *The Shaping of the American High School, 1880–1940.* New York: Harper and Row, 1964.

LANNIE, VINCENT P. *Public Money and Parochial Education: Bishop Hughes, Governor Seward, and the New York School Controversy.* Cleveland, Ohio: The Press of Case Western Reserve University, 1968.

LEE, GORDON C. *The Struggle for Federal Aid, First Phase: A History of the Attempts to Obtain Federal Aid for the Common Schools, 1870–1890.* New York: Teachers College, 1949.

LOGAN, RAYFORD W. *The Negro in American Life and Thought: The Nadir, 1877–1901.* New York: Dial, 1954.

McAVOY, THOMAS T. *The Americanist Heresy in Roman Catholicism, 1895–1900.* Notre Dame, Ind.: University of Notre Dame Press, 1963.

McCADDEN, JOSEPH J. *Education in Pennsylvania 1810–1835 and Its Debt to Roberts Vaux.* Philadelphia: University of Pennsylvania Press, 1937.

MEIER, AUGUST. *Negro Thought in America, 1880–1915: Racial Ideologies in the Age of Booker T. Washington.* Ann Arbor: University of Michigan Press, 1963.

MOSIER, RICHARD D. *Making the American Mind: Social and Moral Ideas in the McGuffey Readers.* New York: King's Crown Press, 1947.

SIMON, BRIAN. *Studies in the History of Education, 1780–1870.* London: Lawrence & Wishart, 1960.

SMITH, TIMOTHY L. "Protestant Schooling and American Nationality, 1800–1850," *Journal of American History,* LIII, 4 (March 1967), 679–695.

SWINT, HENRY L. *The Northern Teacher in the South, 1862–1870.* Nashville, Tenn.: Vanderbilt University Press, 1941.

TAYLOR, WILLIAM R. "Toward a Definition of Orthodoxy: The Patrician South and the Common Schools," *Harvard Educational Review,* XXXVI, 4 (Fall 1966), 412–426.

TYACK, DAVID B. "Education and Social Unrest, 1873–1878," *Harvard Educational Review,* XXXI, 2 (Spring 1961), 194–212.

WELTER, RUSH. *Popular Education and Democratic Thought in America.* New York: Columbia University Press, 1962.

WESLEY, EDGAR B. *NEA: The First Hundred Years. The Building of the Teaching Profession.* New York: Harper and Row, 1957.

WEST, EARLE H. "The Peabody Education Fund and Negro Education, 1867–1880," *History of Education Quarterly,* VI, 2 (Summer 1966), 3–21.

WISHY, BERNARD. *The Child and The Republic: The Dawn of Modern American Child Nurture.* Philadelphia: University of Pennsylvania Press, 1968.

DOCUMENTARY HISTORIES

COON, CHARLES L., ed. *The Beginnings of Public Education in North Carolina: A Documentary History, 1790–1840.* 2 vols. Raleigh: North Carolina Historical Commission, 1908.

FINEGAN, THOMAS E., ed. *Free Schools: A Documentary History of the Free School Movement in New York State.* Fifteenth

Annual Report of the New York State Education Department, 1917–1918, vol. I. Albany: University of the State of New York, 1921.

KNIGHT, EDGAR W., ed. *A Documentary History of Education in the South before 1860.* 5 vols. Chapel Hill: University of North Carolina Press, 1949–1954.

————, and HALL, CLIFTON, eds. *Readings in American Educational History.* New York: Appleton-Century-Crofts, 1951.

RANDALL, S. S. *History of the Common School System of the State of New York, from Its Origin in 1795, to the Present Time: Including the Various City and Other Special Organizations, and the Religious Controversies of 1821, 1822, and 1840.* New York, 1871.

VASSAR, RENA, ed. *Social History of American Education.* 2 vols. Chicago: Rand McNally, 1965.

ACKNOWLEDGMENTS

Like every anthologist who draws on ephemeral primary sources, I am heavily indebted to the libraries and special collections in which they have been preserved. In particular, I have been assisted in the preparation of this volume by the American Antiquarian Society, the Harvard College Library, the Library of Congress, the New York Public Library, the State Library of New York, and the Wisconsin Historical Society. I have also benefited from the courtesies extended to me by the libraries of Bennington College, Clark University, the College of the Holy Cross, Union College, and Williams College.

In addition, I owe a debt of gratitude to friends who have helped me to deal with specific problems created by the anthology. They are Robert D. Cross, Manfred Jonas, and Wallace P. Scott. Last but not least, Virginia Sandy has been of inestimable help in reading proofs with me. If the documents printed here are not letter-perfect versions of the originals, it is only because I have not been able to live up to her high standards of typographical accuracy.

Rush Welter

American Writings on Popular Education

The Nineteenth Century

1.

Report of the Committee on Education, House of Representatives of Pennsylvania, 1810

Like the generation of the founding fathers, the generation that came to maturity during the first decades of the nineteenth century heard frequent appeals to the states to establish truly effective systems of popular education in keeping with their republican institutions. The report that follows, drafted by Nicholas Biddle and presented by him to the Pennsylvania House of Representatives, exemplifies both the high idealism of the second generation of republican leaders and the practical difficulties they confronted. If popular education was indispensable to the safety of the republic and an invaluable asset to an open society, its claims had not yet been fully recognized. It had to contend with a shortage of public funds, a popular prejudice against gratuitous instruction, and a lurking suspicion that it might encroach on religious conscience or ethnic idiosyncrasy. These difficulties were especially prominent in Biddle's Pennsylvania, which had a long tradition of voluntary instruction in church-related schools, and which also suffered from long-standing tensions between its German- and its English-speaking populations. Under the circumstances it is hardly surprising that Biddle's call to action—modest as it may seem in retrospect—met with no success.

. . . Mr. Biddle from the committee to whom was referred on the 10th instant, the fourth item of the Governor's

From *Journal of the Twenty-first House of Representatives of the Commonwealth of Pennsylvania* (Lancaster, Pa., 1810), pp. 108–114.

message, relative to the education of the poor, &c. made report, which was read as follows, viz.

That in the constitution of Pennsylvania, which each member of this house has solemnly sworn to support, there is no injunction more commanding, than that "the Legislature shall, as soon as conveniently may be, provide by law for the establishment of schools throughout the commonwealth, in such manner that the poor may be taught gratis." Nearly twenty years of undisturbed repose and of prosperity beyond all example, have been enjoyed under that constitution; yet, no one school has ever been established by the state; and although the poor have been occasionally assisted, by partial efforts, yet no general or permanent system has ever been adopted for the diffusion of knowledge through the commonwealth.

However they may lament so extraordinary a delay, your committee will not believe that the representatives of a free people can be insensible to the blessings of popular education. In other countries indeed, where the strength of the government is too often only the debasement of the people, every plan for their improvement is cautiously excluded; since it is the obvious policy of the rulers to subdue every spirit, and to depress every feeling that would endanger their own safety, and to extinguish all the lights of instruction which might discover to the nation the deformities of their government. Grave statesmen, therefore, in the old world have pretended, that to instruct the people would only render them vicious and unhappy; that the sober pursuits of industry would be deserted for useless learning; and that the best and happiest condition, of what is fastidiously termed the lower ranks of society, is a state of laborious ignorance. But these are not sentiments worthy of a free nation. The first object of the commonwealth, is the happiness of the people; its highest security their attachment; and that government is alike ignorant of its interests and false to its duty, unless it zealously strives to improve their condition. On ourselves this duty is enjoined by considerations far more important than our own personal advantage, when we observe the wonderful career which Providence has permitted to this nation, or how powerfully its fate must influence the future destinies of freedom. In the revolutions which are still shaking the earth to its centre, almost every government that once asserted the great cause of religious and political liberty, has been prostrated in succession, till there now remains but one republic, the last hope of civilized freedom—the only government that has dared to build its altars on universal toleration, or confided its laws to public virtue. It is for us then to vindicate the dignity of human nature and its capacity for freedom. Our own example must determine whether it be indeed true, that men are unable to enjoy popular government; or, whether after a few years of freedom, due, not to our government, but to local causes, we are to close forever the melancholy list of nations who have vainly attempted to be free. In this situation we should anxiously surround our institutions with every thing that may purify their spirit or contribute to their stability. The founders of the republic have therefore wisely recommended that which alone can ensure its permanency—a general republican system of education. They knew, that if the laws were to be dictated by the intelligence, and executed by the spirit of the people, it was essential to purify at once the sources of power, to qualify the youth of the country for the rich inheritance of its freedom, and to communicate those early impressions which give the government of our native country so commanding an authority over our affections as well as our duties. They felt, that if the slavery of a country be always caused or followed by its ignorance, it is not less true that no country, whose inhabitants are enlightened, can long submit to arbitrary power. A foreign violence might hazard the existence of a free government, or domestic dissensions might modify its forms, but the buoyant spirit of an intelligent educated people would easily survive these disasters; nor can the total overthrow of freedom be ever accomplished but by the decay of virtue, and the corruption of public sentiment.

The advantages of education are, however, by no means confined to the security of the government, it confirms the industrious habits, it purifies the morals, and increases the resources of every part of the community. To give to the citizens education, is in fact to give them wealth, because it supplies the means of acquiring riches, and more than wealth, because it teaches the means of enjoying them. Without such instruction, moreover, many of the political advantages of the constitution cannot be extended to the people. Every citizen has a right to share in the government, yet while that right is practically withheld by refusing the means of qualifying himself for the exercise of it, we only mock the ambition of the poor, with the image of a power, to which they are invited to aspire, but which they can never hope to attain. Our laws have established a political equality, but the privilege is rendered perfectly unsubstantial, while we continue that most odious of all distinctions, the practical inequality between the educated and the ignorant.

With these impressions your committee have maturely deliberated on the form and the extent of which public instruction is susceptible. They have thought in the first place that such instruction would derive much of its value from being systematic and general; from its power to impress a national stamp of character, and to cherish common sympathies among the people. The basis of such a system should therefore be broad and liberal, and its spirit, like the air we breathe, should pervade the remotest parts of the state. The views of the commonwealth ought not to be obscured by any misjudged calculation of expense, where the benefits are incalculable; nor its munificence circumscribed by any political or religious, or sexual distinctions. To educate then, merely those, who are called *the poor*, would be obviously imperfect in itself, and would too much restrict the meaning of the constitution, which in directing that schools should be established throughout the state, considers the instruction of the poor as merely incidental to a more extensive scheme of national education. Such a distinction too, would seem to militate against the principles of equality, every where interwoven through our institutions: on the one hand it offends the natural prejudices of the poor, who reluctantly submit to the humiliating treatment of paupers; on the other it alarms the pride of the rich, who disdain to mingle with the objects of their own charity.—There is, however, an intermediate class of citizens, powerful in numbers, and highly worthy of our attention, to whom the education of their children is burdensome, and who are alike unable to instruct them at their own expense, and unwilling to owe it to the bounty of others. To your committee it seemed most expedient to conciliate these different interests. If it be reasonable that the wealthy should contribute towards establishments highly useful to the state, and which they may themselves enjoy; and if those to whom fortune has denied the means of instruction should be educated at public expense; it is equally reasonable that they who are not absolutely poor should still be assisted by the state. Instead, therefore, of paying large sums from the treasury for the schooling of paupers, it seems advisable to equalise at once the burden and the advantage of public instruction—to promote, as far as possible, a practical equality among the youth of the country; and not merely give gratuitous education to a few, but cheap education to all.

For this purpose, the plan which your committee recommend, is to arrange the different counties of the state into small neighborhoods, so as to place each family within convenient reach of a school. The general superintendence over this school might be entrusted to a few respectable householders, and the expenses of it defrayed by the county—but to the master, should be paid from the county treasury, not his entire emoluments, but such a salary only as would oblige him to teach *gratis* the most indigent, and to lower very considerably the price of tuition to the rest of the neighborhood. Such an arrangement, while it would attract to a cheap school, those who would not frequent a free school, might also quicken the diligence of the master, whose gains would still depend on his conduct and reputation, and who might be careless of both, if his income were placed above contingencies.

To the execution of such a project your committee perceive no obstacles, which may not be surmounted by steadiness and perseverance. The various religious sects into which we are divided, could scarcely be offended with a simple, unassuming institution, to which those of every religious persuasion would have equal access, which would present to the lowest citizen the volume of holy instruction; and where might first be acquired that intelligence and expansion of mind, which are the best foundations of piety. Still less would the difference of language present a difficulty, since the instruction might easily be conveyed in the prevailing language, or in both the languages of a particular vicinity. Nor does there seem to be any very solid objection to making the expense of public instruction equal on all the members of the community. It might not indeed be advisable, or even practicable, to oblige every one to frequent the schools, yet if from pride or from better motives, any individual should decline this advantage, he is not therefore absolved from the duty of bearing his share of the burden. According to our law even those whose religion forbids it, are bound to contribute to the common defence; nor is there scarcely any example of taxation, where the citizen is not compelled to pay for public improvements, in which it is still optional for him to participate.

Your committee found but little embarrassment in fixing the limits of public instruction. The great mass of any people are always so much occupied in the labors of procuring subsistence, so that the acquisition of the learned languages and of abstruse science, must be left to individual leisure and affluence. But there are no occupations without intervals of leisure, when the rudiments of learning may be acquired, as there is no condition in life which may not be benefited by them. Without any ostentation therefore of making a learned people, without any parade of charity, the commonwealth will then perform its duty, and not till then, when it has brought instruction home to every citizen, when it has given him the means of obtaining plain, solid, practical instruction, which in more prosperous circumstances, he may extend and improve.

The details of such a plan will be respectfully submitted if it be the pleasure of the house. But your committee cannot conclude without strenuously recommending the subject of national education, not only as a high constitutional duty, but urged by every feeling for the welfare of our fellow-citizens, as the brightest glory of a free nation, and the firmest foundation of a free government. . . .

2.

Thomas Jefferson, Letter to Joseph Cabell, 1816

No history of American attitudes toward popular education would be complete without some acknowledgment of Thomas Jefferson's views on the subject, yet his recorded opinions probably did as much to hinder as to help the development of a democratic educational system. Two aspects of his thought, both tied to his vision of America as a land of yeoman farmers and both expressed in a letter to Joseph Cabell (his chief lieutenant in the Virginia legislature) produced this ambiguous result.

One aspect was his abiding interest in establishing a comprehensive system of instruction ranging from primary schools to university, which led him to press the claims of the University of Virginia as strenuously as he pressed those of lesser institutions. Although his plan for ward schools compared favorably with schemes actually put into effect in the northeastern states, it was in many respects only an adjunct to his plan for colleges and a university, and in any event it was pushed aside during the campaign to establish a university. The reasons are complicated, but it would seem that the aging statesman assumed that lesser institutions would arise through the voluntary action of local communities. His assumption was plausible enough in a white society made up almost exclusively of large planters and small landholders—each class saw to the educa-

tion of its children by its own means—yet in the long run it tended
to deprecate organized public effort to secure universal literacy.

In addition, Jefferson left a specific legacy of hostility to
political consolidation, one that stood in the way of virtually every
subsequent attempt at educational reform. (For an example, see Document 12, page 85.) Significantly, the letter to Cabell begins with a
discussion of measures intended to encourage popular education and
ends with a tirade against powerful government. In particular, Jefferson had in mind a competing educational plan, sponsored by
Charles Fenton Mercer, calling for an even more elaborate educational system administered by the state, but the grounds of his objection were universal. In effect, the sage of Monticello put liberty
before education, and both before government.

My letter of the 24th ult. conveyed to you the grounds of
the two articles objected to in the College bill.[1] your last presents one of them in a new point of view, that of the commencement of the Ward schools as likely to render the law
unpopular to the county. it must be a very inconsiderate and
rough process of execution that would do this. my idea of the
mode of carrying it into execution would be this. Declare the
counties *ipso facto* divided into wards, for the present by the
boundaries of the militia captaincies; somebody attend the ordinary muster of each company, having first desired the Captain to call together a full one. there explain the object of the
law to the people of the company, put to their vote whether
they will have a school established, and the most central and
convenient place for it; get them to meet & build a log school

From Roy J. Honeywell, *The Educational Work of Thomas Jefferson*
(Cambridge: Harvard University Press, 1931), pp. 228–229. Reprinted by
permission of the publisher.

[1] [On January 24 Jefferson had written Cabell to justify assigning the
proposed University of Virginia two kinds of civil power: jurisdiction over
breach of the peace by its students, and authority to initiate public
elementary schools in Albemarle County. Bracketed notes are the editor's.]

house, have a roll taken of the children who would attend it, and of those of them able to pay. these would probably be sufficient to support a common teacher, instructing gratis the few unable to pay. if there should be a deficiency, it would require too trifling a contribution from the county to be complained of; and especially as the whole county would participate, where necessary, in the same resource. should the company, by it's vote, decide that it would have no school, let them remain without one. the advantages of this proceeding would be, that it would become the duty of the aldermen elected by the county to take an active part in pressing the introduction of schools and to look out for tutors. if however it is intended that the State government shall take this business into it's own hands, and provide schools for every county, then by all means strike out this provision of our bill. I would never wish that it should be placed on a worse footing than the rest of the state. but if it is believed that these elementary schools will be better managed by the Governor & council, the Commissioners of the literary fund, or any other general authority of the government, than by the parents within each ward, it is a belief against all experience. try the principle one step further, and amend the bill so as to commit to the Governor & Council the management of all our farms, our mills, & merchants' stores. No, my friend, the way to have good and safe government, is not to trust it all to one; but to divide it among the many, distributing to every one exactly the functions he is competent to. let the National government be entrusted with the defence of the nation and it's foreign & federal relations; the State governments with the civil rights, laws, police & administration of what concerns the State generally; the Counties with the local concerns of the counties; and each Ward direct the interests within itself. it is by dividing and subdividing these republics from the great National one down thro' all its subordinations, until it ends in the administration of every man's farm and affairs by himself; by placing under every one what his own eye may superintend, that all will be done for the best. what has de-

stroyed liberty and the rights of man in every government
which has ever existed under the sun? the generalizing & con-
centrating all cares and powers into one body, no matter
whether of the autocrats of Russia or France, or the aristocrats
of a Venetian Senate. and I do believe that if the Almighty has
not decreed that Man shall never be free, (and it is blasphemy
to believe it,) that the secret will be found to be in the making
himself the depository of the powers respecting himself, so far
as he is competent to them, and delegating only what is beyond
his competence by a synthetical process, to higher & higher
orders of functionaries, so as to trust fewer and fewer powers,
in proportion as the trustees become more and more oligarchi-
cal. the elementary republics of the wards, the county republics, the State republics and the republic of the Union, would
form a gradation of authorities, standing each on the basis of
law, holding every one it's delegated share of powers, and con-
stituting truly a system of fundamental balances and checks for
the government. where every man is a sharer in the direction of
his ward republic, or of some of the higher ones, and feels that
he is a participator in the government of affairs not merely at
an election, one day in the year, but every day; when there
shall not be a man in the state who will not be a member of
some one of it's councils, great or small, he will let the heart be
torn out of his body, sooner than his power be wrested from
him by a Caesar or a Bonaparte. how powerfully did we feel
the energy of this organization in the case of the Embargo? I
felt the foundations of the Government shaken under my feet
by the New England townships. there was not an individual in
their states whose body was not thrown, with all it's momentum, into action, and, altho' the whole of the other states were
known to be in favor of the measure, yet the organization of
this little selfish minority enabled it to overrule the Union. what
could the unwieldy counties of the middle, the South and the
West do? call a county meeting, and the drunken loungers at
and about the Courthouses would have collected, the distances
being too great for the good people and the industrious gener-

ally to attend. the character of those who really met would have been the measure of the weight they would have had in the scale of public opinion. as Cato then concluded every speech with the words 'Carthago delenda est', so do I every opinion with the injunction 'divide the counties into wards'. begin them only for a single purpose; they will soon shew for what others they are best instruments. God bless you, and all our rulers, and give them the wisdom, as I am sure they have the will, to fortify us against the degeneracy of our government, and the concentration of all it's powers in the hands of the one, the few, the well-born, or but the many.

TH: JEFFERSON

3.

Thomas Cooper, *Lectures on the Elements of Political Economy*, 1826

In his *Lectures on Political Economy* Thomas Cooper sought to convey to the American people principles of liberal economics that he had learned from the Benthamite radicals in his native land. A friend and ally of Thomas Jefferson in his effort to counteract Alexander Hamilton's mercantile economic policies, Cooper later became president of the University of South Carolina, which he made into a southern bastion for republican economics. His *Lectures*, originally delivered at the university, reveal both the logic the Benthamite reformers used to discredit timeworn institutions and the equally rigorous logic with which they approached questions of contemporary social policy and especially of popular education. Cooper's discussion of education is the first of several chapters on police laws and follows a chapter on poor laws; its placement indicates that in his view education is desirable because of its efficiency in promoting social order. By the same token, Cooper praises the monitorial system of instruction advocated by Joseph Lancaster and points to other ways of achieving greater economy in the educational process, almost as if efficiency were more important than pedagogical effectiveness. But it is noteworthy that the criteria of economy and efficiency apply most directly to elementary education, while Cooper goes out of his way to urge generous support for secondary and higher education of the few. Like many republican spokesmen, in short, Cooper viewed universal elementary education as a sort of underpinning for national liberty, which depended as much on the skills of the few as on the literacy of the many.

Chapter 26

OF POLICE LAWS RELATING TO INSTRUCTION AND EDUCATION

It is in vain to talk of equal rights and equal laws—of the obligation of constitutions—the dependency of legislatures —or the responsibility of public officers, to members of a community who can neither read or write.

The first duty of a republic, is to provide for the instruction of its citizens; the next, to exact the evidences of it. The most useful, the most charitable of all contributions, is the contribution of knowledge.

One of the contrivances of an antient tyrant, was to engrave his laws in characters so small, and to hang up the tablets so high that the people who were required to obey them could not read them. The British parliament have acted much in the same way: their criminal code, does not consist merely of the

---

From Thomas Cooper, *Lectures on the Elements of Political Economy* (Columbia, S. C., 1826), pp. 264–271.

common law with the innumerable distinctions and decisions belonging to the penal portion of it, but of seven hundred and fifty verbose, close printed and in many cases incongruous statutes; the inventions for the most part of aristocratical pride, of fiscal necessity, and manufacturing cupidity. Surely for a code of such voluminous fecundity pressing upon the people, the necessity of a national education, is most glaring: yet the benefit of clergy is still a part of the law by which males who can read are exempted from the punishment of crime to which the ignorant poor, and offenders of the female sex are yet subjected. Let it be so there: it ought not to be so here; more especially as we adopt the British maxim, *Ignorantia legis, excusat neminem.*[1]

There is no remedy against mistake or imposition of any kind, political, clerical, medical, or legal, but knowledge. There is no method of attaching the mass of the people to republican institutions, or of inducing them to prefer common sense to mystery, but by giving them information, and enabling them to think and reflect. Ignorance is necessary to the continuance of slavery, whether the object be to keep the mind or the body, or both in chains. Hence throughout Europe, the dread of discussion; the tyrannical extent of the doctrine of libel; the morbid aversion of legitimacy to all mental improvement beyond mere scientific fact. Hence the holy alliance in that quarter of the world between church and state, in which one party says to the other, "if you will preach up and inculcate implicit faith in all the mysteries of politics, and implicit obedience to all the pretensions of government, we will enforce all the theological mysteries that you may deem requisite to a full command over the minds of the people, and a plentiful share of the public wealth." We want no learned men in our dominions, says the present Emperor of Austria; we want none but good subjects; we want no instructors but the worthy priests.

As a member of the holy alliance, he was right. But

---

[1] [Ignorance of the law excuses no one.]

look at the effect of this doctrine, in Spain, Italy, Austria, France, where the priesthood regulates every thing!

It is not sufficient that a knowledge of elementary science should be diffused among every class of the people; they should know also, if time admit, the *elementary* truths of politics, political economy, and ethics. This may seem a great deal, but almost all that is valuable as elementary and demonstrative truths in these branches of knowledge, may be taught in twelve months. If we are to have enlightened legislators we must have enlightened electors; especially in a government where the principle and the practice of universal suffrage is required to prevail. Without this knowledge, that principle and that practice is liable to many very formidable if not insuperable objections; give the knowledge, and the objections are answered: and I think it can be given. The *Mechanic Library Societies*, and the *Mechanic Institutions* for the purpose of affording and acquiring elementary science, now so prevalent in England, and commencing in New York and Philadelphia, show what prodigious benefit can be effected in that way; and a very moderate extension of the principle, will embrace all that is wanted for the purposes of a republican elector. To extend knowledge among the rich, is doing great good: for the truths that have to fight their way in the present generation, will become axioms universally adopted half a century hence: but he is the best patriot who extends the blessings of knowledge among the great mass of mankind; among those whose condition most requires to be improved. If liberty is to be placed on firm ground, it must be by the means here suggested, for there are no other equal to the required effect.

In the present state of public sentiment and public information, the requisites I now propose, will I fear, be more than can be soon acceded to: and it may be wise not to attempt too much. If therefore the state were to open and furnish elementary schools for the purpose of teaching reading, writing, the English grammar, the rules of arithmetic, including vulgar and decimal fractions, mensuration, and the elements of geography, it would be perhaps as far as the temper of the times would admit. Less than this is surely too little. Some history of America and the American revolution, with the Declaration of Independence, the Constitution of the United States and of our own state, should be made school books. Snowden's History of America, or a concise history of the United States (M'Culloch, Philadelphia, 1795) either of them are a good size for the purpose, and sufficiently well compiled.[2]

The great difficulty is to lay down the principles on which the schools should be conducted to make them answer the required purpose. There is great danger of their becoming jobs in the hands of the managers.

1. What is the plan of teaching most convenient to be adopted in our country? In South Carolina?

2. What provisions are necessary in the law to render these means of instruction efficient?

3. What provisions are necessary to secure the due application of the school funds, without defalcation or waste?

4. Should the instruction afforded, be without pay, and without any price exacted from the parents?

5. Can any means be adopted to insure to the public, that every citizen really has been educated to the extent proposed?

As to the first question. It appears to me, that where a dense population, and the number of students will justify it, the Lancasterian monitorial plan of mutual instruction as described in the first number of that excellent work, the Westminster Review, is most efficient and most economical. It is therefore adapted to our large cities, and populous districts. But in country places, in remote townships settled as yet by

---

[2] [The reference is probably to Richard Snowden's *History of North and South America, from its Discovery, to the Death of General Washington.* The first edition was published by Jacob Johnson in Philadelphia in 1806; revised editions continued to appear until 1832. John M'Culloch first published his *Concise History of the United States, from the Discovery of America* in 1787, then re-issued it in 1795.]

scattered inhabitants, the schools should be conducted in the usual way, by single masters, until the population should admit of, or require a change.

As to the second question. The masters appointed, should devote every Saturday to examination into the acquirements of the preceding five days: and the trustees of the school should be required to attend at least all quarterly examinations. This should be a duty exacted under a penalty. At these quarterly examinations, specimens of proficiency, produced on the spot, on momentary requisition, should be demanded from each pupil. The secret of all school proficiency, is frequent and rigid examination.

I am inclined to think that every voter should be bound to declare, at every election, that the ticket by him delivered in, is in his own hand writing.

As to the third question. The expenditure of the money allowed to such school district, if the present plan of free schools, should be permitted to continue, should be rigidly enquired into twice a year, by some independent persons chosen at the general election to be school auditors of the district for the year. This audit should take place within a week after the expiration of the half year, and the result published in the newspaper; or in two newspapers of the place: open to a further audit if necessary, on motion made before the court of common pleas or chancery, shewing sufficient reason for further investigation. School funds are at present liable to great abuse, from collusion between the masters and the managers of the entrusted fund, and for want of some efficient means of rigidly compelling those who receive the money to account for its honest appropriation. This has been too much neglected in this State. But upon the plan I am about to propose, the expence of State schools will regulate itself, and there can be no room for expence arising from peculation or neglect.

As to the fourth question. I do not think that the free schools erected by the state, should be so free as to furnish knowledge without cost or price. This may do in the old countries of Europe, where taxation falls heavily on the poor; but I am persuaded that it is not eligible here. There is no man so poor in this country that he cannot afford half a day's wages per week for the education of his child. There is not an industrious man in the United States who cannot afford twice that contribution.

Moreover, the common feeling among the poorer class in the United States, revolts at an obligation that looks like bestowing of alms. They would rather pay a small sum to a good school, frequented also by the children of more opulent parents, than to send their children to a charity school. This is a feeling fit to be encouraged: and if it be not checked by a system of poor rates, operating as a premium for idleness, and drunkenness, it will universally prevail.

I am inclined therefore to think, that every man however poor should be required to pay a small sum for the education of his children, that he may feel that he has *a right* to have them educated; and take an interest in the management and the success of the school.

The State therefore should furnish no more than a competent teacher, and pay him a moderate salary.* The school house and furniture with wood for firing, should be at the expence of the district; the school books, paper, slates, pens, ink, &c. should be at the charge of the parents. If an assistant teacher be wanted monitors may be appointed to relieve the master. Each parent also, ought to pay a small sum quarterly for each child he sends, which should form an addition to the master's emoluments.

If the master received from the State, 450 dollars a year for each school district, and two dollars a quarter for each pupil sent to school, where one only comes from one family, and one

---

* I think the State also should furnish each schoolhouse with a map of the world, of Europe, of Asia, of Africa, of South America, of the West Indies, of Australasia, and of the United States: to be replaced when damaged by the Township by an order on the county treasurer by the school trustees.

dollar each where two or more are sent, it would amount to a salary sufficient to ensure competent teachers: the trustees of each district (never exceeding in extent five miles square) might be nominated annually by the judge of the first session in the year.[3] Their duty of superintendence, especially at quarterly examinations should be imperative and compulsory. The judge of the district on application of the trustees, might have power to remove a schoolmaster for misconduct or neglect, and appoint another. The schoolmasters might be chosen by the trustees, after examination as to their qualifications by the faculty of the college. The salary to be drawn from the State treasury. At present the State is at an expence of about forty thousand dollars a year for a very inefficient system of free schools, of which the city of Charleston absorbs nearly one half. Nor is any account annually published as it ought to be, of the names of the teachers, and the number of scholars in each district, nor how long each scholar stays at school, or how in particular the monies are expended.

As to the fifth question. I greatly doubt if any compulsory method other than I have now indicated, can be put in force so as to compel the evidences of the required education. For the most part, public example, and good feelings, will suffice to induce every parent to avail himself of the means afforded, because it is plainly his duty and his interest to give these advantages to his children. We may safely leave it therefore to the operation of parental interest.

There is a further question connected with this subject.

Ought the community at the public expence to establish universities, or collegiate seminaries for the teaching of the higher branches of knowledge? Branches to which the poor cannot have access and of which their probable avocations in future life will have no need?

---

[3] [The first session of the county court, which performed in the South many of the tasks that New England practice assigned to town governments.]

I have no hesitation in saying yes. For the following reasons:

First. Knowledge is power. The higher grades of knowledge such as the higher mathematics and astronomy, chemistry, mechanical philosophy, the elements of politics, political economy, ethics, logic, the theory of language, of jurisprudence, of botany, mineralogy, anatomy, physiology and pathology are not only greatly conducive to private comfort and improvement, but they constitute the indispensible [*sic*] basis of all national power, national wealth, prosperity, reputation and happiness. The nations that possess them in the greatest degree, are the most powerful. The facts are too glaring to admit of doubt. Look at Great Britain and France: it is not necessary to look farther. I refer to the discourse of *Cuvier* already cited for the incalculable influence of the higher grades of science and literature on the happiness and prosperity of nations.[4]

Secondly. These acquirements are not merely accessary [*sic*] of themselves and for their own sake, and for home use, but they constitute the main difference between nations in respect of their power and their influence over each other. For the extensive application of the higher branches of knowledge, I need refer not only to the discourse of Cuvier, but to Dupin's account of the prodigious scientific power of Great Britain;[5] to the present state of astronomy and nautical instr[u]ments; to the discoveries and applications of chimistry [*sic*]; to the steam engine; and to the other innumerable labour saving machines guided by the higher mathematics, and the algebraical calcu-

---

[4] [The reference is to "Reflections on the Progress of the Sciences, and their relations with Society," by the eminent French paleontologist, Baron Georges Léopold Chrétien Frédéric Dagobert Cuvier (1769–1832). His paper had appeared in translation in the first volume of Walsh's *American Register* (1817).]

[5] [Between 1820 and 1824 Baron Charles Dupin, a prominent French mathematician and statistician, published six volumes surveying the commerce and industry of Great Britain under the general title *Voyages en Grande-Bretagne de 1816 à 1819*.]

lus, which seems to have subjected to its power the whole range of scientific fact.

Thirdly. The apparatus of every description, buildings, professors, instruments, machines, library, &c. absolutely necessary for instruction in the higher branches of knowledge, are far too expensive for any private speculation. Private persons, if they could command the necessary capital, could never command the price of tuition that would repay such an expenditure. In no nation whatever, have these institutions been attempted, or could they have succeeded without public aid to a great amount; and from the nature of them, they cannot be set up on an efficient scale, but at the public expence. Nor is this a misappropriation of the public money for the benefit of the rich, and to the exclusion of the poor. It is not meant to benefit the rich, or the poor, or both, or either: but as an instrument of national benefit, like an army or navy for public defence. These institutions are absolutely necessary to furnish us with the same advantage derived from the possession of knowledge, that our neighbours enjoy. The terms and conditions on which it is to be communicated, will vary with the condition of the society in which they are erected.

Thirdly. The higher the scale of education in the best society, the higher will be the amount of knowledge required, in every other class from the highest to the lowest. If the quantity of acquired knowledge in the higher ranks of society be but moderate, how can we expect any among the lowest? Experience has fully shewn that the progress and influence of good education is downward. I hope it is not necessary to dwell on these truths, which no man of experience will hesitate for a moment to admit.

In this country of the United States, every state ought to have primary schools, and an university: a military and a naval school also might be desirable for the maritime states. The naval academy of the English, has been found of incalculable advantage.

It is not my business to enter into any details on these subjects, but merely to state what appear to me in this respect the duties of the government toward the people, or rather the duties of the people toward themselves: and what description of institutions rank among the necessary means of national prosperity. All the institutions and apparatus for the diffusion of knowledge among the people, from primary schools to the best appointed University, I consider as entering into the catalogue of expences of the very first and most indispensible necessity: nor can any state be in a high degree either powerful, safe, happy, or wise, whose governors are not alive to the importance of these truths.

4.

De Witt Clinton, Message to the New York Legislature, 1826

Governor De Witt Clinton of New York, a vigorous promoter of increased educational appropriations and of improved teaching methods, could count on a greater degree of public support for elementary education than was common in many of the other states of the Union. Like many of his contemporaries, he looked to the annual income from an augmented Common School Fund to meet the state's obligations to its school districts, but he also relied on the voluntary assistance of the Free School Society of New York City (of which he was a prominent member) to provide gratuitous elementary instruction for many really needy children. Although he had too-great hopes for the monitorial system of instruction, it is noteworthy that he was a pioneer advocate of normal training and that he urged gratuitous secondary education on the monitorial system for meritorious students who could not otherwise afford it. If he was almost totally unaware of the enormous tasks the state would confront when it decided to see to a truly effective education of its people, he nevertheless voiced the early republican concept of popular education at its best.

. . . The first duty of government, and the surest evidence of good government, is the encouragement of education. A general diffusion of knowledge is the precursor and protector of republican institutions; and in it we must confide as the conservative power that will watch over our liberties, and guard them against fraud, intrigue, corruption and violence. In early infancy, education may be usefully administered. In some parts of Great Britain, infant schools have been successfully established, comprising children from two to six years of age, whose tempers, hearts and minds are ameliorated, and whose indigent parents are enabled by these means, to devote themselves to labor without interruption or uneasiness. Institutions of this kind are only adapted to a dense population, and must be left to the guardianship of private benevolence. Our common schools embrace children from five to fifteen years old, and continue to increase and prosper. The appropriations for last year from the school fund amount to $80,670, and an equivalent sum is also raised by taxation in the several school districts, and is applied in the same way. The capital fund is $1,333,000, which will be in a state of rapid augmentation from sales of the public lands and other sources. And it is well ascertained that more than 420,000 children have been taught in our common schools during the last year. The sum distributed by the state is now too small, and the general fund can well warrant an augmentation to $120,000 annually.

An important change has taken place in the free schools of New York. By an arrangement between the corporation of that city and the trustees of the free school society, those estab-

---

From *State of New York. Messages from the Governors,* ed. Charles Z. Lincoln (11 volumes; Albany, N. Y., 1909), III, 114–117.

lishments are to be converted into public schools, to admit the children of the rich as well as of the poor, and by this annihilation of factitious distinctions, there will be a strong incentive for the display of talents, and a felicitous accommodation to the genius of republican government. In these seminaries, the monitorial system has been always used, and it has in other institutions been applied with complete success to the high branches of education.

Our system of instruction, with all its numerous benefits, is still however susceptible of great improvement. Ten years of the life of a child may now be spent in a common school. In two years the elements of instruction may be acquired, and the remaining eight years must either be spent in repetition or in idleness, unless the teachers of common schools are competent to instruct in the higher branches of knowledge. The outlines of geography, algebra, mineralogy, agricultural chemistry, mechanical philosophy, surveying, geometry, astronomy, political economy, and ethics, might be communicated in that period of time by able preceptors, without essential interference with the calls of domestic industry. The vocation of a teacher, in its influence on the characters and destinies of the rising and all future generations, has either not been sufficiently understood or duly estimated. It is or ought to be ranked among the learned professions. With a full admission of the merits of several who now officiate in that capacity, still it must be conceded that the information of many of the instructors of our common schools, does not extend beyond rudimental education;—that our expanding population requires constant accessions to their numbers, and that to realize these views, it is necessary that some new plan for obtaining able teachers, should be devised; I therefore recommend a seminary for the education of teachers in the monitorial system of instruction, and in those useful branches of knowledge which are proper to engraft on elementary attainments. A compliance with this recommendation will have the most benign influence on individual happiness and social prosperity. To break down the

barriers which poverty has erected against the acquisition and
dispensation of knowledge, is to restore the just equilibrium of
society, and to perform a duty of indispensable and paramount
obligation. And under this impression, I also recommend that
provision be made for the gratuitous education in our superior
seminaries of indigent, talented and meritorious youth.

I consider the system of our common schools as the palladium of our freedom; for no reasonable apprehension can be
entertained of its subversion, as long as the great body of the
people are enlightened by education. To increase the funds, to
extend the benefits, and to remedy the defects of this excellent
system, is worthy of your most deliberate attention. The officer
who now so ably presides over that department, is prevented
by his other official duties from visiting our schools in person,
nor is he indeed clothed with this power.[1] A visitatorial authority for the purpose of detecting abuses in the application of
funds, of examining into the modes and plans of instruction,
and of suggesting improvements, would unquestionably be attended with the most propitious effects. . . .

5.

Josiah Holbrook, "Considerations," 1827

One of the methods by which early republican philanthropists sought to promote popular education was the creation of voluntary societies to augment the work of the elementary schools. To a
large extent their mechanics' institutes, libraries, and similar agencies followed the example of the London Mechanics' Institution,

---

[1] [In New York at this time the secretary of state was ex officio superintendent of common schools. The incumbent was John Van Ness Yates.]

founded in England in 1823 to assist aspiring mechanics and other worthy individuals to benefit from the scientific and technological discoveries of their age. The American Lyceum, on the other hand, was a largely indigenous expression of the same impulse, one geared to self and social improvement in virtually every area of contemporary life. As this statement by its most prominent advocate shows, in its early stages it consisted of local associations of interested citizens who met to discuss scientific discoveries, to promote serious conversation, and to disseminate improvements in pedagogy. Some lyceums also undertook to compile town histories, to draft town maps, and to conduct geological surveys or assemble mineral collections, all of which were expected to contribute to the same ends. As the institution spread outside New England it abandoned some of these functions to become instead a well-organized popular lecture circuit, but for many years it remained a powerful vehicle for the diffusion of science, technology, and moral philosophy.

Institutions for Mutual Instruction have some advantages over any others which can be formed.

In the first place, they can diffuse information more generally. They may extend it to nearly every member of the community. The old and young, the male and female, the parent and child, the learned and illiterate, the clergyman and physician, the lawyer and statesman, the merchant, mechanic, and farmer, may each benefit others, and, at the same time, confer a double benefit upon himself.

Secondly—the information they communicate is practical. As each Association, from one meeting to another, chooses their subjects of attention, and, as the instruction is communicated principally by discussion and conversation, they will be likely to be of a practical nature, and directly and thoroughly applied to the various avocations and pursuits of those con-

From *American Lyceum of Science and the Arts, Composed of Associations for Mutual Instruction, and Designed for the General Diffusion of Useful and Practical Knowledge* (Worcester, Mass., 1827), pp. 5–7.

cerned. They also furnish a strong inducement to read, and to apply what they read to their present and future benefit, and thus render a Library a hundred fold more useful.

Thirdly—they have a good moral tendency. This is the most important consideration. Indeed, the morals of the young, in particular, demand, most imperiously, something of this nature; for there are at this moment, in our country, thousands, and many thousands too, the pride and the hope of parents and friends, who are going rapidly to destruction, for the want of some object of sufficient interest to divert their attention from places and practices, calculated to fix upon them habits, which will lead to their ruin with as much certainty as falling bodies are drawn towards the centre of the earth.

It is not frowns, it is not arguments, that will correct or prevent these practices. It is presenting a substitute, which is not less interesting but more useful, that alone will prove an effectual bulwark against vicious habits in the young, and set them in a way that leads to usefulness, respectability and happiness, in this and the future world. Consequently, Associations for mutual improvement in useful knowledge are the best moral societies that can possibly be formed.

Fourthly—they have a good political tendency. The prosperity, and probably the existence, of our Government, depend upon the general diffusion of knowledge. It is upon the ignorant, that the aspiring demagogue acts to effect his designs, and usurp the rights of a nation. The intelligent are better able to see through the pretences and intrigues of a usurper, as well as to understand and support their rights. If all the members of our nation should become enlightened, they would view the principles of their Constitution as inviolable as the mind that planned it, and be ready to defend it with the same boldness and energy as the hand that drew it.

Fifthly—Associations for mutual improvement are economical. If all should unite in them who ought, One Dollar a year each would be sufficient to defray all the current expenses attending them; and, as this dollar is to be appropriated to books and other valuable property, it would be a permanent fund for the future use and benefit of the members and their posterity. In many cases it would be an actual saving of expense; for, as it would turn the attention of the members to subjects of general utility, it would, consequently, divert it from others which are more expensive, and less useful, if not pernicious. The economy of time is not less in their favor: to many it would be a saving of time; to none would it be a loss. And yet, notwithstanding the expense of time or money would in no case be perceptible, and in many there would be an actual saving of both, it is confidently believed that a youth, growing up to manhood, under the advantages and influence of an Association well conducted, would gain more useful, practical information than he would be likely to obtain in a College course.

Sixthly—they may be the means of improving common schools, and establishing in them greater uniformity, both in books and instruction. If these Associations should be formed in most of our towns, and all within a county, or other moderate district, united by a Board of Delegates, the several Boards would have it in their power, not only to adopt regulations for the mutual benefit of their several Branches, but also to take measures for the improvement of common education. There might even be established, under their patronage, institutions for qualifying teachers, and for giving practical instruction on the various subjects fitted to the employments of the farmer and mechanic, if not to those of the legislator, the physician, and the divine. From the several Boards of Delegates in various parts of the country, a general one might be formed, to be called the AMERICAN BOARD OF EDUCATION. Said American Board would, of course, be composed of gentlemen of the most liberal and enlightened views upon the subject of education; and, if they should meet annually, they would bring together a knowledge of the state and improvements of schools and common education in their several districts, and might recommend measures which would have the most salutary influence upon the interests of the rising generation, and, of course, upon the highest and most lasting interests of our nation and the world.

6.

William Carroll, Message to the Tennessee Legislature, 1827

Because the states of the Northeast generally boasted some semblance of a public school system during the early years of the nineteenth century, they were often held up as a model by the advocates of popular education in other regions of the country. Governor William Carroll of Tennessee was one such figure, and the terms in which he addressed the state legislature in 1827 reveal both the pressures state governments everywhere had begun to feel to provide directly for education and the complications that still attached to the idea. On the one hand, Carroll testified to the worth of universal education and the necessity of providing it gratis or nearly gratis even in a society of yeoman farmers. On the other hand, he apparently hoped to achieve it without requiring either state or local taxation for the purpose, and (in common with many contemporaries) he looked upon the public domain as a potential source of educational funds. The erstwhile frontier state of Tennessee was neither hostile to education nor willing as yet to pay for it.

. . . In a government like ours, founded upon, and supported by, the will of the people, it is of the utmost consequence to the stability of our civil institutions, that the yeoman[r]y of the country—the cultivators of the soil, should be enlightened by education. It improves their moral condition, takes away incentives to vice; establishes habits of sobriety,

---

From *Tennessee House Journal*, 1827, pp. 10–12.

industry and a cheerful obedience to the laws; and enables them to acquire a knowledge of the salutary principles of our government. Nor is this all. Under the happy influence of a system of education extending its benefits to every one, genius and talent are brought forth to usefulness, which would otherwise remain in obscurity. This interesting subject is every day, attracting more and more attention in all parts of the Union, and is diffusing its blessings throughout the land. In New England, the plan of common schools is carried to great perfection. The counties are divided into small districts, in each of which there is a school, where every citizen whether he be rich or poor, has a right to send his children. The funds for the support of those schools, in most places, are principally derived from a tax upon real property, so that the expense of educating the poor falls upon the wealth of the country. By this plan of instruction, indigent youth are prepared to be useful and respectable citizens here, and are qualified for happiness hereafter. In New York, upwards of four hundred thousand children, at least one fourth of the whole population of the state, are instructed in common schools. In the metropolis of that great state, more than ten thousand children are annually educated by the charity of its citizens at free schools; and, it is said, a solitary instance has not occurred, of any one taught at those institutions having been convicted of crimes. This circumstance furnishes an interesting lesson in support of a general diffusion of knowledge. Indeed all experience proves the happy effects of education upon the morals of society. Of Scotland, where great attention is paid to education, an eloquent writer says, 'that there is no country of Europe, in which in proportion to its population, so small a number of crimes fall under the chastisement of the criminal law.' How dark is the opposite side of the picture? What is the condition of those, who, for want of opportunities of learning, are kept in a state of ignorance? A great portion of them seek enjoyment in midnight revels, gaming and every species of dissipation, which allures them from the paths of honor, and they sink into an untimely grave, without even the regrets of the community or of those who are bound to them by the ties of kindred. In addition to this, a fact may with propriety be mentioned, to show the baleful effects of ignorance, and a want of learning. A large portion of the unfortunate inmates of penitentiaries and prisons in the United States, were, when committed, almost wholly destitute of education. Feeling a lively interest in this matter, I cannot but hope that you will cause a fund to be set apart, in addition to those already designated for that purpose, for the support of common schools, academies and colleges. A portion of the revenue of the state could not be applied to a nobler object, and I propose the measure for your deliberate consideration. The residue of the lands in the Western District, after the satisfaction of North Carolina claimants, will be of no great value —not of sufficient importance, perhaps, to the general government, to justify the expense they must necessarily incur to use them for the general benefit, but yet might be so appropriated by them towards all these objects, as to aid much in the attainment of the ends proposed.[1] Ought not a vigorous effort to be made, to procure a relinquishment of claim to them by Congress for these purposes? . . .

---

[1] [The Western District was the area that now comprises the western third of Tennessee. It was withheld from sale in 1806 when the United States, Tennessee, and North Carolina signed a compact assigning unappropriated lands in the eastern two-thirds of Tennessee to that state on condition that she appropriate a stipulated acreage to education and that she honor land titles issued by North Carolina before Tennessee had been established as a separate state. From 1824 on the state legislature solicited Congress to assign it control over the reserved lands.]

7.

Report of a Committee of Philadelphia Workingmen, 1830

Much of the pressure for educational reform during the first decades of the nineteenth century came from well educated publicists and officials who either feared or regretted the consequences of popular ignorance. With the advent of the workingmen's movement, however, the character of agitation for educational reform began to change. Many of its spokesmen were fairly prosperous citizens, as were many of the workingmen themselves; they united more often to block economic and social innovations than to secure the rights of an industrial proletariat. Nevertheless, as this statement by a committee of Philadelphia workingmen indicates, they also indicted as "anti-republican" or undemocratic many of the educational institutions that a generation of republican spokesmen had taken for granted. In their eyes, universal elementary education at public expense was the only appropriate way to overcome inequalities of birth and to destroy the unfair advantages that well-to-do citizens derived from academies and colleges supported in large part by public funds. Some workingmen also looked to the creation of public boarding schools to prevent adventitious distinctions from being carried into the classroom, and they were often sympathetic to manual labor schools on the Swiss model as a way of helping to support secondary education and as a mode of practical instruction in the dignity of labor. In the long run these innovations failed to attract significant support even among workingmen, but the early agitators did succeed in making republican concern for the education of the people into a powerful argument for the establishment of truly common schools.

Report of the Joint Committees of the City and County of Philadelphia, appointed September, 1829, to ascertain the state of public instruction in Pennsylvania, and to digest and propose such improvements in education as may be deemed essential to the intellectual and moral prosperity of the people.

It is now nearly five months since the committees were appointed to co-operate on this arduous duty. But the importance of the subject; the time expended in research and enquiry, in order to procure information relative to it; and the multiplied discussions and deliberations necessary to reconcile and correct their own different and sometimes conflicting views, will, they believe, constitute a reasonable apology for this long delay.

After devoting all the attention to the subject, and making every enquiry which their little leisure and ability would permit, they are forced into the conviction, that there is great defect in the educational system of Pennsylvania; and that much remains to be accomplished before it will have reached that point of improvement which the resources of the state would justify, and which the intellectual condition of the people and the preservation of our republican institutions demand.

With the exception of this city and county, the city and incorporated borough of Lancaster, and the city of Pittsburgh, erected into "school districts" since 1818, it appears that the entire state is destitute of any provisions for public instruction, except those furnished by the enactment of 1809. This law requires the assessors of the several counties to ascertain and return the number of children whose parents are unable, through poverty, to educate them; and such children are per-

---

From *Working Man's Advocate,* March 6, 1830, reprinted in John R. Commons *et al.,* eds., *A Documentary History of American Industrial Society* (10 volumes; Cleveland, Ohio, 1910–1911), V, 94–107. Second edition, with new prefaces, New York: Russell & Russell, 1958.

mitted to be instructed at the most convenient schools at the expense of their respective counties.

The provisions of this act, however, are incomplete and frequently inoperative. They are, in some instances, but partially executed; in others, perverted and abused—and in many cases entirely and culpably neglected. The funds appropriated by the act, have, in some instances, been embezzled by fraudulent agents; and in others, partial returns of the children have been made, and some have been illegally and intentionally excluded from participating in the provisions of the law. From a parsimonious desire of saving the county funds, the cheapest, and consequently the most inefficient schools have been usually selected by the commissioners of the several counties.

The elementary schools throughout the state are irresponsible institutions, established by individuals, from mere motives of private speculation or gain, who are sometimes destitute of character, and frequently, of the requisite attainments and abilities. From the circumstance of the schools being the absolute property of individuals, no supervision or effectual control can be exercised over them; hence, ignorance, inattention, and even immorality, prevail to a lamentable extent among their teachers.

In some districts, no schools whatever exist! No means whatever of acquiring education are resorted to; while ignorance, and its never failing consequence, crime, are found to prevail in these neglected spots, to a greater extent than in other more favored portions of the state.

The "three school districts," however, which have been alluded to, are not liable to these objections. Much good, in particular, has resulted from the establishment of the first of these, comprising this city and county, and which owes its establishment to the persevering efforts of a few individuals, who, in order to succeed, even so far, were compelled to combat the ignorance, the prejudices, and the pecuniary interests of many active and hostile opponents.

But the principles on which these "school districts" are founded, are yet, in the opinion of the committees, extremely defective and inefficient. Their leading feature is pauperism! They are confined exclusively to the children of the poor, while there are, perhaps, thousands of children whose parents are unable to afford for them, a good private education, yet whose standing, professions or connexions in society effectually exclude them from taking the benefit of a poor law. There are great numbers, even of the poorest parents, who hold a dependence on the public bounty to be incompatible with the rights and liberties of an American citizen, and whose deep and cherished consciousness of independence determines them rather to starve the intellect of their offspring, than submit to become the objects of public charity.

There are, also, many poor families, who are totally unable to maintain and clothe their children, while at the schools; and who are compelled to place them, at a very early age, at some kind of labor that may assist in supporting them, or to bind them out as apprentices to relieve themselves entirely of the burthen of their maintenance and education, while the practice formerly universal, of schooling apprentices, has, of late years, greatly diminished and is still diminishing.

Another radical and glaring defect in the existing public school system is the very limited amount of instruction it affords, even to the comparatively small number of youth, who enjoy its benefits. It extends, in no case, further than a tolerable proficiency in reading, writing, and arithmetic, and sometimes to a slight acquaintance with geography. Besides these, the girls are taught a few simple branches of industry. A great proportion of scholars, however, from the causes already enumerated, acquire but a very slight and partial knowledge of these branches.

The present public school system, limited as it is to three solitary school districts, makes no provision for the care and instruction of children under five years old. This class of children is numerous, especially among the poor, and it frequently happens that the parents, or parent, (perhaps a widow) whose only resource for a livelihood is her needle or wash tub, is compelled to keep her elder children from the school to take charge of the younger ones, while her own hands are industriously employed in procuring a subsistence for them. Such instances are far from being rare, and form a very prominent and lamentable drawback on the utility of the schools in these districts. The care thus bestowed on infants, is insufficient and very partial. They are frequently exposed to the most pernicious influences and impressions. The seeds of vice, thus early scattered over the infant soil, are too often permitted to ripen, as life advances, till they fill society with violence and outrage, and yield an abundant harvest for magdalens and penitentiaries.

An opinion is entertained by many good and wise persons, and supported to a considerable extent, by actual experiment, that proper schools for supplying a judicious infant training, would effectually prevent much of that vicious depravity of character which penal codes and punishments are vainly intended to counteract. Such schools would, at least, relieve, in a great measure, many indigent parents, from the care of children, which in many cases occupies as much of their time as would be necessary to earn the children a subsistence. They would also afford many youth an opportunity of participating in the benefits of the public schools, who otherwise must, of necessity, be detained from them.

From this view of the public instruction in Pennsylvania, it is manifest that, even in "the school districts," to say nothing of the remainder of the state, a very large proportion of youth are either partially or entirely destitute of education.

It is true the state is not without its colleges and universities, several of which have been fostered with liberal supplies from the public purse. Let it be observed, however, that the funds so applied, have been appropriated exclusively for the benefit of the wealthy, who are thereby enabled to procure a liberal education for their children, upon lower terms than it could otherwise be afforded them. Funds thus expended, may serve to engender an aristocracy of talent, and place knowledge, the chief element of power, in the hands of the privileged few; but can never secure the common prosperity of a nation nor confer intellectual as well as political equality on a people.

The original element of despotism is a monopoly of talent, which consigns the multitude to comparative ignorance, and secures the balance of knowledge on the side of the rich and the rulers. If then the healthy existence of a free government be, as the committee believe, rooted in the will of the American people, it follows as a necessary consequence, of a government based upon that will, that this monopoly should be broken up, and that the means of equal knowledge, (the only security for equal liberty) should be rendered, by legal provision, the common property of all classes.

In a republic, the people constitute the government, and by wielding its powers in accordance with the dictates, either of their intelligence or their ignorance; of their judgment or their caprices, are the makers and the rulers of their own good or evil destiny. They frame the laws and create the institutions, that promote their happiness or produce their destruction. If they be wise and intelligent, no laws but what are just and equal will receive their approbation, or be sustained by their suffrages. If they be ignorant and capricious, they will be deceived by mistaken or designing rulers, into the support of laws that are unequal and unjust.

It appears, therefore, to the committees that there can be no real liberty without a wide diffusion of real intelligence; that the members of a republic, should all be alike instructed in the nature and character of their equal rights and duties, as human beings, and as citizens; and that education, instead of being limited as in our public poor schools, to a simple acquaintance with words and cyphers, should tend, as far as possible, to the production of a just disposition, virtuous habits, and a rational self governing character.

When the committees contemplate their own condition, and that of the great mass of their fellow laborers; when they look around on the glaring inequality of society, they are constrained to believe, that until the means of equal instruction shall be equally secured to all, liberty is but an unmeaning word, and equality an empty shadow, whose substance to be realized must first be planted by an equal education and proper training in the minds, in the habits, in the manners, and in the feelings of the community.

While, however, the committees believe it their duty to exhibit, fully and openly, the main features and principles of a system of education which can alone comport with the spirit of American liberty, and the equal prosperity and happiness of the people, they are not prepared to assert, that the establishment of such a system in its fullness and purity, throughout the state, is by any means attainable at a single step. While they maintain that each human being has an equal right to a full development of all his powers, moral, physical, and intellectual; that the common good of society can never be promoted in its fullness till all shall be equally secured and protected in the enjoyment of this right, and that it is the first great duty of the states, to secure the same to all its members; yet, such is now the degraded state of education in Pennsylvania, compared with what, in the opinion of the committees, education for a free people should be, that they despair of so great a change as must be involved in passing from one to the other, being accomplished suddenly throughout the state. No new system of education could probably be devised with consequences so manifestly beneficial, as to awaken at once in the public mind, a general conviction and concurrence in the necessity of its universal adoption.

The committees are aware, also, that it is their duty to consult the views, the feelings, and the prejudices, not of a single district or county merely, but of the state in general. The measure which it is their business to propose, is one designed to be of universal extent and influence, and must, to be successful, be based upon the manifest wishes of nearly the whole commonwealth. It is not, therefore, to what would constitute a perfect education only, but also, to what may be rendered practicable—it is not with a view, exclusively, to the kind of education every child of Pennsylvania ought to have, but likewise to what it is possible, under existing circumstances, views, and prejudices, every child of Pennsylvania may and can have, that they have drawn up a bill or outline of what they deem a system of public education, adapted to the present condition and necessities of the state in general.

The principal points in which the bill for establishing common schools, accompanying this report, differs from the existing system of free schools, are as follows:

1. Its provisions, instead of being limited to three single districts, are designed to extend throughout the commonwealth. 2d. It places the managers of the public schools, immediately under the control and suffrage of the people. 3d. Its benefits and privileges will not, as at present, be limited as an act of charity to the poor alone, but will extend equally and of right to all classes, and be supported at the expense of all. 4th. It lays a foundation for infantile, as well as juvenile instruction. And lastly, it leaves the door open to every possible improvement which human benevolence and ingenuity may be able to introduce.

While, however, the committees would urge the establishment of common elementary schools throughout the state, as comprising, perhaps, the best general system of education which is at present attainable, it is but just to exhibit, also, some of the defects as well as the advantages of such schools; and to suggest such further measures as appear calculated to obviate such defects.

The instruction afforded by common schools, such as are contemplated in the bill for a general system of education, being only elementary, must, of necessity, produce but a very limited development of the human faculties. It would indeed diminish, but could not destroy, the present injurious monopoly of talent. While the higher branches of literature and science remain accessible only to the children of the wealthy, there must still be a balance of knowledge, and with it a "balance of power," in the hands of the privileged few, the rich and the rulers.

Another radical defect in the best system of common schools yet established, will be found in its not being adapted to meet the wants and necessities of those who stand most in need of it. Very many of the poorest parents are totally unable to clothe and maintain their children while at school, and are compelled to employ their time, while yet very young, in aiding to procure a subsistence. In the city of New York, a much more efficient system of education exists than in this city, and common schools have been in successful operation for the last ten or twelve years; yet there are at the present time upwards of 24,000 children between the ages of 5 and 15 years, who attend no schools whatever, and this apparently criminal neglect of attending the schools is traced, chiefly, to the circumstance just mentioned. It is evidently therefore, of no avail, how free the schools may be, while those children who stand most in need of them, are, through the necessity of their parents, either retained from them altogether, or withdrawn at an improper age, to assist in procuring a subsistence.

The constitution of this state declares that "the legislature shall provide schools in which the poor may be taught gratis." If this signifies that the poor shall have an opportunity afforded for instruction, it must involve means equal to the end. The poverty of the poor must be no obstruction, otherwise the constitution is a dead letter—nay, worse, an insult on their unfortunate condition and feelings.

The committees, therefore, believe, that one school, at least, should be established in each county, in which some principle should be adopted, calculated to obviate the defects that have been alluded to, and by which the children of all who desire it, may be enabled to procure, at their own expense, a liberal and scientific education. They are of the opinion that a principle fully calculated to secure this object, will be found in a union of agricultural and mechanical with literary and scientific instruction; and they have therefore, in addition to a plan of common elementary schools, drawn up and appended to this report, the substance of a bill providing for the establishment of high schools, or model schools, based upon this principle, which they also present for public deliberation.

Believing, as the committees do, that upon an equal education and proper training to industry, sobriety, and virtue, hangs the liberty and prosperity of the new world, and, perhaps, the ultimate emancipation of the old; and believing, as they do, that the union of industry with literature and science constitutes the only desideratum by which an equal education can be supplied and secured to all classes, they experience the most sincere pleasure in discovering that this good and great principle is gaining in popularity and dominion throughout the world. Not only are institutions of this kind established in France, Prussia, Germany, and Great Britain, in imitation of the original Hofwyl institutions in Switzerland, but in the United States, also, there are several. At Whitesborough, N.Y., there is one with from 30 to 40 pupils; at Princeton, Ky., another containing 80; a third exists at Andover, Mass., that accommodates 60 pupils; a fourth at Maysville, Tenn.; and a fifth has recently been established at Germantown, in this county. At Monmouth, N.J., and at Cincinnati, Ohio, very extensive establishments, based upon this principle, have been or are about commencing.

The Germantown establishment had been commenced only seven months when its first report was made, in November last. The pupils are instructed in literature, the sciences, languages, morals, and manual labor. The latter consists of agriculture, gardening, and some mechanic arts. They are permitted to labor little or much, as their dispositions may incline them or their necessities dictate. The institution, at its commencement, on the 1st of May, 1829, had but four pupils—at the date of the report it had 25. By an estimate made by the board of managers, as early as July last, it appeared that the balances against several of them for board and tuition were but very small, and that some of them, by their labor, had almost cleared their expenses. They generally work from two to five hours per day.

The first institution in which manual labor appears to have been combined with literature and science, was established many years since by Fellenberg, at Hofwyl, in the Canton of Bern, Switzerland.

The pupils of this institution, in addition to a common or elementary education, were instructed in almost every branch of literature and science. They were taught agriculture, gardening, and the mechanic arts, and their choice of the latter was greatly facilitated by the numerous workshops on the premises. The elements of drawing, surveying and geometry, botany, mineralogy, music, and athletic exercises formed a part of their amusements.

Hofwyl was an independent, selfgoverning community, regulated by a constitution and bylaws formed by the pupils themselves. It had its code of laws; its council of legislation; its representatives; its civil officers; its treasury. It had its annual elections, and each member had an equal vote; its labors and duties in which all took an equal share. It proposed, debated, and enacted its own laws independent even of Fellenberg himself, and never, writes one of the pupils after he had left it, "never perhaps were laws framed with a more single eye to the public good, nor more strictly obeyed by those who framed them."

The same writer considers this circumstance of forming the school into an independent juvenile republic, as the great lever that raised the moral and social character of the Hofwyl establishment to the height it ultimately attained. It gave birth, he says, to public spirit and to social virtues. It awakened in the young republican an interest in the public welfare, and a zeal for the public good, which might in vain be sought in older but not wiser communities. . . .

There is one point in which the committees believe that the gradual extension and ultimate universal adoption of this system of education will produce a benefit, the value of which no human calculation can ascertain. It is but too well known that the growing effects of intemperance—that assassinator of private peace and public virtue, are in this country terrific; and that this fearful pestilence, unless checked in its career by some more efficient remedy than has yet been resorted to, threatens to annihilate, not only the domestic peace and prosperity of individuals, but also the moral order and political liberties of the nation. No people can long enjoy liberty who resign themselves to the slavery of this tyrant vice. Yet does it appear to the committees, that all efforts to root this moral poison from the constitution of society will prove futile until the trial shall be made upon our youth. When we behold the hundreds, perhaps thousands of youth, who, between the ages of 14 and 21 are daily and nightly seduced around or into the innumerable dens of vice, licensed and unlicensed, that throng our suburbs, we are constrained to believe that in many if not in most cases, the unconquerable habit that destroys the morals, ruins the constitution, sacrifices the character, and at last murders both soul and body of its victim, is first acquired during the thoughtless period of juvenile existence. This plan of education, however, by its almost entire occupation of the time of the pupils, either in labor, study, or recreations; by the superior facilities it affords for engrossing their entire attention, and by its capability of embracing the whole juvenile population, furnishes, we believe, the only rational hope of ultimately averting, the ruin which is threatened by this extensive vice.

The committee are aware that any plan of common and more particularly of equal education that may be offered to the public, is likely to meet with more than an ordinary share of opposition. It is to be expected that political demagogism, professional monopoly, and monied influence, will conspire as hitherto (with several exceptions more or less numerous) they ever have conspired against every thing that has promised to be an equal benefit to the whole population. Nevertheless, the appearance, that something will now be done for the intellectual as well as every thing for the physical improvement of the state are certainly very promising. The public mind is awake and favorably excited, while the press also is somewhat active on this subject. Our present legislature and chief magistrate appear likewise earnestly desirous of producing a reform in the system of public education, and we believe they are waiting only for the public sentiment to decide on the principles and character of that reform.

When this decision shall be fully made, and openly and firmly supported by the public voice, we doubt not but our representatives will cheerfully give their legislative sanction to those measures of educational reform, which shall appear manifestly based upon the will of the people.

8.

William Ellery Channing, "Remarks on Education," 1833

While the criticism workingmen and other agitators leveled against established educational practices on the grounds that they were inegalitarian was one factor in changing American attitudes, another lay in the criticisms pedagogical innovators leveled against time-honored methods of instruction. One of the major influences on this development was William Ellery Channing, the leading spokesman for New England Unitarianism, who depicted teaching as a sort of secular ministry to the souls of children through which in the long run all good would come to a free society. In equating teaching with pastoral duties he stood close to his orthodox forebears and contemporaries, but in assuming the primacy of spiritual

freedom and the corollary importance of the sympathetic development of each child's character, he lent support to radical innovations
in educational methods. It followed from his principles that every
teacher must be trained to perform his tasks with great skill, and
beyond this that the state might provide the means of such training
even while it abandoned other forms of legislation in order to promote voluntary efforts at personal and social amelioration. The
essay below, which illustrates these implications of his thought, is
an abridged version of a review of William C. Woodbridge's
American Annals of Education and Instruction—itself a vehicle of
pedagogical innovations.

. . . We are aware, that there are some, who take an attitude of defence, when pressed with earnest applications on the
subject of education. They think its importance overrated. They
say, that circumstances chiefly determine the young mind, that
the influence of parents and teachers is very narrow, and that
they sometimes dwarf and distort, instead of improving the
child, by taking the work out of the hand of nature. These remarks are not wholly unfounded. The power of parents is often
exaggerated. To strengthen their sense of responsibility, they
are often taught, that they are competent to effects, which are
not within their reach, and are often discouraged by the greatness of the task to which they are summoned. Nothing is gained
by exaggeration. It is true, and the truth need not be disguised,
that parents cannot operate at pleasure on the minds and characters of the young. Their influence is limited by their own
ignorance and imperfection, by the strength and freedom of the
will of the child, and by its connexion, from its first breath, with
other objects and beings. Parents are not the only educators of
their offspring, but must divide the work with other and numerous agents; and in this we rejoice; for, were the young confined to domestic influences, each generation would be a copy

From *Christian Examiner*, XV, 3 (November 1833), 258–263, 265–268,
274–276.

of the preceding, and the progress of society would cease. The child is not put into the hands of parents alone. It is not born to hear but a few voices. It is brought at birth into a vast, we may say, an infinite school. The universe is charged with the office of its education. Innumerable voices come to it from all that it meets, sees, feels. It is not confined to a few books anxiously selected for it by parental care. Nature, society, experience, are volumes opened every where and perpetually before its eyes. It takes lessons from every object within the sphere of its senses and its activity, from the sun and stars, from the flowers of spring and the fruits of autumn, from every associate, from every smiling and frowning countenance, from the pursuits, trades, professions of the community in which it moves, from its plays, friendships, and dislikes, from the varieties of human character, and from the consequences of its actions. All these, and more than these, are appointed to teach, awaken, develope the mind of the child. It is plunged amidst friendly and hostile influences, to grow by coöperating with the first, and by resisting the last. The circumstances in which we are placed, form, indeed, a most important school, and by their help some men have risen to distinction in knowledge and virtue, with little aid from parents, teachers, and books.

Still the influence of parents and teachers is great. On them it very much depends, whether the circumstances which surround the child shall operate to his good. They must help him to read, interpret, and use wisely the great volumes of nature, society, and experience. They must fix his volatile glance, arrest his precipitate judgment, guide his observation, teach him to link together cause and effect in the outward world, and turn his thoughts inward on his own more mysterious nature. The young, left to the education of circumstances, left without teaching, guidance, restraint, will, in all probability, grow up ignorant, torpid in intellect, strangers to their own powers, and slaves to their passions. The fact, that some children, without aid from parents or schools, have struggled into eminence, no more proves such aid to be useless, than the fact, that some have grown strong under physical exposures which would destroy the majority of the race, would prove the worthlessness of the ordinary precautions which are taken for the security of health.

We have spoken of parents, as possessing, and as bound to exert, an important influence on the young. But they cannot do the whole work of education. Their daily occupation, the necessity of labors for the support of their families, household cares, the duty of watching over the health of their children, and other social relations, render it almost impossible for parents to qualify themselves for much of the teaching which the young require, and often deny them time and opportunity for giving instruction to which they are competent. Hence the need of a class of persons, who shall devote themselves exclusively to the work of education. In all societies, ancient and modern, this want has been felt; the profession of teachers has been known; and to secure the best helps of this kind to children, is one of the first duties of parents, for on these the progress of their children very much depends.

One of the discouraging views of society at the present moment is, that whilst much is said of education, hardly any seem to feel the necessity of securing to it the best minds in the community, and of securing them at any price. A juster estimate of this office begins to be made in our great cities; but generally it seems to be thought, that any body may become a teacher. The most moderate ability is thought to be competent to the most important profession in society. Strange, too, as it may seem, on this point parents incline to be economical. They who squander thousands on dress, furniture, amusements, think it hard to pay comparatively small sums to the instructer [*sic*]; and through this ruinous economy, and this ignorance of the dignity of a teacher's vocation, they rob their children of aid, for which the treasures of worlds can afford no compensation.

There is no office higher than that of a teacher of youth, for there is nothing on earth so precious as the mind, soul, character of the child. No office should be regarded with greater respect. The first minds in the community should be encouraged to assume it. Parents should do all but impoverish themselves, to induce such to become the guardians and guides of their children. To this good, all their show and luxury should be sacrificed. Here they should be lavish, whilst they straiten themselves in every thing else. They should wear the cheapest clothes, live on the plainest food, if they can in no other way secure to their families the best instruction. They should have no anxiety to accumulate property for their children, provided they can place them under influences, which will awaken their faculties, inspire them with pure and high principles, and fit them to bear a manly, useful, and honorable part in the world. No language can express the cruelty or folly of that economy, which, to leave a fortune to a child, starves his intellect, impoverishes his heart. There should be no economy in education. Money should never be weighed against the soul of a child. It should be poured out like water, for the child's intellectual and moral life.

Parents should seek an educator for the young of their families, who will become to them a hearty and efficient friend, counsellor, coadjutor, in their work. If their circumstances will allow it, they should so limit the school, that the instructer may know intimately every child, may become the friend of each, and may converse frequently with them in regard to each. He should be worthy of their confidence, should find their doors always open, should be among their most welcome guests, and should study with them the discipline which the peculiarities of each pupil may require. He should give the parents warning of the least obliquity of mind which he discovers at school, should receive in return their suggestions as to the injudiciousness of his own methods in regard to one or another child, and should concert with them the means of arresting every evil at its first manifestation. Such is the teacher we need, and his value cannot be paid in gold. A man of distinguished ability and virtue, whose mind should be concentrated in the work of training as many children as he can thoroughly understand and

guide, would shed a light on the path of parents for which they
often sigh, and would give an impulse to the young, little comprehended under our present modes of teaching. No profession
should receive so liberal remuneration. We need not say how
far the community fall short of this estimate of the teacher's
office. Very many send their children to school, and seldom or
never see the instructer, who is operating daily and deeply on
their minds and characters. With a blind confidence, perhaps
they do not ask how that work is advancing, on which the dearest interests of the family depend. Perhaps they put the children under the daily control of one, with whom they do not
care to associate. Perhaps, were they told what they ought to
pay for teaching, they would stare as if a project for robbing
them were on foot, or would suspect the sanity of the friend,
who should counsel them to throw away so much money in
purchasing that cheapest of all articles, that drug in every
market, instruction for their children.

We know not how society can be aided more than by
the formation of a body of wise and efficient educators. We
know not any class which would contribute so much to the stability of the state, and to domestic happiness. Much as we respect the ministry of the gospel, we believe that it must yield in
importance to the office of training the young. In truth, the
ministry now accomplishes little for want of that early intellectual and moral discipline, by which alone a community can
be prepared to distinguish truth from falsehood, to comprehend
the instructions of the pulpit, to receive higher and broader
views of duty, and to apply general principles to the diversified
details of life. A body of cultivated men, devoted, with their
whole hearts, to the improvement of education, and to the most
effectual training of the young, would work a fundamental revolution in society. They would leaven the community with just
principles. Their influence would penetrate our families. Our
domestic discipline would no longer be left to accident and impulse. What parent has not felt the need of this aid, has not
often been depressed, heart-sick, under the consciousness of
ignorance in the great work of swaying the youthful mind!

We have spoken of the office of the education of human beings, as the noblest on earth, and have spoken deliberately. It is more important than that of the statesman. The statesman may set fences round our property and dwellings; but how much more are we indebted to him, who calls forth the powers and affections of those for whom our property is earned, and our dwellings are reared, and who renders our children objects of increasing love and respect. We go further. We maintain, that higher ability is required for the office of an educator of the young, than for that of a statesman. The highest ability is that, which penetrates farthest into human nature, comprehends the mind in all its capacities, traces out the laws of thought and moral action, understands the perfection of human nature and how it may be approached, understands the springs, motives, applications, by which the child is to be roused to the most vigorous and harmonious action of all its faculties, understands its perils, and knows how to blend and modify the influences which outward circumstances exert on the youthful mind. The speculations of statesmen are shallow, compared with these. It is the chief function of the statesman to watch over the outward interests of a people; that of the educator to quicken its soul. The statesman must study and manage the passions and prejudices of the community; the educator must study the essential, the deepest, the loftiest principles of human nature. The statesman works with coarse instruments for coarse ends; the educator is to work by the most refined influences on that delicate, ethereal essence, the immortal soul. . . .

One great cause of the low estimation in which the teacher is now held, may be found in narrow views of education. The multitude think, that to educate a child, is to crowd into its mind a given amount of knowledge, to teach the mechanism of reading and writing, to load the memory with words, to prepare a boy for the routine of a trade. No wonder, then, that they think almost every body fit to teach. The true end of education, as we have again and again suggested, is to unfold and direct aright our whole nature. Its office is to call forth Power of every kind, power of thought, affection, will, and outward action; power to observe, to reason, to judge, to contrive; power to adopt good ends firmly, and to pursue them efficiently; power to govern ourselves, and to influence others; power to gain and to spread happiness. Reading is but an instrument; education is to teach its best use. The intellect was created, not to receive passively a few words, dates, facts, but to be active for the acquisition of Truth. Accordingly, education should labor to inspire a profound love of truth, and to teach the processes of investigation. A sound logic, by which we mean the science or art, which instructs us in the laws of reasoning and evidence, in the true methods of inquiry, and in the sources of false judgments, is an essential part of a good education. And yet how little is done to teach the right use of the intellect, in the common modes of training either rich or poor. As a general rule, the young are to be made, as far as possible, their own teachers, the discoverers of truth, the interpreters of nature, the framers of science. They are to be helped to help themselves. They should be taught to observe and study the world in which they live, to trace the connexions of events, to rise from particular facts to general principles, and then to apply these in explaining new phenomena. Such is a rapid outline of the intellectual education, which, as far as possible, should be given to all human beings; and with this, moral education should go hand in hand. In proportion as the child gains knowledge, he should be taught how to use it well, how to turn it to the good of mankind. He should study the world as God's world, and as the sphere in which he is to form interesting connexions with his fellow creatures. A spirit of humanity should be breathed into him from all his studies. In teaching geography, the physical and moral condition, the wants, advantages, and striking peculiarities of different nations, and the relations of climate, seas, rivers, mountains, to their characters and pursuits, should be pointed out, so as to awaken an interest in man, wherever he dwells. History should be constantly used to exercise the moral judgment of the young, to call forth sympathy with the fortunes of the human race, and to expose to indigna-

tion and abhorrence, that selfish ambition, that passion for dominion, which has so long deluged the earth with blood and
woe. And not only should the excitement of just moral feeling
be proposed in every study. The science of morals should form
an important part of every child's instruction. One branch of
ethics should be particularly insisted on by the government.
Every school, established by law, should be specially bound to
teach the duties of the citizen to the state, to unfold the principles of free institutions, and to train the young to an enlightened patriotism. From these brief and imperfect views of the
nature and ends of a wise education, we learn the dignity of
the profession to which it is entrusted, and the importance of
securing to it the best minds of the community.

On reviewing these hints on the extent of education, we
see that one important topic has been omitted. We have said,
that it is the office of the teacher to call into vigorous action the
mind of the child. He must do more. He must strive to create a
thirst, an insatiable craving for knowledge, to give animation to
study and make it a pleasure, and thus to communicate an impulse which will endure, when the instructions of the school are
closed. The mark of a good teacher is, not only that he produces great effort in his pupils, but that he dismisses them from
his care, conscious of having only laid the foundation of knowledge, and anxious and resolved to improve themselves. One of
the sure signs of the low state of instruction among us is, that
the young, on leaving school, feel as if the work of intellectual
culture were done, and give up steady, vigorous effort for
higher truth and wider knowledge. Our daughters at sixteen
and our sons at eighteen or twenty have *finished* their education. The true use of a school is, to enable and dispose the
pupil to learn through life; and if so, who does not see that the
office of teacher requires men of enlarged and liberal minds,
and of winning manners, in other words, that it requires as
cultivated men as can be found in society. If to drive and to
drill were the chief duties of an instructer, if to force into the
mind an amount of lifeless knowledge, to make the child a

machine, to create a repugnance to books, to mental labor, to
the acquisition of knowledge, were the great objects of the
school-room, then the teacher might be chosen on the principles which now govern the school-committees in no small part
of our country. Then the man who can read, write, cypher, and
whip, and will exercise his gifts at the lowest price, deserves
the precedence which he now too often enjoys. But if the human being be something more than a block or a brute, if he
have powers which proclaim him a child of God and which
were given for noble action and perpetual progress, then a
better order of things should begin among us, and truly enlightened men should be summoned to the work of education. . . .

[*After commenting critically on corporal punishment
in the schools and urging teachers to cooperate with parents
in awakening nonsectarian religious principles in the young,
Channing points out statistical evidences—reported in the*
Annals of Instruction—*of deficiencies in the best American
school systems when compared with Prussia's recent achievements.*]

. . . The view now taken of education in our country shows
us, that, whilst we boast of free institutions, their happiest
influence and chief end is little understood. Their greatest
glory is, to furnish abundantly the means of moral and intellectual developement, to enlarge and ennoble the human mind.
Free institutions should constantly and powerfully tend to
produce a state of society, in which there shall be no populace,
no lower class, no common people; in which the multitude
shall not be looked down upon as an inferior race by the
more prosperous members of the community; in which the
only important distinctions, those of the intellect and heart,
shall be placed within reach of all; in which refined manners,
liberal sentiments, and the pleasures of taste and imagination
shall be more and more diffused throughout all conditions and
vocations; in which justice shall be done to human nature in

whatever sphere it may be placed. This is the true good, the grand purpose of free institutions, and to this they should make constant approaches. And is such their tendency here? Let the great proportion of our population, given up to ignorance and degradation, answer. Let the thousands and ten thousands of our children, growing up without the ordinary means of education, answer. Let the thousands and ten thousands of our children, who, whilst sent to school, receive a mechanical education which gives no force to the intellect, answer. Let the thousands of adults in our cities, who are unimproved in intellect, immersed in sensuality, untaught in the duties of citizens, coarse in manners, and fit tools for demagogues to work with, answer. The best fruits of free institutions are found but sparingly among us, and yet we boast of our freedom.

To meet these wants, to improve our modes of teaching, to make instruction more efficient and extensive, is the object of the "Annals of Education." Its editor perhaps understands better the state of education in this and other countries than any man among us, and his whole heart is in his work. The aim of this periodical has been, to give just ideas of the extent of a wise and good education, to show that it proposes at once the physical, intellectual, moral, and religious advancement of the human being, to show the distinction between mechanical instruction and that which quickens the mind and brings it into vigorous action, to show the importance and to teach the methods of the latter, and to recommend and teach the moral and religious care of the young, without entering into the peculiarities of any body of Christians.—The work has been complained of as wanting interest, but we believe that the blame rests on the reader as much as on the author. The Editor has probably given ground for this complaint, in consequence of the supposition, very natural to an ardent mind, that the community, and especially the body of teachers, were prepared to enter into the subject with his own zeal. Returning from Europe, after a patient examination of the most approved modes of teaching, he imagined that nothing was needed to attract attention, but a simple exposition of his observations. He especially supposed, that a minute account of the school of Fellenberg, the most celebrated in the world, would be gladly received from one, who had spent months on the spot, and enjoyed every opportunity of studying its spirit and details. The experiment, however, has shown, that little disposition exists among us to study the improvements of other countries.—Another obstacle to the popularity of the work may be found in the simplicity of the object. People grow weary of one subject. The repetition of one word, though that word be Education, and though it include an infinite variety of subjects, has the effect of monotony. So serious is this difficulty, that did not education come home to the bosom of every parent and family, we should despair of its being overcome.—Another fault found with the book has been, that it is too much adapted to professed teachers, and not enough to parents. In this respect, we believe, an improvement will be made. Indeed, we are confident that the Editor, if encouraged, will spare no effort to made [sic] his work more acceptable and useful, and we trust encouragement will not be denied.

We are aware that the free disclosures we have made of the defects of our institutions, and the free strictures we have made on them, will not find favor with those, who think it every man's duty to speak well of his country. We think, on the contrary, that those best serve their country, who speak the truth, be it in praise or in blame. We care not how widely our defects are made known, for we see not how else the remedy is to be applied. We do indeed deserve the reproaches of Europe in regard to education, and let them be heaped on us, until shame, if not a better principle, shall lead us to reformation. The single fact, that a vast multitude of uneducated and poorly educated children are growing up among us, afflicts us inexpressibly more than all the calumnies, which have been forged against us by European travellers and politicians. We are indignant, indeed, when we hear, that falsehood in relation to this country is industriously propagated abroad, for the purpose of bringing reproach on free institutions. But this indignation almost passes from our minds, when we consider our own unfaithfulness to our high trust; when we consider that a generation is growing up, to which our civil and religious liberties cannot safely be committed. This people ought to be awakened to their treachery to the holy cause of freedom and humanity. Our politicians are crying Peace, when there is no peace, and our orators soothing the country with honied accents of praise. We hope, that impartial judges and fearless reprovers will arise among us, and that truth, taught by a voice more powerful than ours, will bring conviction to a people, who are violating their obligations to themselves and to their children, to freedom and to mankind.

9.

Transactions of the Western Literary Institute, 1836

Although Massachusetts Unitarians were to occupy a prominent place in the movement for educational reform, there was neither a denominational nor a regional monopoly of the cause. One early vehicle for educational innovations was the Western Literary Institute and College of Professional Teachers, founded in Cincinnati in 1831 to promote both the diffusion of education and the improvement of teaching methods in Ohio and the Old Northwest generally. The founders of the Institute included a good many transplanted easterners who looked with equal disdain on Unitarian heterodoxy, Catholic orthodoxy, and Jacksonian Democracy, and their efforts at pedagogical reform were often correspondingly conservative if not reactionary. (One of the members was William H. McGuffey, whose *Readers* are justly celebrated today for having sought to inculcate painfully old-fashioned virtues.) Nevertheless, their number also included Alexander Campbell, a founder of the Disciples of Christ and at least initially a prominent supporter of Andrew Jackson, whose impromptu address to the members in 1836 is printed here. His words suggest both the extraordinary hopes that even religious fundamentalists attached to educational reform and the nativist fears that often helped to stimulate their interest—in the East as well as in the West.

Closing Address

BY ALEXANDER CAMPBELL

Gentlemen:—Called upon, as I have just now been, in conclusion of our very agreeable, and I trust, very useful session, to offer a few valedictory remarks; without any preparation, and at the impulse of the moment, I cannot expect to offer any thing worthy of your consideration. We have, indeed, much reason to congratulate one another for the good temper, general harmony, and kind feelings which have characterized all our proceedings; and for the happy issue to which our various labors and deliberations have come. To myself, the recollection of this week will be always pleasing and acceptable; and I doubt not we will all regard it as one of the most useful appropriations of all the weeks of the year. The acquaintance which we have formed with each other, the kindred sentiments, views and wishes which have been exchanged on this

From *Transactions of the Sixth Annual Meeting of the Western Literary Institute and College of Professional Teachers, 1836* (Cincinnati, Ohio, 1837), pp. 253–256.

floor, our sympathies and our cordial co-operation in the sacred cause of education, cannot but interest us more in one another, and in the general prospects of our beloved country in literature, science, morality and religion. We shall all separate, I doubt not, with a better opinion of one another, than we entertained on our coming together, and this may authorize the conclusion, that from a better and still more intimate acquaintance, we might yet rise higher in mutual friendship and esteem.

Pardon the egotism while I say, that I congratulate myself on having seen attempted, and that with much promise of success, what I once regarded as, in the present generation, wholly impracticable. Engaged as I was some fifteen years ago, in the profession of teaching, in which calling I have spent several years, I have found innumerable defects in books, in theories, and in plans of teaching, all of which I considered in a great measure irremediable, because of the want of public zeal, discrimination and taste; and because I saw no way of rousing the community to the necessity and the importance of a radical, if not an entire change of the whole system. Books without philosophy, and teachers without science, or of art, if they were only at a low price, seemed to have the universal sway; and fathers, having, as they imagined, done well with a very small literary capital, conjectured that their children with the same outfit in literature, and a little more cash, might still do better than they had done.

But from the developments of this College, from what is already done and in the way of being done, I can see it possible, practicable, and indeed, comparatively easy, by the machinery now in operation, to regenerate the schools, and to elevate the literary taste, character and attainments of the whole West, of the Union, and ultimately of the whole world; provided only the same spirit, effort and enterprize, shall be perseveringly kept alive, and advance in the ratio of the success which will doubtless crown the experiment.

I had heard something, I had heard much of the value

and promise of this project; but as the Queen of the South said of the wisdom and magnificence of Solomon and his court, I am constrained to say, "the half has not been told me." Still I admit we have yet but the "embryo blossom;" much is yet to be done, and the effort must be unremitting as life, and as untiring as the flux of time.

But what is too hard for intelligent and moral co-operation? The very greatest events on the wonderful page of history may be traced to the smallest beginnings. But a co-operation of counsel, talent, or of propitious circumstances, have always explained the phenomena of every splendid and successful consummation.

You have, gentlemen members of this College, begun a good and a great work; and its claims upon your perseverance strengthen with the bright prospects which in the distance already open to your view. For my own part, I feel constrained to lend my feeble energies to the promotion of the benevolent objects which you have in contemplation. I see the destinies of unborn millions may be more or less happily involved in the fortunes of this grand literary institution for the reformation of books and schools and colleges and teachers and society. I therefore feel it a duty which I owe the great family of man to lift up my voice and to put forth my hand in this magnificent undertaking, and shall do it as far as my influence and opportunity will allow.

I control one press,[1] and by it I intend in the current and coming year, to lay before some thousands of my fellow citizens, the nature, objects and progress of this philanthropic institution, and I will (because I can do it sincerely and conscientiously) commend it to the consideration and furtherance of such of the humane and benevolent, as happen to be enrolled on my list of readers, and these are found in every state of this Union, as well as in foreign countries.

---

[1] [In 1823 Campbell had established a press at his home, where he published the *Christian Baptist* and, subsequently, the *Millennial Harbinger*.]

Let each of us, then, gentlemen, in our respective vicinities and spheres of action, inquire what we can do to promote this all-absorbing interest, and whenever and wherever an opportunity occurs to say a word in support of the claims of this College upon public patronage and regard, let it be said with all candor, and with all the authority of truth and reason and morality.

Every wind is carrying to our shores, hundreds and thousands of human beings from distant and oppressed countries, alike ignorant of things human and divine, calling for our sympathies and our means of promoting their cultivation, both in things intellectual and moral; and shall we suffer them to appeal to our humanity and our religion in vain? Our own interests, indeed our political safety, our personal security from wrong and outrage, demand our best efforts to neutralize that mass of ignorance and corruption which otherwise must accumulate on our borders, or grow up in the bosom of our society, so long as the rights of hospitality and of citizenship are tendered to men, of all climes and languages and religions under heaven. To transmit to our posterity the rich blessings which we enjoy; it behooves us therefore, not knowing by whose hands the "rod of empire" may yet be swayed in this our happy land, to give not only our suffrage, but our efforts to the cause of education, and to use all lawful means to facilitate the diffusion of knowledge and the influence of morality and good order, through every ramification of society.

To this greatest and best of causes, which has the temporal and eternal destiny of future generations in its aspirations, we have given some pledge of our devotion. In bidding each other adieu for another year, we do it indeed, in the expectation of meeting again with renewed zeal, with improved energies and increased faculties for advancing the great interest of education. May our hopes not be disappointed, and our efforts eminently successful, in an enterprize which is alike honorable to our religion, and beneficial to our fellow creatures!

10.

The Public School Society of New York,
The Public Schools, Public Blessings, 1837

The Public School Society of New York City was only one of many urban groups that sought to combat illiteracy and its accompanying evils by offering free elementary education to any children who were willing to accept it. Chartered in 1805 as the Free School Society, it became the Public School Society in 1826 when the state legislature designated it as the sole recipient of public grants made in support of elementary education in New York City. In the long run the practice of giving public aid to a private agency in order to stimulate popular education alienated almost everyone, the more so as it involved discrimination against competing educational institutions and against Catholic children whose parents resented the nondenominational but none the less Protestant bias of its instruction. (See Document 13, page 98.) In addition, many of the Society's purported beneficiaries were either too poor or too parsimonious to seek any education at all. (The Society expected those who could afford it to help meet the cost of its schools.) Its little tract of 1837, the first half of which appears here, represents one way of dealing with the problem. Significantly, it appeals to parents to send their children to school mainly for reasons of personal profit and individual success; but it does so in terms that indicate a lurking social bias—didactic, paternalistc, and even elitist—on the part of its sponsors. Events were to demonstrate that public education must be visualized in more clearly egalitarian terms before it could claim the loyalty of ordinary men and women.

My Friend,

Are you a father, or mother,—or have you children under your care? Will you permit a fellow-citizen to say a few words to you about them, for your and their good?

I have, myself, a large family. You and I are deeply interested in the welfare of our children. What a comfort it will be to us, should they all grow up to become intelligent, virtuous, and respectable citizens! What an unspeakable, public blessing, if all the children in the land should be so educated as to grow up and have this character! Then we might expect that our country would continue to be flourishing and happy; and that its privileges would be enjoyed by our children's children, without fear of losing them.

Do your Children go to School? If they do not, or if they are not constant and punctual in their attendance,—permit me to ask if you have thought upon this subject as much as its importance demands? Perhaps you have been so much taken up with other things, that you have not considered what you and your children certainly must *lose,* if they do not have good schooling; and what, if they have it, they will be in the fair way of *gaining.*

Suppose we attend to this subject, a few minutes. Or, if you are too busy to do it now, you can take up the book again when you are less engaged, and then give me your patient attention. If you will do so, I think, I shall show you clearly that the subject is one of the greatest importance both to you and your children.—You love them, and wish to do all that you can for their good; and we shall see, as we go along, that one of *the very best things* you can do for them, is to send them to School.

Should your children grow up, without learning how to read and write; to cipher and keep accounts; and to under-

From *The Public Schools, Public Blessings* (New York, 1837), pp. 5–14.

stand something of geography, grammar, and the other useful things that are taught in our Public Schools;—how can they ever expect to *rise in the world,* to acquire property, and to gain respectability and influence.

We will take the *boys* first. Unless they know these things,—or, at least, some of them,—and live to be young men, how can they get good situations; or hope, by and by, to do business for themselves? Who will like to take them as apprentices and clerks?—Who will be willing to trust them with any important concerns?—How will they acquire the good opinion and confidence of others?

Young men cannot jump into employment and business at once. Even those that have had good schooling, have to get along step by step. They must let those around them see that they are worthy of being trusted on account of their good conduct, useful attainments, industry, and skill in doing business. And there are so many who are taught at our Public Schools, and who leave them with an excellent character, that they will always be preferred to *the ignorant.* So that for these reasons, a lad who cannot even read, write, and cipher, will find it very, very hard to *begin* to get forward in the world.

Besides, what possible chance will such an ignorant lad ever have, of becoming *a partner in trade* with some one who is looking out for a smart, intelligent, and upright young man to aid him in carrying on, and enlarging his business? Such instances often happen in this great city. How sorry both you and your sons will be, to see other boys of their acquaintance, as they grow up, securing such situations, and they, because they are so ignorant, cut off forever from them.

Those who wish to employ young persons, either your sons or daughters, or who can place them in good situations, are getting to be more and more particular about these things. And, unless some peculiar misfortune prevents parents from giving their children good schooling, (especially when the Public Schools are open to all, without any expense,) if it is found that a boy, or girl, of a suitable age, has made no progress in learning, it is always considered *a very bad sign* against them. People will think there must be something wrong about it, and doubt very much whether the character of the young person is what it should be.

On the other hand, where they find good schooling has been given to the child, they will, so far, think well of *the child and parent both,* and be much more ready to believe other good things that may be told them about your son or daughter.

And, believe me, this is a thing of no small importance in this changing and dying world. For you know not how soon your children may be left without your care, to get along as well as they can; when, under the blessing of God, every thing may depend upon their *character,* and the favorable opinion that kind and respectable persons may form of them.

Let us now consider a little the case of the *girls.* In whatever way they may wish to get their living as they grow older,—they will certainly lose many, very many advantages by not having had good schooling. Every body loves to be treated well, and to be respected by others. And the young woman who has gone to one of our Public Schools for a few years, and been attentive to her studies; and acquired habits of industry, neatness, punctuality and order; and conducted well; will be sure of having good treatment and respect, whatever her situation may be. She will be *sought after;* and will always find useful an[d] profitable employment. At this very time, nine of the Primary Schools, which the younger children attend, are taught by *young women who were not long since scholars in our Public Schools;*—and they have good salaries. Such young women, also, are often employed in families to teach the children; and in private schools, as assistants; or they may set up such schools themselves.

Other situations in some of the various trades, will be open, too, for such young women. And in managing business for others, or in attending to their own concerns, as they get along in the world, they will have great advantages, in being able to read and know what is going on around them;—to write a good hand, so that they can both understand letters and answer them: and to use figures and keep accounts correctly.

Now an ignorant girl, or young woman, in this land of intelligence and of schools, who cannot even read and write, will never be thus treated and respected. It will be very difficult, if not impossible, for her to rise above some of *the lowest stations.* From the advantages and expectations which I have been describing, she must be forever cut off. People will not employ such an one for such situations. Indeed, if she could obtain one of them, her sad ignorance would soon be found out, and she would only suffer disappointment, mortification, and disgrace.

Think, what you[r] daughters must *lose,* if by your neglect in not sending them to school, they should be deprived of the prospects which I have mentioned. As you and they grow older, you will see other young women of your acquaintance, who have had good schooling, rising to places of respectability and usefulness. Such places your children would be equally well fitted to fill by their natural talents and capacity; but they will lose them just for *the want of that amount of learning* which they might easily have acquired at our Public Schools. What sorrow and regret both you and they will feel. But it will come too late. They will be *too old* to think of going to school. They must be content to plod on through life, with little or no hope of ever overtaking those whose *good schooling,* when young, has favored them with so many advantages.

And all these considerations apply with equal force to one other subject, connected with the future prospects of your daughters, which must not be passed over in silence. The time will come, when young men will be looking out among them, and other young women, for *companions for life.* Some of these young men will have had good schooling themselves, and will understand how important it is that a wife and mother should have had it also. They will know how often a wife who can read, and write a letter, and use figures, can be of great service to her husband, when he is hurried, or unwell, or called away from home. They will know, too, what a difference it will make in their families, and in the bringing up of their children, whether the mother is *an ignorant woman,* or has had some education. In addition to this, every man knows that his respectability is increased by the respectability of his wife;— that his influence is;—that his friends are;—that his very business often is. Then he wants an intelligent and pleasant companion at home; one that can entertain and improve him by her conversation; who can *understand* him when he reads to her, and who can sometimes *read* to him when he is tired or ailing. How many husbands would thus love to spend their leisure hours *at home,* and make their families happy, and be kept from ruinous temptations if their wives were such as I have been describing.

The fact is, young men are getting more and more education *themselves,* and will feel more and more the need of it in their *wives.* And if you let your daughters grow up without giving them suitable instruction at school, *they will stand a very poor chance of getting husbands that are at all worth having.*

I wish you had time to consider a number of other things concerning the schooling of your children, which I should like to state. I hope however, you will be able to attend to a few more. Or, if you must stop, you know you can put the book carefully away, and take it up again, in the course of the day or evening.

And then I will not detain you long.[1]

---

[1] [Part Second of the pamphlet reiterates these arguments and then explains the organization and practices of the Society's schools.]

11.

The *Connecticut Common School Journal* and *The Common School Journal,* 1839 and 1840

As educational enthusiasts in other parts of the Union frequently observed, Connecticut and Massachusetts boasted effective systems of common schools when other states were only beginning to secure elementary education for all their children. By the fourth decade of the century, however, educational reformers in both states were aware that there were serious gaps in the established systems and that the level and character of instruction were often inadequate. They reacted by urging state-wide boards of education, pressing for the creation of normal schools, and sponsoring state educational journals, as well as campaigning for increased tax support and the elimination of rate bills (partial charges for tuition).

Henry Barnard was instrumental in establishing a state board of education in Connecticut and served as its secretary until political controversy forced him out of office and sent him to Rhode Island to occupy a similar post. (He was later to return to Connecticut as Superintendent of Common Schools.) Two editorials from the second volume of his *Connecticut Common School Journal,* printed here, exemplify the appeals it made to philanthropy, local patriotism, and the idea of progress in support of the highest possible standards of public instruction. In addition it served as a compendium of useful information and practical advice to teachers.

Horace Mann played much the same role in Massachusetts, spending twelve years in improving public schools and schooling until he resigned from the Board of Education to become a Whig congressman (a Conscience Whig) and, subsequently, the first president of Antioch College. The "Appeal to the Citizens of

Massachusetts," written for the second volume of his *Common School Journal*, is typical of that magazine's hortatory style and content. (So is the fact that Mann called his publication *The Common School Journal*, although it first appeared four months after Barnard's more prosaic enterprise.) These differences aside, both journals testify to the strides educational reform had begun to make as a concomitant to the democratization of American society.

Connecticut Common School Journal, August 1839

WHAT CONNECTICUT WOULD BE WITH GOOD SCHOOLS

It is truly agreeable to fancy what happy changes a good and thorough improvement in our common schools would effect in this state. How favorably situated is the population! not thinly scattered over the soil, with great distances intervening,—not unfurnished with roads, bridges, or the means of conveyance,—not composed of heterogen[e]ous materials, as in some parts of the Union, difficult to sympathize and to be brought into a co-operation,—not prejudiced against education, ignorant of its importance, or unaccustomed to the arrangements necessary to secure attendance and regularity. Such is not the state of our citizens. On the contrary, quite the opposite is the fact; so that we find around us as many facilities, as in other regions are found obstacles and discouragements. We every where witness, also, effects of common schools, long in general and active operation; and we can, therefore, form some judgment of what their influences would be, if they were raised to a high state of improvement.

In the first place, every town, village, and district would have at least one edifice in good taste,—in a conspicuous and

From *Connecticut Common School Journal,* II, 1 (August 1839), 8–9.

agreeable situation,—a correct model of architecture,—pleasing to the eye of every spectator, and agreeable to those for whom the school house is designed. Early childhood would feel attracted towards the place of learning by the beauty of its aspect. Here would be studiously combined the symmetry of art, with the beautiful variety of nature. Umbrageous foliage, and fragrant flowers, would unite to shelter and perfume the spot where the young received the instruction necessary to prepare them well for this life and the next. How would such edifices adorn our streets, and arrest the eye of the travellers along our roads, rivers, and sea coast! What an influence, also, would models of this kind soon exercise on the taste of our people, and their views of domestic architecture, and the arrangement of their own grounds!

But as the apparatus of education within the school, with the matter taught, and the modes of instruction, would be far more important than every thing exterior, so we might expect to find the intellectual and moral influence of real improvement far transcending any of their physical or external effects. Let each of us but ask himself what would probably have been the advantage to me if I had been trained from early childhood by well taught instructors,—educated on system to teach systematically,—prepared by an enlightened and well adapted course of study, example and practice, to instruct well,—liberally sustained and encouraged by intelligent virtuous, and public-spirited men, acting as inspectors under a well devised and approved system,—furnished with good apparatus, and dexterous in its use, and enjoying in the public opinion that elevated rank, and high estimation which are the natural due of their station when well filled? How much greater would our own progress have been in knowledge! How much more thorough, at the same time!—how much more practical our acquisitions, and how much better qualified we should have been, as well as more disposed, to continue the pursuit of knowledge through life! Which of us would not have entered business far better prepared, and made much greater advances than we have done, in increasing our store of useful learning? There can be no more doubt, that we should, at this time, have been more intelligent and capable advocates of public education; and, if there were now a few thousands, or even a few hundreds, or scores, of men in the state, who had been educated in the manner spoken of, is it not probable, that Connecticut would have already reached a point in improvement of which we have, as yet, hardly allowed ourselves to dream?

It would be easy for a good teacher to give his pupils in a common school as good an education as is actually possessed by many of the young men who have proceeded from colleges; for in those institutions, it is well known, not a few, for want of proper diligence and faithfulness, fail to enjoy much of the benefit which is offered to them. But besides, the moral habits and character may be easily well formed and guarded in a district school; where there are few temptations to evil, and the youth are alternately under the care of their teachers and parents. In this important department of morals, therefore—this most important department—the good influences of improved common schools would be signally displayed. And what benefits would flow from a thorough and universal system of good moral education, founded on the principles of Christianity? let every mind, capable of forming an estimate, candidly enquire.

The useful arts of life would speedily receive an impulse from the more energetic and well directed exercise of the minds of men. The principles of mechanics and agriculture,— the numerous and interesting truths of chemistry and natural history, most intimately connected with so many useful plans, methods and processes, being familiarly known, would be applied with great results. Soils and plants, vegetables and animals, would be studied and understood. Experiments would bring to light many efficient and economical ways of performing labor, and increasing the necessaries and comforts of life.

At the same time the tone of intercourse between men would be raised, and many an hour now spent in frivolity or solitude, —in vacuity or hurtful occupations, would then be devoted to solid reading, rational conversation, or well directed labor.

Extended views of human ability, duty and resource, would also aid in training better freemen. We should be able to understand and appreciate our rights, and the best way to enjoy and secure them. Party spirit would not have so much power to blind our eyes, or to veil or misdirect our vision; and the real friends of the state would be less in danger of misunderstanding and distrusting each other.

Good common schools would do more than we can easily calculate, to increase the resources of the state and its population. For one of its most natural tendencies would be, to multiply the means of life; and this would detain at home many of those valuable young men who would otherwise be attracted to distant places. In proportion, too, as the state of society became more elevated by intelligence, morality and religion, Connecticut would be more dear to the best portion of her citizens; and thus her population might multiply, improve and strengthen, to an indefinite degree.

But it is time to bring these remarks to a close, though the subject is a pleasing, and almost a boundless, one. Our readers may pursue it further at their leisure, and it is desirable that it should be more considered than it has been, for one of the things we have most to fear, is, that in undertaking improvements, we may set out with too low a standard, and effect much less than we ought, for the want of a mark sufficiently elevated.

THE BENEFITS OF NORMAL INSTITUTIONS

The advantages which we should derive from good seminaries for teachers, are more various and numerous than one might at first imagine.

In the first place, it would be necessary that a system should be formed for conducting them. But, before this could be properly devised, the true objects and principles of common education, needed by our youth, must be understood. We are all ready to say that this should be a good one. But how good; —that is, how elevated or extensive, or exactly how far it ought to be carried;—such a question might lead us to silent reflection, rather than to a hasty answer. If then the question be asked, what branches of learning can and ought to be taught in our common schools, who would be ready to reply? If this question were settled, next come a crowd relating to the methods of teaching, the nature and forms of discipline, &c. &c., which have never yet been arranged in any distinct manner, nor indeed, by most, treated as if they all needed it. Yet a normal institution could not properly open its doors before all these points had been settled, a system of common school instruction planned, even in all its details, and a system of instruction for teachers erected upon that, with its proper adaptation in every part and particular.

The principles of such a system must of course be known and approved, or public opinion would not be enlisted in favor of the enterprize—a point indispensable to its success. If these principles were at once as deep and as lofty, as just and practical as they ought to be, the people would approve as soon as they comprehended them; and the mere elevation of such a standard, and the acclamations of the State in its favor, would give an exciting and healthful thrill through the whole population. The truth is, we believe, that the true value of commo[n] schools have never been fully appreciated, unless by their founders, and such individuals as have seriously and with great deliberation, reflected on their nature. That the great mass of the people of our country, and even of our State have not, appears to us clear beyond a doubt. Their value however is great—inestimable; and, the more we learn to estimate it, the higher does it rise. We speak now of what they are capable of becoming. Too much has it been habitual with us to consider ·common schools, as being necessarily what they are. So long as this idea prevails, we may despair of their improvement.

The promulgation of a properly elevated plan for their arrangement and conduct, made by a respectable institution for the instruction of teachers, would enlighten many of our eyes, and lead to maturity of opinions. Those who are reflecting on education, would find great assistance in forming correct estimates and conclusions; persons engaged in instruction, even in the most retired situations, find a plan and manual placed in their hands, which they might apply with greater or less advantage even without leaving their homes; while parents would soon begin to regard the improved common school as an object of great value, and court its benefits for their children, as if it contained money, houses or lands. Nay more. They would perceive that it could train well and furnish the mind, form and consolidate the character, establish christian principles, form moral habits, and thus prepare for usefulness, prosperity and happiness. The views of the people concerning the scope and nature of a common school would then be changed. Such remarks would pass current as we now may hear made every day, even by persons well informed on other matters: "Learn to read, write and cipher, study geography and grammar, and you will be fit to engage in business;"— "We have a first rate teacher: he makes his pupils mind and study well." We should not hear such points underrated; but we should find them no longer regarded as the sum total of common education. On the contrary, we might expect this meagre list used as a criterion between the old and the new standard. Those teachers who should continue to limit their plans to this narrow circle, would find themselves regarded as far in the back ground, and be compelled, by the force of an active demand, to increase their stock.

In the mean time, a number of teachers would be preparing to prosecute the management of schools, under the training of a seminary; and when the system and methods of a good normal institution had begun to produce their direct effects on schools, and their results are carried to towns and villages, laid before the eyes of the people, and their children are made subjects of the experiments, how will they rise in the estimate of the public! If the people of Connecticut can see so much that is lovely and valuable in the training of children in such buildings as many of our school houses are, amidst all their defects and deficiencies; if they consider the common school teacher a personage of such indispensable importance, that they cannot dispense with him, when he has had no regular preparation for his task, and is so far sunk by discouragements and obstacles as to seem but the shadow of himself, how highly will they appreciate those institutions of their fathers, and him their favorite functionary, invested by them, at Plymouth Rock, with such dignity and authority; when both shall be elevated to the rank originally designed for them, and be seen dispensing those intellectual and moral blessings which they were formed to confer.

By means of the cultivated and well directed intelligence of the instructers [*sic*], operating with the machinery of good methods, the phenomena of society will be explained to the young, its frame-work and processes in some degree made known, the principles taught by which men and women ought to be guided in life. Instead of banishing every thing from the school house, except the bare rudiments of knowledge, as it is commonly expressed, and regarding every thing as extraneous and intrusive which is not reading, writing, ciphering, grammar, geography or history, every thing which may serve as a useful illustration of their principles, or afford a means of their application, will be regarded as admissible; and the training of the affections will be treated as an object of such paramount importance, and pursued on such a sound christian basis, that the child will feel, from his first introduction, that the great objects of common schools are, to mould the character after the model drawn out in the scriptures, and to give it not only the knowledge which is profitable to the life that now is, but to that also which is to come.

The Common School Journal, February 1840

AN APPEAL TO THE CITIZENS OF MASSACHUSETTS, IN BEHALF OF THEIR PUBLIC SCHOOLS

Fellow Citizens,—I have before me the 'Abstract of the Massachusetts School Returns, for 1838–9,' prepared by the Secretary of the Board of Education. It is a valuable and interesting book, containing a comprehensive view of the actual condition of the Common Schools in the State, and of the sums raised by taxes in each town, for their support. The statement, on the whole, is humbling to our pride and self-complacency. We boast of being a cultivated people, but how small are the sacrifices we are willing to make, to perpetuate the blessings of universal education! While our resources are doled out with so niggard a hand, it is impossible that our schools should accomplish the great purposes for which they were established.

There are, however, many honorable exceptions to this remark. In a considerable number of towns, we may observe a liberality worthy of all praise; the annual appropriations for the current expenses of the schools being from one dollar to one dollar and fifty cents, for each of the whole population. But in a great proportion of the interior towns, the tax on the inhabitants, for the support of public schools, does not exceed the miserable sum of twenty-five or thirty cents ! ! !

There may be a frugality which is not economy. A community, that withholds the means of education from its children, withholds the bread of life, and starves their very souls.

From *The Common School Journal,* II, 4 (February 15, 1840), 54–56.

I fear that there is, in this bragging age, a great falling off from the noble spirit and aims of our ancestors. *They* deemed no sacrifices too great, to secure a sound education of the whole people. They were willing to throw their "two mites into the treasury" of wisdom, even when it was all their living. In their rude forest homes, they were glad to do battle with necessity, to higgle with their appetites, to be meanly clad, and coarsely fed, that they might endow a college *"to the end that good learning may not be buried in the graves of our fathers."* Two hundred years ago, when the young institution was the object of the people's hope and prayer, we find that gifts were pouring in from every quarter,—of a few sheep, a piece of cloth, a pewter dish, five shillings, nine shillings, one, two, or five, pounds, in money. "The gifts were small, but the people were poor; it was the contribution of liberal, enlightened, virtuous penury," a sacrifice of the present to the future,—of the material to the spiritual. The poor came up with their humble free-will offerings,—the fruits of their labor or self-denial.

And these are the men,—these pilgrim fathers,—who, in the midst of want, and hardship, and danger, laid the foundation of that Common School system, which is the pride and hope of the country, the support of intelligence, freedom, and virtue. Would it have been credible to them, that their posterity, two centuries after, when God had blessed the land with abundance, would be so regardless of the rich legacy bequeathed to them, would so meanly estimate its object and its worth, that some towns actually *pay less for the support of all their teachers* in a year, than would be necessary to feed and clothe *a single able-bodied pauper* for the same time?

Men of Massachusetts, are you not ashamed of this sordid parsimony? Is this the way to carry out the plans of the generous and far-sighted wisdom of your forefathers? Are there no superfluities, from which you may retrench somewhat, for this great object? Are there no artificial wants, which you can leave unsatisfied, for the sake of the necessities of the opening mind? Are there no imperious claims of habit, that can be

set aside, by a resolute will? If nothing can be spared from
luxury, nothing from hoarded treasure, then let poverty come
up to the help of the cause, with its scanty gatherings; let
beggary divide its loaf, for the sake of imparting the bread of
life; let severer frugality create new means for this great end.
Drive hard bargains with your house-keeping; stint yourselves
of the meat in the larder, of the meal in the barrel; pinch, save,
if need be, in every thing; do every thing that you honestly
can, that you honorably can, to enable you to vote a liberal
appropriation for your schools. But do not stint and starve the
immortal mind of your children. If I could go into your town
meetings the coming March, and be permitted to plead this
cause, I would entreat you by your love of country, by your
love of man, by your love of those whom God has made dearer
to you than life, to lift up your minds to the height and grandeur
of this great interest,—the one object, I might almost say, for
which you live. Open your hearts, I beseech you; open your
hands, open your pockets. Make *large* appropriations, that you
may pay instructers liberally for their work, and obtain such as
are worth the pay. I use only the sober and earnest language
of truth when I say, that your chief concern here is, not to lay
up a fortune for your children; but to rear a generation of wise
and virtuous citizens, of clear-headed and right-hearted men,
of intelligent and cultivated women, who shall, in turn, be
fathers and mothers to a generation, more enlightened and
better than themselves. "This is your business, your duty, the
thing you came into the world to do." Will you do it? Fellow-
citizens, will you do this duty, at whatever cost and sacrifice,
or will you be "accessary before the fact" to all the unimagin-
able mischiefs, which your ignorant and brutal successors will
most surely bring upon themselves and their country? This is
the great concern of humanity. The voices of your children's
souls cry out to you; spirits of the unborn are crying out to you;
the country, with dim, prophetic foresight of unknown evils,
is uttering inarticulate cries to you, for help. And will you hear
nothing, do nothing, give nothing? You want not facts and

argument, to convince you, so much as a loud trumpet-blast, to rouse you to this great duty. *You cannot hope to educate your children without the means.*

It cannot, I think, be necessary to insist, that public prosperity and private happiness depend upon the intelligence and virtue of the people. Without disciplined and cultivated minds, the many, like the laboring population of Europe, will become slaves and victims of their employments. We can avert this peril only by insisting that *we will have* schools of a high order, fit for the education of free citizens; and what is more, fit for the education of the heart and conscience of immortal beings, who have capacities for great thought, great action, and immeasurable progress. We have a right to insist, that all the resources of the country, now held by stewards of the Divine bounty, shall be sacredly pledged to their support, so that the children of every man, the poorest even, may have opportunity to obtain a liberal culture, equivalent, at least, to what is received in the best academies. *Make the public schools better than the academies,* and you will draw to the former the resources now expended upon the latter; and thus nearly double the pecuniary means of common education.

By education, I do not mean a mere capacity to read, write, and cipher; but some faithful training of the power of thought, some generous unfolding of the whole spiritual being, which shall lay a foundation for a vigorous and noble manhood. I would give every poor and friendless boy a chance to grow up a strong-minded and right-hearted man,—independent, free, able to bear himself well in the great struggle of life, and subdue refractory circumstances to his resolute will. We have a right to insist, nay, it is our sacred duty to insist, that our towns shall furnish the means of such training and discipline, for all their children, in their early years. And then, when they become older, they will hunger and thirst after knowledge, till they be filled. They will love to sit at the feet of Wisdom, more than to enjoy any of the pleasures of sense.

Friends, and fellow-citizens, are you prepared to say

that you have done your duty in this great matter? Will you go
to the question, next month, with no more enlarged views
than you had, last March,—with no more liberal vote? I am
earnest and urgent with you, because I feel a deep sympathy
with the people,—the whole people. The welfare of my brethren is *my* welfare. I am bound up, for weal or wo, with the
destinies of my fellow-creatures. I yearn to see the long-de-
ferred hope of humanity fulfilled, when the work of the hands
shall not preclude refinement of manners, nor dignity of soul. I
long to see the whole generation of men educated, in some
measure, according to their capacities as rational and immortal
beings, children of the Infinite Father. Let there be no *low class*
among us; no man can be dishonored by any thing save what
rises out of his own character. I would have the rising generation cultivated, because it will be a generation of free citizens,
sovereigns of the country, who will have great duties. Yet not
for this only, or chiefly. I reverence the human soul; I have
faith in its sublime possibilities. I cannot bear to see it buried
in ignorance, and degraded by vice. I would not have the
Image of God defaced and broken, by our negligence or parsimony. I would insist upon the cultivation of every individual
man, not so much as an instrument, as an end, and for his own
sake.

But I believe, also, and hope in the culture and elevation
of society,—of a whole people. There are persons, however,
not without worth and influence, who have no faith in the
progress of humanity. They regard all efforts for public improvement, as visionary. They call themselves practical men,
who have the wisdom of experience. But they make little
account of the wants of our higher nature. As they view the
matter, man lives to work with spade or axe, with trowel or
pen, with figures of arithmetic or figures of speech, and works
only that he may live; thus is the little orbit of his being complete, though there is no ministration to his mind or soul. They
keep a running account with Earth and Heaven, and require
always a balance in their favor, that can be counted out, in the

current coin of the country, or notes of specie-paying banks. They like not to invest capital in mental cultivation, which brings no quick and visible return, never reproducing its exchangeable value with usury. They are unwilling to sow the seeds of public improvement, because the harvest is distant, and they may not live to see it. Like the farmer in Maine, who dug up his potatoes for his table, the week after they were planted, they "hate to give long credits."

Such men will try to persuade you to have cheap schoolhouses, cheap teachers, cheap knowledge for your children,— and little of it; they will urge you to be sparing, when it is truest economy to be liberal. Often the wisdom of hope is better than the wisdom of experience. Never be discouraged by the slow growth of your hopes. The greatest effects are often long in ripening. Every generation must work in part, for those which shall come after. We are surrounded by the accumulations of many ages. We gather the fruit, and sit under the shadow, of trees which our great grandfathers planted. We must do for our children, as our ancestors have done for us.

12.

Two Criticisms of Educational Reform in Massachusetts, 1840

At times educational innovators like Mann and Barnard made it seem that the chief purpose of educational reform was to combat the excesses of democracy. Partly for this reason, and partly because the reformers obviously sought to change established local practices, spokesmen for the insurgent democracy often took issue with their educational innovations. In Massachusetts, Governor Marcus Morton—the first Democrat to hold that post—used the occasion of his annual message to the state legislature in 1840 both to press the claims of the common schools and to praise local control of education as a fundamental democratic principle. The Committee on Education of the House of Representatives, composed of Whigs as well as Democrats and including among its members orthodox clergymen who were offended by Mann's Unitarianism, responded dutifully with an attack on the Board of Education and on the state's normal schools cast in terms of the Democratic party's hostility to monopoly and to the Whig propensity to intrude government into areas best left to regulate themselves. Many of the committee's complaints now seem to have been ill-tempered if not disingenuous, but they also reflected a genuine popular concern lest a system of schools conceived by its patrons as an instrumentality of democratic social ends be converted into an agency serving the consolidation of political power, the regimentation of public opinion, and the obliteration of denominational distinctions. Nevertheless, the critics failed by a narrow margin to destroy either the Board or its normal schools, and in the long run they would be compelled to accept both as the only plausible means of maintaining an effective system of public education. Governor Morton himself betrayed the weakness of their position in placing such a high value on the common schools. To concede this value, when it was becoming increasingly obvious that traditional provisions for education were inadequate to cope with novel social problems, was to concede the necessity for committing the state to the improvement as well as the diffusion of popular education.

Marcus Morton, Message to the Massachusetts Legislature, 1840

. . . The education of the people, is a subject which has commanded so much of the public consideration, and been

From "Address of His Excellency Marcus Morton, to the Two Branches of the Legislature, on the Organization of the Government, for the Political Year . . . 1840," *Documents Printed by Order of the House of Representatives of the Commonwealth of Massachusetts, 1840,* Number 9, pp. 29–31.

so often and so ably presented to successive legislatures, that it will not fail to command your earliest attention and most anxious deliberations. Its importance in a democratic government, which must be sustained by the intelligence and virtue of the people, cannot be too highly appreciated. The system of free schools which has been transmitted from generation to generation, has improved in its progress, and is now in a high degree of perfection. But it is capable of still further improvement. Recently, great labor has been bestowed upon and great advancement made in some departments of education. But the very improvements in the higher branches, and in the more elevated seminaries, excite the ambition and engross the attention of those most active in the cause of education, and thus expose the common schools to fall into neglect and disrepute. To arouse that strong and universal interest in them, which is so necessary to their utility and success, an interest that should pervade both parents and children, the responsibility of their management should rest upon the inhabitants of the towns. And the more immediately they are brought under the control of those for whose benefit they are established, and at whose expense they are supported, the more deep, and active will be the feelings engendered in their favor, and the more certain and universal will be their beneficial agency. In the town and district meetings, those little pure democracies, where our citizens first learn the rudiments and the practical operation of free institutions, may safely and rightfully be placed the direction and the government of these invaluable seminaries. In my opinion, the main efforts and the most unceasing vigilance of the government should be directed to the encouragement of the primary schools. These are the fountains whence should flow the knowledge that should enlighten, and the virtue that should preserve, our free institutions. Let them ever be kept free and pure.

   The instruction of the common mind should be the common concern. Let the whole people be educated and brought up to the standard of good citizens and intelligent and moral members of society. Let the government care for those who have no one else to care for them. The poor, the weak, the depressed and the neglected, have the greatest need of the protecting arm and the succoring hand of the Commonwealth. Let the children of such be deemed the children of the republic, and furnished with suitable means of instruction, that their powers, mental and physical, may be developed, and they be converted into ornaments and blessings to the community. Let the town schools be open to all, and made so respectable and so useful, that all may desire to enter them.[1] The district school, properly governed and instructed, is a nursery of democratic sentiments. It strikingly illustrates the fundamental principle of our government. There, before the pride of family or wealth, or other adventitious distinction has taken deep root in the young heart, assemble upon a perfect level, children of all circumstances and situations of life. There they learn that rewards and honors, do not depend upon accidental advantages, but upon superior diligence, good conduct and improvement. There they have practically written upon their tender minds, too deeply to be obliterated by the after occurrences and changes of life, the great principles of equal rights, equal duties, and equal advantages.

It is the illumination of the universal mind that is the sure foundation of democracy. It is the elevation of every rational soul into moral and intellectual consciousness and dignity, that is to carry onward improvements in our social and civil institutions. To this end should be directed the highest aims and efforts of the legislature. . . .

---

[1] [The Massachusetts school system had originated in the requirement, first adopted by the colonial legislature in 1647, that every town of fifty families should employ a teacher of reading and writing, and every town of one hundred families a Latin master. During the eighteenth century most towns substituted district schools for centralized elementary schools to accommodate their increasingly dispersed populations.]

Report of the Committee on Education of the House of Representatives

House of Representatives, March 7th, 1840.

The Committee on Education having been directed by an order of the House of the 3d inst., to consider the expediency of abolishing the Board of Education and the Normal Schools, and to report by bill or otherwise, have attended to that duty, and respectfully submit the following

REPORT:

In entering upon the duties entrusted to them, your Committee were fully aware of the difficulties with which it is encompassed. Their inquiry extends to the principles, operation and probable effects of an institution, organized by a former Legislature, to promote the great interest of common schools. A period of nearly three years has elapsed, since the act of the Legislature which established the Board of Education; two successive legislatures have acquiesced in its existence, and the three annual reports of the Board and their Secretary, have borne strong testimony to its beneficial influence. Under these circumstances, for your Committee to give an opposite testimony, might seem to savor of temerity—not to say, of presumption. But your Committee, in the faithful performance of their duty, do not shrink from encountering this charge;—they cannot allow themselves to be deterred from expressing the deliberate conclusions of their judgment, by

From *Documents Printed by Order of the House of Representatives of the Commonwealth of Massachusetts, 1840,* Number 49.

the fear of this or any other imputation. Their apprehensions spring from a different source. An attempt may be made to identify the interests of common schools with the existence of the Board of Education, and any objections to that Board, may, perhaps, be regarded by some, as a covert assault upon our long established system of public instruction. But since our system of public schools did not owe its origin to the Board of Education, but was in existence for two centuries before that Board was established, a proposal to dispense with its further services cannot be reasonably considered as indicating any feelings of hostility or of indifference, towards our system of common schools. It is, indeed, the attachment of your Committee to that system, which has induced them to investigate, with care and attention, the tendencies of the Board of Education. And it is the conclusion to which they have arrived, that the operations of that Board are incompatible with those principles upon which our common schools have been founded and maintained, that leads them to make this report.

The first question to be considered, is, what is the power of the Board of Education? Upon this point very great differences of opinion appear to prevail. By the terms of the act, the board seems to have only a power of recommending, but it is the opinion of many that this power of recommendation, exercised by such a board, must of necessity be soon converted into a power of regulation; and even if it were not, the vantage ground which such a board occupies, must obviously give it, for all practical purposes, an equivalent power. One manifest means by which this power of recommending measures, may become, and, in several instances, has already become equivalent to a power of regulation, is to be found in the circumstance that the Legislature will naturally lend a ready ear to the suggestions of the board, and will be apt, without much examination, to clothe with a legal sanction such rules and regulations, as the board may recommend. It would thus appear, that the board has a tendency, and a strong tendency, to engross to itself the entire regulation of our common schools, and practically to convert the Legislature into a mere instrument for carrying its plans into execution. If, however, this result should be disclaimed, and the Legislature is left as independent as before, and with the same feeling of responsibility for all enactments on the subject of schools, the Board seems to be useless, for the Legislature will not lack suggestions from a variety of other quarters, equally well adapted to furnish them. If, then, the board has any actual power, it is a dangerous power, trenching directly upon the rights and duties of the Legislature; if it has no power, why continue its existence, at an annual expense to the Commonwealth?

As a mere organ for the collection and diffusion of information on the subject of education, the board seems to your Committee to be, in several respects, very much inferior to those voluntary associations of teachers, which preceded the existence of the board, and which, perhaps, suggested the idea of it. In these voluntary associations a vast number of persons are interested; a spirit of emulation exists, and each member is anxious to distinguish himself by his contributions to the common cause. Indeed the Board of Education has found itself obliged to have recourse to these very associations, as a principal means for carrying out its plans. But it is obvious to your Committee, that conventions of teachers called by authority, and subjected to a foreign control, will not feel themselves free to act, they will not feel a due responsibility, and will not share the zeal and emulation to be expected in associations purely voluntary. As your Committee have already stated, these associations of teachers were in existence before the Board was established, and, from the best information your Committee have been able to obtain, instead of increasing they have, in some places, declined in interest and utility, since they were taken under the patronage of the Board.

Considering the degree of interest which pervades this community on the subject of education, and the large number of intelligent persons whose lives are devoted to that profession, your Committee do not apprehend that any discoveries, which may be made in the art or science of teaching, will remain undisseminated, through want of zeal to spread information or of disposition to acquire it. Your Committee can well imagine that in a different state of society,—such as is to be found in the newly settled States,—where common schools are a novelty and teachers are generally ill qualified for their office, some artificial means, such as a Board of Education, might be useful, in stimulating a spirit of inquiry and in disseminating knowledge. But among us, with so many accomplished teachers, a public Board, established for the benefit of the profession of teaching, seems as little needed as a public Board for the benefit of Divinity, Medicine, or the Law. Undoubtedly, in all these professions, great improvements might be made, but it is better to leave them to private industry and free competition, than for the Legislature to put them under the superintendence of an official Board.

The true way to judge of the practical operations of the Board of Education, is not merely to consult the statutes by which the Board is established, but also to examine its own reports. They will furnish an unquestionable means of discovering what are the objects, which the Board actually proposes for itself. A very cursory examination of these documents, will suffice to show that, so far from continuing our system of public instruction, upon the plan upon which it was founded, and according to which it has been so long and so successfully carried on, the aim of the Board appears to be, to remodel it altogether after the example of the French and Prussian systems.

These systems have a Central Board, which supplies the ignorance and incapacity of the administrators of local affairs, and which models the schools of France and Prussia, all upon one plan, as uniform and exact as the discipline of an army. On the other hand, our system of public instruction has proceeded upon the idea, that the local administrators of affairs, that is to say, the school committees of the several towns and districts, are qualified to superintend the schools, and might best be trusted with that superintendence. This different method of operating is not confined to public schools, but extends to every other department of life. In France or Prussia, the smallest bridge cannot be built, or any village road repaired, until a Central Board has been consulted,—a plan, which, in its practical operations, and notwithstanding the science of the Central Board, and the skill of the engineers whom it has at command, is found not at all comparable with our system of local authority.

De Tocqueville, whose work upon America has been so much admired, dwells at great length and with great emphasis, upon the advantages which New England derives from its excellent system of local authority; while he points out the want of local public spirit in the countries of Europe, and the deficiency of interest in local affairs, as the greatest obstacle in the way of public improvements. This system of local authority, is as beneficial to the schools, as to any thing else. It interests a vast number of people in their welfare, whose zeal and activity, if they find themselves likely to be overshadowed by the controlling power of a Central Board, will be apt to grow faint. Improvements, which a teacher or school committee have themselves hit upon, will be likely to be pushed with much more spirit, than those which are suggested, or, as it were, commanded, by a foreign and distant power.

After all that has been said about the French and Prussian systems, they appear to your Committee to be much more admirable as a means of political influence, and of strengthening the hands of the government, than as a mere means for the diffusion of knowledge. For the latter purpose, the system of public common schools, under the control of persons most interested in their flourishing condition, who pay taxes to support them, appears to your Committee much superior. The establishment of the Board of Education, seems to be the commencement of a system of centralization and of monopoly of power in a few hands, contrary, in every respect, to the true spirit of our democratical institutions, and which, unless speedily checked, may lead to unlooked for and dangerous results.

As to the practical operation of this centralizing system, your Committee would observe, that some of the rules and regulations already devised by the Board of Education, and, doubtless, considered by it as of a very useful tendency, have proved, when carried into execution in the schools, very embarrassing, and have engrossed much of the time and attention of the teachers, which might better have been bestowed upon the instruction of their pupils, than in making out minute and complicated registers of statistics. The Board passes new regulations respecting the returns to be made out by the school committees, and sends forth its blanks; the school committees are abruptly notified of them, without being informed of the reasons upon which they are founded. The rules and regulations become so numerous and complicated, as to be difficult of apprehension as well as of execution. Indeed, a periodical commentary seems necessary, from the secretary of the board, in order to enable school committees to discharge their duties. Your committee are strongly of opinion, that nothing but a prevailing impression, well or ill founded, that a compliance with the rules and regulations of the Board, is necessary to secure to towns their annual share of the school fund, has enabled those rules and regulations to be at all regarded. The multiplicity and complexity of laws, with respect to any subject, are matter of just complaint; and this is especially the case with respect to common schools, the teachers of which have a great variety of arduous duties, which must, of necessity, be performed, and which ought not to be aggravated by any requirements, not essential to the welfare of the schools. A Central Board, the members of which are not practical teachers, will be easily led to imagine, that minute statistical facts and other like information, may be obtained at a much less expense of valuable time, than is actually needed for procuring them.

Your Committee have already stated, that the French

and Prussian system of public schools, appears to have been devised, more for the purpose of modifying the sentiments and opinions of the rising generation, according to a certain government standard, than as a mere means of diffusing elementary knowledge. Undoubtedly, common schools may be used as a potent means of engrafting into the minds of children, political, religious and moral opinions;— but, in a country like this, where such diversity of sentiments exists, especially upon theological subjects, and where morality is considered a part of religion, and is, to some extent, modified by sectarian views, the difficulty and danger of attempting to introduce these subjects into our schools, according to one fixed and settled plan, to be devised by a Central Board, must be obvious. The right to mould the political, moral and religious opinions of his children, is a right exclusively and jealously reserved by our own laws to every parent; and for the government to attempt, directly or indirectly, as to these matters, to stand in the parent's place, is an undertaking of very questionable policy. Such an attempt cannot fail to excite a feeling of jealousy, with respect to our public schools, the results of which could not but be disastrous.

A prominent measure, already brought forward by the Board of Education, as a means of moulding the sentiments of the rising generation, is the project of furnishing, under the sanction of the Board, a school library for each district in the Commonwealth. It is professed, indeed, that the matter selected for this library, will be free both from sectarian and political objections.[2] Unquestionably, the board will endeavor

---

[2] [A law of 1837 authorized school districts to levy taxes to support school libraries, but a law of 1827, confirmed in 1835, barred them from acquiring sectarian books. Mann sought both to improve the libraries and to overcome the gaps left by the law of 1827 by having the Board of Education recommend lists of books to the school districts. In order to avoid sectarian bias he arranged to have the Board make its nominations only with the unanimous consent of its members, who represented a variety of denominations.]

to render it so. Since, however, religion and politics, in this
free country, are so intimately connected with every other subject, the accomplishment of that object is utterly impossible,
nor would it be desirable, if possible. That must, indeed, be an
uninteresting course of reading, which would leave untouched
either of these subjects; and he must be a heartless writer, who
can treat religious or political subjects, without affording any
indication of his political or religious opinions. Books, which
confine themselves to the mere statement of undisputed propositions, whether in politics, religion, or morals, must be meagre
indeed; nor is it possible to abstract, from treatises on these
subjects, all that would give offence, without abstracting, at
the same time, the whole substance of the matter. Mere abstract propositions are of very little interest—it is their practical application to particular cases, in which all readers, and
especially young readers, are principally interested. It is not
sufficient, and it ought not to be, that a book contains nothing
which we believe to be false. If it omit to state what we believe
to be true; if it founds itself upon vague generalities, which will
equally serve the purpose of all reasoners alike, this very omis-
sion to state what we believe to be the truth, becomes, in our
eyes, a fault of the most serious character. A book, upon politics,
morals, or religion, containing no party or sectarian views, will
be apt to contain no distinct views of any kind, and will be likely
to leave the mind in a state of doubt and skepticism, much more
to be deplored than any party or sectarian bias.

If a taste for reading exist in our common schools, considering the cheapness and multiplicity of books, and the vast
number of pens devoted to the supply of intellectual wants, it
cannot be doubted that, according to the ordinary rules of
demand and supply, books adapted for the purpose of a school
library will be furnished, as fast as they are needed; and out of
the books, thus produced, every school committee would be at
liberty to make a selection, adapted to the wants and wishes
of their district. The question whether the public money

should be appropriated to aid the school districts in providing themselves with books, is a question as to which your Committee do not feel themselves called upon to express any opinion. That question, however, is very different from the question whether the Commonwealth shall aid, by an appropriation of the public money, and by lending its countenance and patronage to give an artificial circulation, to a particular set of books. Your Committee have no doubts as to the inexpediency of such a proceeding.

Another project, imitated from France and Prussia, and set on foot under the superintendence of the Board of Education, is the establishment of Normal schools. Your Committee approach this subject with some delicacy, inasmuch as one half the expense of the two Normal schools already established, has been sustained by private munificence.[3] If, however, no benefit in proportion to the money spent, is derived from these schools, it is our duty, as legislators, in justice not only to the Commonwealth but to the private donor, to discontinue the project. Comparing the two Normal Schools already established with the Academies and High Schools of the Commonwealth, they do not appear to your Committee to present any peculiar or distinguishing advantages.

Academies and High Schools, cost the Commonwealth nothing, and they are fully adequate, in the opinion of your Committee, to furnish a competent supply of teachers.[4] In years past, they have not only supplied our own schools with competent teachers, but have annually furnished hundreds to

---

[3] [In 1827 James Carter opened a normal school in Lancaster, using a public building but meeting other costs out of his own pocket. In 1838 the legislature finally agreed to appropriate public funds for normal instruction when Edmund Dwight (a member of the Board of Education) offered the state $10,000 for the purpose if it would provide matching funds. The first two state schools were opened in 1839.]

[4] [Academies and high schools were supported by private funds and municipal taxation, respectively, or by a combination of the two.]

the west and the south. There is a high degree of competition existing between these Academies, which is the best guaranty for excellence. It is insisted by the Board, however, that the art of teaching is a peculiar art, which is particularly and exclusively taught at Normal Schools; but it appears to your Committee, that every person, who has himself undergone a process of instruction, must acquire, by that very process, the art of instructing others. This certainly will be the case with every person of intelligence;—if intelligence be wanting, no system of instruction can supply its place. An intelligent mechanic, who has learned his trade, is competent, by that very fact, to instruct others in it, and needs no Normal School to teach him the art of teaching his apprentices.

Considering that our District Schools are kept, on an average, for only three or four months in the year, it is obviously impossible, and, perhaps, it is not desirable, that the business of keeping these schools should become a distinct and separate profession, which the establishment of Normal Schools seems to anticipate.

Even if these schools did furnish any peculiar and distinguishing advantages, we have no adequate security that the teachers, thus taught at the public expense, will remain in the Commonwealth; and it seems hardly just that Massachusetts, in the present state of her finances, should be called upon to educate, at her own cost, teachers for the rest of the Union.

If it be true, that the teachers of any of our District Schools, are insufficiently qualified for the task, the difficulty originates, as it appears to your Committee, not in any deficiency of the means of obtaining ample qualifications, but in insufficiency of compensation. Those districts which are inclined to pay competent wages, can at all times be supplied with competent teachers; and the want of means or inclination to pay an adequate salary, is not a want which Normal Schools have any tendency to supply.

From the number of scholars who have hitherto attended the Normal Schools, established by the Board of Education, it does not appear, that any want of such institutions, is seriously felt. The number of pupils falls far short of the average number in our Academies and High Schools.

It may be suggested, that to abolish these Normal Schools, when they have been in operation for so short a time, is not to give the experiment a fair trial. But the objections of your Committee, as will appear from the considerations above submitted, are of a general and fundamental nature, and they do not consider it advisable to persevere in an experiment, of the inutility of which they are perfectly satisfied. In fact, these schools do not appear to your Committee, to have any stronger claims on the public treasury, for an appropriation of two thousand dollars a year, than many of our Academies and High Schools.

Should the Normal Schools be discontinued by the Legislature, it is but just and reasonable, in the opinion of your Committee, that the sums advanced by the individual, who has generously contributed to the support of those schools, should be refunded; which might be done, by an appropriation of probably five or six hundred dollars, in addition to the money not yet expended, in the hands of the treasurer of the fund.

The Secretary of the Board of Education, stated, in his argument before your Committee on the subject of Normal Schools, that engagements with the teachers of those schools and other parties interested, had been entered into for a term of three years; and he argued, that it would be improper for the Legislature to disturb these contracts. With respect to these contracts, your Committee are decidedly of opinion, that they ought never to have been made, except with the express understanding of a liability to be rescinded or modified, at the pleasure of the Legislature. If, however, they have been otherwise made, and if any individuals shall appear to have any reasonable claim to be remunerated for any disappointment, occasioned by discontinuing the schools, the Legislature have the power to make such remuneration; and your Committee believe, that the sooner such a settlement is made, the better,—inasmuch as an increase in the number of the schools, as contemplated by the board, would increase the difficulty and cost of such a settlement.

In conclusion, the idea of the State controlling Education, whether by establishing a Central Board, by allowing that Board to sanction a particular Library, or by organizing Normal Schools, seems to your Committee a great departure from the uniform spirit of our institutions,—a dangerous precedent and an interference with a matter more properly belonging to those hands, to which our ancestors wisely entrusted it. It is greatly to be feared, that any attempt to form all our schools and all our teachers, upon one model, would destroy all competition,—all emulation, and even the spirit of improvement itself. When a large number of teachers and school committees, are all aiming at improvement, as is doubtless the case to a great extent in this Commonwealth, improvements seem much more likely to be found out and carried into practice, than when the chief right of experimenting is vested in a Central Board.

With these views, your Committee have come to the conclusion, that the interests of our common schools would rest upon a safer and more solid foundation, if the Board of Education and the Normal Schools were abolished. Your Committee would, therefore, recommend the passage of the following bill.

For the Committee,

ALLEN W. DODGE

13.

The Public School Controversy in New York City, 1840

The incipient organization and consolidation of the public school system not only gave many rural democrats cause for concern; it also seemed to threaten the rights of Roman Catholics, who came in ever greater numbers to inhabit the cities of the eastern seaboard. From the Catholic point of view, no public schools were acceptable so long as they forced Protestant principles and Protestant prejudices on Catholic children, and Catholic leaders began to explore ways of protecting their communicants from Protestant importunities. In New York City, where public education remained a function of the Public School Society (See Document 10, page 62), they petitioned that public funds be distributed to Catholic schools that met the educational standards of the Society. In their petition (the first of the documents printed here) they not only dwelt on the obvious bias that books used by the Public School Society expressed toward Roman Catholics, but also insisted that correction of their errors could not meet the requirements of conscience. In doing so, they pointed up the dilemma that the effort to maintain nonsectarian instruction in the public schools created: if such education were to be truly nonsectarian, it would by definition exclude Christianity and thereby promote "infidelity"—two consequences few contemporaries were willing to acquiesce in; while if it were to retain a distinctly religious character, it would in fact be sectarian and therefore be no more eligible for public funds than avowedly Catholic education.

The petitioners' insistence on this point strengthened resistance to their complaints. While spokesmen for the Public School

Society were willing to alter the texts used in their schools, they would not agree that a nonsectarian Protestant education need be offensive to any patriotic American, and the Common Council of the city sustained them in their determination. (The Report of its Special Committee appears as the second document.) More important, Protestant spokesmen rallied to their support. Although many orthodox Protestants had been critical of nonsectarian public education on the grounds that only a truly religious education could overcome the dangers of godlessness, they accepted nondenominational Protestant education as a necessary alternative to the recognition of sectarian differences in the allocation of public funds. The Memorial of a committee of Methodist clergymen, printed as the last document here, illustrates this tendency as well as the outright nativism that characterized most Protestant reactions to Catholic criticisms of the public schools.

Petition of the Catholics of the City of New York

At a meeting of the Catholics of the City of New York, held at St. James' Church, on Monday evening, the 21st of September, inst., Thomas O'Connor was appointed Chairman; Andrew Carrigan, Gregory Dillon and Peter Duffy, Vice Chairman; and B. O'Connor, S. M. Laughlin and James Kelly, Secretaries.

The Right Reverend Bishop Hughes, from the Committee selected at a former meeting, presented the following petition on behalf of the Catholics of the City of New York; which was, on motion, unanimously adopted, and ordered to be presented

---

From *Documents of the Board of Aldermen, of the City of New York,* VII, 40 (1840–1841), 569–579.

to the Board of Aldermen, after having been signed by the officers of the meeting.[1]

To the Honorable the Board of Aldermen of the City of New York:

THE PETITION OF THE CATHOLICS OF NEW YORK RESPECTFULLY REPRESENTS:

That your petitioners yield to no class in their perform-ance of, and disposition to perform, all the duties of citizens. They bear, and are willing to bear their portion of every com-mon burthen; and feel themselves entitled to a participation in every common benefit.

This participation, they regret to say, has been denied them for years back, in reference to common school education in the City of New York, except on conditions with which their conscience, and, as they believe, their duty to God, did not, and does not leave them at liberty to comply.

The rights of conscience, in this country, are held by both the Constitution and universal consent, to be sacred and inviolable. No stronger evidence of this need be adduced than the fact, that one class of citizens are exempted from the duty or obligation of defending their country against an invading foe, out of delicacy and deference to the rights of conscience which forbids them to take up arms for any purpose.

---

[1] [John Joseph Hughes, coadjutor-bishop of New York, was instrumental in rousing his people to demand their fair share of public school funds. An Irish immigrant who had come to America just after the War of 1812, he spoke for a new Catholic population who rapidly outnumbered the earlier French strain. In practice he was willing to accept completely secular schools for the time being, but in the long run he gave a great impetus to the building of Catholic parochial schools.]

Your petitioners only claim the benefit of this principle, in regard to the public education of their children. They regard the public education which the State has provided as a common benefit, in which they are most desirous, and feel that they are entitled, to participate; and therefore they pray your Honorable Body that they may be permitted to do so, without violating their conscience.

But your petitioners do not ask that this prayer be granted without assigning their reasons for preferring it. In ordinary cases men are not required to assign the motives of conscientious scruples in matters of this kind. But your petitioners are aware that a large, wealthy, and concentrated influence is directed against their claim by the corporation called the Public School Society. And that this influence, acting on a public opinion already but too much predisposed to judge unfavorably of the claims of your petitioners, requires to be met by facts which justify them in thus appealing to your Honorable Body, and which may, at the same time, convey a more correct impression to the public mind. Your petitioners adopt this course the more willingly, because the justice, and impartiality which distinguish the decisions of public men, in this country, inspire them with the confidence that your Honorable Body will maintain, in their regard, the principle of the rights of conscience, if it can be done without violating the rights of others, and on no other condition is the claim solicited.

It is not deemed necessary to trouble your Honorable Body with a detail of the circumstances by which the monopoly of the public education of children in the City of New York, and of the funds provided for that purpose at the expense of the State, have passed into the hands of a private corporation, styled in its act of charter, "The Public School Society of the City of New York." It is composed of men of different sects or denominations. But that denomination, Friends, which is believed to have the controlling influence, both by its numbers and otherwise, holds as a peculiar *sectarian principle* that any formal or official teaching of religion is, at best, unprofitable.[2] And your petitioners have discovered that such of *their* children as have attended the public schools, are generally, and at an early age, imbued with the same principle—that they become intractable, disobedient, and even contemptuous towards their parents—unwilling to learn any thing of religion—as if they had become illuminated, and could receive all the knowledge of religion necessary for them, by instinct or inspiration. Your petitioners do not pretend to assign the cause of this change in their children: they only attest the fact, as resulting from their attendance at the public schools of the Public School Society.

This society, however, is composed of gentlemen of various sects, including even one or two Catholics. But they profess to exclude all sectarianism from their schools. If they do not exclude sectarianism, they are avowedly no more entitled to the school funds than your petitioners, or any other denomination of professing Christians. If they do, as they profess, exclude sectarianism, then your petitioners contend that they exclude Christianity; and leave to the advantage of infidelity the tendencies which are given to the minds of youth by the influence of this feature and pretension of their system.

If they could accomplish what they profess, other denominations would join your petitioners in remonstrating against their schools. But they do not accomplish it. Your petitioners will show your Honorable Body that they do admit what Catholics call sectarianism, (although others may call it only religion,) in a great variety of ways.

In their 22d report, as far back as the year 1827, they tell us, page 14, that they *"are aware of the importance of early*

---

[2] [Friends had played a large part in the founding of the city's first Free School for Girls, in 1802. Many of the same families were involved in organizing the Free School Society in 1805 in order to educate children not already provided for by any religious society.]

RELIGIOUS INSTRUCTION"—and that none but what is "exclusively general and scriptural in its character should be introduced into the schools under their charge." Here, then, is their own testimony that they did introduce and authorize "religious instruction" in their schools. And that they solved, with the utmost composure, the difficult question on which the sects disagree, by determining *what kind* of *"religious instruction"* is *"exclusively general and scriptural in its character."* Neither could they impart this "early religious instruction" themselves. They must have left it to their teachers—and these, armed with official influence, could impress those "early religious instructions" on the susceptible minds of the children, with the authority of dictators.

The Public School Society, in their report for the year 1832, page 10, describe the effect of these "early religious instructions," without, perhaps, intending to do so; but yet precisely as your petitioners have witnessed it, in such of their children as attended those schools. "The age at which children are usually sent to school, affords a much better opportunity to mould their minds to peculiar and exclusive forms of faith than any subsequent period of life." In page 11, of the same report, they protest against the injustice of supporting "religion in any shape" by public money: as if the "early religious instruction" which they had themselves authorized in their schools, five years before, was not "religion in some shape," and was not supported by public taxation. They tell us again, in more guarded language, "The Trustees are deeply impressed with the importance of imbuing the youthful mind with religious impressions, and they have endeavoured to attain this object, as far as the nature of the institution will admit." Report of 1837, page 7.

In their 33d Annual Report they tell us, that "they would not be understood as regarding religious impressions in early youth as unimportant; on the contrary, they desire to do all which may with propriety be done, to give a right direction to the minds of the children entrusted to their care. Their schools are uniformly opened with the reading of the Scriptures, and the class books are such as recognise and enforce the great and generally acknowledged principles of Christianity." Page 7.

In their 34th Annual Report, for the year 1339 [1839], they pay a high compliment to a deceased teacher for "the moral and RELIGIOUS influence exerted by her over the three hundred girls daily attending her school," and tell us that "it could not but have had a lasting effect on many of their susceptible minds." Page 7. And yet in all these "early religious instructions, religious impressions, and religious influence," essentially anti-catholic, your petitioners are to see nothing sectarian; but if in giving the education which the State requires, they were to bring the same influences to bear on the "susceptible minds" of their *own* children, in favor, and not against, their *own* religion, then this society contends that it would be sectarian ! !

Your petitioners regret that there is no means of ascertaining to what extent the teachers in the schools of this society carried out the views of their principals on the importance of conveying "early religious instructions" to the "susceptible minds" of the children. But they believe it is in their power to prove, that, in some instances, the Scriptures have been explained, as well as read, to the pupils.

Even the reading of the Scriptures in those schools your petitioners cannot regard otherwise than as sectarian; because Protestants would certainly consider as such the introduction of the Catholic Scriptures, which are different from theirs; and the Catholics have the same ground of objection when the Protestant version is made use of.

Your petitioners have to state further, as grounds of their conscientious objections to those schools, that many of the selections in their elementary reading lessons contain matter prejudicial to the Catholic name and character. The term "POPERY," is repeatedly found in them. This term is known and employed as one of insult and contempt towards the

Catholic religion, and it passes into the minds of children with the feeling of which it is the outward expression. Both the historical and religious portions of the reading lessons are selected from Protestant writers, whose prejudices against the Catholic religion render them unworthy of confidence in the mind of your petitioners, at least so far as their own children are concerned.

The Public School Society have heretofore denied that their books contained any thing reasonably objectionable to Catholics. Proofs of the contrary could be multiplied, but it is unnecessary, as they have recently retracted their denial, and discovered, after fifteen years enjoyment of their monopoly, that their books do contain objectionable passages. But they allege that they have proffered repeatedly to make such corrections as the Catholic Clergy might require. Your petitioners conceive that such a proposal could not be carried into effect by the Public School Society without giving just ground for exception to other denominations. Neither can they see with what consistency that society can insist, as it has done, on the perpetuation of its monopoly, when the Trustees thus avow their incompetency to present unexceptionable books, without the aid of the Catholic, or any other Clergy. They allege, indeed, that with the best intentions they have been unable to ascertain the passages which might be offensive to Catholics. With their intentions, your petitioners cannot enter into any question. Nevertheless, they submit to your Honorable Body, that this society is eminently incompetent for the superintendence of public education, if they could not see that the following passage was unfit for the public schools, and especially unfit to be placed in the hands of Catholic children.

They will quote the passage as one instance, taken from Putnam's Sequel, page 296:

"Huss, John, a zealous reformer from Popery, who lived in Bohemia, towards the close of the fourteenth, and the beginning of the fifteenth centuries. He was bold and persevering; but at length, trusting himself to the deceitful Catholics, he was by them brought to trial, condemned as a heretic, and burnt at the stake."[3]

The Public School Society may be excused for not knowing the historical inaccuracies of this passage; but surely assistance of the Catholic Clergy could not have been necessary to an understanding of the word "deceitful," as applied to all who profess the religion of your petitioners.

For these reasons, and others of the same kind, your petitioners cannot, in conscience, and consistently with their sense of duty to God, and to their offspring, entrust the Public School Society with the office of giving "a right direction to the minds of their children." And yet this society claims that office, and claims for the discharge of it the Common School Funds, to which your petitioners, in common with other citizens are contributors. In so far as they are contributors, they are not only deprived of any benefit in return, but their money is employed to the damage and detriment of their religion, in the minds of their own children, and of the rising generation of the community at large. The contest is between the *guarantied* rights, civil and religious, of the citizen on the one hand, and the pretensions of the Public School Society on the other: and whilst it has been silently going on for years, your petitioners would call the attention of your Honorable Body to its consequences on that class for whom the benefits of public education are most essential—the children of the poor.

This class (your petitioners speak only so far as relates to their own denomination) after a brief experience of the schools of the Public School Society, naturally and deservedly withdrew all confidence from it. Hence the establishment by your petitioners of schools for the education of the poor. The expense necessary for this, was a second taxation, required,

---

[3] [The reference is to Samuel Putnam's *Sequel to the Analytical Reader* (Portland, Me., 1828).]

not by the laws of the land, but by the no less imperious demands of their conscience.

They were reduced to the alternative of seeing their children growing up in entire ignorance, or else taxing themselves anew for private schools, whilst the funds provided for education, and contributed in part by themselves, were given over to the Public School Society, and by them employed as has been stated above.

Now your petitioners respectfully submit, that without this confidence, no body of men can discharge the duties of education as intended by the State, and required by the people. The Public School Society are, and have been at all times, conscious that they had not the confidence of the poor. In their twenty-eighth report, they appeal to the ladies of New York to create or procure it, by the "persuasive eloquence of female kindness;" page 5. And from this they pass, on the next page, to the more efficient eloquence of coercion, under penalties and privations to be visited on all persons "whether emigrants or otherwise," who being in the circumstances of poverty referred to, should not send their children to some "public or other daily school." In their twenty-seventh report, pages 15 and 16, they plead for the doctrine, and recommend it to public favor by the circumstance that it will affect but "few natives." But why should it be necessary at all, if they possessed that confidence of the poor, without which they need never hope to succeed. So well are they convinced of this, that no longer ago than last year, they gave up all hope of inspiring it, and loudly call for coercion by *"the strong arm of the civil power"* to supply its deficiency. Your petitioners will close this part of their statement with the expression of their surprise and regret that gentlemen who are themselves indebted much to the respect which is properly cherished for the rights of conscience, should be so unmindful of the same rights in the case of your petitioners. Many of them are by religious principle so pacific that they would not take up arms in the defence of the liberties of their country, though she should call them to her aid; and yet, they do not hesitate to invoke the "strong arm of the civil power" for the purpose of abridging the private liberties of their fellow citizens, who may feel equally conscientious.

Your petitioners have to deplore, as a consequence of this state of things, the ignorance and vice, to which hundreds, nay, thousands of their children are exposed. They have to regret, also, that the education which they can provide, under the disadvantages to which they have been subjected, is not as efficient as it should be. But should your Honorable Body be pleased to designate their schools as entitled to receive a just proportion of the Public Funds, which belong to your petitioners, in common with other citizens, their schools could be improved, for those who attend; others now growing up in ignorance, could be received, and the ends of the Legislature could be accomplished—a result which is manifestly hopeless, under the present system.

Your petitioners will now invite the attention of your Honorable Body, to the objections and misrepresentations that have been urged by the Public School Society, to granting the claim of your petitioners. It is urged by them, that it would be appropriating money raised by general taxation, to the support of the Catholic religion. Your petitioners join issue with them, and declare unhesitatingly, that if this objection can be established, the claim shall be forthwith abandoned. It is objected, that though we are taxed as citizens, we apply for the benefits of education, as "Catholics." Your petitioners, to remove this difficulty, beg to be considered in their application in the identical capacity in which they are taxed, viz: as citizens of the Commonwealth. It has been contended by the Public School Society, that the law disqualifies schools, which admit any profession of religion, from receiving any encouragements from the School Fund. Your petitioners have two solutions for this pretended difficulty. *First*—Your petitioners are unable to discover any such disqualification in the law, which merely delegates to your Honorable Body, the authority and discretion of determining what schools or societies shall be entitled to its bounty. *Second*—Your petitioners are willing to fulfil the conditions of the law, so far as religious teaching is proscribed, during school hours. In fine, your petitioners, to remove all objection, are willing that the material organization of their schools, and the disbursements of the funds allowed for them, shall be conducted, and made, by persons unconnected with the religion of your petitioners; even the Public School Society, if it should please your Honorable Body to appoint them for that purpose. The public may then be assured, that the money will not be applied to the support of the Catholic religion.

It is deemed necessary by your petitioners, to save the Public School Society the necessity of future misconception, thus to state the things which are *not* petitioned for. The members of that society, who have shown themselves so impressed with the importance of conveying *their* notions of "early religious instruction" to the "susceptible minds" of Catholic children, can have no objection that the parents of the children, and teachers in whom the parents have confidence, should do the same: provided, no law is violated thereby, and no disposition evinced to bring the children of other denominations within its influence.

Your petitioners, therefore, pray that your Honorable Body, will be pleased to designate, as among the schools entitled to participate in the Common School Fund, upon complying with the requirements of the law, the ordinances of the Corporation of the city, or for such other relief, as to your Honorable Body shall seem meet—St. Patrick's School, St. Peter's School, St. Mary's School, St. Joseph's School, St. James' School, St. Nicholas' School, Transfiguration Church School, and St. John's School.

And your petitioners further request, in the event of your Honorable Body's determining to hear your petitioners, on the subject of their petition, that such time may be appointed, as may be most agreeable to your Honorable Body, and that a full session of your Honorable Board be convened for that purpose.

And your petitioners, &c.

THOMAS O'CONNOR,
Chairman,
GREGORY DILLON,
ANDREW CARRIGAN,
PETER DUFFY,
Vice Chairmen,

B. O'CONNOR,
JAMES KELLY,
J. MCLOUGHLIN,
Secretaries.

Of a general meeting of the Catholics of the City of N. York, convened in the school room of St. James' Church, 21st September, 1840.

Report of the Special Committee of the Board of Aldermen

The Special Committee, to whom were referred the petition of the Catholics of New York, relative to the distribution of the School Fund, the several remonstrances and other documents connected with the subject, together with the above resolution of instructions, respectfully submit the following

REPORT:

In pursuance of the instructions contained in the resolution, they employed two entire days in visiting the public schools, accompanied by a Committee of the petitioners, and also of the Public School Society, with a view to ascertain if any defects exist in their organization; and after a thorough

---

From *Documents of the Board of Aldermen, of the City of New York,* VII, 40 (1840–1841), 558–563.

scrutiny, in which all parties participated, your Committee not only failed to discover anything strikingly defective in the system, but became strongly impressed with a conviction that the public schools under their present organization, are admirably adapted to afford precisely the kind of instruction for which they were institnted [*sic*]. It is deemed essential to the welfare and security of our government, that the means of mental cultivation should be extended to every child in the community. The rising generation are destined to be the future rulers of the land, and their happiness can only be secured by such an education as will constitute them an intelligent community, prepare them to guard against the machinations of demagogues, and so to exercise the rights and franchises of citizens as not to deprive themselves of the invaluable privileges which are their birthright. That the public school system, as now organized, is calculated to effect these objects, your Committee do not entertain a doubt; but, though they regard it as an incalculable public blessing, if they could be persuaded that it trespassed upon the conscientious rights of any portion of our citizens, they would begin to doubt the propriety of its continuance: they cannot, however, conceive that it is justly amenable to such a charge, so long as sectarian dogmas and peculiarities are excluded from the schools, and no pupils are either admitted into them, or excluded from them, against the consent of their natural or legal guardians. The system has grown up under the auspices of a voluntary association of individuals usually known as "The Public School Society," formed for the purpose of promoting education, and admitting to membership any citizen of good moral character, who is not a clergyman, upon a contribution of ten dollars to its funds. This society has watched with indefatigable vigilance and untiring assiduity over the rise and progress of the system, and by their unrequited labors it has been nurtured into maturity. In its present aspect, it is a monument of disinterestedness and public spirit, of which our city has reason to be proud. Your Committee hereby acknowledge their indebtedness to the members of that society, for the prompt manner in which they responded to every call made upon them, and they cannot but hope that the spirit of candor which they have displayed, and which the petitioners in the same spirit acknowledge, will ultimately remove every barrier, which, through misapprehension, as your Committee believe, has hitherto retarded the entire success of their benevolent and patriotic exertions. It has been objected on the part of the petitioners, that the books used in the public schools contain passages that are calculated to prejudice the minds of children against the Catholic faith. This objection, your Committee discovered to be not wholly unfounded; but we are happy to have it in our power to add, that the School Society fully agree with us in the opinion that nothing in the books or usages of the schools should be continued that is calculated in the remotest degree to wound the feelings or prejudice the minds of children in favor of or against any religious sect whatever; that they have expunged such passages in the books as they have been able to discover in any way objectionable; that they desire to continue, and earnestly solicit the aid and co-operation of the petitioners, in the work of expurgation, until every really objectionable feature shall be entirely obliterated. The extreme difficulty of this undertaking, is illustrated by the fact that some of the very same passages quoted by the petitioners as particularly objectionable, and which have been obliterated in the public school books, were found by your Committee entirely unobscured in the books used in one of the Catholic schools. It is a melancholy fact, that in neighborhoods where Catholic children are numerous, the public schools number but few children whose parents profess the Catholic faith; but after the arduous task of expurgation shall have been completed, and every well grounded objection removed, your Committee fondly hope that the school houses will be filled with children, and that no parents or guardians, be their religious feelings what they may, will refuse to avail themselves of the benefits of the public schools for the education of their children, being fully persuaded that many years would elapse before any new system of instruction could be organized, with advantages equal to the one now equally available to every child in the community. If, with such a system, any portion of the children should be left uneducated, it cannot be justly chargeable to a want of comprehensiveness in the system, but is more fairly attributable to imperfections which human legislation cannot remedy. The general objections to sectarian public schools, do not apply to cases where children are supported by charity, and necessarily confined to a particular locality, and not open to all children. Your Committee think that all such establishments might enjoy the benefits of education, at public expense, without an infringement of the principles contended for; and the rule being made general, their participation in the benefits of the School Fund would not necessarily constitute a public recognition of their religious sectarian character. No school system can be perfect which does not place the means of education within the reach of every child who is capable of receiving instruction; and such, your Committee believe, to be the design and capacity of the system now in use in this city.

The Public School buildings are constructed upon a uniform model; the books used are the same in all the schools, and the classes and departments in each are so similarly constituted and provided, that the removal of a pupil from one school to another, will not interrupt his studies or retard his progress. Though religion constitutes no specific part of the system of instruction, yet the discipline of the schools, and the well arranged and selected essays and maxims which abound in their reading books, are well calculated to impress upon the minds of children, a distinct idea of the value of religion; the importance of the domestic and social duties; the existence of God, the creator of all things; the immortality of the soul; man's future accountability; present dependence upon a superintending providence; and other moral sentiments, which do not conflict with sectarian views and peculiarities.

The different classes examined in several schools by your Committee, exhibited an astonishing progress in geography, astronomy, arithmetic, reading, writing, &c.; and indicated a capacity in the system for imparting instruction, far beyond our expectations; and, though the order and arrangement of each school would challenge comparison with a camp under a rigid disciplinarian, yet the accustomed buoyancy and cheerfulness of youth and childhood, did not appear to be destroyed, in any one of them: such were the favorable impressions forced upon our minds by a careful examination of the public schools.[4] It is due to the Trustees, to add, that not one of our visits was anticipated, and no opportunity was afforded to any of the teachers, for even a momentary preparation. In the course of our investigations, we also visited three of the schools established by the petitioners, and for the benefit of which, a portion of the School Fund is solicited. We found them, as represented by the petitioners, lamentably deficient in accommodations, and supplies of books and teachers: the rooms were all excessively crowded and poorly ventilated; the books much worn as well as deficient in numbers, and the teachers not sufficiently numerous; yet, with all these disadvantages, though not able to compete successfully with the public schools, they exhibited a progress, which was truly creditable; and with the same means at their disposal, they would doubtless soon be able, under suitable direction, greatly to improve their condition. The object of the petitioners, is to supply these deficiencies from the fund provided by the bounty of the State, for the purposes of common school education. But however strongly our sympathies may be excited in behalf of the poor children assembled in these

---

[4] [The Lancasterian system of education depended upon the services of older children who had already made some progress in the subject being taught. They were assigned the responsibility of monitoring the work of less knowledgeable pupils under the general supervision of an adult instructor who stood at the head of the schoolroom. For this reason, and because learning took the form of rote responses to the instructor's commands, the ideal schoolroom closely resembled a contemporary factory in which all the workers were compelled to labor on assigned tasks at an established speed.]

schools, such is the state of the public mind on this subject, that if one religious sect should obtain a portion of the School Fund, every other one would present a similar claim, and it would be a signal for the total demolition of the system, which has grown up under the guidance of many years of toilsome experience; attaining a greater degree of perfection, than has perhaps, ever before been achieved, and which is probably extending a greater amount of instruction at smaller expense than can possibly be imparted by any other school system, that has been devised. This result of such a disposal of the School Funds, would most probably, be followed by a counteraction in the public mind, which would lead to a revocation of the Act, by a succeeding Common Council, and the awakening of a spirit of intolerance, which, in our country, is of all calamities, the one most to be dreaded. Political intolerance, is an unmitigated evil; but the experience of past ages ought to admonish us to guard, with unceasing vigilance, against religious intolerance, as an evil greater in magnitude, in proportion as eternal consequences exceed those of time. So long as government refuses to recognise religious sectarian differences, no danger need be apprehended from this source; but when it begins to legislate with particular reference to any particular denomination of christians, in any manner which recognises their religious peculiarities, it oversteps a boundary which public opinion has established; violates a principle which breath[e]s in all our Constitutions; and opens a door to that unholy connection of politics with religion, which has so often cursed and desolated Europe. Under these impressions of the impossibility of granting the prayer of the petitioners, without producing the most fatal consequences, and impressed, at the same time, with an anxious desire to remove every obstacle out of the way of the public education of their children, if it could be done without sacrifising [*sic*] any fundamental principle, your Committee invited the School Society and the petitioners, to appoint delegates to meet them, with a view to effect a compromise, if possible. The invitation was promptly responded to, and several meetings were held, at which the subject was fully and very courteously discussed, in all its bearings, and though we extremely regret to report, that the conferences did not result as favorably as we had hoped, yet the spirit and tenor of the following propositions, submitted at our request, by both the School Society and the petitioners, encourage a belief, that our labor may not have been entirely in vain.[5]

Memorial of a Committee of the Methodist Episcopal Church

To the Honorable the Common Council of the City of New York.

The undersigned Committee, appointed by the Pastors of the Methodist Episcopal Church in this City, on the part of said pastors and churches, do most respectfully represent:

That they have heard with surprise and alarm, that the Roman Catholics have renewed their application to the Common Council, for an appropriation from the Common School Fund, for the support of the schools under their own direction; in which they teach, and propose still to teach, their own sectarian dogmas; not only to their own children, but to such

---

From *Documents of the Board of Aldermen, of the City of New York,* VII, 40 (1840–1841), 580–585.

[5] [In these propositions, the Catholic spokesmen undertook to subordinate their schools to the discipline, pedagogical system, and financial control of the Public School Society and to bar doctrinal teaching from them, provided that the schools' trustees might appoint their own teachers, subject to confirmation by the Society. In reply, the Public School Society undertook to remove books offensive to Catholics from Society schools, to deal justly with other Catholic complaints and proposals, and to buy one of the Catholic school buildings for use as a Society school.]

Protestant children as they may find means to get into their schools.

Your memorialists had hoped that the clear, cogent, and unanswerable arguments, by which the former application for this purpose was resisted, would have saved the Common Council from further importunity.

It was clearly shown that the Council could not legally make any sectarian appropriation of the public funds; and it was as clearly shown, that it would be utterly destructive of the whole scheme of public school instruction to do so, even if it could be legally done. But it seems that neither the Constitution of the State, nor the public welfare, are to be regarded, when they stand in the way of Roman Catholic sectarianism and exclusiveness.

It must be manifest to the Common Council, that if the Roman Catholic claims are granted, all the other Christian denominations will urge their claims for a similar appropriation; and that the money raised for education by a general tax, will be solely applied to the purposes of proselytism through the medium of sectarian schools. But if this were done, would it be the price of peace? or would it not throw the apple of discord into the whole Christian community? Should we agree in the division of the spoils? Would each sect be satisfied with the portion allotted to it? We venture to say that the sturdy claimants who now beset the Council, would not be satisfied with much less than the lion's share; and we are sure that there are other Protestant denominations, besides ourselves, who would not patiently submit to the exaction. But when all the Christian sects shall be satisfied with their individual share of the public fund, what is to become of those children whose parents belong to none of these sects, and who cannot conscientiously allow them to be educated in the peculiar dogmas of any one of them? The different Committees who on a former occasion approached your Honorable Body, have shown that to provide schools for these only, would require little less than is now expended; and it requires little arithmetic to show that when the religious sects have taken all, nothing will remain for those who have not yet been able to decide, which of the Christian denominations to prefer. It must be plain to every impartial observer, that the applicants are opposed to the whole system of public school instruction; and it will be found, that the uncharitable exclusiveness of their creed, must ever be opposed to all public instruction, which is not under the direction of their own priesthood. They may be conscientious in all this; but though it be no new claim on their part, we cannot yet allow them to guide and control the consciences of all the rest of the community. We are sorry that the reading of the Bible, in the public schools, without note or commentary, is offensive to them; but we cannot allow the holy scriptures to be accompanied with *their* notes and commentaries, and to be put into the hands of the children, who may hereafter be the rulers and legislators of our beloved country; because, among other bad things taught in these commentaries, is to be found the lawfulness of murdering heretics; and the unqualified submission in all matters of conscience to the Roman Catholic Church.

But if the principle on which this application is based should be admitted, it must be carried far beyond the present purpose.

If all are to be released from taxation when they cannot conscientiously derive any benefit from the disbursement of the money collected, what will be done for the Society of Friends, and other sects, who are opposed to war, under all circumstances. Many of these, beside the tax paid on all the foreign goods they consume, pay direct duties at the Custom House, which go to the payment of the army and to purchase the munitions of war. And even when the Government finds it necessary to lay direct war taxes, these conscientious sects are compelled to pay their proportion, on the ground that the public defence requires it. So it is believed the public interest requires the education of the whole rising generation; because it would be unsafe to commit the public liberty, and the perpetuation of our republican institutions, to those whose ignorance of their nature and value would render them careless of their preservation, or the easy dupes of artful innovators; and hence every citizen is required to contribute in proportion to his means to the public purpose of universal education.

The Roman Catholics complain that books have been introduced into the public schools, which are injurious to them as a body. It is allowed, however, that the passages in these books, to which such reference is made, are chiefly, if not entirely, historical; and we put it to the candour of the Common Council to say, whether any history of Europe, for the last ten centuries, could be written, which could either omit to mention the Roman Catholic Church, or mention it without recording historical facts unfavorable to that church? We assert that if all the historical facts in which the Church of Rome has taken a prominent part, could be taken from writers of her own communion, only, the incidents might be made more objectionable to the complainants, than any book to which they now object.

History itself, then, must be falsified for their accommodation; and yet they complain that the system of education adopted in the Public Schools does not teach the sinfulness of lying! They complain that no religion is taught in these schools, and declare that any, even the worst form of Christianity, would be better than none; and yet they object to the reading of the Holy Scriptures, which are the only foundation of all true religion. Is it not plain, then, that they will not be satisfied with any thing short of the total abandonment of public school instruction, or the appropriation of such portion of the public fund as they may claim, to their own sectarian purposes.

But this is not all. They have been most complaisantly offered the censorship of the books to be used in the Public Schools. The Committee to whom has been confided the management of these schools, in this city, offered to allow the Roman Catholic Bishop to expurgate from these books any thing offensive to him.

But the office was not accepted; perhaps, for the same

reason that he declined to decide on the admissibility of a book of extracts from the Bible, which had been sanctioned by certain Roman Catholic Bishops in Ireland. An appeal, it seems, had gone to the Pope on the subject, and nothing could be said or done in the matter until his Holiness had decided. The Common Council of New York will therefore find that when they shall have conceded to the Roman Catholics of this city, the selection of books for the use of the Public Schools, that these books must undergo the censorship of a foreign potentate. We hope the time is far distant when the citizens of this country will allow any foreign power to dictate to them in matters relating to either general or municipal law.

We cannot conclude this memorial without noticing one other ground on which the Roman Catholics, in their late appeal to their fellow citizens, urged their sectarian claims, and excused their conscientious objections to the Public Schools. Their creed is dear to them, it seems, because some of their ancestors have been martyrs to their faith. This was an unfortunate allusion. Did not the Roman Catholics know that they addressed many of their fellow citizens who could not recur to the memories of their own ancestors, without being reminded of the revocation of the Edict of Nantz; the massacre of Saint Bartholomew's day; the fires of Smithfield; or the crusade against the Waldenses?[6]

---

6 [The Massacre of St. Bartholomew's Day was a slaughter of French Calvinists (Huguenots) instigated by Catholic members of the French court on the saint's day in 1572 just after the marriage of Henry of Navarre, the Protestant claimant to the French throne, to Margaret of Valois. Despite Catholic opposition, Henry succeeded to the throne in 1589, and in 1598 issued the Edict of Nantes guaranteeing freedom of worship to the Huguenots even though he had abandoned Protestantism. In 1685, however, Louis XIV, who had long since determined to stamp out Protestantism as a force hostile to his consolidation of royal power, revoked the Edict and thereby spurred on persecutions that ultimately drove the Huguenots out of France, many to England and America.

The Waldensians were medieval French Protestants, condemned by Pope Lucius III in 1184, against whom Pope Innocent III preached and the

We would willingly cover these scenes with the mantle of charity; and hope that our Roman Catholic fellow citizens will, in future, avoid whatever has a tendency to revive the painful remembrance.

Your memorialists had hoped that the intolerance and exclusiveness which had characterized the Roman Catholic Church in Europe, had been greatly softened under the benign influences of our civil institutions. The pertinacity with which their sectarian interests are now urged, has dissipated the illusion. We were content with their having excluded us, "ex cathedra," from all claim to heaven, for we were sure they did not possess the keys, notwithstanding their confident pretensions; nor did we complain that they would not allow us any participation in the benefits of Pugatory; for it is a place they have made for themselves, and of which they may claim the exclusive propriety; but we do protest against any appropriation of the Public School Fund for their exclusive benefit, or for any other sectarian purposes whatever.

Assured that the Common Council will do, what it is right to do in the premises, we are, gentlemen, with great respect,

Your most obedient servants,

N. BANGS,
THOMAS E. BOND,
GEORGE PECK.

French armies conducted a crusade of extermination of 1487. Smithfield Market in London was the site on which public authorities burned English Protestant leaders at the stake during the reign of "Bloody Mary" (1553–1558), who sought to nullify the English Reformation initiated by her father, Henry VIII.]

14.

Henry A. Wise, Address to His Constituents, 1844

In general, Whigs were quicker than Democrats to press for universal elementary education at the public expense, and Henry A. Wise of Virginia was no exception. In 1844 the Whig congressman, named Minister to Brazil by President John Tyler, took the occasion of his retirement from the House of Representatives to exhort his constituents on the subject of popular education. Significantly, he insisted that tax support for schools was both necessary and feasible, and he rebuked typically republican provisions for the public education only of the indigent. Doing so, he also testified to sectional differences within Virginia that had so far blocked all efforts to create a state-wide system of schools, and at least by implication he depicted a combination of rural parsimony and rural skepticism toward book-learning (common also in the North) that discouraged even yeoman farmers from demanding schooling for their children.

If I had an archangel's trump—the blast of which could startle the living of all the world—I would snatch it at this moment and sound it in the ears of all the people of the debtor

From *Report of the Commissioner of Education for the Year 1899–1900* (Washington, D.C., 1901), I, 397–403. No source is indicated in the Commissioner's *Report,* which erroneously dates the address 1856. For the correct date, see Barton A. Wise, *The Life of Henry A. Wise of Virginia, 1806–1876* (New York, 1899), p. 105.

States and of the States which have a solitary poor "unwashed and uncombed" child untaught at a free school.

Tax yourselves.

First. To pay your public State debt.

Second. To educate your children—every child of them —at common primary free schools at State charge.

That is my legacy of advice to you before I leave my country's shores to return, perhaps, no more forever.

Distrust all attempts to disturb the operations of a tax bill already passed. Disbelieve any set of men who come before you with false promises of freedom from taxation. Listen only to those sincere friends who will honestly tell you that you must be taxed, how much you ought to be taxed, and who will counsel freely and fully with you beforehand as to the mode and subjects of taxation. In a word, learn to love taxation as the only means of accomplishing such objects as those of paying the public debt and of educating your children, rich and poor. See to it well that no revenue raised for legitimate purposes is wasted; see that it is all faithfully applied to the true ends of government, but be sure to raise enough and amply enough for every kind of State necessity, usefulness, and honor. There is no easy mode of taxation, no royal road to paying debts or to education. Industry, honesty, economy, and education alone can make you a free and happy people.

Educate your children, all your children—every one of them!

Do you know how education languishes with us [in twelve counties having 37,230 free white persons, of whom 17,809 were over 20 years of age]?

First. The fact appears that of the whole number of free white persons nearly one-eighth can not read and write.

Second. That of the whole number of free white persons over 20 years of age more than one-fourth can not read and write.

Third. That you have but 17 academies and 101 primary

schools, making 118 in all, when you ought to maintain at least 259, leaving a deficiency of 141 common schools.

Fourth. That you have 2,628 scholars in your primary schools and but 695 children in them at public charge, when you ought to have at least 7,448 children at from 7 to 15 years of age, all at public charge, in free schools, leaving 4,175 children of that age unaccounted for.

Fifth. That this number of 4,175 children of that age presumed not sent to school is nearly the precise number of adults, 4,514, who in this generation have grown up ignorant of letters.

Sixth. That this number of adults, 4,514, who can not read and write exceeds even the number of voters, 4,379, in the district.

Seventh. That, allowing $12 to each scholar, you are now expending but $38,646 per annum for common schools, when you ought to expend the sum of $89,376, leaving a deficiency of funds amounting to $50,730 per annum.

Eighth. That this sum of $50,730 must be raised and expended in some way to make the rising generation more learned than their fathers.

This is a lamentable condition of education among us. I would never have exposed it to the scoff or pity of the world, but our own census takers have already made report thereof to the Department of State of the United States, and Congress has printed these facts at public expense. I know that a very large body of our people is among the most intelligent, and some of them among the most learned, of the country; I know how much credit and honor is due to some of our parents, who have not only rubbed nature's rust off their sons at common schools, but have polished their minds bright not only at our own colleges and universities, but in the universities of Europe. I know what a body of well-instructed gentlemen we have who would do honor to any society of any Athens in the land; how gracefully they live in all the means of the light of learning; what a

venerable alma mater of great men we have in old William and
Mary College; what a select corps of professors and teachers
become our seminaries and academies; what a fine body of
young graduates yearly come out of our own and the Northern
schools; what an eminent professional corps, both in law and
medicine, ministers to our minds as well as our physical and
pecuniary cases; what active industry, enterprise, and intelligence there is among the great body of our farmers, planters,
and mechanics. I know how to account for much of the lack of
learning among our people from their geographical location,
living, as many of them do, on islands and long peninsulas in-
convenient to schools, and how much ignorance is to be attributed to the valuable labor of poor children whose poor parents
can not spare their time at school, precious as it is, to procure
for them their daily bread. I know all these consoling excuses,
but still the fact stares us frightfully in the face that more than
4,000 poor children in our district are growing up in the night
of ignorance. Most of these doubtless are female children, and
the touching fact is presented that many mothers of the generation to follow will not be able to teach their sons and daughters
how to read and write. We can not mend the present generation of fathers and mothers, but we may provide intellectual
food enough, and to spare, for the health and happiness of
those who are to come after us.

The first and greatest error of our present system is that
it proceeds upon the principle of charity. Common school education should not be a State charity, but it should be the chief
element of the freedom of the State. The poor man pays taxes,
renders military and civil service, is subject to fines, must obey
the laws, and in return he should have the protection of the
laws, the ordinary privileges of citizenship, such as the right
of voting, and I say he should have his children educated as of
right, free of charge. And in all these respects the rich and poor
should be placed on precisely the same equal footing. There
should be no distinction between the children of a republic.
They are not in the school sense the children of their parents,

but the State is parens patriæ,[1] and they should all be regarded as sons and daughters of Mother Commonwealth. The taxes, it is true, will have to be raised chiefly from the property of the rich; but at last the school revenue is distributed as funds of the State, and when with her liberal and equal hand they are distributed impartially to all there is no feeling of dependence in any. They all alike look up to the benign State mother for the mental bounty, all praise her only and love her supremely for it, and thus is laid a foundation of amor patriæ[2] ever-during as the reminiscences of schoolboy days and fervent as the fondest recollections of life and gratitude can ever be in the human heart.

As our system now is, in schools mixed of children whose parents pay for schooling them and of those who are sent by the school commissioners of the State, the child of charity is humbled by the comparison of itself with those who pay. The school is not pleasant to this child, and the pride of parents so revolts at the dependence and inequality in the school that they often refuse to allow their children to enter. While the school is free of charge, still it is not free. The true course is to make it free to all, make it the school of the State, and let all her children come, "without money and without price." Then no human pride will militate against education, but, on the contrary, every little checked apron will be washed and ironed and every little fly-flap bonnet will be stiffened and straightened for the "school parade." Funds and the universal school are all that are wanting to enlighten every child among us and to array human pride on the side of the school.

You need not, my friends, wait for the tardy action of our legislature. If we wait for that, I fear we will wait forever. What then? Organize yourselves by counties and districts. All that you have need to ask of the legislature is to pass an act for every county which will adopt a system for itself, incorporating

---

[1] [Father of the country.]

[2] [Love of country.]

for it a board of education with powers similar to those of the county courts for county levies and other purposes. Let this board be elected biennially by the votes of all the male parents and guardians, having a member for every hundred voters, according to districts to be laid off by the board.

Let this board be required to levy taxes sufficient to educate every white child between the ages of 7 and 15 years, at common free schools, at the rate of $12 per annum for each child, and allowing 30 scholars to each teacher, and to pay expenses of assessment and superintendence. Let it lay off the county in districts of 30 scholars, and 1 teacher to each district.

Let it have power to appoint one assessor to take annual census of the persons and property to be taxed for the school fund; of one collector of the fund, to give bond and security; and one superintendent to visit quarterly each school, to take regular account of the system of teaching, of the number of pupils, and of the qualifications and conduct of teachers and to make report thereof to the board; with reasonable compensation to each of those officers.

Let this board have power to fine and to collect fines of parents and guardians, rich or poor, who fail or refuse to send their children or wards to some schools of their own selection. And let it meet quarterly or as often as it chooses, with power to pass by-laws for its own government.

For every county that will thus tax itself to educate itself the State should, out of the literary fund, build all the additional schoolhouses required. It should do more, and what is all essential—it should take upon itself to furnish competent teachers in a reasonable course of time to every county in the Commonwealth. And this can easily be done. The university and the colleges, particularly, must be more liberally patronized. The universities and colleges are the fountains of good teachers. They must be upheld and encouraged, and the most munificent and beneficent mode of doing this, in my humble opinion, is for the State, out of the literary fund and by taxation, if necessary, to support at the respective colleges a number of our own Virginia youths equal to twice the number of delegates and senators in the legislature, and to require these youths, when they have obtained certificates of competency, to teach in the primary and common free schools, at the rate allowed for each scholar ($12) as long as they have been maintained at college at State charge. Let them enter into indentures to the State, and then they will obtain their education and will have worthily paid for it. Each youth of this description will cost not more than $250 per annum for his board, tuition, and incidental expenses.

The number proposed is 332, and the cost to the literary fund would be $83,000 per annum. This would give to each university and college 25 State students, and distribute to each the patronage of $6,385 per annum. This would give to the State in the term of three years, say, a corps of 332 competent teachers, certain to be engaged in the work of tuition for a period of three years more, and shedding the light of their knowledge into every recess of the State and exciting the thirst for mental improvement everywhere by their example, and when done teaching, abiding ornaments of the State.

The State, too, should furnish the books for the free schools, and should have two general superintendents, one for eastern and one for western Virginia.

I call upon the learned professors of William and Mary and of the academies and schools; I call upon the reverend clergy of every denomination; I call upon my brethren of the bar; I call upon the humane faculty of medicine; I call upon our most excellent farmers and mechanics; I call upon parents and guardians; I call upon women who would be the mothers of scholars, philosophers, sages, and great men; I call upon all ages and sexes; I call upon the rich man and the poor man, and upon men of all conditions, to stir—to "live, move, and have their being" in this vital subject. Knowledge is power; it is the greatest of all power. It is the power which overcomes all social obstacles; it is the power which prostrates all political inequalities; it is the power which overcomes all physical obstructions in the way of man; castes and ranks and grades bow before it; wealth is impotent against it; it subdues the earth, and it humbles tyrants. And if knowledge is power, ignorance is weakness—utter, impotent weakness. We say we were all born free and equal. That may be so; but if we were born so, the state of freedom and equality does not last long in life if one man is to be cultivated in his mind whilst the other is permitted to grow up in ignorance. How is the man who can not read and write the equal in power of any sort, except muscular power, of the man of letters? No. Ignorance among the people destroys the liberty and equality of the people; it makes inequalities in the social state; it gives one man a preeminence and preference among men over another in the political state; it makes the very weeds of the earth too strong for man's physical might to earn his bread; it makes the rich richer and the poor poorer, the strong stronger and the weak weaker; it is the sycophant and slave of tyrants and the foundation of despotism; it not only enslaves the citizen, but enervates the State.

Does anyone suppose that if education had been diffused universally among our people Virginia would have increased in the last ten years in white population some 20,000 or 30,000 only? That her agriculture and mechanic arts would be in the low state they are now in? That the rich bowels of her inexhaustible mountain mines of iron and coal would be undug and almost unexplored? That her manufactures would have languished as they do? That the big bend of the Ohio River would not have been tapped long ago, and that the mighty Miami country, and an interminable back country besides, would not ere this have built us an Eastern city to consume our products at home? That emigration would have flowed from us to lands not half so precious, to homes not half so sacred? Oh, my friends, the theme is full of facts, figures, and feeling.

To the poor, ignorant man I say, let no man tell you that a "little learning is a dangerous thing." The least of it is not half so dangerous as that ignorance that can not read and write. If Patrick Henry once said "natural parts are better than all the learning in the world," don't believe it, though he said it. What would he not have been had he possessed only half the learning of the world? Of what would the power of his "natural parts" have stopped short in human greatness, in human eloquence, if he had been possessed of the purchase of the lever of learning? The self-made man may boast—I love to admire him rising by the lone power of his genius—but I despise his self-sufficiency when he boasts against "the books." Not once in an age does it happen that one self-made man stamps the age with his genius. But, at last, how can any man be said to be self-made? Those who claim to be self-made are so made by the books, if not by the schoolmaster. Tell me the knowledge that anyone of you all has which was not derived, directly or remotely, from the books? None. There is none in law, none in medicine, none in agriculture, none in mechanic arts not traceable to the books. And, my friends, if you would only yourselves go to the books, they would inform you much better than you are now instructed, by tradition, or second-hand informers. Look for yourselves; learn for yourselves. To the books! to the books! and be self-made yourselves if you will.

But the schoolmaster must teach you how to read and write. Remember that the books are sealed to those who can not read and write. I will not descant upon the pauperism and the crime which "a little learning" would diminish. No, there is a much more interesting class than that of inmates of poorhouses and of jails to be discussed. I mean one of the best classes of men on God's earth—a class with whom "the gods" are said to take part in their struggles through life—that class of good men who, notwithstanding they were never taught, are so endowed by nature with noble instincts as to perform their whole duty worthy of themselves, worthy of the State, and worthy of their eternal destiny. Men whom ignorance does not debase, whom it does not enervate nor make to despair, men who work in the world against all odds of ignorance and win a crown of earthly honor and of eternal glory. I know who they are. I know every one of them in my old district by name. I would have a word

with them. They are the good, hard-working, honest class of
men who, notwithstanding they can not read and write, can
"make their marks" in the world. May God bless them! I know
an aged man, small in stature, his head is silvered over with the
white frost of years, with a lively, joyous face and a twinkling
blue eye that needs no glass for its keen vision, an honest heart
and a hand as hard as ax helve and plow handle would have it,
who does "not know a letter in the book," and who yet is rich
in the stores of practical wisdom and of real wealth. Some one
near Guilford, in Accomac, can guess who I mean. I would have
a word with that good old friend of mine. I speak to his noble
example. I speak to him because I love him and he belongs to a
class by whom I wish to be heard. I speak to him for his class.
Listen to me good old man. I see you smile and swear you are
not old. Well, that is exactly like you, but I am serious. You are
great in my eye. You can not read and write; you will have to
get some one to read what I write to you and all like you, but
you have, without learning, achieved a conquest in life[.] You
began a neglected, penniless, friendless boy. You have worked,
honestly worked at hard labor, until your hand is as hard as your
heart is soft and tender. "Scorn can not point her slow-moving
finger" at you. There is no blot on your name. You have dug the
earth for your living and lived literally by the sweat of your
brow. You have lived honestly, you have paid your debts with
the cash down, you owe no man anything but good will, your
industry has been untiring, a thousand and a thousand sturdy
blows you have struck with a freeman's "right good will" for the
"glorious privilege of being independent." Every way by which
you have won "geer"[3] is justified by honor. You have oppressed
no man. You have been just to every man and have never robbed
the poor, or the widow, or the orphan. You are a happy old man,
there is jollity in your very eye, and temperate habits have made
you healthfully buoyant and cheerful. God has given you children and grandchildren, and your sons and daughters are like

---

[3] [A variant of "gear," meaning movable property; hence wealth.]

a thick forest around you. The kind, hospitable partner of your bosom and of your journey through life still abides with you on earth, and you have laid up plenty, plenty, and have peace with it for your good old age. This is a mastery; this is a self-made man.

Now, tell me, good and great old man, what would you not have been had you held in your grasp the lever of knowledge? Ah! you know what it is to have a handspike at a log-rolling or a house raising. You know what a "purchase" of power is. Knowledge, learning, is all that, and more. How many blind licks it would have saved you. How many thousands and tens of thousands more than you have now in your old "blue chest" you would have had could you have seen by "learning's light" the dark ways of nature. Do you know that learning made your ax helve, your plow handle; that it applies in the most proper way that very handspike, your ox chain; that it prepares the very best manure; that it can beat you all hollow in applying it to the soil; that it knows more than you do all about the soil of every field you plow, and can tell you of every plant which grows on it and the food it craves? Did you know that learning saves labor, sells your grain, fixes the price, and carries it away for you? Ah! you shake your head and say, "Well, I would not give my poor, weak experience for all your book learning." Do you say that? Well, if that be so, if you know something that the books don't teach, I am the more urgent still. You must write it down for the rest of the world, for your own posterity. Write it, record it; you are bound to do so for the sake of some poor fellow who is to come after you in your way of life and who hasn't your experience. But you can't write. Pity! pity! You know something, then, which you can't communicate to more than the few who hear the sound of your voice. Learning would enable you to do that much, at least. Suppose you go and get some one to write it down for you—your experience in cultivating corn, potatoes. You told me once tobacco was a valuable medicine for horses. Write it, I say, and have it printed, and bind it, and what then does it become but book learning? Book learning to be dispensed by somebody else, perhaps, in the present or coming generation; and what is poor, despised "book learning" at last but somebody's discovery, somebody's experience of nature's laws and nature's truths?

Don't despise it my friends; but go to that old, long-used, well-worn, leathern bag or stocking-leg purse in that same old blue chest, and take from it 12, just 12, of those hard dollars, for which you have labored so honestly and so hard, for each and every child and grandchild you have, put it in his satchel, and send him to school.

15.

Report of the Committee on Education, Louisiana Constitutional Convention, 1845

The triumph of democratic political principles during the decades immediately preceding the Civil War was epitomized in the activities of state constitutional conventions, which sought to institutionalize such contemporary innovations as white manhood suffrage, an elective judiciary, and limitations on the powers of the legislature. Many of these conventions also undertook to promote elementary schooling by establishing state superintendencies of instruction, by placing established common school funds beyond the reach of reckless legislators, and by committing the proceeds of future land sales to the support of education. The Louisiana convention of 1844–45, the second in a great wave of revisionist conventions that occurred throughout the United States between 1844 and 1853, was typical only in that its members pressed public schools even more enthusiastically than its committee on education, whose report to the delegates is printed here. (Article 134 of the constitution as finally adopted reads: "The legislature shall establish free public schools throughout the State, and shall provide means for their support by taxation on property, or otherwise.") In all likelihood the delegates' zeal reflected anxiety, also expressed in the committee's report, that education must be provided at home in order to obviate the necessity and the perils of acquiring it in the North.

Mr. Mayo[1], chairman of the committee on education, submitted the following report and resolutions, viz:

As it is through the medium of education that the intellectual faculties of man are cultivated, and his physical and mental powers regulated and perfected, the subject would appear to justify as much attention and care as any other that can engage the attention of the legislator.

This State has for many years acted with a degree of liberality in making appropriations for the erection and support of colleges and academies, and for the education of indigent children.

By the report of the State treasurer, dated 11th January, 1844, it appears that the sum of $1,710,559 40-100, from the year 1812 to the 31st December, 1844, has been expended by the State for the support of public schools, colleges, academies, seminaries, and asylums; and by the same report it appears that $463,791 71-100, which is more than one-fourth of the whole sum, has been expended for the building and support of the colleges of Louisiana and Jefferson.[2] The first of which is not

---

From *Proceedings and Debates of the Convention of Louisiana, which assembled at the city of New Orleans, January 14, 1844* [i.e., 1845], Robert J. Ker, reporter (New Orleans, 1845), pp. 316–319.

[1] [George Mayo was one of the convention's major figures, a leading Democrat and an insistent reformer.]

[2] [The College of Louisiana, privately established in 1825, received state funds originally assigned by the territorial legislature to the College of Orleans. However, because the College of Orleans had served the territory's French population, whereas the College of Louisiana served an English-speaking population, the state legislature had found it neces-

now in operation; and owing to the want of a regular system of education, has not produced results that ought to have been expected from so large an amount of expenditure.

The college of Jefferson is in operation, and has seventy or eighty students, as appears from the report of the committee of the house of representatives on the subject of education, lately made to that body.

The annual appropriation for that institution being $10,-000, the annual expenditure for each student, supposing the number to be eighty, is $125, paid by the State, in addition to all the expenses of tuition, board, &c., which is paid by individuals.

These facts are stated for no other purpose than to bring to view the disproportion in the expenditure, and actual waste of public money for want of a well regulated system of education.

A large portion of the State is in a situation, in relation to schools, which is truly to be lamented; produced by various causes, some of which are peculiar to local situations where the population is extremely sparse, rendering it impracticable to support schools in the neighborhood, for want of sufficient number of children to attend them without sending them from home to board, which many persons of large families either have not the means to do, or if they have, are not disposed to appropriate them for that purpose, in other neighborhoods where schools could be supplied if the people desired. No interest or zeal appears to be felt on the subject, and children are permitted to grow up in ignorance, for want of a disposition on the part of the parent to educate them. The money that has been expended for the support of schools has in many, if not a majority of the par-

---

sary in 1831 to establish another French institution. This was the College of Jefferson. Both colleges survived the withdrawal of state funds in 1845, the College of Louisiana as Centenary College of Louisiana and the College of Jefferson as a private institution operated by the Marist fathers.]

ishes,[3] failed to produce the beneficial results which were intended. Incompetent men have been employed as teachers, whose object has been to get the public money, more than improve the children under their care; and when the public money, to which a school has been entitled, has been exhausted, the schools in many instances have been broken up, and no more taught in the neighborhood until another supply of money has been expected from the State to pay the teacher.

Owing to facts like these, the children that have occasionally attended the schools have received, in many places, but little benefit from them. One of the causes of the failure in the expenditure of the funds of the State, distributed to the parishes generally, has been that indigent children only have been entitled to the benefits of the public funds. Men of the high sentiments and noble feelings that characterize the citizens of this State feel a repugnance at the thought of educating their children by the use of a fund that none but the poor and needy can be partakers of. Hence it is believed that many persons, unable to educate their children at their own expense, have too much pride and feel that it would be humiliating to themselves and their children to partake of a bounty thus offered. When the fact of partaking furnishes of itself evidence of their poverty and indigence; and though this may to some extent arise from false pride, still the fact exists, and the effect is the same as though the objection were a good one. Another cause of the failure has been that large expenditures have been made for building colleges and academies for the promotion of the higher branches of literature, before providing the means for teaching the first rudiments of a common education.

The necessary steps ought first to be taken to place within the reach of the mass of the children throughout the State, such an education as will fit them for the higher branches, and in such a manner as to place all on an equal footing in the enjoyment of

---

[3] [The parish is the equivalent of the county in other states.]

the benefits to be derived from the funds of the State. This would create a laudable ambition between those whose progress and advancement would fit them for the higher schools; and thus the higher as well as the lower would be supported. The progress of the child in the acquisition of a substantial education, would emulate the parent; parents would encourage each other; and when the spirit of education could be fairly put into operation, it is believed that it would here, as it has done in many of the States of the United States, and in Prussia and Germany, carry with it public opinion, which in this country is all that is necessary to sustain any measure that promises to be permanently useful.

The people must see and feel the importance of the subject, the necessity of action. The subject must receive their approbation; excite their interest and zeal; they must act together with their influence and money to carry it into operation. The public mind in this State has never been sufficiently aroused to the importance of educating the youth. Any system that may be organised, not calculated to enlist the feelings and receive the cordial approbation and support of a majority of the citizens, cannot be relied upon to effect the object desired, viz: that of furnishing to the greatest number of the rising generation, upon equal terms, the best education that the resources of the State, and of its citizens generally, will justify.

To overcome these difficulties would require a system more in detail, than it would be proper to incorporate into the constitution, and which would often have to be changed and improved, as circumstances and observation might require.

Provision ought to be made by the State for as large a fund for immediate use as its financial condition will permit, and also for a permanent fund for future use, large enough if possible to afford the means to all the children in the State of obtaining a knowledge of reading, writing and arithmetic; branches which are indispensably necessary to every citizen in his intercourse with his fellow man and with the world.

Your committee have, by a provision which they report herewith, endeavored to lay the foundation for a permanent fund, which will have the power of increase within itself; to meet the increase of children, and of expenditure that improvements may require, as will be seen by the provisions reported.

A provision is also contained in the report providing for the appointment of a superintendent of education; the object of which is to secure an efficient officer whose sole business shall be to attend to the duties of that office, and who shall constitute the head of an organized school department of the State. By another section it is made the duty of the legislature to encourage the institution of common schools throughout the State, for the promotion of literature and the arts and sciences, and to provide means for their support. By enjoining the encouragement and support of education upon the legislature, it will be part of the duty which every member of that body will be sworn to perform, to give it attention.[4]

The cultivation of the mental faculties for the promotion of wisdom, morality and virtue, is amongst the first duties of a State. The chief object of constitutions and laws being to render its citizens secure in their lives, liberty and property, the importance of a good education to each individual, to every community, and to the State, cannot be too highly valued. It is certainly of too great value to be estimated by any pecuniary consideration.

From the genius, nature and spirit of republican government, it is and must be based upon public opinion; which to be salutary in its operation must be virtuous and enlightened.

The permanence of our institutions ever have, and must continue to depend upon the genius of our constitution and laws, sustained by that spirit of freedom which actuates every man who is truly an American.

---

[4] [The following eight paragraphs are direct quotations or paraphrases from contemporary exhortations to educate as a republican necessity.]

Upon education we may safely confide as the conservative power of the State, that will watch over our liberties and guard them against fraud, corruption and decay.

Without morality, virtue and intelligence to regulate the genius and spirit of republicanism, the latter [are] constantly exposed to be swept away by the iron rule of ignorance and vice, when wielded by demagogues, to destroy our liberties.

Morality and virtue may exist without the peculiar culture of schools; but a man can hardly be said to be intelligent without knowing how to read, and without that kind of knowledge that generally has its source in an education acquired at school. Without intelligence, virtue and morality would cease to perform their legitimate functions, and to have that influence upon the body politic which it is necessary they should exert. Without these necessary ingredients to sustain the purity and harmony of our constitution and laws, unless the people know and appreciate their rights, and know how to maintain and protect them, the vicious and disorderly will protect and screen each other from the operation of the laws; the restraining influence of the social and political compact will be annihilated, and dissolution and ruin will be the inevitable result.

There can be no security, the true spirit of liberty cannot exist where vice, ignorance and immorality predominate.

Where a right direction is given to the young and tender mind, correct principles inculcated and impulses given, morality, virtue and reason commence their reign, and with the necessary culture fit their possessors to be useful to themselves, ornaments to society, and safe-guards to the State. The strength of the State and the happiness of its people increase with the increase of useful knowledge. Without knowing their rights and duties men become dangerous to the State, nuisances to the community, and burdensome to themselves. By laying the foundation of a system susceptible of being carried into practical operation, and which will secure to the rising generation the means by which they may be educated [*sic*].

The greatest degree of social and individual prosperity

will be secured to our posterity, and a strong guarantee of protection to our constitution and laws.

Louisiana should possess the means of educating her youths at home. Southern men should have southern heads and hearts, with sentiments untarnished by doctrines at war with our rights and liberties. It is of the first importance that correct impressions be made upon the minds of children; for it is difficult to unlearn what has been learned amiss.

When our children return from the north, after having received an education there, they have to be re-acclimated, and not unfrequently fall victims to the effects of the change. Many of the most promising youths of the State have been swept away within a very short period after their return with an accomplished education, from the effects of a change of climate. Youths who were the fondest hopes of their parents, and promised to be ornaments, not only to them, but to the State, and whose loss to both is irreparable.

All this can be remedied by entering upon the work ourselves, with a determination to accomplish it. A good education furnished to the rising generation, will afford us a better guarantee of protection than fleets and armies. Shall we not then be inexcusable for neglect to make the trial?

It is said that a man will give all he has for his life. If so, ought he not, with equal read[i]ness, give the same price, if necessary, to secure his life, liberty and happiness, and the prospect of conferring upon his posterity the same blessings, enriched and ennobled by the highest degree of intellectual attainments?

All of which is respectfully submitted, together with the accompanying provisions and resolutions.

[Signed]   G. MAYO,
                                                  Chairman.

Report of the committee on the subject of education:

Sec. 1. The governor shall nominate, and by and with the advice and consent of the senate, appoint a superintendent of education, who shall hold his office for two years; whose duties shall be prescribed by law; and who shall receive such compensation as the legislature may direct.

SEC. 2. The legislature shall encourage the institution of common schools throughout the State, for the promotion of literature and the arts and sciences, and shall provide means for that purpose and for their support.

SEC. 3. The proceeds of all lands that have been or hereafter may be granted by the United States to this State, for the use and support of schools, and of all land that may have been or may hereafter be granted by the United States, or by any person or persons, body politic or corporate, to this State, and not granted expressly for any other purpose, which shall hereafter be sold or disposed of, and all estates of deceased persons to which the State may be or hereafter become entitled by law, shall be held by the State as a loan, and shall be and remain a perpetual fund, on which the State shall pay an annual interest of—per cent., which interest, together with all the rents of the unsold lands, shall be inviolably appropriated to the support of schools and institutions of learning throughout the State, until the rents or interest, or both together, shall amount to the sum of ——— per annum; after which the annual excess of such rents and interest may be applied by the legislature to other objects.

SEC. 4. The funds arising from the rents or sales, which may hereafter be made, of any lands heretofore granted by the United States to this State, for the use of a seminary of learning, and of any land that may hereafter be granted for that purpose, and any interest that may accrue upon such funds, shall be inviolably applied to the use specified, or that may be specified in the grant.

And your committee recommend the adoption of the following resolution:

Resolved, That our representatives and senators in congress be requested to use their best efforts to procure the passage of a law, granting to this State the unsold lands within this State, belonging to the United States, or as large a portion thereof as possible, for the purpose of education; and to co-operate, if necessary to effect that object, with the representatives and senators in congress from other States.

16.

Nathan S. S. Beman, *The Influence of Freedom on Popular and National Education*, 1846

In general, antebellum advocates of popular education found it necessary to supplement the efforts of such voluntary agencies as lyceums and libraries with systematic provision for public schooling. At the same time, these agencies of informal education continued to flourish, and with them an extraordinary belief that in some fashion the practice of self-culture (as Channing had called it) extended not only to ambitious individuals but also to the society as a whole. One of its most striking expressions is found in the contention, voiced here by a Presbyterian minister and president of Rensselaer Polytechnic Institute before the Young Men's Association of Troy, New York, that democratic institutions in America (manhood suffrage, political deliberations, participation in the processes of politics) are themselves a guarantee of popular education. The idea was not unprecedented—Thomas Jefferson and Charles Jared Ingersoll, among others, had adumbrated it—but it was significant because it indicated how far Americans even of a generally conservative persuasion might go toward grounding education in democracy as well as democracy in education.

. . . The structure of society, in this country, is friendly to popular education,—to the training of mind. It differs from all other lands, in this respect. In Europe, as a general fact, and especially in Catholic countries, they have no *people*. I do not mean, that their kingdoms and states are without inhabitants, but society is often a monster, having a head joined to the lower extremities, and no body between them. The more elevated classes and the rabble, and especially the last named, may be found everywhere; but, in our sense of the term, there are no people. The first thing that attracts the eye of an American traveler when he lands on the shores of the old continent,—and the same is partly true even of England,—is the multitude of men and women who seem rather to *vegetate,* than to exercise the functions of animal life, and the still higher agencies of intelligence and reason. How a system of popular and universal education can be carried out, in such countries, and the frame work of society remain what it now is, presents a problem difficult to be solved. Take Great Britain,—a country as favorable for such a work as almost any other in Europe, and where the theme is on every tongue,—and two or three facts are sufficient to prove, to a moral certainty that the national mind can never be educated, so that the great masses shall become a reading, thinking, reasoning people, while society is organized on the present model. The day is far distant when their twenty-eight millions will become so far enlightened as to understand their moral and social relations, their personal and civil rights, the geography and history of their own kingdom, the application of mind to the physical elements around them, so that they shall minister to the comforts of life, the blessings of education to their children, and their still higher and more enduring relations to God and another world, unless the social edifice is

---

From Nathan S. S. Beman, *The Influence of Freedom on Popular and National Education: A Lecture, delivered at the Opening of the Association Lecture Room, in the Athenaeum, Troy, February 24, 1846* (Troy, N. Y., 1846), pp. 14–25.

essentially re-modeled from the deep foundations to the heaven-aspiring pin[n]acle! There are in Great Britain four millions of paupers,—one seventh part of the population of the empire. One in every seven, a pauper. Since 1815—thirty years—they have been taxed for the support of these paupers £200,000,000 —or $1,000,000,000. And yet the annual income of a single noble lord is estimated at 400,000 pounds sterling, or two millions of dollars. In such a country universal education is out of the question.—But with us the case is entirely different. The means of mental and moral culture are within the reach of almost every member of the community. Hardly any man need remain in ignorance. As a general fact, property is more equally diffused among the people,—furnishing a beautiful illustration of the Republican principle,—and very few are borne down and oppressed by the calamities either of poverty or wealth.

The tyranny of caste which, in its segregating influence, has always put its stern veto on popular education, is less severe and exclusive, in this country, than in almost any other. Jealousies, growing out of social conditions and established ranks, cannot exist to any considerable extent among us, and what do occasionally spring up, are altogether gratuitous and uncalled for, because no such distinctions belong to our country. Our nobility, if we have any, is that of nature. God made it, and not man, and it is not as easily tainted by contact with humanity, as the artificial and spurious! It belongs to the "inner man," and is not the creature of human law, statute or common. Men are not here stereotyped, in the condition of their parents, and in which they themselves,—without their own consent,—may have been born. We acknowledge no such arbitrary and unyielding customs of society. The mind within—the immortal of man—is permit[t]ed to expand itself, and throw off the crushing disabilities which may weigh it down, and make and occupy its own level, as graduated by intelligence and attainment, by activity and worth. I do not say, that it always is so. But it may be so. There is nothing in the usages of society to prevent it. Here a man may make, or unmake himself, in half a life-time.

This must operate as a stimulus to mind,—to the activity of thought, to the acquirement of knowledge, to general and diffusive education. It permits a man to feel that he is a *man,* and not another man's shadow! This is the natural form of human society, symmetrical and beauteous, as ordained of heaven,—where mind is unchained and free, like the air that breathes around the mountain-tops, or the gushing streams that leap from their sublime declivities, and course along their sides, and water the green, fertile vales. Educate mind,—leave it unshackled,—and it will find its own level. Had this been the case, in some other countries,—many a peasant would have become a prince, and many a nobleman, a postillion or a lackey. As long as the barriers of caste continue to seperate [sic] the different orders of society from each other, as by walls of brass or adamant,—walls which are too solid to be broken through and too high to be leaped over,—what I mean by the education of a people, is out of the question. And it matters not whether that caste assumes its perfect form, as among the semi-barbarians of India, or aspires only at an humble imitation, as among the more enlightened and polished of England, France and Italy.

But these are not our only peculiarities. While the education and discipline of mind—the acquirement and the uses of knowledge, are among the great objects of our being, no people are more abundantly furnished with the necessary means, than ourselves. The comparative ease with which the necessaries and conveniencies of life may be obtained,—and indeed many of its little delicacies too,—leaves almost every one in possession of time for reading and study. Not only the professional man, but the merchant, the clerk, the mechanic, the apprentice, the farmer, the day laborer, may all find abundant leisure for training their higher powers,—for acquiring not only that knowledge adapted to their own peculiar calling, but to become well informed on many general subjects. But those who would accomplish this, must not be satisfied with bodily activity, and mental indolence. They must con-

sider time more than *money*,—they must look upon it as intellectual and moral wealth. Their intervals of business and labor
must be devoted, not to self-indulgence and dissipation, but
to reading, reflection, and mental discipline. Books too are
within the reach of every one. If we have any reason to complain, it is, that they are too cheap, especially if they were not
better than many which come, at the present day, like the
frogs of Egypt, croaking from the press, and find their way
"into the bed-chambers," if not into the very "kneading
troughs," of both city and country. One of the first objects of
every young man should be to procure, little by little, a well
selected library. In twenty years, it will become a rich treasure,—more valuable than bank-stock, or a splendid wardrobe,
or extravagant expenditures upon self-created and factitious
appetites. With a good library and intercourse with cultivated
minds, any young man may educate himself.

There is another process, always going on, in our Republic, which should be noticed in this connection. The discussions which never fail to interest a free people, and stir up
the hidden and spiritual man within, cannot but have their
effect upon mind; nor is this influence confined to any one
portion of the community. It is a power, pervading and diffusive, having intense relations to every part and to every
member of the entire body politic. As the government and
people are one, every great interest which comes before the assembled representatives, comes before the nation. There is
an amazing educational power, in all this, which has not been
duly estimated by writers on government and systems of mental training. The free discussion of every subject which is presented to the American Congress, every year, and consequently
to the millions of our people, is itself an important process of
education. Men read attentively, feel deeply, and speak frankly,
on these subjects of thrilling interest. While their own minds
become awakened and excited, the effect is certain. The various powers are stirred up, and the training process goes on.
The information thus gained, for its own sake, and its in-

cidental and certain effect on the human mind, can hardly
be overrated. A free people form a national academy, in which
the process of self-education is carried on, by the spontaneous
action of its own essential elements. Every thing which relates
to agriculture, manufactures and commerce, to our domestic
and foreign relations, to peace and war, to internal improvements, to taxation and expenditures, to freedom and oppression, to the safety, protection and happiness of the Republic,
comes before the nation, and must interest every individual.
These things are "not done in a corner." They all stand out
before the eyes, and are proclaimed in the ears, of the people.
Here, then, we have a kind of national education of itself. If
this were all that could be said, on this point, you would be
likely to have, in this country, a people of more than ordinary
intelligence. But this is not all. We have, in these things, only
the alphabet of the lessons taught,—the title-page of the deep
and instructive volume. Open that volume, and read still
farther.

The state of mind produced by these discussions is less
important, in its direct than its incidental relations. The mental
excitement, thus produced, is necessary to the education of a
people. No nation was ever well instructed in the art of thinking and reasoning, in the application of knowledge to the
abridgment of labor and to the increase of the comforts of life,
in their relations to man and God, to earth and heaven, without freedom of inquiry and discussion. This lies at the basis
of all training, human and divine. Man is a thing, and not a
moral agent, without it. You can educate a free people, and
no other. The awakened mind loves thought,—lives on investigation,—expands by its own exercises,—becomes impatient to see, and know, and comprehend,—and luxuriates in
the discovery of facts and the revelations of truth! If our
system of government, its free discusssions, and the deep national participation in the great topics which are addressed
to all, and which embody the interests and existence of all,
shall fail eventually to secure the education of this people, it

will be our own fault. The philosophy of the position I have assumed, I have no doubt, is sound, and will be ordinarily sustained by experience. A failure, if it occur, must be charged to an abuse of the principle.

And what, I ask, are systems of education under the more arbitrary forms of government? They are very different from what they are, or should be among us.—They are restricted to classes, as such,—so that it is little more than a drilling for the destiny marked out for each class, by the usages of society. It teaches the son to walk in the footsteps of the father, as mechanically as one quadruped, be his ears long or short, follows another, in the beaten track, around the bark-mill. And the things taught, are often such as can hardly constitute a system of education. They do not train mind. They have little or nothing to do with the power of thought. They often consist of the mere dogmas of the exerting government and the established forms of religion. It may be fairly questioned, whether the peculiar zeal which has been recently kindled up, in some parts of Europe, for the education of the people, has not for its leading object, political discipline, for the support of the throne and the mitre, rather than the expansion of mind, the diffusion of light and intelligence, the growth of liberal sentiments, and the happiness of the people.

The elective franchise cannot but have its influence upon mind, and its cultivation. As the safeguard of civil rights, this subject has been so often and so ably discussed, and is so well understood in this country, that it may be left to stand upon its own basis. It should be dear to a nation, as "the apple of the eye." In all the essential interests of a social existence, it is the right arm of personal protection. Without it, man *may* be free by the mere sufferance of others, but he has no bond to secure him. The first revolution of the wheel may crush his hopes and his inheritance, with himself, to the dust! That it belongs to the people, there can be no doubt; and yet no nation should bestow it too heartily upon mere adventurers who have no knowledge of the government, no interest in the soil, and nothing to gain or lose by any possible contingencies. It is too rich a pearl to be thrown away with romantic wantonness, or bartered for the warblings of a mere political song.

But I do not refer to it here as a mere matter of politics. It has much higher and more sacred relations. It is a stimulus to intellect, a promoter of thought, the handmaid of education; and where the great body of the people are freemen, and have a right to march up, with the face and front of men, to the ballot-box, you have stirring motives to intellectual culture— to the analysis of mind—to its progress and perfection in knowledge, which never exist where human beings are enrolled as political cyphers. Where the law and public sentiment make something of a man, he will, as a general fact, make something of himself; and there is no surer way to annihilate mind, and efface the last vestage [*sic*] of humanity from his immortal essence, than to put the stigma of inferiority upon him, and then let pride and scorn stand, and point the finger at him! In these circumstances, he feels like a cashiered soldier, an outlawed citizen, a whipped slave! He is an exile from home, in the midst of the surrounding multitude; and he cannot stand up among those who should be his compeers, with the conscious feeling of manliness, and meet the claims of others upon him, and discharge, with a becoming spirit, the various duties of social life. Destroy self-respect and personal confidence, and his mental executions will be feeble and vapid, and even his corporeal will be the promptings of necessity, rather than the spontaneous movings of a free spirit. Body and mind are both chained. This has been the course of our world and its governments, from olden time. The *people* have been made the POPULACE beneath its Stygian shades and leaden sceptre. Despotism, in every age, has built and maintained his throne, and so has his royal consort ignorance too, by excluding the people from all participation in the affairs of government. They have been looked upon as too low and too vulgar to intermeddle with such deep and sacred mysteries. And *when* and *where* have nations, thus governed, ever been educated? NEVER, and NOWHERE! The school-house and the ballot-box be-

long to the same category,—and universal intelligence will
never prevail where men are not freemen.

But if the elective franchise has its power over mind, by
inspiring self-respect and manliness of purpose, as I have already, though feebly traced, much more of the same character
may be asserted respecting the mode in which our government
is administered. I refer to its popular administration, or the
appointment of its effective agencies. Popular elections, no
doubt, have their incidental evils, but they are necessary evils,
for the purpose of securing the greater good. Men are not
born rulers here. And why should they be? It is one of the
anomalies of human society, that it is so anywhere! We have
no kings. We want none. Our fathers left their old homes, and
fled across the ocean, and took shelter in the wilderness, in
order to escape from their merciless grasp: and we shall not
soon forget the story. We have no queens here, except those
who are elected by individual suffrage, and that only to reign
over a very *select* and *limited* territory. The only crown they
wear, is their own native excellence, and as they are not usur-
pers, no one should wish to depose them. We have no heredi-
tary nobles, deriving their claims to priority of rank from some
successful military chieftan, and enriched by the spoils of the
nation. We never can have such an order of men here, without
a revolution which shall first lay the constitution in the sep-
ulchre, and chant its funeral dirge, and hang the country
around with mourning! Rulers here are only a portion of the
people, selected for the time being, and for a very limited
period too, to carry out the will of the community. When this
agency is finished, they are mere citizens again, and have no
other distinctions than those which are created by real or
reputed worth. A ruler here, whatever office he may fill, is no
demi-god. I did not say *demagogue*, for he may be that! The
senator, the judge, the governor of a State, the president of
the Republic, are all citizens, filling to be sure, by the de-
signation of the people, dignified and responsible offices, but
they receive no servile homage, they affect no 'pomp and circumstance,' but are merely the head and hand and mouth-

piece of the nation. They are "the servants of the people." This description of rulers has been much ridiculed in older and more stately governments, but it asserts the true principle. It is beautifully announced and illustrated by one of the greatest and best of men, and in a connection quite analog[o]us to the one now before us. The gifted and immortal Paul, speaking of himself and his fellow-apostles, says,—"*Ourselves your* SERVANTS,"—and yet they were both rulers and teachers.

That this state of things should affect mind, and promote inquiry, and give impulse to education,—I mean popular and national education, any one can see by a single glance of thought. The highest offices of state, are open to all. Every man in the nation may be a competitor. No one is excluded, except he may have been guilty of the involuntary crime of wearing a black skin, or the *voluntary*, and probably the still deeper crime—*because voluntary*—of wearing a black coat![1] All others are eligible to any office,—to every office. These things have their effect. The nation feels it. It makes a vivid— thinking—reading—active people. All are pushing forward to something higher and better. The nation is agitated. Mind is electrified. The face brightens, in all its features. The eye speaks. The tongue is eloquent. You see nothing of that profound dullness which characterizes the lower classes in some of the kingdoms of Europe,—those dead, plaster-of-Paris faces where a struggling thought from within has never yet reached the surface. A man, among us, may choose his own position, if he will submit to the necessary toil. He may pave his own way, and then walk in it. The plough-boy, of to-day, may, in thirty years, be the President of the United States. Some of our best legislators and magistrates have once been our enterprising merchants, or our laborious farmers, or active mechanics. Nobility may curl the lip, and princes may shake the proud head and turn away the scornful eye, and pronounce all this unbecoming and vulgar,—but it will not hurt us. We claim to be a nation of noblemen and princes,—veritable and

---

[1] [i. e., of being a clergyman.]

legitimate monarchs—born to govern ourselves. This state of things makes an appropriate and successful appeal to the hidden spirit of man; and it is producing a national activity of thought, a desire for information, self-denials and sacrifices in its pursuit, and actual attainments too, rarely to be found among any people, on Island or Continent, in circumnavigating the globe. It is true, we are a youthful people, and, in the estimation of some of the hoary headed nations, perhaps a little *green;* but time will cure this, and there can be no doubt but a ripe and dignified manhood is before us. And that manhood, we trust, if it be not perpetual as the earth itself, will be followed only by a far distant and vigorous old age. But this prediction, if prediction you call it, can be verified only by the fact, that this generation, and each succes[s]ive generation, shall make the most of themselves and their circumstances. . . .

17.

Debate in the Constitutional Convention of Ohio, 1850

By 1850, most public figures in the North were clearly committed to public elementary education, although they often fought bitterly over how to implement it. This fact was nowhere more apparent than in the Ohio Constitutional Convention of 1850–1851, which struggled over such issues as the limits of the state's right to educate, the necessity or desirability of stipulating what appropriations the legislature must make in support of public schools, the right of Negroes and mulattoes to attend common schools (or any public schools at all), and the right of sectarian institutions to share public funds. Nevertheless, the convention's deliberations on these matters suggest that most of the quarrels were disagreements over detail—few delegates were willing to gainsay either the value of education or the state's obligation to provide for it. Only the question of the rights of Negroes created a significant division among the members, one that was resolved (as were many other questions involving Negroes during that troubled era) by evasion.

As the debates indicate, the convention's appointed committee on education initially proposed a comprehensive article on education requiring an elective superintendent of common schools, safeguards for the school fund, and public appropriations to augment that fund to the point at which all children might be educated gratis. It also proposed to bar sectarian participation in school funds. In the event, the convention agreed only to preserve the school fund and to require that the legislature provide a thorough and efficient system of common schools, subject to the prohibition on appropriations to sectarian schools. Even so, the legislature revived the state superintendency in 1853, when it also abolished school fees, thereby establishing in practice what the committee had sought to establish in principle.

Among the delegates who took part in the debates, Harmon Stidger, Samuel Quigley, and James W. Taylor were members of the committee on education. Both Taylor and Norton S. Townshend were Free Soil Democrats and outright advocates of Negro suffrage, while Stidger, Quigley, and Charles Reemelin were Locofocos and William Sawyer and Joseph McCormick were loyal Democratic liberals in economic matters. Samson Mason was a prominent Whig, then congressman from Springfield.

Fifty-fifth Day.

WEDNESDAY, December 4, 1850.

On motion by Mr. REEMELIN the Convention resolved itself into a Committee of the whole, Mr. HORTON in the Chair, and proceeded to the consideration of the report of the standing committee on education.

From *Report of the Debates and Proceedings of the Convention for the Revision of the Constitution of the State of Ohio, 1850–1851.* J. V. Smith, official reporter to the convention (2 volumes; Columbus, Ohio, 1851), II, 10–17.

The first section is as follows:

> The General Assembly shall provide for the election by the people, of a Superintendent of Common Schools, whose term of office, duties and compensation, shall be prescribed by law; and shall provide for the election or appointment of such assistants, or other officers, as may be found necessary, prescribe their duty, term of office and compensation.

This section was adopted unanimously and without amendment.

The second section was then read:

> The General Assembly shall encourage by suitable means, the promotion of moral, intellectual, scientific and agricultural improvement.
>
> The proceeds of the sales of all lands that have been, or may hereafter be granted by the United States for educational purposes, and all lands or other property given by individuals, for educational purposes, and all lands or other property given by individuals for like purposes, together with the surplus revenue[1] deposited with this State by the United States (until reclaimed) shall be, and forever remain, a permanent and irreducible fund; the interest and income therefrom, shall be faithfully applied to the specific objects of the original grant, gift or appropriation.

Mr. STIDGER. I will remark that it was intended to provide that the *proceeds* of the several funds named in the report just read, should be applied for educational purposes—not the funds themselves.

---

[1] [An act adopted by Congress in 1836 provided that the financial surplus in the United States Treasury as of January 1, 1837, would be deposited with the states in proportion to the electoral vote of each. It was tacitly assumed that this deposit would never be recalled. Because of the Panic of 1837, only three of four projected quarterly installments were paid.]

Mr. SAWYER. I move to strike out the first paragraph of this section. It is this "The General Assembly shall encourage, by suitable means, the promotion of moral, intellectual, scientific and agricultural improvement." I do this sir, in order to elicit from the Chairman (Mr. STIDGER) of the Committee on Education, an explanation of the intention of the Committee in embodying this exceedingly broad and comprehensive sentence in their report. There may be more in those words than strikes the eye at first sight. The expression seems to me vague and too general in its character. We had better leave "the encouragement of science and agriculture" to the legislature. I cannot quite conceive what connection the subject of agriculture has with that of popular Education.

Mr. STIDGER. If we should leave every thing to the Legislature, why not adjourn this Convention *sine die*, at once? But the gentleman from Auglaize cannot see what connection the subject of Agriculture has with that of Education. I would remark, in the words of the distinguished lecturer of last evening (Cassius M. Clay) that this is an age of progress, and that it is a feature of the century in which we live that science has come to the aid of the agriculturist, and that it has become almost as necessary to the farmer to understand the principles of chemistry as to possess muscular strength to sow and reap. I would also remark to the gentleman from Auglaize, that in other parts of the state, Agriculture means something more than the raising of *hoop poles*. (Laughter.)

Mr. QUIGLEY. It was the earnest purpose of the committee to report an article full in all its parts, and commensurate with the advanced position of society. Agricultural progress and good morals are intimately connected with the subject of Education. A knowledge of Chemistry and Geology for instance, are necessary to the agriculturist.

Mr. REEMELIN. I should myself have risen and moved to strike out the sentence now in debate, but I had almost come to the conclusion that this convention would never close its labors, and therefore, that all efforts to amend the Constitution would be wasted.

But sir, the first sentence of this section is entirely too comprehensive in its character; it needs definiteness and restriction. If we adopt it as a part of the new constitution, the legislature will, under its general terms, have all power to do every thing within the range of Government. There is entirely too much power granted in the words "The General Assembly shall encourage, by suitable means, the promotion of moral, intellectual, scientific and agricultural improvement," and I shall vote to strike them from the section.

The question being upon the motion to strike out the first sentence of the section, the same was disagreed to.

The third section was then taken up, and is as follows:

> The General Assembly shall make such provision by taxation and other means (in addition to the income arising from the irreducible fund) as will secure a thorough and efficient system of Common Schools, free to all children in the State.

Mr. Sawyer. I move to insert the word "white" between the word "the" and the word "children," so that the section will provide for the education of all the *white* children in the State. That is the only class of children in the State of Ohio for whose education I am willing to make provision in this Constitution.

Mr. Taylor. I confess, sir, that I am surprised. I did not expect that a motion of this kind would be made by any gentleman on this floor. I did not, on the other hand, suppose that any proposition to extend the political rights of the colored citizens of Ohio would be adopted; but I had supposed that a knowledge of the law of self-preservation would have suggested to the gentleman from Auglaize [Mr. Sawyer] and to every gentleman upon the floor, that it would be good policy to give to all within the reach of our laws a good moral and intellectual training. I knew that this Convention was not prepared to increase the political rights of the black man; but I had hoped that all were willing to provide against his becoming the pest of society, by being deprived of all opportunities for education. Shall we not secure protection to ourselves and our children by relieving the colored population of Ohio, from the absolute necessity of growing up in vice and ignorance? Shall we, by the adoption of the amendment of the gentleman from Auglaize, constitute a class who will become the inmates of our poor houses, and the tenants of our jails? I think it must be clear to every reflecting mind that the true policy of the statesman is to provide the means of education, and consequent moral improvement, to every child in the State, the offspring of the black man equally with that of the white man, the children of the poor equally with the rich. But I am told that the Negro belongs to a degraded and inferior race; so much the more reason, sir, for their education and improvement. Leave them to grow up without moral and intellectual training, and they become a positive curse as well as a burthen upon society. Educate them, and they become useful members of the community that has cared for them.

I repeat that I had not heard that we were positively to retrograde in this matter by commencing a system of persecution upon the colored population of the State, already, one would think, sufficiently unfortunate. I beg gentlemen to be consistent in this regard—let them proclaim their real designs —if the black man is to be driven across our borders at the point of the bayonet, let them say so.

I believe that a majority of the members of this Convention are not prepared to deny to our colored population all opportunities for moral and intellectual training for the duties of life; although they may not be willing to extend to that class the right to exercise the elective franchise. Education will tend to make men moral and useful members of society, therefore let us provide for the education of every child in the State.

Mr. SAWYER. I have but a few words to say, sir, upon this subject. I am sure that I would go quite as far as the gentleman from Erie, (Mr. TAYLOR,) to do justice to the negro race. When he hears my views upon the subject, he may find that we do not differ very widely. Under our present laws, the negro is not taxed for the support of schools to which his children are denied admittance. True, the negro is taxed for school purposes, but it is exclusively for the benefit of his own children, when he desires it should be thus applied. There is therefore no injustice, no inhumanity, if gentlemen choose to place the matter upon that ground. And, sir, I am willing to extend to the negro the same exemption from taxation for the support of white schools, for all time to come. But, sir, while I will oppose any measure for the oppression of the blacks now in the State, I will as strenuously oppose every proposition which, in its practical effect, will tend to encourage the emigration of blacks into the State. And, sir, while I would desire to injure the feelings of no gentleman who holds sentiments opposite to my own, I must say that I rejoice in the passage of the fugitive slave bill; for I believe it will have the effect to rid the free States of the curse of a negro population, intermixed with the whites. . . .[2]

Mr. President, while I sit here, to assist in framing a Constitution for the people of Ohio, I must look first, to the interests of the white race. With this view, I will not encourage the emigration of blacks into this State, nor will I make it so much the interest of that class to remain here, that there will be no disposition for them to emigrate to Liberia. And, in this I am actuated by no hatred of the negro race—no desire to oppress them. I have declared before, and I repeat it now, that I am willing that the negro shall have every privilege and every right that I myself enjoy. I am willing that he shall vote; I am willing that he shall be a justice of the peace, or governor, a judge, or a member of Congress. Aye, sir, I am willing that he

---

[2] [The Fugitive Slave Act, part of the Compromise of 1850, sought to strengthen the federal constitutional provision guaranteeing the recovery of runaway slaves by creating United States commissioners with power to issue warrants for the arrest of fugitives on affidavit of their masters.]

shall be President of a Republic. I am willing that the language of our sublime Declaration of Independence, shall apply to the negro as well and as fully as to myself. But sir, I am unwilling that he shall enjoy these privileges in this country, preoccupied as it is, by a different and a higher race. I am willing that he shall enjoy all these rights and privileges in his native country. Is there anything either unjust or inhumane in this? . . .

I shall insist upon protecting the negro in the enjoyment of all the rights now guarantied to him by the laws of Ohio. In this I will go as far as the gentleman from Erie, (Mr. TAYLOR,) but, at the same time, I declare my unalterable resolution to hold out no inducements to their farther emigration into the State. Virginia and Kentucky have passed stringent laws, making it a criminal offence for free negroes to remain in those States. The effect of this is to drive all the old, worn out, broken down slaves into the free States for support, after they have ceased to be productive property. This they shall not do with impunity, if I can help it. If slavery is a blessing, let them have the whole of it. If they will eat the meat let them pick the bones. . . .

Mr. TOWNSHEND. I did not rise, Mr. Chairman, to reply to the remarks of the gentleman from Auglaize on the Fugitive Slave Bill. I don't see what that bill has to do with Common Schools in Ohio; but sir, as that gentleman has kindly given us his opinion, I will just take the opportunity to give mine, which is, that the Fugitive Law in all its distinctive features, is utterly and teetotally damnable.

But I rose, Mr. Chairman, to correct one or two mistakes into which that gentleman has unfortunately fallen. The first relates to the feelings with which the people of Canada regard the fugitives who escape from this country. I do not believe that the people there are alarmed at the "black cloud" of fugitives that comes up from the States. On the contrary, [I] know that they treat them with great humanity, furnishing them with food, clothing, and employment. But, sir, Canadians feel, and have a right to feel indignation and contempt for the government and people, that, in spite of the loudest pretentions to freedom and justice, nevertheless drives a portion of the human family to take refuge under the protection of Monarchical Institutions. The gentleman alluded to the temper of Canadian papers. I think, sir, I have seen the paper to which allusion was made, and if I am correctly informed, the articles are not written by any native of Canada or Great Britain, but by a negro hater from the United States.

Another mistake which I wish to correct, is the assertion that the property of negro and mulatto persons is not taxed for school purposes. There was a time, sir, when in this State colored persons were taxed for school purposes and excluded from the benefits of our Common School System. Subsequently to that, the property of colored persons was exempted from such taxation. But two years ago, all the existing laws, conferring especial privileges or imposing especial disabilities on such persons, were repealed. The School law passed at the same time, taxes all persons alike, but provides that in certain cases, colored schools may be established separately, and the money raised from colored persons in such localities, may all be appropriated to the support of such schools. I know, sir, that in the village where I live, the children of colored persons are included in the general enumeration, and the tax raised from colored persons goes into the same fund, and there is not prejudice against color enough to make the establishment of colored schools necessary.

The other mistake I wish to notice, is the assertion of the gentleman, that there are, comparatively, no colored persons in the free soil counties, and that therefore, all the sympathy felt in those counties, is for a class of persons which we, in such counties, don't have among us; and of the evils of whose presence we know nothing. Now, sir, I think it will be conceded that we have *some* free soil in Lorain, and there, sir, we have quite a sprinkling of colored persons. I don't pretend to know the exact number, but I should think but little, if any, less than one hundred in the village where I live, and a still larger number in another village but a few miles off. The census of 1840 is in error on that subject, possibly because with us we don't call a man black, unless he is absolutely and unequivocally so; nor a man a mulatto unless we know enough of his pedigree to satisfy us that he is exactly half and half. But, sir, we have less prejudice against colored persons, not because we don't know them, but because we do. In Lorain county there is a Collegiate Institution, which has, in its several departments, about six hundred students, and to all the privileges of that Institution colored youth are admitted as freely as white.³ And, sir, I have attended the Commencement Exercises of that College for several years, and I know that the young colored men who have graduated have stood as high and acquitted themselves as well as the other students in the same class. This year one colored young lady graduated from the Ladies' Department, who was second to none of the ladies that graduated at the same time, and the address delivered by her on that occasion, would, I think, have done good even to the gentleman from Auglaize, could he have heard it. Our sympathy, sir, for colored persons does not spring from our ignorance of them, but from the conviction that they are human beings, and therefore entitled to all the rights and privileges and sympathies due to humanity, and from the conviction that they, equally with other men, are susceptible of intellectual and moral elevation. . . .

Mr. NASH moved to strike out all after the word "schools," in the third section, which would cut off the words, "free to all children in the State." He remarked that he made this motion in order to leave the question free from all extraneous matters.

Mr. BATES. I am not in the habit of making speeches, but I am desirous of expressing my views upon the subject now before the convention. I must express my regret and astonishment at the vote given a few minutes since, by which the word "white" was inserted in the third section. I shall vote for the motion of the gentleman from Gallia to strike out all after the

³ [Oberlin College, founded in 1833 as the Oberlin Collegiate Institute, admitted black students as early as 1835.]

word "schools," so that the section would provide a thorough and efficient system of common schools proscribing no class, and leaving the details of the system to be fixed by the Legislature. The second section of this report declares that the Legislature shall encourage moral, intellectual, and scientific improvements, and, by the insertion of the word "white" you have declared that a certain class *shall not* receive any of the benefits arising from the common school fund.

View this question as you will—as a matter of morality or of political economy, a question of right or expediency, the State would materially suffer if a provision to exclude any class of children from the benefits of common schools, should be engrafted in the new Constitution. The experience of the past has shown that morality and virtue keeps pace with education and that degradation and vice are the inevitable results of ignorance. Good policy, humanity, and above all, the spirit of the Christian religion, demands that we should provide for the education of every child in the State.

I shall therefore vote for the pending motion, which would secure the benefits of common schools to all, leaving the details of the system to be fixed by future legislatures, who can adapt the system to the ever varying circumstances of society.

Mr. Dorsey. While I believe that the benefits of a system of common schools should be extended to all, I desire to avoid doing any thing to encourage the emigration of negroes into the state. I trust that before the close of this session, a provision will be adopted authorizing the Legislature to appropriate a sum of money annually, for the purpose of assisting negroes and mulattoes to leave the State.

I would move to amend the amendment of the gentleman from Gallia, (Mr. Nash,) by adding the following after the word "schools," "and such schools shall be open for the reception of scholars, students, and teachers of every grade, without any distinction or preference whatever, contrary to the intent of such provision."

Mr. Archbold. Though I feel reluctant to mingle at all in debate, I must express my dissent from the views as well as the amendment of the gentleman from Miami, and my hope that the original amendment, (Mr. NASH's) will prevail. I am opposed to all minute legislation by this Convention.

Mr. SMITH of Warren, called for a division of the question, and the same turning first on the motion to strike out all after the word "School,"

The Convention agreed to strike out.

The question then being upon Mr. Dorsey's amendment,

Mr. MASON, moved as a substitute, the following: "Provision shall be made by law for the separate establishment and support of schools for the instruction of the children of black and mulatto persons."

Mr. MANON, remarked that he should vote against the substitute, the amendment, and the whole system, if it were not made plainer and more intelligible than at present.

He desired a simple system of public instruction, and that schools should be kept for at least eight months in the year.

Mr. MASON's amendment was disagreed to.

The question then being upon the adoption of Mr. Dorsey's amendment, the same was disagreed to.

Mr. McCORMICK moved to amend by striking out the two first lines of the pending section, and amend so that the whole section would read as follows:

> SEC. 3. The permanent common school fund shall be augmented by taxation and otherwise to such sum as shall, in addition to the funds heretofore provided, produce an annual revenue of————dollars which shall be annually applied to secure a thorough and efficient system of common schools, free to all the children in the State.

[*Subsequently, Nash moved to fill the blank with $500,000. Manon then moved that it be not less than $1,-500,000 and the convention concurred.*]

Fifty-sixth Day.

THURSDAY, December 5, 1850.

Mr. QUIGLEY. . . . The Committee were . . . led to the conclusion that all that was necessary in the fundamental law, was provision for the safe keeping of the irreducible funds, and grant power to the Legislature to raise by taxation, as the growing population and other circumstances may from time to time require, and carry out in detail, such measures as will secure a good and efficient system of Common School Education. I ask what is required in a fundamental law on this subject? I answer, to provide for the safe keeping of the present School Funds and such irredeemable Funds as by donation or otherwise may inure to the State for School purposes, and inculcating upon the Legislature the necessity of raising by tax or otherwise, funds, from time to time, sufficient to secure a thorough and efficient system of Common School Education. I would also ask permission to remark on the whole report, a privilege which has been granted to others on former occasions. So far as I was concerned in the report, I might here state, that I was impressed with the necessity of reporting in favor of a Superintendent, and giving latitude to the Legislature to furnish assistants to constitute an efficient board of Superintendents, from the fact that some, and especially school laws making no provision for Superintendants [sic], are liable to be neglected, and fall into disuse. The great and important business of securing a general education, and of conducting a well regulated system of common schools, requires perseverance, energy and vigilance, and will languish into neglect without a suitable supervision, and we may justly fear that without the fostering care of an active, zealous and faithful Superintendant, laws for the promotion of education will be passed in vain. We were also impressed with the importance of giving

the Legislature ample room to encourage education without
any violation of the Constitution, and in the first clause of the
Report, have left to the wisdom of future Legislatures to
encourage, by suitable means, the promotion of moral, intellectual, scientific and agricultural improvement, language sufficiently liberal to meet the views of the most zealous and
sanguine on the great cause of education. . . .

The third section of the report directs the Legislature to
make full and ample provision for securing a thorough and
efficient system of common school education, free to all the
children in the State. The language of this section is expressive
of the liberality worthy a great State, and a great people. There
is no stopping place here short of a common school education
to all the children in the State. That this is an age of improvement and progress is admitted by all who are acquainted with
the great and important transactions of the present century.
That a spirit of education is increasing in our beloved country
is known from common observation, and should not only be
hailed, but cherished with delight.

Science has dispelled the darkness from our land which
for ages benighted the inhabitants of the old world, and gave
the tyrant power to sway an iron sceptre over their subjects,
and by discouraging instruction and keeping them in ignorance,
perpetuated their servitude—continued them in degradation—
shackled with despotic chains, not knowing that they were men
capable of becoming free and governing themselves. This condition of things has become changed—intelligence, the truth of
divine revelation—liberty of conscience—self-government—
freedom of the press—free and fair discussion, together with
freedom of thought, have brought our free citizens from under
the dominion of tyranny, declaring and demonstrating to the
world that great truth, that men are born free and equal and
capable of governing themselves. Had not knowledge been
shed upon the human understanding, all would have remained
in the darkness of heathenism, and governed by superstition
and fanaticism, our country would have still borne testimony to

savage cruelty; the banks of our majestic Ohio would have been the theatre of the war dance and deeds of savage cruelty.

The fair portion of our inhabitants would have been kept in as servile degradation as the aboriginal females of our former wildness. But how great—how glorious the change. Instead of toiling under heavy loads heaped upon them by those task-masters under the name of fathers, brothers, husbands —doomed to linger out a miserable existence in privation, hardship and drudgery—what ease—what elegance—what happiness—what accomplishment is everywhere visible—what intelligence, what engaging loveliness beams from their eyes now become the ornaments of society, charitable to a fault (if charity is susceptible of a fault,)—foremost in the encouragement of all that is moral—religigious [*sic*] virtuous and good —calculated in a very eminent degree to solace and sustain their friends under every difficulty, to pour into their desponding souls the balm of consolation, to cheer them through life —administer comfort in sickness and death, and to spread happiness and joy all around. Thus by civilization, religion and intelligence, are they prepared to carry out their high destiny as distinguished ornaments in the social system.

Nor does education lavish all its ennobling qualities upon the fair sex. The male sex are also elevated to a place among the intelligent throng—and although all may not arrive at the full course of classical education, yet in our land of liberty, all may be competitors on the great theatre of talent and advancement, knowledge and aggrandizement; each in his turn may be a philosopher, an orator, a sage, or a statesman.

Intelligence is the foundation-stone upon which this mighty Republic rests—its future destiny depends upon the impulse, the action of the present generation in the promotion of literature. Will we not, are we not, as patriots, bound in solemn duty to use our energies, our influence to forward this greatest of interests to present and future generations; and especially will the great State of Ohio fall short in so mighty an enterprise—so essential and indispensable a duty? Shall Ohio be remiss in an endeavor to compete with her sister States? Massachusetts and New York are ahead now, and several other States are rapidly gaining upon us, if not already in advance. Arouse, then, citizens of Ohio, to your best interests, and show that you are not only able to compete in agriculture, in public improvement, in commerce—yes, and in the battle field, with other States, but also in intelligence.

Will it be necessary to appeal to the generosity of her citizens to pay tax for such purposes? Certainly not. Her noble sons would blush to hesitate—and her yet more philanthropic daughters will become tributary to the great cause which leads to the development of the rich resources of nature—prepares the mind for the investigation of philosophy, morals, religion and virtue, and enables it to study nature in all its beauty and grandeur, and realize the important work that has been done, and still going on, in making the wilderness and solitary places glad, and the desert to bud and blossom as the rose, and not only so, but to elevate the thoughts above the home of the sunbeam, and contemplate the Creator and meditate on things Heavenly and divine. Prompted by such exalted motives and pleasing anticipations, taxation will not be considered onerous.

Massachusetts raises annually for school purposes between seven and eight hundred thousand dollars—New York some eight hundred thousand; Connecticut about ten thousand dollars for common and Normal schools. Pennsylvania appropriates above seven hundred thousand, more than five hundred thousand dollars of which is raised by taxation. Mississippi and Louisiana are proportionally liberal. Other States are fast on the advance, and I ask again, can it be that Ohio will remain an exception, and not assist in so great an enterprise? The answer, I doubt not, will be returned—*she will not.*

The fourth section provides for the safety of school funds against sectarian innovation, and forever bars access to exclusive control by sectarianism, and needs no comment. Thus having briefly given the views which governed me in this report, and hoping that it will be found to contain all that is necessary in a constitutional provision to secure the best interests of education among us, it is submitted to the consideration of the committee.

Mr. McCormick wished to be heard upon the amendment, not upon his own account, but for the sake of those, in the future who might desire to be benefited by the laws of the State, for the promotion of Education. The day in which he himself was to be benefited by such laws was long past. He spoke for those who in all future time are to constitute the people, the law makers the members of the Government of Ohio. We may construct the laws of the State as we please; unless the minds of the people are educated, the legislation is in vain. As we improve in general intelligence we shall approximate to that point where legislation may be dispensed with. Educate the mind of man, and the heart, and little legal restraint upon his conduct will be required.

The amendment under consideration was offered with this view. The object sought to be attained is [t]he establishment of a permanent and efficient system of education in the State, which shall constantly furnish a supply to the ever increasing demand for education in the State. The sum proposed in it, looks perhaps large to some. It is in fact too small to answer the purpose. If the statistics of the report of the Secretary of State can be relied on, there are, instead of fifty four thousand, as has been stated, over three hundred and sixty seven thousand children in Ohio. To educate this immense number, there is provided, under our present law, the astonishing sum of two hundred and ninety-five thousand dollars—almost the enormous amount of three quarters of a dollar a piece annually for the purposes of education. And under this state of circumstances, gentlemen of this Convention sit down with conscience satisfied at having provided efficiently for so important an interest.

Mr. Quigley interposed some remarks not understood by the reporter.

Mr. McCormick, continued. Gentlemen of the Convention seem to be unwilling to fix any feature of a system of public education in the Constitution. They desire to leave everything to be fixed by the General Assembly. But let us look at past legislation done upon this subject. The present Constitution imposes upon the Legislature the duty of establishing a system of public education; and in forty-eight years it has succeeded in building up a plan of benevolence, which gives the amount of seventy-five cents per annum, for school purposes, to each child in the State. How long will it take for active legislation of this character, to raise a sum sufficient to educate all the children in the State, who, in fact, instead of three hundred and sixty-seven thousand, number over five hundred thousand. He did insist that we should act upon this measure, and act upon it advisedly. We have been deceived by a rapid series of legislative, systems, each less efficient and valuable than its predecessor, and the last system brought into existence is far inferior in the length of time which it furnishes schools, and in efficiency, to its predecessor, or any prior law. He did not propose by this amendment to limit the amount to be appropriated by the Legislature for educational purposes. He desired only to establish a minimum. One and a half millions would, at the present time, be about three dollars for each scholar in the State—as small an amount as could by any possibility secure the necessary result. Looking at the sum itself, it seems large; but when we look at the magnitude of the cause, and its importance, it is not large. Massachusetts gives a larger sum in proportion to the number; Connecticut also a larger; and what is the result? It is a recommendation—a letter of credit to a man, to have been born and educated upon the soil of Massachusetts. It is well known, that with a higher grade of intelligence they have far less crime to punish—less public and private follies to repent and be ashamed of. He would make the State of Ohio superior even to Massachusetts. He would devote for that purpose, all the funds that can be raised. He would cut down, as far as possible, all the other expenses of the government, until we can accumulate a fund of thirty, forty, or even fifty millions, within the coming half century—a sum which, however enormous it may seem, is not, in comparison with the importance of the cause, too large. In behalf, therefore, of ourselves, posterity, and future history, let us make adequate provisions to supply this important, this primary necessity. . . .

Mr. MANON did not suppose that the acts of the Convention in this behalf would do much good; but he would do all in his power to educate the children of Ohio. He had heard of a gentleman who, traveling among the barren hills of Vermont, inquired of a boy, by the road-side, what they raised. He answered—"Men." He wished to do the same in Ohio.

Mr. NASH said that after awhile all these things will practically be controlled by public opinion. If legislation is against public opinion, it is powerless, and in such a case you array public opinion against you, and against this Constitution, and will sink it and the system together. Leave such questions to the General Assembly, and that body will act under the influence of that general sentiment, which after all, is the great sanction of the law of the land. If we descend to legislation upon mere questions of policy, we shall inevitably defeat the very object which we seek to promote. If enough has not been hitherto done for education, it is because public sentiment has not demanded it; and if we attempt to go in advance of that sentiment, we shall not be followed, and shall be forced to retreat.

Mr. HAWKINS liked the section, in the main, as it is. He thought with a little modification, it would suit the opinions of nearly every member. Enjoin upon the Legislature the duty of establishing an efficient system, and we shall have done our duty. He agreed in the main with the remarks of the gentleman from Adams (Mr. McCORMICK,) upon the importance of education; but he had not been in the habit of esteeming the morals of New England, so far as it results from mere learning, so very high. He admitted their learning, but doubted whether, after all, in so high a sense, they could be considered and [*sic*] educated people. He was opposed to too great minuteness in the detail of our constitution; but at the same time we are warranted by public sentiment in requiring at the hands of the General Assembly a full, complete and efficient system of public education.

Mr. RANNEY thought the subject a very importan[t] one, and worthy of all the consideration that has been given it. He concurred heartily in the plan of the gentleman from Adams, (Mr. McCORMICK.) He did not profess to say what the minimum sum should be; but that a sum should be enjoined to be raised, sufficient for the purpose, he had no doubt. The gentleman from Gallia, (Mr. NASH) was opposed to too great particularity in the provisions of this Constitution. That was the reason why he objected to portions of this report. There is too great generality in it. It recommends something, suggests much, and provides nothing at all. What are we here for? Merely to declare in a few words the general topics upon which a Legislature shall act? or to fix a form of government? If the former is only our duty, we may as well go home again. It is unnecessary for us to declare that the Legislature shall establish a Judiciary system. They know that already. We are to do more. We are to mark out the boundaries of a Legislative, Executive, and Judiciary system, and to define and limit the powers of a government. Now I came here to aid in establishing a legislative department of this government, in the same manner as any other branch of the government. I desire to lay a plan such as within certain limits the Legislature shall be bound to carry out. It is clearly and unquestionably right that government has a right to establish a system of education that shall reach every poor, every ragged, every destitute child in the State; and if we believe that the people are desirous to establish such a system, let us go forward and do it, and have no fears the people will not respond to it with enthusiasm. I go for an efficient provision, not for any extravagance.

Mr. TAYLOR said, his objection to the amendment was, that if we placed any sum in the constitution, it might be looked upon as limiting the legislature, who might be disposed to give more liberally. It seemed to him, that there was a prospect that the people would progress faster than we anticipate, and would make a far more ample provision than any constitutional sum that we are able to fix. He hoped therefore that no sum would be fixed, but that it would be left to the progressive spirit of the age and of the people. Let there be a guaranty that the school be kept open a specific time, and the objects sought would be gained as far as we are able to secure them.

Mr. McCORMICK moved to fill the blank in his amendment with the sum of one million dollars.

Mr. REEMELIN said that he had not desired to take part in this debate, but he desired to correct the ideas of some gentlemen, upon the subject of what Ohio has done in the cause of education. He ventured to assert, that in no community in the world, has there been so much done, in proporiion [*sic*] to the means, as in the State of Ohio. He had ever taken a great interest in education, and had ever been a laborer in the cause, and he was desirous to state what has been the great impediment to a more rapid advance of the cause among us.

One great reason is the rivalry of schools, established by different sects. Another reason is the want of efficient teachers. These difficulties are to be overcome by time; and we are not prepared to establish that comprehensive and complete system of education, which we shall eventually come to. He desired to say to those gentlemen who speak so poorly our progress in education, and too highly of that of Massachusetts, that they do injustice to our State. Let them institute a comparison beween Massachusetts at fifty years of age, and Ohio; and his word for it our system would be found as good as theirs.

He thought the time had not come for the elaboration of a perfect system of education in Ohio, and that by fixing provisions in the Constitution, that it may be necessary to alter in future, we shall involve ourselves in a dilemma very unfortunate, and from which it will be difficult to escape. There are also many reasons why a general system, established by general rules, without exceptions, might be injurious to the interests of some portions of the State. For instance, in this city, it would be better to leave it all to the local authorities.[4] He wanted to see such a system that should present the means of education to every child in Ohio; but let us not go too fast.

Mr. R. continued by saying that he hoped all the amendments would fail, and that he hoped all attempts to create a system would be left to the General Assembly. . . .

Mr. REEMELIN moved to strike out of the fourth section, in the first line, the word "exclusive," and to substitute the word "any" in its place, which was agreed to.

Mr. LARSH moved the following amendment, to come in at the end of the same section: Or of any of the schools, seminaries or institutions of learning, under the patronage of the State.

Mr. MASON hoped that before this amendment was adopted, the committee would examine and see what it was doing. This amendment proposes to extend the provisions of the section which provides that all religious denominations— the whole religious community, in fact, shall be forever excluded from any participation in the school fund of the State; and that, because they are religious. You take care of the convicts in your penitentiary, and provide for their religious and moral instruction; but the religious of the country are as a class proscribed. You may say that you do not intend any such thing; but if you do it, it is of little consequence what is intended.

Mr. NASH did not understand the section as it was interpreted by the gentleman from Clark (Mr. MASON.) Every citizen has, and will have a right to part[i]cipate in the means of education; but the intention of the provision merely is, that no organized body of christians, as such, shall be entitled to lay its hand upon the school funds of the State, and appropriate it to the furtherance of its own peculiar views. He did not understand that it goes any further than the old constitution. The

---

[4] [The convention had been meeting in Cincinnati since the second of December.]

amendment of the gentleman from Preble, (Mr. LARSH,) merely adds a few superfluous words to what? There is in the section no exclusion of any individual. It means merely, that neither the Presbyterian, the Episcopalian, nor the Catholic church shall have the power to seize upon the public funds and appropriate them to suit itself.

Mr. DORSEY agreed with the gentleman from Clark (Mr. MASON) in his construction of the section. The presidents of our universities cannot, under this provision, be members of any church. It goes further. It uses the word "party," and it would seem that no member of any party—no whig, democrat or free-soiler can participate in the benefits of the fund. The gentlemen would seem to exclude all sects and parties, and have no use for the money.

The amendment was then disagreed to.

Mr. HUNT moved a reconsideration of the vote agreeing to the amendment of Mr. Reemelin, to strike out of the fourth section, the word "exclusive," and substitute the word "any."

Mr. REEMELIN thought, in the interpretation which gentlemen had given to the amendment proposed by him, they had discovered a mare's nest. It would bear no such construction. No boy who went to school would ever be inquired of as to his religion. No one would say to a Presbyterian schoolmaster, go away, you have no business here. No sect or party have, or can have any exclusive right. Any boy who had been one hour at a common school, would know better than to believe any such story as this.

Mr. DORSEY inquired if the words "any right," does not exclude all persons of whatever religion?

Mr. REEMELIN did not believe that his amendment excluded any child in Ohio. . . .

18.

Horace Bushnell, *Common Schools*, 1853

Horace Bushnell's *Discourse* stands as a landmark in the development of American attitudes toward the common schools. It said nothing that was unfamiliar to his generation, and it echoed long-standing controversies between Protestants and Catholics that were to continue to agitate American politics, but in tone as well as argument it epitomized the consensus that a great majority of Americans had reached on the place of education in their democracy and of religion in that education.

On the religious side, and despite its obvious antagonism toward Roman Catholicism, Bushnell's sermon is less often anti-Catholic than antitheocratic; the scion of New England Congregationalists has embraced American denominationalism—the collaborative effort of all Protestant sects to forward the work of the Lord—and with it the propriety of relying upon the common schools to teach an indispensable but not a sectarian morality. In most respects, that is, his anti-Catholicism is better seen as pro-Protestantism, and (like many of his contemporaries) he looks forward to a time when the whole world will have adopted the American way in religion because it is the true Christian way, at once liberal and devout. The schools are an important vehicle of this consummation.

The expression Bushnell gives to the political assumptions of his generation is no less striking. His arguments for the social necessity of common schools draw on a long tradition associating popular education with social control, and they express the commonplace anxiety of conservative social commentators lest class antagonism destroy the social order. Yet they do so in such liberal terms as to be almost unexceptionable. In effect, Bushnell argues that both social control and social justice will be the voluntary achievements of free men trained to the task in common schools, and he even suggests how much a reformed pedagogy (itself responsive to his own liberal theology) will contribute to that result. Hence his Americanism, coercive as it may in fact have been toward Catholics and secularists, is at bottom an expression of the nation's almost unanimous confidence in a reformed public education as the palladium of American liberties.

> *Lev. 24:22. Ye shall have one manner of law,*
> *as well for the stranger,*
> *as for one of your own country:*
> *for I am the Lord your God.*

It is my very uncommon privilege and pleasure to speak to you, for once, from a text already fulfilled, and more than fulfilled in the observance. For we, as a people, or nation, have not only abstained from passing laws that are unequal, or hard upon strangers, which is what the rule of the text forbids, but we have invited them to become fellow-citizens with us in our privileges, and bestowed upon them all the rights and immunities of citizens. We have said to the strangers from Germany, France, Switzerland, Norway, Ireland, and indeed of every land, "Come and be Americans with us, you and your children; and whatsoever right or benefit we have, in our free institutions and our vast and fertile domain, shall be yours."

Thus invited, thus admitted to an equal footing with us, they are not content, but are just now returning our generosity by insisting that we must excuse them and their children from being wholly and properly American. They will not have one law for us and for themselves, but they demand immunities that are peculiar to themselves, and before unheard of by us; or else that we wholly give up institutions for their sake that

From Horace Bushnell, *Common Schools: A Discourse on the Modifications Demanded by the Roman Catholics, Delivered in the North Church, Hartford, March 25, 1853* (Hartford, Conn., 1853).

are the dearest privileges of our birthright. They accept the common rights of the law, the common powers of voting, the common terms of property, a common privilege in the new lands and the mines of gold, but when they come to the matter of common schools, they will not be common with us there— they require of us, instead, either to give up our common schools, or else, which in fact amounts to the same thing, to hand over their proportion of the public money, and let them use it for such kind of schools as they happen to like best; ecclesiastical schools, whether German, French, or Irish; any kind of schools but such as are American, and will make Americans of their children.

It has been clear for some years past, from the demonstrations of our Catholic clergy and their people, and particularly of the clergy, that they were preparing for an assault upon the common school system, hitherto in so great favor with our countrymen; complaining, first, of the Bible as a sectarian book in the schools, and then, as their complaints have begun to be accommodated by modifications that amount to a discontinuance, more or less complete, of religious instruction itself, of our "godless scheme of education;" to which (as godless only as they have required it to be) they say they can not surrender their children without a virtual sacrifice of all religion. Growing more hopeful of their ability, by the heavy vote they can wield, to turn the scale of an election one way or the other between opposing parties, and counting on the sway they can thus exert over the popular leaders and candidates, they have lately attempted a revolution of the school system of Michigan, and are now memorializing the legislatures of Pennsylvania and Ohio, and urging it on the people of these states to allow a change or modification of theirs that amounts to a real discontinuance; viz., to make a distribution of the public school money to all existing schools, of whatever description, according to the number of their scholars; and the moment this is done, plainly nothing will be left of the common school system but a common fund, gathered by a common tax on property, to support private schools.[1]

Evidently the time has now come, and the issue of life or death to common schools is joined for trial. The ground is taken, the flag is raised, and there is to be no cessation, till the question is forever decided, whether we are to have common schools in our country or not. And accordingly, it is time for us all, citizens, public men and Christians, to be finding the ground on which we expect and may be able to stand. In one view the question is wholly a religious question; in another it is more immediately a civil or political question. And yet the lines cross each other in so many ways that any proper discussion of the topic must cover both aspects or departments, the religious and the political. I take up the question at this early period, before it has become, in any sense, a party question, that I may have the advantage of greater freedom, and that I may suffer no imputation of a party bias, to detain me from saying any thing which pertains to a complete view of the subject.

As this day of fasting is itself a civil appointment,[2] I have always made it a point to occupy the day, in part, with some subject that pertains to the public duties and religious concerns of the state or nation. I propose, therefore, now to anticipate, as it were, the pressure of this great subject, and discharge myself, once for all, of my whole duty concerning it; and I hope to speak of it under that sense of responsibility, as well as in

---

[1] [During the early 1850s, Roman Catholic voters in every major city flooded their respective state legislatures with petitions demanding exclusion of the King James Bible from the public schools and renewing the claims of Catholic schools to share public appropriations. Their campaign was widely believed to have been stimulated by a series of articles published in 1853 in the *Freemen's Journal,* Bishop Hughes' organ in New York City.]

[2] [Since colonial times, the Connecticut legislature had appointed an annual fast day as a public observance of religious faith.]

that freedom from prejudice, which one of the greatest and
most serious of all American subjects requires. I wish I might
also speak in a manner to exclude any narrow and partial or
sectarian views of it, such as time and the further consideration
of years might induce a wish to qualify or amend.

I will not undertake to say that our Catholic friends
have, in no case, any just reason for uneasiness or complaint. A
great many persons and even communities will very naturally
act, for a time, as power is able to act, and will rather take
counsel of their prejudices than of reason, or of the great principles that underlie our American institutions. Consideration, as
a rectifying power, is often tardy in its coming, and of course
there will be something unrectified, for so long a time, in the
matter that waits for its arrival.

Meantime the subject itself is one of some inherent difficulty, and can not be expected to settle itself upon its right
foundation, without some delay or some agitation, more or less
protracted, of its opposing interests and reasons. We began our
history in all but the single colony of Baltimore, as Protestant
communities; and, in those especially of New England, we
have had the common school as a fundamental institution from
the first—in our view a Protestant institution—associated with
all our religious convictions, opinions, and the public sentiment
of our Protestant society. We are still, as Americans, a Protestant people, and many are entirely ignorant, as yet, of the fact
that we are not still Protestant states also, as at the first; Protestant, that is, in our civil order, and the political fabric of our
government. And yet we very plainly are not. We have made
a great transition; made it silently and imperceptibly, and
scarcely know as yet that it is made. Occupied wholly with a
historic view of the case, considering how the country and its
institutions are, historically speaking, ours; the liberality and
kindness we have shown to those who have come more recently
to join us, and are even now heard speaking in a foreign accent
among us; the asylum we have generously opened for them and
their children; the immense political trust we have committed

to them, in setting them on a common footing, as voters, with ourselves; and that now we offer to give a free education to their children, at the public expense, or by a tax on all the property of the state—considering all this, and that we and our fathers are Protestants, it seems to be quite natural and right, or even a matter of course, that our common schools should remain Protestant, and retain their ancient footing undisturbed.

But we shall find, on a second consideration, that we have really agreed for something different, and that now we have none to complain of but ourselves, if we have engaged for more than it is altogether pleasant to yield. Our engagement, in the large view of it, is to make the state or political order a platform of equal right to all sects and denominations of Christians. We have slid off, imperceptibly, from the old Puritan, upon an American basis, and have undertaken to inaugurate a form of political order that holds no formal church connexion. The properly Puritan common school is already quite gone by; the intermixture of Methodists, Quakers, Unitarians, Episcopalians, and diverse other names of Christians, called Protestants, has burst the capsule of Puritanism, and, as far as the schools are concerned, it is quite passed away; even the Westminster catechism is gone by, to be taught in the schools no more. In precisely the same manner, have we undertaken also to loosen the bonds of Protestantism in the schools, when the time demanding it arrives. To this we are mortgaged by our great American doctrine itself, and there is no way to escape the obligation but to renounce the doctrine, and resume, if we can, the forms and lost prerogatives of a state religion.

But there is one thing, and a very great thing, that we have not lost, nor agreed to yield; viz., *common schools.* Here we may take our stand, and upon this we may insist as being a great American institution; one that has its beginnings with our history itself; one that is inseparably joined to the fortunes of the republic; and one that can never wax old, or be discontinued in its rights and reasons, till the pillars of the state are themselves cloven down forever. We can not have Puritan com-

mon schools—these are gone already—we can not have Protestant common schools, or those which are distinctively so; but
we can have common schools, and these we must agree to have
and maintain, till the last or latest day of our liberties. These
are American, as our liberties themselves are American, and
whoever requires of us, whether directly or by implication, to
give them up, requires what is more than our bond promises,
and what is, in fact, a real affront to our name and birthright
as a people.

    I mean, of course, by common schools, when I thus
speak, schools for the children of all classes, sects and denominations of the people; so far perfected in their range of culture
and mental and moral discipline, that it shall be the interest of
all to attend, as being the best schools which can be found;
clear too, of any such objections as may furnish a just ground
of offense to the conscience or the religious scruples of any
Christian body of our people. I mean, too, schools that are established by the public law of the state, supported at the public
expense, organized and superintended by public authority. Of
course it is implied that the schools shall be under laws that are
general, in the same way as the laws of roads, records, and military service; that no distribution shall be made, in a way of
exception, to schools that are private, ecclesiastical or parochial; that whatever accommodations are made to different
forms of religion, shall be so made as to be equally available to
all; that the right of separate religious instruction, the supervision, the choice of teachers, the selection of books, shall be provided for under fixed conditions, and so as to maintain the fixed
rule of majorities, in all questions left for the decision of districts. The schools, in other words, shall be common, in just the
same sense that all the laws are common, so that the experience
of families and of children under them, shall be an experience
of the great republican rule of majorities—an exercise for
majorities, of obedience to fixed statutes, and of moderation
and impartial respect to the rights and feelings of minorities—
an exercise for minorities of patience and of loyal assent to the

will of majorities—a schooling, in that manner, which begins at the earliest moment possible, in the rules of American law, and the duties of an American citizen.

And this, I undertake to say, is the institution which we are not for any reason to surrender, but to hold fast as being a necessary and fixed element of the public order, one without which our American laws and liberties are scarcely American longer; or, if we call them by that name, have no ground longer of security and consolidated public unity.

In the first place, it will be found, if we closely inspect our institutions, that the common school is, in fact, an integral part of the civil order. It is no eleemosynary institution, erected outside of the state, but is itself a part of the public law, as truly so as the legislatures and judicial courts. The school-houses are a public property, the district committees are civil officers, the teachers are as truly functionaries of the law as the constables, prison-keepers, inspectors and coroners. We perceive then, if we understand the question rightly, that an application against common schools, is so far an application for the dismemberment and reorganization of the civil order of the state. Certain religionists appear, in the name of religion, demanding that the state shall be otherwise constructed. Or, if it be said that they do not ask for the discontinuance of the common schools, but only to have a part of the funds bestowed upon their ecclesiastical schools, the case is not mended but rather made worse by the qualification; for in that view they are asking that a part of the funds which belong to the civil organization shall be paid over to their religion, or to the *imperium in imperio,* their religion so far substitutes for the civil order. It is as if they were to ask that the health wardens should so far be substituted by their church wardens, or the coroner's inquest by their confessional, and that the state, acknowledging their right to the substitution demanded, should fee the church wardens and confessors, in their behalf. If an application that infringes on the civil polity of our states, in a manner so odious, is to be heard, the civil order may as well be disbanded, and the people given over to their ecclesiastics, to be ruled by them in as many clans of religion as they see fit to make. Are we ready, as Americans, to yield our institutions up in this manner, or to make them paymasters to a sect who will so far dismember their integrity?

This great institution, too, of common schools, is not only a part of the state, but is imperiously wanted as such, for the common training of so many classes and conditions of people. There needs to be some place where, in early childhood, they may be brought together and made acquainted with each other; thus to wear away the sense of distance, otherwise certain to become an established animosity of orders; to form friendships; to be exercised together on a common footing of ingenuous rivalry; the children of the rich to feel the power and do honor to the struggles of merit in the lowly, when it rises above them; the children of the poor to learn the force of merit, and feel the benign encouragement yielded by its blameless victories. Indeed, no child can be said to be well trained, especially no male child, who has not met the people as they are, above him or below, in the seatings, plays and studies of the common school. Without this he can never be a fully qualified citizen, or prepared to act his part wisely as a citizen. Confined to a select school, where only the children of wealth and distinction are gathered, he will not know the merit there is in the real virtues of the poor, or the power that slumbers in their talent. He will take his better dress as a token of his better quality, look down upon the children of the lowly with an educated contempt, prepare to take on lofty airs of confidence and presumption afterward; finally, to make the discovery when it is too late, that poverty has been the sturdy nurse of talent in some unhonored youth who comes up to affront him by an equal, or mortify and crush him by an overmastering force. So also the children of the poor and lowly, if they should be privately educated, in some inferior degree, by the honest and faithful exertion of their parents; secreted as it were, in some back alley or obscure corner of the town, will either grow up in a fierce, inbred hatred of the wealthier classes, or else in a mind cowed by undue modesty, as being of another and inferior quality, unable, therefore, to fight the great battle of life hopefully, and counting it a kind of presumption to think that they can force their way upward, even by merit itself.

Without common schools, the disadvantage falls both ways in about equal degrees, and the disadvantage that accrues to the state, in the loss of so much character, and so many cross ties of mutual respect and generous appreciation, the embittering so fatally of all outward distinctions, and the propagation of so many misunderstandings, (righted only by the immense public mischiefs that follow)—this, I say, is greater even than the disadvantages accruing to the classes themselves; a disadvantage that weakens immensely, the security of the state, and even of its liberties. Indeed, I seriously doubt whether any system of popular government can stand the shock, for any length of time, of that fierce animosity, that is certain to be gendered, where the children are trained up wholly in their classes, and never brought together to feel, understand, appreciate and respect each other, on the common footing of merit and of native talent, in a common school. Falling back thus on the test of merit and of native force, at an early period of life, moderates immensely their valuation of mere conventionalities and of the accidents of fortune, and puts them in a way of deference that is genuine as well as necessary to their common peace in the state. Common schools are nurseries thus of a free republic, private schools of factions, cabals, agrarian laws and contests of force. Therefore, I say, we must have common schools; they are American, indispensable to our American institutions, and must not be yielded for any consideration smaller than the price of our liberties.

Nor is it only in this manner that they are seen to be necessary. The same argument holds, with even greater force, when applied to the religious distinctions of our country. It is very plain that we can not have common schools for the purposes above named, if we make distributions, whether of schools or of funds, under sectarian or ecclesiastical distinctions. At that moment the charm and very much of the reality of common schools vanish. Besides, the ecclesiastical distinctions are themselves distinctions also of classes, in another form, and such too as are much more dangerous than any distinctions of wealth. Let the Catholic children, for example, be driven out of our schools by unjust trespasses on their religion, or be withdrawn for mere pretexts that have no foundation, and just there commences a training in religious antipathies bitter as the grave. Never brought close enough to know each other, the children, subject to the great well known principle that whatever is unknown is magnified by the darkness it is under, have all their prejudices and repugnances magnified a thousand fold. They grow up in the conviction that there is nothing but evil in each other, and close to that lies the inference that they are right in doing what evil to each other they please. I complain not of the fact that they are not assimilated, but of what is far more dishonest and wicked, that they are not allowed to understand each other. They are brought up, in fact, for misunderstanding; separated that they may misunderstand each other; kept apart, walled up to heaven in the inclosures of their sects, that they may be as ignorant of each other, as inimical, as incapable of love and cordial good citizenship as possible. The arrangement is not only unchristian, but it is thoroughly un-American, hostile at every point, to our institutions themselves. No bitterness is so bitter, no seed of faction so rank, no division so irreconcilable, as that which grows out of religious distinctions, sharpened to religious animosities, and softened by no terms of intercourse; the more bitter when it begins with childhood; and yet more bitter when it is exasperated also by distinctions of property and social life that correspond; and yet more bitter still, when it is aggravated also by distinctions of stock or nation.

In this latter view, the withdrawing of our Catholic children from the common schools, unless for some real breach upon their religion, and the distribution demanded of public moneys to them in schools apart by themselves, is a bitter cruelty to the children, and a very unjust affront to our institutions. We bid them welcome as they come, and open to their free possession, all the rights of our American citizenship. They, in return, forbid their children to be Americans, pen them as foreigners to keep them so, and train them up in the speech of Ashdod among us.[3] And then, to complete the affront, they come to our legislatures demanding it, as their right, to share in funds collected by a taxing of the whole people, and to have these funds applied to the purpose of keeping their children from being Americans.

Our only answer to such demands is, "No! take your place with us in our common schools, and consent to be Americans, or else go back to Turkey, where Mohammedans, Greeks, Armenians, Jews are walled up by the laws themselves, forbidding them ever to pass over or to change their superstitions; there to take your chances of liberty, such as a people are capable of when they are trained up, as regards each other, to be foreigners for all coming time, in blood and religion." I said go back to Turkey—that is unnecessary. If we do not soon prepare a state of Turkish order and felicity here, by separating and folding our children thus, in the stringent limits of religious non-acquaintance and consequent animosity, it will be because the laws of human nature and society have failed.

Besides, there are other consequences of such a breach upon the common school system, implied in yielding this demand, which are not to be suffered. A very great part of the children, thus educated, will have very inferior advantages. They will be shut up in schools that do not teach them what, as Americans, they most of all need to know, the political geography and political history of the world, the rights of humanity, the struggles by which those rights are vindicated, and the glo-

---

[3] [Ashdod was one of the principal cities of the ancient Philistines. It repeatedly asserted its independence—of Judah, Assyria, the Chaldeans, and the Romans.]

rious rewards of liberty and social advancement that follow. They will be instructed mainly into the foreign prejudices and superstitions of their fathers, and the state, which proposes to be clear of all sectarian affinities in religion, will pay the bills!

It will also be demanded, next, that the state shall hold the purse for the followers of Tom Paine, and all other infidels, discharging the bills of schools where Paine's Age of Reason, or the Mormon Bible, or Davis' Revelations are the reading books of the children.[4]

The old school Presbyterian church took ground, six years ago, in their General Assembly, at the crisis of their high church zeal, against common and in favor of parochial schools. Hitherto their agitation has yielded little more than a degree of discouragement and disrespect to the schools of their country; but if the Catholics prevail in their attempt, they also will be forward in demanding the same rights, upon the same grounds, and their claim also must be granted. By that time the whole system of common schools is fatally shaken. For, since education is thrown thus far upon the care of individual parents, still another result is certain to follow in close proximity, viz., the discontinuance of all common schools, and of all public care of education; and then we shall have large masses of children growing up in neglect, with no school at all provided to which they can be sent; ignorant, hopeless and debased creatures; banditti of the street; wild men of anarchy, waiting for their leaders, and the guerilla practice of the mountains; at first the pest of society, and finally its end or overthrow. A result that will be further expedited, by the fact that many children, now in our public schools, will be gathered into schools of an atheistic or half pagan character, where they will be educated in a contempt of all order and decency, to be leaders of the ignorance and brutality supplied by the uneducated. How different

---

4 [*Principles of Nature, Her Divine Revelations, and a Voice to Mankind,* published in 1847 by Andrew Jackson Davis, the clairvoyant and spiritualist (1826–1910).]

the picture from that which is now presented by our beautiful system of common schools—every child provided with a good school, all classes and conditions brought together on an equal footing of respect and merit, the state their foster-mother, all property a willing and glad contributor for their outfit in life, and their success in the ways of intelligence and virtue!

Take it then for a point established, that common schools are to remain as common schools, and that these are to be maintained by the state as carefully as the arsenals and armed defenses of the country—these and no other. Just here, then, comes the difficult question, what we are to do, how to accommodate the religious distinctions of the people, so as to make their union in any common system of schools, possible— how the Catholics, in particular, are to be accommodated in their religion, in those societies and districts where Protestants are the majority; how Protestants, where Catholics are the majority?

The question how Pagans, Mohammedans, and Atheists, are to be accommodated, is, in my view, a different question, and one, I think, which is to be answered in a different manner. They are to be tolerated, or suffered, but in no case to be assisted or accommodated, by acts of public conformity. I can not agree to the sentiment sometimes advanced, that we are not a Christian nation, in distinction from a Pagan, Mohammedan or Infidel. Indeed I will go further, assuming the fact of God's existence, I will say that no government can write a legitimate enactment or pass a valid decree of separation from God. Still, after the act is done, God exists, God is the only foundation it has of public right or authority. The state, indeed, is a fiction, a lie, and no state, save as it stands in him. And then as Christianity is only the complete revelation of God, otherwise only partially revealed, it follows that the state can not be less than a Christian state, can not any more disown or throw off its obligations to be Christian, than an individual can. Nor in fact has our government ever attempted to shake off

Christianity, but has always, from the first day till now, taken the attitude and character of a Christian commonwealth—accepting the Christian Sabbath, appointing fasts and thanksgivings, employing military and legislative chaplains, and acknowledging God by manifold other tokens. Accordingly our schools are, to the same extent, and are to be Christian schools. This is the American principle, and as we have never disowned God and Christ, as a point of liberty in the state, or to accommodate unbelievers, so we are required by no principle of American right or law to make our schools unchristian, to accommodate Turks and Pagans, or rejectors and infidels.

Common schools, then, are to be Christian schools— how Christian? In the same sense, I answer, that Catholics and Protestants are Christians, in the same sense that our government is Christian, in the same that Christendom is Christian, that is, in the recognition of God and Christ and providence and the Bible. I fully agree with our Catholic friends regarding what they say in deprecation of a godless system of education. Dr. Chalmers, engaged in a society to establish Catholic schools in Glasgow, went so far as to say that if he had not been able to obtain "favorable terms from the priest, that is, the liberty of making the Bible a school-book," he would still have persevered, "on the principle that a Catholic population, with the capacity of reading, are a more hopeful subject than without it."[5] Perhaps he was right, but the statistics reported in France, a few years ago, showing that public crimes, in the different departments, were very nearly in the ratio of education, increasing too in the ratio of the increase of education, are sufficient to throw a heavy shade of doubt on the value of all attempts to educate, that increase the power of men, and add no regulative force of principle and character. It is, to say the least, a most perilous kind of beneficence. The chances are far

---

[5] [Thomas Chalmers (1780–1847), a prominent Scottish theologian and philanthropist, was a leading figure in the movement to extend religion to the "home heathen" of Great Britain.]

too great that knowledge, without principle, will turn out to be only the equipment of knaves and felons.

The greater reason is there that our Catholic fellow-citizens should not do what they can to separate all the schools of the nation from Christian truth and influence, by requiring a surrender of every thing Christian in the schools, to accommodate their sectarian position. Or, if they reply that they would wholly supplant the common schools, leaving only parochial and sectarian schools in their place, on the ground that our government can not, without some infringement on religion, be made to coalesce with any thing Christian, then is it seen they are endeavoring to make the state "godless" in order to make the school Christian. Exactly this, indeed, one of their most distinguished and capable teachers in Pennsylvania is just now engaged to effect; insisting that the civil state has no right to educate children at all; not only controverting a constituent element of our civil order, but claiming it as a Christian right that the state shall exercise no Christian function. Which then is better, a godless government or a godless school? And if his own church will not suffer a godless school, what has it more earnestly insisted on than the horrible impiety of a state separated from God and religion, and the consequent duty of all kings and magistrates to be servants and defenders of the church? The Catholic doctrine is plainly in a dilemma here, and can no way be accommodated. If the state is godless, then it should as certainly withdraw from that as from the school, which, if it persists in doing, it as certainly does what it can, under the pretext of religion, to empty both the state and the schools of all religion.

The true ideal state manifestly is, one school and one Christianity. But it does not follow that we are to have as many schools as we have distinct views of Christianity, because we have not so many distinct Christianities. Nor is any thing more cruel and abominable than to take the little children apart, whom Christ embraced so freely, and make them parties to all our grown up discords whom Christ made one with himself

and each other, in their lovelier and, God forgive us if perchance it also be, their wiser age. Let us draw near rather to
the common Christ we profess, doing it through them and for
their sake, and see if we can not find how to set them together
under Christ, as his common flock.

In most of our American communities, especially those
which are older and more homogeneous, we have no difficulty
in retaining the Bible in the schools and doing every thing
necessary to a sound Christian training. Nor, in the larger
cities, and the more recent settlements, where the population is
partly Catholic, is there any, the least difficulty in arranging a
plan so as to yield the accommodation they need, if only there
were a real disposition on both sides to have the arrangement.
And precisely here, I suspect, is the main difficulty. There may
have been a want of consideration sometimes manifested on
the Protestant side, or a willingness to thrust our own forms of
religious teaching on the children of Catholics. Wherever we
have insisted on retaining the Protestant Bible as a school book,
and making the use of it by the children of Catholic families,
compulsory, there has been good reason for complaining of our
intolerance. But there is a much greater difficulty, I fear, and
more invincible, on the other side. In New York the Catholics
complained of the reading of the Protestant Scriptures in the
schools, and of the text-books employed, some of which contained hard expressions against the Catholic church. The Bible
was accordingly withdrawn from the schools and all religious
instruction discontinued. The text-books of the schools were
sent directly to Archbishop Hughes, in person, to receive exactly such expurgations as he and his clergy would direct.
They declined the offer, by a very slender evasion, and it was
afterward found that some of the books complained of were in
actual use, in their own church schools, though already removed from the schools of the city. Meantime the immense and
very questionable sacrifice thus made, to accommodate the
complaints of the Catholics, resulted in no discontinuance of
their schools, neither in any important accession to the common

schools of the city, from the children of Catholic families. On the contrary, the priests now change their note and begin to complain that the schools are "godless" or "atheistical"—just as they have required them to be. In facts like these, fortified by the fact that some of the priests are even denying, in public lectures, the right of the state to educate children at all, we seem to discover an absolute determination that the children shall be withdrawn, at whatever cost, and that no terms of accommodation shall be satisfactory. It is not that satisfaction is impossible, but that there is really no desire for it. Were there any desire, the ways in which it may be accomplished are many and various.

1. Make the use of the Bible in the Protestant or Douay version, optional.

2. Compile a book of Scripture reading lessons, by agreement from both versions.

3. Provide for religious instruction, at given hours, or on a given day, by the clergy, or by qualified teachers such as the parents may choose.

4. Prepare a book of Christian morality, distinct from a doctrine of religion or a faith, which shall be taught indiscriminately to all the scholars.[6]

Out of these and other elements like these, it is not difficult to construct, by agreement, such a plan as will be Christian, and will not infringe, in the least, upon the tenets of either party, the Protestant or the Catholic. It has been done in Holland and, where it was much more difficult, in Ireland. The British government, undertaking at last, in good faith, to construct a plan of national education for Ireland, appointed Archbishop Whately and the Catholic Archbishop of Dublin, with five others, one a Presbyterian and one a Unitarian, to be a board or committee of superintendence. They agreed upon a selection of reading lessons from both translations of the Scriptures, and, by means of a system of restrictions and qualifica-

---

[6] [An extensive footnote is omitted here.]

tions, carefully arranged, providing for distinct methods and times of religious instruction, they were able to construct a union, not godless or negative, but thoroughly Christian in its character, and so to draw as many as 500,000 of the children into the public schools; conferring thus upon the poor neglected and hitherto oppressed Irish, greater benefits than they have before received from any and all public measures since the conquest.

I can not go into the particulars of this adjustment, neither is it necessary. Whoever will take pains to trace out the particular features of the plan, will see that such an adjustment is possible. Enough is it for the present to say, that what has been can be, and that if there is a real and true desire in the two parties to this coming controversy, to settle any plan that will unite and satisfy them both, it will be done. It may never be done in such a manner as to silence all opposition or attack from the ultra Protestant party on one side, and the ultra Catholic on the other. Bigotry will have its way, and will assuredly act in character here, as it has in all ages past and does in Ireland now. The cry will be raised on one side, that the Bible is given up because it is read only at the option of the parents, or because only extracts from it are read, though the extracts amount to nearly the whole book, or because they are, some of them, made from the Catholic and some from the Protestant version; whereas, if only this or that catechism were taught, with not a word of Scripture, no complaint of a loss of the Bible would be heard of, or if the Psalter translation were read, instead of the Psalms, it would be regarded as no subject of complaint at all. On the other, the Catholic side, it will be insisted that the church authority is given up, though every word and teaching is by and from it, or that religion itself is corrupted by the profane mixtures of a Protestant proximity and intercourse. Probably the bigots, on both sides, will have much to say, in deprecation of the "godless system of education," and yet there will be more religious teaching, and more impression made of true religion, by that cordial and Christian adjustment of differences, which brings the children of two hostile bands together, in this manner, than by whole days and weeks of drill and catechism in separate schools.

There is a great deal of cant in this complaint of godless education, or the defect of religious instruction in schools, as Baptist Noel, Dr. Vaughan, and other distinguished English writers, have abundantly shown.[7] It is not, of course, religious instruction for a child to be drilled, year upon year, in spelling out the words of the Bible, as a reading book—it may be only an exercise that answers the problem how to dull the mind most effectually to all sense of the Scripture words, and communicate least of their meaning. Nay, if the Scriptures were entirely excluded from the schools, and all formal teaching of religious doctrine, I would yet undertake, if I could have my liberty as a teacher, to communicate more of real Christian truth to a Catholic and a Protestant boy, seated side by side, in the regulation of their treatment of each other, as related in terms of justice and charity, and their government as members of the school community, (where truth, order, industry and obedience are duties laid upon the conscience, under God,) than they will ever draw from any catechism, or have worn into their brain by the dull and stammering exercise of a Scripture reading lesson. The Irish schools have a distinct Christian character, only not as distinctly sectarian as if they were wholly Protestant or wholly Catholic. They are Christian schools, such as ours may be and ought to be, and, I trust, will be, to the latest generations, nor any the less so that they are common schools.

Neither is it to be imagined or felt that religion has lost its place in the scheme of education, because the Scriptures are

---

[7] [Baptist W. Noel (1798–1873) was a Scottish preacher especially active in home missions and elementary public education. In 1840, before his conversion to Baptism, he made studies of elementary schooling in Birmingham and Manchester. Robert Vaughan (1795–1868), a Welsh Congregationalist, wrote *Popular Education in England* (1846).]

not read as a stated and compulsory exercise, or because the higher mysteries of Christianity as a faith or doctrine of salvation, are not generally taught, but only the Christian rules of conduct, as pertaining to the common relations of duty under God. What is wanting may still be provided for, only less adequately, in other places; at home, in the church, or in lessons given by the clergy. It is not as when children are committed to a given school, like the Girard College, for example, there to receive their whole training, and where, if it excludes religion, they have no religious training at all.[8]

I do then take the ground, and upon this I insist, as the true American ground, that we are to have common schools, and never to give them up, for any purpose, or in obedience to any demand whatever—never to give them up, either by formal surrender, or by implication; as by a distribution of moneys to ecclesiastical and sectarian schools. The state can not distribute funds, in this manner, without renouncing even a first principle of our American institutions, and becoming the supporter of a sect in religion. It may as well support the priests of a church, as support the schools of a church, separated from other schools, for the very purpose of being subjected to the priests.

But while we are firm in this attitude, and hold it as a point immovable, we must, for that very reason, be the more ready to do justice to the religious convictions of all parties or sects, and to yield them such concessions, or enter into such arrangements as will accommodate their peculiar principles and clear them of any infringement.

But it will be objected by some, that while this should be done, if there were any thing to hope from it, there is really no hope that our concessions or modifications will be of any avail, and therefore that they should not be made at all; for

---

[8] [Girard College opened in Philadelphia in 1848 to educate poor white male orphans. Under the terms of Stephen Girard's will, no minister might enter the grounds.]

they will only so far abridge the value of our schools without yielding any recompense for the loss. Then let us offer the modifications, offer any terms of union that can be offered without a virtual destruction or renunciation of the system; and then if they are not accepted it will not be our fault. I very much fear they will not be, that an absolute separation of the Catholic children from our schools is already determined, and that no revision of the sentence can be had. Still it is much for us to take away every excuse for such a determination, and every complaint or pretext by which it is justified.

Then, having done it, we can take the ground explicitly, and clear of all ambiguity, that they who exclude themselves are not Americans, and are not acting in their complaints or agitations, on any principle that meets the tenor of our American institutions. Nothing will be more evident, and they should be made to bear the whole odium of it. If to keep their people apart from the dreaded influence of Protestant Christianity, they were to buy townships of land, or large quarters in our cities, to be occupied only by Catholics, walled in by their own by-laws, and allowing no Protestant family, or tradesman, or publican, to reside in the precinct—no one to enter it without a pass; and then to come before our legislatures in petition that we will distribute moneys to support their roads, and pay their constables and gate-keepers; they would scarcely do a greater insult to our American society than they do in these separations from our common schools, and the petitions they are offering to be justified and rewarded in the separation.

But we tax them, it will be said, for the support of the common schools, and then, receiving no benefit from the tax they pay, they are obliged to tax themselves again, for schools of their own. It is even so, and for one, apart from all resentment, I rejoice in it; unless they have grievances put upon them by the organization of our schools, such as justify their withdrawal. We tax the Quakers for defect of military service, and bachelors who have no children, and we ought, much more, to tax the refractory un-American position taken by these Catholic strangers, after we have greeted them with so great hospitality, and loaded them with so many American privileges. If now they will not enter into the great American institution, so fundamental to our very laws and liberties, let them pay for it, and measure their deserts by their dissatisfactions. If they will be foreigners still among our people, let them have remembrances that interpret their conduct to them in a way of just emphasis.

Meantime let us be sure also of this, that a day is at hand when they will weary of this kind of separation, and will visit on their priests, who have required it, a just retribution. One generation, or possibly two, may bear this separation, this burden of double taxation, this withdrawal of their children from society and its higher advantages, to be shut up or penned as foreign tribes in the state, thus to save the prejudices of a discarded and worthless nationality; but another generation is to come who will have drunk more deeply into the spirit of our institutions, and attained to a more sufficient understanding of the hard lot put upon them, in this manner, by a jealous and overbearing priesthood. Then comes a reaction, both against them and their religion; then a flocking back to the schools to reap their advantages; and it will be strange if the very measure now counted on as the means of their preservation, does not, of itself, become one of the strongest reasons for the alienation of their children from it. Of this we may be quite sure, and it ought not to be any secret to them, that their children of the coming time will at last find a way to be Americans; if not under the Pope and by the altars, then without them.

Neither let it be said that this is a matter which lies at the disposal of politics, and that our political demagogues will sell any thing, even our birthright as a people, to carry the vote of a campaign. The experiment has just been tried in Detroit, with a most signal and disastrous failure.[9] In cases where the

---

9 [In the municipal elections of March 1853, a slate of independent Democrats running with the tacit support of the Whigs overwhelmed the regular Democrats, whom they charged with having supported a bill to

issue touches no religious interest or feeling of the Protestants, and the Catholics can be gained to throw a casting vote on one side or the other, the politicians will not deal so absurdly, if they consent to buy that vote by some great promise, and I have so little confidence in many of them, under the prodigious temptations of a canvass, as to have it for granted, that they will stick at nothing which is possible. But here, thank God, is one thing that is impossible, and whatever politician ventures on the experiment, will find that he has not worked his problem rightly—that if Catholics can be often united and led in masses to the vote, so Protestants will sometimes go in masses where they are not led, save by their principles. That our legislatures can not and will not be gained to allow the ruling out of the Scriptures, and all religious instruction from the schools, as in New York city, I am by no means certain—I very much fear that they will—but that they can ever become supporters and fund-holders to ecclesiastical schools, or be induced to give up common schools, I do not believe.[10] Whatever politician or political party ventures on that experiment, will find that he has rallied a force manifold greater against him than he has drawn to his aid. A point so thoroughly un-American, so directly opposite also to the deepest convictions of the great Protestant majorities of the country, can not be carried, and, if pressed, will suffice to fix a stigma that is immovable upon any leader who is desperate enough to try the experiment.

Here I will close. The subject is a painful one, and not any the less so that the line of our duty is plain. It can not be said by any, the most prejudiced critic, that our conduct as a

---

divide the state's educational appropriations among competing denominations including Roman Catholics. I am indebted to Lewis A. Erenberg, doctoral candidate in History at the University of Michigan, for information about this election.]

10 [As a result of the controversy surrounding the Public School Society of New York (see Document 13, pages 97–120), the state legislature forbade religious instruction of any sort in the public schools.]

people, to strangers and men of another religion, has not been
generous and free beyond any former example in the history
of mankind. We have used hospitality without grudging. In one
view it seems to be a dark and rather mysterious providence,
that we have thrown upon us, to be our fellow-citizens, such
multitudes of people, depressed, for the most part, in character,
instigated by prejudices so intense against our religion. But
there is a brighter and more hopeful side to the picture. These
Irish prejudices, embittered by the crushing tyranny of England, for three whole centuries and more, will gradually yield
to the kindness of our hospitality, and to the discovery that it
is not so much the Protestant religion that has been their
enemy, as the jealousy and harsh dominion of conquest. God
knows exactly what is wanting, both in us and them, and God
has thrown us together that, in terms of good citizenship, and
acts of love, we may be gradually melted into one homogeneous people. Probably no existing form of Christianity is perfect—the Romish we are sure is not—the Puritan was not, else
why should it so soon have lost its rigors? The Protestant, more
generally viewed, contains a wider variety of elements, but
these too seem to be waiting for some process of assimilation
that shall weld them finally together. Therefore God, we may
suppose, throws all these diverse multitudes, Protestant and
Catholic, together, in crossings so various, and a ferment of experience so manifold, that he may wear us into some other and
higher and more complete unity, than we are able, of ourselves
and by our own wisdom, to settle. Let us look for this, proving
all things, and holding fast that which is good, until the glorious result of a perfected and comprehensive Christianity is
made to appear, and is set up here for a sign to all nations. Let
us draw our strange friends as close to us as possible, not in any
party scramble for power, but in a solemn reference of duty to
the nation and to God. I can not quite renounce the hope that a
right and cordial advance on our part—one that, duly careful
to preserve the honors of Christianity, concedes every thing
required by our great principle of equal right to all, and as

firmly refuses to yield any thing so distinctively American as this noble institution, identified with our history as the blood with the growth of our bodies—will command the respect and finally the assent of our Catholic friends themselves. And since God has better things in store even for religion, than the repugnant attitudes of its professed disciples can at present permit, I would even hope that he may use an institution so far external to the church, as a means of cementing the generations to come in a closer unity, and a more truly catholic peace; that, as being fellow-citizens with each other, under the state, in the ingenuous days of youth and youthful discipline, they may learn how also to be no more strangers and foreigners, but fellow-citizens with the saints and of the household of God.

19.

"The States' Duties in Regard to Popular Education," *DeBow's Review,* 1856

Before the Civil War, northerners debated whether to admit free Negroes to their common schools; southerners usually took it for granted that slaves could not and should not be educated. When they examined the question more fully under the impact of antislavery agitation, they often sought to prove that only a society in which manual labor was performed by an inferior race could avoid the dangers to be apprehended from popular ignorance. Consequently, as this excerpt from *De Bow's Review* indicates, they turned the national campaign for popular education on its head. While northern Negrophobes were concerned primarily with excluding blacks from schools that they took to be the common property of whites, southern proslavery writers described an hierarchical social order in which different kinds of schooling would be provided (respectively) for those born to command, for others born to occupy the middle ranks of society, and for still others born to labor. In one sense, they only restated in more invidious terms a commitment to social elitism that an earlier generation of republican social theorists had also expressed, but on a more basic level they appealed to the idea and fact of a social elite to refute northern democratic pretensions to both liberty and education. In effect, they seceded from the northern democratic crusade to extend democratic institutions just as it reached its height.

It is an old saying, and one as beautiful as true, that "He who labors prays." And just as it happens to him who prays, that whether his prayer be granted or not, he has yet placed his soul in harmony with God's purpose, and is ready to rejoice with humility or to submit with joy; so, to him who labors earnestly in any of the manifold varieties of human occupation, whether that labor be crowned with success or not, it happens that toil brings its own reward; and that all work binds the worker by ties of gentler and more enduring fellowship to that wide human society which, absorbing, almost unheeded, his humble effort in its great results, is laboring forever on to the final consummation of God's vast providence. And when you remember that, underlying the great men and the great deeds which make the pageantry of history, there always have been, there always must be, the unwearying millions whose obscure toil creates the material of national wealth, whose simple sentiments concentrate into national opinion, whose rude life forms, in fact, national character, and yet whose only teachers are the field and the factory—you surely will admit, in view of its influence on the discipline of life that, however political economy may consider it, labor should, in its highest and truest charac-

---

From *DeBow's Commercial Review of the South and West*, XX, 2 (February 1856), 143–144, 146–151. The magazine tentatively attributed its article to J. H. Thornwell, South Carolina's chief advocate of educational reform.

ter, be regarded as one, perhaps the chiefest, of the moral elements of national life.

But while, in God's economy, hard daily labor is thus made the schoolmaster of the poor, to teach them those lessons of moral duty which are perhaps the highest education, it cannot be denied that there are aspects under which the necessity of constant toil gives to humble life a most dreary and repulsive coloring. There are hundreds of thousands to whom this world, in all the richness of its beauty, is but a weary workshop; to whom the blessed sun shines only as a factory lamp to light them to hopeless, aimless, endless toil, and to whom the calm and holy night brings no refreshment on her shadowy wings. They live—they work—they die. When they fall, they fall as in battle, and the ranks of the innumerable army of workmen close and trample over them, no heart to pity and no time to mourn. And yet society seems to require this eternal sacrifice; as if the creation and existence of a nation, like the formation of the coral islands of southern seas, demand that generation after generation of workers shall perish unknown and unrewarded, before its foundations are made secure, and its soil, raised into light, shall be fertilized and quickened for the fruits and flowers of a perfect civilization. And if, looking at this subject more in detail, you dwell upon the strange and terrible revelations of such books as "London Labor and the London Poor," or the recent parliamentary reports, you will realize in all its fearful fulness the importance to every society of the character of the labor which supports it.[1] But while the condition of labor in every country exerts an

---

[1] [*London Labour and the London Poor* was a detailed account of the habits and economic circumstances of the hawkers and performers who thronged the streets of London during the 1840s and 1850s. Compiled by Henry Mayhew, a humorous writer who helped to found *Punch*, it began as a miscellaneous exercise in urban journalism but metamorphosed into an almost obsessive treatment of the condition of the poor. Hence it paralleled and augmented the reports of parliamentary investigations into the condition of the working classes.]

immediate influence upon the character of its civilization, there is another element not less direct, nor less powerful in its action, and that is its intellect. For, after all, labor is but a means and must have an object; and it is as well the conception of those objects as the character of those means, which must determine the eminence of a nation's place in history. Intellect and labor, therefore, are both absolutely necessary to the development of either. A nation of mere scholars, each man working for abstract truth, is impossible; a nation of mere laborers, each man working only for his daily bread, is inconceivable. And the condition, therefore, which it should be the object of every society to establish, is that the intellect of the State should be as practically active, and the labor of the State as practically intelligent, as is consistent with the nature of these two agents—for it is only the joint action of the two that can produce an advanced civilization. A people may be refined and intelligent without energy, like some of the people of southern Europe; they may be energetic, but ignorant and savage, like our own Indians; they may be neither, like many of the South American people. . . .

The educational system of any State may I think fairly be considered as representing its intellect; and the question which I would discuss is, how far should that system be modified by the character of the State's labor, in order to secure the best and concerted action of the two. I neither wish nor intend to discuss it as an abstract question; but I propose to examine its bearings and consequences in reference to the fundamental institution—slave labor—upon which our society rests. This subject—the relation between learning and working—has of late attracted the serious attention of statesmen in the old world. The immense mass of ignorant, suffering, and vicious labor upon which their complicated society rests, calls for wise and speedy action. Men too are beginning to feel that independent of their selfish interest in the condition of these vast masses, there is a fellowship in their common humanity which no difference of social condition can entirely destroy;

and that there must be something wrong in a system which condemns the great majority of any people to perpetual, and, in many cases, degrading and insufficient labor, in order that the minority may enjoy the honors and pleasures of a highly refined cultivation. There have been, in consequence, many and most commendable efforts to establish a system of education for the working classes, to found schools and even colleges for workmen, and thus to afford to the humblest means of improvement and an opportunity to share those more refined enjoyments, a taste for which education alone creates. But besides the religious question involved in this experiment, and which, in all States possessing an established church, still remains unanswered, there are two difficulties which seem almost insuperable. In all countries of the old world the distinction of class is not based upon distinction of race, and the millions who labor are identical in blood and capacity with the few thousands who, as a privileged and governing class, enjoy the fruit of this labor. In all these countries there is also a large surplus laboring population. The endeavor to educate this laboring class, therefore, is met first by the fact, that this surplus population reduces the wages of labor to starvation point; and to make barely enough to support daily life requires, on the part of the majority of laborers, unremitting work from the rising of the sun even to the going down thereof; and the overlabored workman has neither the time nor the temper to profit by the opportunities offered him. In the next place, so long as hard and distasteful work is the necessary rule of his life, it is questionable how far you are really serving him when you foster and develop in the laborer capacities which he can never exert, tastes which he can never indulge. History has recorded more than one revolution which has sprung from the restlessness of large social classes, dissatisfied with the existing order of things, because they feel that their higher faculties are shut out from the natural field of exercise. And wherever such a feeling is prevalent, revolution is, in the very nature of things, inevitable. Now, if the great throng of men who live and die working for no higher end than daily subsistence, and who are yet capable of being roused to the hopes and passions of a nobler life, should be carefully educated for a sphere of wider action, and trained to the exercise of their loftier faculties, while the material interests and old organization of society refuse them admission into that sphere and forbids them the use of those faculties, no power under heaven could prevent wild and ruinous social convulsion.

Fortunately for us, our institutions are free from this fundamental difficulty. The great mass of coarse and unintellectual labor which the necessities of the country require, is performed by a race not only especially fitted for its performance, but especially unfitted and disqualified for that mental improvement which is generally understood by the term education. This class of people, therefore, do not require any place in the educational system of the State. Nay, more; their habits, capacities, and natures are such, that the only and best education which they are capable of receiving, is just that which their labor itself furnishes—namely, an education of character, rather than an education of mind. And, talking to southern men, as I am now, I may safely assume, what any practical knowledge of the subject amply confirms, that a well-managed estate, where debt calls for no unusual and strained effort to force labor to its extremest point of production, while a necessary economy allows the least possible expenditure upon the comforts of the laborer—where the master's eye directs the work and watches the morals of his people—where the great and simple truths of Christianity are freely but orally taught to the slave, (and for simple minds oral instruction is the best and wisest)—where, in a word, slavery is the institution, and not merely an investment—there the whole discipline of his condition develops in the slave the highest moral life of which he is capable, and his education is perfected by industry, obedience, and loyal affection to his master. And every one of you must have seen and known slaves trained under this system, whose courtesy, fidelity, and simple wisdom, would put to shame the result of a more liberal and more boastful education. It does occasionally happen that in certain occupations white and black labor trench upon each other, but this in our society is exceptionable in a very limited circle; and it may be safely laid down as a political axiom with us that these classes should never be confounded, for it inevitably tends to the degradation of the white and the demoralization of the black; as the only wholesome condition under which the two classes can labor together is, that the white shall control and direct the labor of the black. The character of our labor, therefore, draws a broad line between the class who merely labor and the white population of the State, who are thus created a governing, privileged class. This distinction lies at the basis of our society. We can neither ignore nor oppose it. Its natural consequences, if allowed legitimate development, are eminently advantageous; and the State cannot safely refuse to accept them or to adopt, in a slaveholding community, a political theory based upon the principle of free labor. In establishing, then, a system of education for a slave State, there are two principles which may be placed as the foundations upon which to build:

1. That the State is *not* required to provide education for the great bulk of its laboring class.

2. That it *is* required to afford that degree of education to every one of its white citizens which will enable him intelligently and actively to control and direct the slave labor of the State.

If we take the white population of the State as the class for whom the State should provide education, that education must, of course, be adapted to the necessities of its scholars; and while all the members of that class are politically equal, they are distributed in various conditions of life, and destined to occupations requiring very different kinds of knowledge. With one section of that class—the large slave owners employed in agriculture, the great merchants and bankers who represent the commercial capital of the State, the learned professional men who make and administer its laws, and its men of science—education is not only a matter of necessity, but a matter of luxury. Wealth and leisure offer the opportunity an[d] inducement for higher and more abstract studies than can be afforded by the large majority of any people. For these, therefore, and the few outside of these, to whom exceptional tastes and minds are given, are required and provided colleges and universities, where the course of education is as wide and discursive as the mind itself, and where the means and appliances of learned labor are supplied to those who will use them. But university education, vastly important as it is to the State, does not properly come within the scope of that popular education, the character and necessity of which I am now discussing. In this State, as every where else, every man who does not inherit a fortune has to work for a living. Commerce and the learned professions furnish remunerative employment to but a limited number, and even these, as a general rule, require an advance of capital, or a long and expensive education. Our practical question, therefore, is, to what degree, and how are the rest of the numerous class of citizens to be educated? And it must be recollected that the distinction of rich and poor is not with us a social distinction—that the one consist of sons, brothers, relatives of the other. The task of the State is, therefore, double. It has to educate these men for work, but it has also so to educate them as to maintain their position as members of the white, privileged class of our society; and it should be the only sure test of the healthy condition of the State, that the natural development of its resources finds employment for this class of its citizens, while its system of education fits them for the discharge of these employments. Let me illustrate by examples: Suppose the interest of the State requires the building of a new railroad to open fresh markets to our commerce. In a proper state of things, the capital for the enterprise would be supplied by one class of citizens—the hard, material work of raising embankments, laying the track, &c., would be executed by our slave labor, while the preliminary surveying, the practical direction of the work, the control of the labor employed, would be in the hands of the very class I have been describing, and whom the State would have educated for the work. Again, the agriculture of this State employs a large class of intermediate agents for the actual superintendence of its works, and there are hundreds of men whom the State, by furnishing the elements of a scientific agricultural education, would fit for this field of honorable and useful action. So with all mechanical employment. Give him the proper education, and you make the mechanic not a mere laborer, but a master workman. He may have to go through the practical apprenticeship necessary to teach him the application of scientific principles to his business; but once that he has obtained a proper education, ever after his mind works as well as his hands, and he is fit to direct the labor which our slave institutions supply. The object, then, of the State system of popular education should be to train and fit for practical usefulness that large class of her citizens who, born on her soil, and having neither fortune nor the taste for professional life, are yet fully entitled to draw sustenance from her bosom—whose lives and whose labor are one great source of her strength and prosperity, and in whose work and character her fame and fortune are both involved. To effect this object, her system must accomplish three things:

1. It must afford a sound, thorough, and practical knowledge of those arts and sciences which are directly concerned in the discovery and development of the material interests of the State.

2. It must, by the general scheme and tone of its studies, liberalize and enlarge the mind of the student so that he will never sink the man in the workman.

3. It must impress upon his whole moral nature the consciousness that work is his duty as a citizen, and that all education is worthless that does not teach every man, in that

condition of life in which it has pleased God to call him, how to work wisely and vigorously.

The importance of this subject cannot be overrated. The institution of slavery is a great blessing to society, for it is the only practicable method of obtaining the advantages of associated labor without the evils of socialism. But slavery has its inexorable requirements, and the safety of a slave society depends upon their strict performance. And its very first requirement, its indispensable consequence where it is true to itself, is the elevation of white labor. Under this institution, the white race must preserve its superiority by making its work mental as well as bodily. The State cannot with justice or safety allow the white man to come into competition with the black simply as a laborer. By the laws of the land, by our strongest instincts, by the very nature of things, there is an immense, an impassable gulf between the lowest and humblest form of white labor and the highest development of black. And the only way to preserve this distinction is to give to every workman in the State the education of a responsible citizen, adapted, in its details, to that sort of work which his condition in life requires. And this principle, if faithfully carried out, will give to white labor a character, efficiency, and dignity that it has possessed nowhere else in the world. Every society rests upon its own principles; is governed by its own fixed laws. If its legislation is not based upon the same principles, or ventures to run counter to these laws, social disorganization is the result, sure, and not slow. Now this State has been laboring for years on the subject of popular education, and with scarcely any success. Why? My firm belief is, because she has started from false principles. We have been studying and imitating foreign systems, based, and in their cases necessarily based, upon the principle of free labor, instead of doing our work in conformity with the nature of our own material. And I believe that if the State will only act consistently with herself she is able to create, and will finally develop, such a system of popular education as none but a slave society can afford—a system which will draw social harmony from materials apparently discordant, and in which every social element will find a field for its peculiar activity. Then, indeed, shall we have successfully vindicated the wisdom and purposes of slavery, so long veiled. Our whole political fabric will rest securely upon the broad basis of slave labor, improved and organized as no labor has ever been before; while every white freeman of the State, realizing his position, and educated for his duty as one of the privileged class of citizens, will feel the dignity of work, which, in its humblest shape, must then, with us, represent the intellect, as well as the labor, of the State.[2]

20.

Colonel Christopher C. Andrews, Address at Little Rock, Arkansas, 1863

Southern criticisms of northern society along with southern delays in the development of common school systems fed the hostile perspectives in which northern critics viewed both slavery and other southern institutions. Once the Civil War had broken out, therefore, differences in educational practice helped northerners to explain why war had come and why rebel leaders were able to maintain the loyalty of their people in spite of the obvious rectitude of the Union cause. It followed that when Union troops began to occupy Confederate territory, northern leaders would turn to the education of the

---

[2] [The remainder of the article, apparently a commencement address, celebrates the work of academies devoted to industrial rather than academic pursuits.]

South to rectify its past errors as well as compensate for its present distresses. The following speech, delivered in Little Rock by the colonel commanding the Union forces there, exemplifies the ways in which alleged southern illiteracy became at one and the same time a datum of history, an explanation of secession, and a challenge to northern energies.

. . . We are carrying on this war not to explore and define new principles, but to preserve and vindicate time-honored principles. The people of the United States undertook to suppress the rebellion because they were bound by every sense of honor to maintain the unity and nationality of their country; because, having enjoyed the blessings, they had complete faith in the success of popular self-government; and because, having the manhood of true Americans, they could not and would not surrender the liberties and the nationality inherited from noble sires. They saw that the rebellion was a step backward—a step toward aristocratic doctrines—a step toward the feudal ages. They saw that if the uneasy suicidal doctrine of secession was tolerated, it would finally lead to unending war and chaos—to war between States; to war between counties. The rebellion was not resistance to any oppression or intolerable grievance. It was a haughty, disdainful, contemptuous, and malignant breaking fellowship with men who held progressive views. And therefore we are testing the question whether a set of conspirators, who had been nourished into too much importance by previous indulgence, can successfully accomplish their nefarious plot.

The rebellion was started not in the hours of cool reflection, but at a time of intense political excitement. None of you would think of buying a yoke of oxen, much less a

From *Early Steps in Reconstruction. Speeches by General C. C. Andrews, of Minnesota, In Texas and Arkansas* (Washington, D. C.: Union Republican Congressional Committee, n.d.), pp. 5–7.

farm, with your minds so excited. How absurd then to think of changing the destinies of a great nation under the influence of transient political excitement. The spirit and behavior of the conspirators showed their inherent antagonism to the principles of popular government. They refused to compromise on any terms. And then the absurdity of their pretexts for dissolving the Union! Some of them put it on the ground of the personal liberty bills, some on the tariff, some on danger apprehended to slavery, some on fishing bounties! And yet they knew very well that Congress and the Supreme Court had freshly fortified the rights of slaveholders; they knew that Abraham Lincoln was pledged to execute the fugitive slave law; they knew that out of regard for the sensitiveness of slavery the Government had continuously refrained from acknowledging the independence of Hayti.

I acknowledge the splendid valor and the tenacity of purpose which the Southern army has shown, and which are worthy a better cause. But the excesses tolerated and the policy of warfare pursued by the leaders betray significantly the spirit of despair. On the land they have practised robbery, and piracy on the sea. Worse than Sylla, who cut down the sacred groves of the academy, they in Tennessee broke into the temple of knowledge and stole away the precious fund for common schools. They have organized the system of guerrilla warfare so repugnant to the laws of war. It is thus they burn and lay waste the country. They are your worst enemies, and they are making war more upon the unarmed and peaceable people of the South than against the United States. Is it a light matter to burn down houses and turn familes [*sic*] out of doors? But what is this to burning vessels at sea? There are many people who spend nearly all their lives on the sea, and who may be said to live on the deep. But so far as the rebels are able they capture and burn our vessels, carrying the crews and passengers who survive into strange ports, to get back if they can, or to linger and die in want. It is a fact well proved that the guerrillas, or "partisans," as they are called in the Richmond

war office, are paid by dividing their plunder among themselves. They are mere robbers. They never show fight to our
men unless they out number us four to one. I say, therefore,
that the wings of the rebellion are piracy on the sea and robbery on the land.

This quarrel must be finished sometime. We had better
do the fighting in the present war than to leave it to break out
in ten or twenty years from now. The truest economy and the
highest duty now is for the nation to *do its best*, which it has
not yet done. Let all differences be healed among ourselves.
Let the strength and talent of the country be used against
the enemy. Let the power of the press and the eloquence of
our orators be employed to awaken more fervent and universal patriotism. Let us first crush the rebellion, and then, and
not till then, discuss and settle political issues which can only
arise after the rebellion is crushed. It is wisdom to do the
work presently before us to be done. The duty of our armies
is to fight. The duty of patriots at home is to reinforce our
armies.

Peace! It is drivelling madness to talk of peace now.
There can be no peace till there is complete submission to the
Government of the Union. To whom does our country belong
that any set of men now living have a right to barter it away?
Is our system of free government an invention of this generation that it can be compromised away by us? On the contrary;
it is the result of the struggles and sacrifices of many centuries
past. It belongs to future generations as well as to us. It is
the glorious legacy which we are bound to preserve as the
highest hope of a progressive civilization. And even if we could
forget the past, if we could forget Plymouth Rock, if we could
forget the revolution of 1688, if we could forget the scaffold
on which Sidney died, if we could forget the dungeons where
freedom's martyrs have languished, if we could forget the
struggles of our Revolutionary ancestors, if we could forget
the warning of Washington and Franklin, yet the sublime
example of the tens of thousands who in rosy youth or in full

manhood have already in this war laid down their lives should inspire us to sacrifice everything in the cause.

I beg your attention to a most important topic. It is that our troubles are greatly owing to the want of free schools in the South. I would not depreciate the culture of the South. She has had her noble colleges and schools. I recollect visiting as fine schools in Mobile as can be found on the continent. But I am speaking of the laboring country people, who do not enjoy such schools. In order to have a popular government successful the people must be educated. Because the masses were not enlightened the republics of Greece and Rome relapsed into anarchy or tyranny. The same common people who had climbed up to towers and roofs—aye, to chimney tops—to see great Pompey pass the streets of Rome, and who shook the Tiber with their shouts when they saw his chariot but approach, afterward strewed flowers in the way of Cæsar when he came in triumph over Pompey's blood. When the light of antiquity seemed again to dawn on the world in the glory of Venice, Genoa, and Florence, we see it was but a transient flame. Its rays after a while began to glimmer and expire, because the torch of liberty can only be kept trimmed and burning by the eternal vigilance of intelligent people. "Remember that the learning of the few is despotism, the learning of the multitude is liberty, and that intelligent and principled liberty is fame, wisdom, and power." Let me tell you that if you want to preserve popular representative government; if you want this country to live and be great, you must keep the people—the great mass of the people—enlightened. Knowledge elevates and cultivates human nature. It enlarges our ideas, moderates our judgment, quickens our sympathies and affections; and, while it teaches proper dependence, also inspires proper resolution and heroism. Aristotle was employed to instruct Alexander the Great. And long before his day it was an admitted truth that those who rule should be educated. Under popular governments the people are rulers, and they ought therefore to be educated.

Now in my opinion the rebel leaders never could have precipitated the South into such an extensive and outrageous revolution if the laboring white people of the South—the masses—had enjoyed the benefits of free schools. In the little experience I have had since the war commenced I have seen many soldiers in the confederate army who could neither read nor write; and have seen poor white men in the South who harbored the strange delusions that the Constitution of the United States expressly authorizes States to secede! It is a fact that the rebellion derived its start and compulsive force from falsehood. And such gross falsehood as was used never could have exerted so potent an influence among educated and reflecting people. Had the poor white people of the South been in the "elevated temples of the wise, well fortified by tranquil learning," they could have resisted the sway of false leaders. But a bold, blatant knave of some talent can lead a dozen men who are without the moral resources of defence or attack which are afforded by education. The citizen who cannot read can poorly confute the errors of his neighbor. He goes to the ballot-box timid. If unable to fortify his judgment by facts and reasons, he is too easily awed into acts which his conscience condemns. It was thus in a great measure that in some instances political scoundrels, and in other instances able and sincere fanatics, raised such a storm in the South.

Here, then, in this rebellion, we have seen one remarkable instance of the want of success under a popular government for the want of education among the masses. Peru, Mexico, and the Central American States have, also, furnished similar instances. What is it that has deprived the poor white men of the South of the advantages of free schools? Slavery. Slavery has prevented the establishment of free schools. The plantation, or slave system, seems specially antagonistic to free schools. You remember an early colonial Governor of Virginia wrote home to the mother country that he thanked God they had not been cursed with any such evil as free schools in

Virginia.[1] Slavery tends to keep such sentiments alive. We have found slavery a destructive element in popular government; and, principally, because it tends to keep the masses ignorant. I am, therefore, heartily glad to see it expiring. It must and will go under. The war has demonstrated one fact, at any rate, that the blacks prefer liberty to slavery. I have sympathy for the many humane slaveholders who will suffer pecuniary loss; but their loss is nothing in contrast with the sacrifice of life which so many have made for their country. I have heard slaveholders here, who have lost $30,000 in slave property, say, and I have heard the wealthiest planters of Mississippi say, they had no tears to shed over the grave of slavery. They say there is no use of crying for spilled milk. This State is older than Iowa. But slavery has kept you far behind Iowa. You have as opulent resources and as salubrious a climate as a State could wish, and with free labor and free schools your future career may be bright and glorious. I think men who are prudent and sagacious will act on the theory henceforward that free labor and free schools will take the place of slavery in Arkansas.

21.

Henry Ward Beecher, "Universal Suffrage," 1865

With the Civil War drawing to a close, former abolitionists and Radical Republicans joined in pressing the North to reinforce emancipation of the slaves and destruction of the southern aristoc-

---

[1] [The reference is to Governor William Berkeley, who had replied in this fashion to one of many questions put him by the Commissioners of Foreign Plantations in 1671.]

racy by extending suffrage to the freedmen. In doing so they confronted a significant practical question: was it safe to extend the vote to an illiterate people only one step removed from bondage? An earlier generation of reformers would have been sure that it was not, but this sermon preached by Henry Ward Beecher in Plymouth Pulpit in February of 1865 indicates how some enthusiasts resolved the question in favor of the Negroes. In effect, they conceded the necessity of popular education but also insisted upon the prior right of suffrage, and they ended by appealing to an extraordinary vision of democracy as itself an educational institution, which Nathan S. S. Beman had also expressed, to justify the widest possible extension of democratic rights. In this sense the Civil War only reinforced the identification Americans of many persuasions made between democracy and education.

> *"Princes shall come out of Egypt; Ethiopia*
> *shall soon stretch out her hands unto God."*
>
> —Psalm LXIII. 34.

No other people can trace back their history farther than the African; and in the periods before written history, they seem to have been in advance of other nations in civilization. No other people save the Jews ever suffered more dispersion throughout the globe, or a harder fate; and not even the Jews have borne their misfortunes with more endurance and more docility than they. There is a prophecy which, through the long night of ages, has beamed upon this darkness. That prophecy seems on the eve of fulfilment.

As we shall soon be called, as citizens, to determine the nation's policy respecting this people, we ought to seek knowl-

---

From *Universal Suffrage, and Complete Equality in Citizenship, The Safeguards of Democratic Institutions: Shown in Discourses by Henry Ward Beecher, Andrew Johnson, and Wendell Phillips* (Boston, 1865), pp. 5–11.

edge betimes, that we may be prepared to perform as Christians should our civil duties.

It is true that the war is not yet over; but does any one longer doubt the issue? It is true that peace has not yet dawned; but, thanks to our President's integrity and sagacity, we have not been entrapped into a snare, and we are sure that when peace does come, it will stand on foundations of justice. It is true that all slaves are not free, but slavery is wounded unto death, beyond a doubt. With the purgation of the fundamental law of the land, is established liberty for every human being in this nation, save when forfeited by crime. And now the great question on every mind is, what shall be done with the blacks? To this I propose to devote the evening.

I begin by saying, that the difficulty in the case of the Anglo-African is not at all one of principle, or of policy, but almost wholly a practical trouble of working out in detail a very clear policy, and an unmistakable principle. This is a great fact, if it be true.

I may say, further, that the difficulty, such as it is, belongs, not to the blacks, but to the races that surround them. It is not inherent; it is extrinsic. In other words, our troubles are *white* troubles, and not *black* ones. Were this a fierce and turbulent people, like the tribes of Algeria; were they a race as unsusceptible of culture and amelioration as the North American Indians have proved to be, there would be less hopefulness in their case; but the Anglo-Africans are a kind, docile, civilizable stock, they are peculiarly susceptible to culture, and they are remarkably endowed with moral susceptibilities; so that, if ever again we are to have prophets and seers and rapt mystics, we shall find them of their blood.

Now that the multitude of lies are swept away which slavery wove as a blanket to cover its own abomination, we begin to see and to know more of the truth of this most interesting and most abused people.

Our first work is one of removing wrongs and disabilit[i]es. We are to recognize this people as a part of that human family for which Christ died. From the face of that truth will fly away all those guilty and hideous lies which have denied their humanity, and ranked them with beasts. They are *Men.* In that one word we have a solution for ten thousand troubles. We are in an age that believes in human nature. If unoppressed, if free, if incited to education and moral culture, we believe that human nature is competent to all its necessities, and to its destiny. And with the sentence, *They are men,* is cleared up a thousand sophisms and shameful excuses for wrong; and they are to have the benefit at once of those general truths respecting man which have been gradually evolved, and are in our hands as the legacy and history of all past generations. The faith which we have in human nature, and the zeal which the certainty that man, though poor, may be born of the Spirit and educated, enkindles, are for them. We have immeasurable confidence in the common people, if only they are educated, and morally inspired, and left free, under our institutions. No one thinks of doubting the results when white men are brought under the Gospel. To all this comes now the black man. Once admit that he is a *man,* and then whatever you would think of the white man, think of him.

The whole question, then, is narrowed, and is a question, not of this race, but of general human nature. Whatever is true of *men,* is true of *black* men. There may be some specific differences between the blacks and the whites; but there are no more than exist between the various races of white men. It is our duty to have faith and courage for their future. To doubt their well being is to doubt the laws of God's moral government.

If I were to put into one single sentence a prescription for that people, it would be this: *Make them full American citizens.* Take away whatever hinders it, and add whatever is needful to it. Make them citizens, and *they* are safe, and *you* are safe.

To give this more in detail I would say,—

1. Give them land in fee simple, with ample protection in shape of a wise self-protecting economy. For it seems to have been a part of the divine purpose that land should be a means of education, and that the ownership of it should be indispensable to the production of the best forms of manhood.

2. Provide for them all those means of improvement which we so solicitously secure for our white population— schools, churches, books, and papers. We organize societies for our new States. We send home missionaries, school-masters, school-mistresses, and all the apparatus required for education, to our newer communities. We ask for the blacks no more than that: just that, and only that.

3. Open up for them a right to use their own faculties and their own skill in honest competition, in all trades and professions, with all comers, whoever they be; and then let them stand or fall by their own capacity to endure the ordeal. I do not propose to dandle the black man, or shield him in any kind of protection, just because he is black. I simply claim that you should give him the same chance that you give to any-body else. Take him as you take any man, making no distinction one way or the other; and then let him stand where he can place himself, neither putting him higher nor lower by privilege or preferment. Give him no prerogatives nor privileges; put upon him no disabilities nor hindrances. Place him on the broad ground on which we put other men as citizens.

4. Give to the blacks that right which belongs to every born creature—the right to take part in determining the laws, the magistracies, and the public policy under which they and their children are to live.

In short, I demand that the broad and radical democratic doctrine of the natural rights of men shall be applied to all men, without regard to race, or color, or condition. Let me see the Democrat that will face me and deny this doctrine! What is the reason that it should not be applied to every living creature, without regard to condition, race, or color? I demand faith in our own national principles, and courage to trust them in their practical application.

I shall be met, at once, with the honest, but mistaken declaration, that it is not safe to put the vote into the hands of the black man; that the elective franchise is too important to be committed to rude hands.

My reply is, that it has been committed to the hands of black men. They are voters in New York. They are voters in Massachusetts. They are voters in other States. They were voters in Virginia and Tennessee until within comparatively recent periods. And when has there ever been an allegation that they were unfaithful to their trust? that they were less than competent to hold it? There is abundant evidence to prove that they have shown themselves to be both faithful to it, and competent to hold it. It has never been dreamed that they were not.

And if it be said that the case is different when you sweep in vast masses of the uneducated black men of the South, I reply, that there may be special cases in which there will be mischief worked, but that the general result cannot but be true to this great democratic principle of the safety of putting trust in common men.

But I give a more general answer than this—for this is a prudential answer. The citizen's suffrage is not a privilege or a prerogative, but a right. Every man has a right to have a voice in the laws, the magistracies, and the policies that take care of him. That is an inherent right; it is not a privilege conferred. It is a part of liberty. It is a very precious part of citizenship, to which all men are entitled, except they forfeit it by crime; and when you say, "It is not safe to trust the vote in these men's hands," I reply that it is not for you to determine. It is a part of that which is their right; and they come to you, and say, "Why do you withhold from us that which God gave to us?"

On no ground, except that of crime, can you deny the

elective franchise to any class, without admitting the monarchial doctrine, that civil rights and authority descend from the superior classes or rulers, and that they have a right to *confer,* as a privilege, that which the democratic doctrine teaches belongs to all men in common. Our doctrine is, that all rights and prerogatives belong to the whole people, and that they may be delegated by them to superior classes. The European doctrine is, that rights and prerogatives belong to the better classes, and that people may have them only as they are delegated to them by these classes. According to our doctrine, it is safe for rights and prerogatives to rest with the people. According to the European doctrine, it is not safe. In England, education is called free; but it is free only as a charity or a dole is free. There are not in Great Britain what we understand by *common schools;* namely, schools provided by the common people for themselves, as a part of their rights; but the State may open schools without pay, as a mode of giving charity to their poor. Our doctrine is, that civil rights inhere in the people, and that, if they rise to the hands of superior classes, they are powers delegated to them, and that they evermore come back to the people. As the clouds draw their rain from the ocean, and, pouring it down upon the ground, return it to the ocean again, so authority goes from the common people to their rulers, and returns to the common people again. And the doctrine that the superior classes are exclusively fitted for holding powers and prerogatives, is a supreme arrogance. It is a part of the impertinence of aristocracy. When, therefore, any part of our people demand their rights as citizens, and we talk about the unsafety of giving these rights to them, we assume the positions and doctrines of monarchial governments and aristocratic classes.

A little more minutely, I would say, that an ignorant, and poor, and inexpert man has an inherent interest in his own affairs as much as though he were expert, and rich, and educated. The life of every man, no matter how poor or ignorant he may be, is as dear to him as yours is to you. The prosperity of his children is of as much importance to him as the prosperity of your children is to you. The laws which affect his peace, and comfort, and well-being are as much his concern as yours. And he has as much right to be consulted as to what shall be his fate as you have. And in ten thousand matters of common daily life, he is as apt to be right, and as surely right, as if he were a born philosopher.

I claim, again, that in a free republic, though it is manifestly dangerous to multiply ignorant voters, yet, it is far more dangerous to have a large under-class of ignorant and disfranchised men who are neither stimulated, educated, nor ennobled by the exercise of the vote. The best government, the wisest laws, the discreetest institutions, and the ablest administration of them, will not save us from perils. There is danger in every thing; and to have an ignorant class voting is dangerous, whether white or black; but to have an ignorant class, and not have them voting, is a great deal more dangerous. In other words, a great mass at the bottom of society that have none of the motives, none of the restraints, none of the appeals to conscience and to manliness that come with the necessity and duty of voting, are more dangerous in critical periods than they could possibly be if they were made citizens; and the remedy for the unquestionable dangers of having ignorant voters lies in educating them by all the means in our power, and not in excluding them from their rights. The safety of the State consists in the virtue, liberty, and power of its whole citizenship. Civil safety is but another term for civil rights. The old policy has been, and in Europe it still is, to attach the population to the State by as few rights as possible, and chiefly to secure him by inculcating blind submission to law, under a motive mostly of fear. But our American doctrine abhors this view, and teaches that the citizen should be attached to the State by every conceivable just expedient. It is best for the State that every single citizen should be a property-holder; should aid in determining the policy of the State; should assist in selecting its magistrates; should have open to him, and to his children, all the honors and powers which any may justly covet or seek; in short, that he be a *stockholder,* and learn to study the public weal as part of his own.

It is not wise to treat thousands of men as if they had no interest in the State, or only a subordinate one. It is not wise to create a class-feeling by giving to one man political power, and withholding it from another. The voter stands in a class above the non-voter. To say that universal suffrage is dangerous is a platitude or a sophism. Limited voting is dangerous. Voting at *all* is dangerous. Living is dangerous. Every thing is dangerous. It is dangerous to have laws, a State, and magistrates. *Not* to have them is *more* dangerous! We *must* have them and combat and overrule all the dangers! If to give half a million men the vote is perilous, how will it be to have them lying at the bottom of society in a state of savagery, looking on laws as enemies, and government as despotic, and bound to their fellows more by a sense of wrong than by common duties, interests, and ambitions?

Does any one say, "First prepare these people, and *then* give them the vote." But who will prepare them? Will the Government undertake their education? Will you assume the burthen? Will their late masters and poor white neighbors take up the cross, and seek to enlighten the blacks? In this land, a poor man without a vote is like a vagabond king hiding for his life; and a poor man with a vote is honored and courted by all. A hundred voteless black men will be consigned to contempt; but a hundred black men with a vote will be a school, and every candidate play schoolmaster to them, and expound and argue the annual questions of policy. Comprehensively viewed, voting carries with it civil education.

Nothing so much prepares men for intelligent suffrage as the exercise of the right of suffrage. You cannot educate a man for liberty in any way so well as by making him use it. What would you think of teaching a child to walk without allowing him to put his foot to the ground? Would you keep a child ignorant of how to walk till he was old enough to understand the anatomy of the legs, and read that to him, and have him sit in a chair and make the motions of walking with his feet, before trying to walk? The best way of educating a child to walk is to let him walk.

It is with voting as it is with many another art; for voting is an art of which political philosophy is the science. It is being accustomed to tools that gives aptness in their use. It is not the theory of construction that makes men good mechanics: it is practice that gives facility to their hands, and carries with it that second nature on which their skill depends; and that which is true in the mechanic arts is true in the matter of voting. There are nations in Europe that have the right of suffrage accorded to them who know not how to use it: they have a tool in their hands which they do not know what to do with; and what we need to give aptness in the use of the franchise is to accord to men the right of suffrage at an early period,—for it is using it that teaches men how to use it.

It is true, I suppose, that some are not benefited by the exercise of the right of suffrage,—such may be counted as the tare and tret of society; but the great mass of men *are* benefited by the simple use of the vote. When, for instance, in a crowd, where men are genial, there is a shouting for some object which they wish to attain, let some one call out the names of five men, proposing that these men shall be a committee to deliberate upon the subject in which they are all concerned, and report what they shall deem to be the best mode of procedure under the circumstances. Up to this time, these men were, like all the rest of the crowd, noisy, disorderly, undignified; but the moment the responsibility is put upon them of thinking for others, they are sobered. They feel differently, because more interests than simply their own are in their hands. And it is natural. You cannot undertake to think for one man, and still less for a community of men, without being conscious that there is a pressure upon you.

Now, the moment a man becomes a voter, he begins

to feel that there is devolved upon him a duty that reaches beyond himself and his family, to the town where he lives, or, it may be, to the party to which he belongs. He is a thinker and an actor for others; and the moment he begins to think and act for others he is an officer of some sort, raised, dignified, and made conscious of an importance that he had not before. In the science of educating a common people, nothing is more essential than that which makes a man feel that he is personally important. One reason why the family has such a civilizing and elevating influence upon society, is because the father is the head, and has the interests of all the members to look after. And the peculiar tendency of putting the vote into a man's hand is to inspire him with conscious importance. The result at first may be slight; but in the long run it is vast. The appeals that are made to the voter's understanding, from first to last, are a great education. Consider, for instance, the discussion of public topics during the last ten years. How universal, how pervading, how intense it has been! That man must be scarcely distinguishable from the beasts of the field into whose head have not, during the last ten years, penetrated many thoughts, and doctrines, and truths, that pertain to the individual and to society.

Consider how any class of the community becomes redeemed from abuse by the power of the vote. Let a town be filled with five hundred freshly-imported Irishmen, who cannot vote, and who cares for them? How easily men curse them! How, if they interfere with men's plans, and desires, and interests, are they treated as the offscouring of the earth! But let them become citizens, and be allowed to vote, and how polite candidates are to them! How instantly their wishes are consulted! How important it is found to be that they should have their rights! The motive that actuates the candidate may be selfish and insincere; but see the result. The rights of those men become respected; and it is held that Irishmen have rights that candidates are bound to respect!

Protecting the rights of the poor is more important than

protecting the rights of the rich; for the poor, being in the majority, give to the community its character. The condition of the poor is the gauge by which to measure the condition of the community. And the way to educate them, and raise them in the scale of being, is to let them vote. For he that votes, and is free to vote, is wanted by both parties. The community, therefore, become a jury, and all party speakers become advocates pleading a case before them; and they are made to sit in judgment; and their vote is their decision. And this process cannot be carried on from year to year without educating men.

So firm is my belief in this, that I would—perhaps after a little combing and washing—have our immigrants vote at once. It would be dangerous, I know, to have them vote immediately; but it would be more dangerous not to have them vote then. I would have them vote at once, first, because I think we have institutions which will bear the strain of bad voting,—for they would vote badly. It would be strange if they did not. Put me in a cabinet shop, and tell me to make a bureau, and the probabilities are that I shall spoil the lumber and the tools that are given me to work with. Put me into the trench to earn my bread by under-draining, and it is likely, not only that my earnings will amount to little or nothing, but that I shall spoil much work. Now, put an Irishman at practicing the art of self-government before he has had any experience in that art, and it will be strange if he does not spoil some tools and some work; but he is a *learner*. He is not to be compared with an old citizen till he has had an opportunity to make himself proficient in his new calling. This country is a great academy of civil government and human rights, and there come to us thousands and thousands of scholars; and the only way for us to deal with them is, to put them to the work of participating in the administration of public affairs. Their first efforts will be bungling; but our system of government will stand the disadvantages of their want of skill while they are being educated. And very soon they will begin to vote better. You may not see the result,—fresh importations may cover it up; but you may take the lowest of

them and let them vote for five years, and you will see that at
the end of that time they will vote with more thought and vim,
if not with more conscience, than they did in the beginning.
Let them grow; let them begin to amass property; let them feel
the influences of the family, and you will find that they are
ameliorating in the character of their vote as well as in their
social condition. And when they have been here and voted for
twenty-five years, show me one of them, if you can, that does
not vote as well as our own countrymen. I hold that it is better
to put them to school at once, and give them to understand
that it is a political school that this nation is keeping, and that
we can afford to have scholars, though they spoil many writing-
books in learning to write.

It is said that there are great interests of society at stake
which cannot safely be trusted to such hands. I reply that this
is true in some countries, and eminently untrue in our country.
In countries where there are *separate political classes,* where
the interests of these classes are not reciprocal, but antagonistic,—in countries, for instance, where there is a monarchy, an
aristocracy, a rich middle class, or plutocracy, and a laboring
class, and they are sharply demarked, having their own special
prerogatives and rights,—I can understand that in such countries it is dangerous to have the vote go below a certain point.
I can understand why, in England, they do not believe in universal suffrage.

But how is it in this country? We have a government
that has been formed, in its laws and institutions and policy, by
poor men for poor men; by exiles for the sake of those that
everywhere should be in exile; by the common people for the
common people. And I hold that in a country where there are
no authorized classes, and where all laws and economies have
been made by the great mass for the benefit of the great mass,
they are not going to be disturbed by those who compose that
great mass. And it is safe to submit our laws and institutions to
the vote of the common people, clear down to the bottom. I
will risk it. I do not fear it. I have faith, if not in the conscience,

yet in the free instincts, of the common people. If there ever was a trial, a test, of a nation's stability, that has been one through which we have been passing during the last five or six years. What is the result? Is the faith of the world shaken in the safety of allowing the common people to take care of their own affairs? Is it not, on the contrary, vindicated beyond all peradventure?

I advocate, then, the giving to all men, black and white, the right of suffrage, first, because it belongs to them; second, because it is safe and beneficial; and, third, because only in this way can we have peace. We cannot have peace in any other way, because no question is ever settled that is not settled right. It is easily disturbed. If justice is refused, you may be sure that you will have agitation. You cannot hush up a principle. And as to compromising, often it is wise and expedient to compromise where *things* are concerned; but never is it wise or expedient to do it where *principles* are concerned. If you do it, you only rake up the fire, that it may break out again to-morrow. And the only way to settle a question of this character is to ask, What are the principles on which we should build? When you have settled a question thus, you have settled it right, and you are done with it. *Of the questions which came up for settlement by our fathers, those in which they touched principles were settled forever, and they never gibber or fit; but those questions where, instead of touching principles, they only touched the quicksand of expediency, have been all our lives agitating and tormenting us.* And if there was ever a people that ought to have learned that to touch the ground of principle is safe, and that to come short of that is unsafe, we are that people. So let us not commit another mistake.

I, then, advocate suffrage for the black people, because I believe they have given evidence that they will make a good use of it. They are intelligent enough to do it.

I advocate it, too, because they have earned and deserved this boon, even if it were not their right. I allude to their singularly good conduct in the trying situations of the last five years; to the wonderful sagacity which has marked them during all that time; and to their invariable love and tender care shown to our soldiers. I do not believe there is a soldier that, escaping from Southern captivity, has been ministered to, night and day, by the blacks, has had his wounds dressed by them, and has in no case been betrayed by them; I do not believe your son, who escaped through the fidelity of these people; I do not believe any soldier who, in the midst of suffering and peril, has been succored and relieved by them, would, if the question were to come up as to whether the negro should be permitted to vote, or be denied the right of voting, go for denying that right.

Then, for their heroic military services, I think the blacks have deserved the right of suffrage. And here let me tell you what was Gen. Grant's testimony about colored soldiers. Said Gen. Grant, "For picket duty, for guard duty, for the march, and for assault, the colored soldiers are surpassed by none in the world, and equalled by few." "Well, then, General," it was asked, "what do they lack? They seem to have every qualification that a soldier requires." Gen. Grant replied, "They may not have the power to endure continuous fighting like that of the forty-five days' struggle from the Wilderness to the James. This has not yet been proved; but it may turn out that they possess this element also."

They are more faithful than white soldiers in guard duty. The bread of the army under the bayonet of the black man is safer than under the bayonet of the white man. And it is not long to be disguised or disputed that these men make as good soldiers as soldiers need be. And when, coming from the plantation, without having had the advantages of education, they are able to maintain themselves by the side of white men that have been brought up in the common schools, how much do they deserve of praise! Let Gen. Sherman be heard: "Though I think the white race a superior one, and that it ought to rule this continent for itself, yet if you admit the negro to this struggle for any purpose, he has a right to stay in for all, and when the fight is over, the hand that drops the musket cannot be denied the ballot."

Moreover, they deserve the right of suffrage by reason of their unswerving fidelity to the Union; and on this ground I demand that they should be recognized as citizens. Talk of their unfitness to hold the destiny of the nation, when, in fifteen States, while the white population have proved recreant to the Government, they have remained constant in their adherence to it! While fifteen millions of white men betrayed their trust, and brought eternal infamy upon their history, these four million blacks, though subjected to severe trial, both of life and limb, were faithful to law, to Union, to the Constitution, to liberty, to the old flag, and all that that flag symbolizes; and in the name of fidelity, I demand that they who have done so much for this nation shall not be denied the right of citizenship in it.

I demand it on one ground more: I demand it for the sake of the white Union men in the South. For, ere long, when again the rebellious States are, by the flash of the sword, wheeled into line; when again things resume their old way, the white men that have been faithful to the Union in those States will be in a sad condition. When local affairs again pass into the hands of the citizens there, those men, who are but a handful, if left by themselves, will be ground as between an upper and lower millstone. But if the slaves are allowed to vote, they and the white Union men will be more than a match for their adversaries. And I demand that you shall not sacrifice the minority of white men in the South, by withholding the vote from these their natural allies, that, if allowed to exercise the rights of citizenship, will always go with them.

I know it is said, "This will make the black man equal to the white." Well, if God made him equal to the white, you cannot help yourselves. If God did not make him equal to the white, then I do not. Whatever God made him capable of becoming, let him become. That is all I ask. I do not express any opinion as to whether he is or is not equal to the white. I am willing to take my chance with him. Are you willing to do the same, or, are you afraid he will outrun you in a fair race?

It is said, too, "If he may vote, then he may be voted for, and may hold office." Why not, if anybody wants to vote for him, and wants to put him in office? Do you suppose that this is the particular danger? Do you suppose that, the moment black men are allowed to vote and to be voted for, every body will insist on having them made officers? One would think, to hear men talk, that, if the way was opened for it, the whole community would rise up and fill every public station with a colored man! Why, do not you know that such is the cloud of prejudice against the negro, that such a thing as the election to office of a colored man would be next to impossible? If it ever did take place, it would be the highest conceivable testimony of the man's fitness for the position to which he was raised. What impertinent objections are these!

But, it is said, "If you take such steps as these, and give citizenship to the blacks, then all distinction will be abolished, and miscegenation will be the result." It seems to me that the whites are an excellent stock in their way and kind, and that the blacks are an excellent stock in their way and kind; and I am not myself in favor of mingling them. There are a great many that for years have insisted upon doing it. All that I have to say is, if it *must* be done, let it be done lawfully, by marriage, and not by adultery. That is all I insist upon. If any man *will* have a black woman for a companion, there ought not to be any law to prevent him, but he should *marry* her. I do not undertake to say that the mingling of these races will deteriorate one or the other. I leave that as a question for physiologists, who, I think, have not facts enough to settle it. The South have had the imprudence to taunt us with that as a doctrine which we abhor in them, and which they not only hold as a doctrine, but put into practice. This is an objection the most unwarranted and unwarrantable.

I am in favor of two laws: first, that, if a man does not wish to marry a black woman, nothing shall compel him to;

and, second, that, if a man wants to marry a black woman, nothing shall hinder him! It seems to me that under such laws this question will be perfectly safe.

I know not that it is necessary for me to go further into objections that are frivolous in the light of the great doctrines of the American people.

I stand, to-night, to plead for the rights of men; and I plead for them all the more willingly because they are the rights of men that are unable to plead for their own rights. They are emerging from bondage. I thank God, as for the best gift of my life, that I have lived to see the day when the chain is broken, and the shackle has fallen, and the African has gone free. Now, if my life has been spared to see that despised creature of the plantation inducted into the fullness of his right as a citizen, religiously taught, and made industrious by the ownership of land, and by the application of those motives that make us industrious; if I have lived to see that nation born in a day, I can say, with Simeon, "Now, Lord, let thy servant depart in peace; for mine eyes have seen thy salvation."

And all this, not because it is a negro, but because it is a *man*. It is not because of his color, but simply because of that which is in him in common with you and me. It is because he came from God, and goes to God again. It is because he was remembered in Gethsemane, and his sins were washed away upon Calvary. I accept him as my brother, because Christ is his Redeemer and mine, and God is his Father and mine; he is my blood kindred. And I assert for him, in the name of Christianity, in the name of liberty, and in the name of civilization, the rights that God gave him, that men have taken away from him, and that it is your privilege to restore to him.

22.

Debate in the Constitutional Convention of South Carolina, 1868

During Reconstruction, Radical Republicans sought to establish democracy in the South by calling state constitutional conventions in which reformers would be able to write into fundamental law the political and social principles that had been institutionalized by northern constitutional conventions during the 1840s and 1850s. The South Carolina convention of 1868 is the most interesting of these bodies because it was controlled by its Negro members, whose deliberations read in most cases like an epitome of all the deliberations that had preceded them. One major innovation lay in the fact that the delegates identified familiar political ends with Republicanism rather than Democracy. Another lay in their concern for the status and prospects of their race, a concern which was nowhere more apparent than in their discussions of public education, to which they turned to achieve all the values that liberal democrats had previously expected of it. "Republicanism has given us freedom, equal rights, and equal laws," John A. Chesnut declared during debate over the principle of compulsory education. "Republicanism must also give us education and wisdom."

At the same time, compulsion gave even advocates of education pause. By 1868 the northern industrial states had begun to move toward requiring children of a certain age to attend school for a given number of months each year, but their measures were frequently tinged with nativism and they raised considerable opposition not only from libertarian democrats but also from the working-class families they were intended to reach. In South Carolina, compulsion could be expected to arouse much the same antagonism from the whites if not the blacks, and in addition it involved the threat if not the fact of forcible integration of the races. As the extended extract printed here indicates, the debates do not make clear to what extent the delegates who advocated compulsory education visualized it as an instrument of integration, but it is plain that they would not permit opposition to racial mingling to stand in the way of universal literacy. Significantly, when the convention decided that all schools and colleges supported even in part by public funds must be open to applicants of any race, only four of its members voted in the negative.

Among the advocates of compulsory education, Henry E. Hayne, Alonzo J. Ransier, Francis L. Cardozo, John A. Chesnut, and (apparently) William E. Johnston were southern Negroes. Benjamin Franklin Randolph and Robert B. Elliott were northern Negroes, while Reuben G. Holmes, Justus K. Jillson, and Benjamin Franklin Whittemore were northern whites. Among the opponents, Robert C. DeLarge and Richard H. Cain were southern Negroes; Jonathan J. Wright was a northern black; Charles P. Leslie was a northern white; and B. O. Duncan was a southern white. Among the blacks, Hayne, Ransier, Cardozo, Cain, Elliott, and Wright subsequently served in state-wide or national office, as did Jillson among the whites. DeLarge and Whittemore were elected to the United States House of Representatives but were denied their seats on the grounds (respectively) of election frauds and of the sale of appointments to the Military Academy.

Forty-first Day.

TUESDAY, March 3, 1868.

. . . Mr. H. E. HAYNE called for the next Special Order, which was the report of the Committee on Education.

From *Proceedings of the Constitutional Convention of South Carolina, Held at Charleston, S. C., beginning January 14th and ending March 17th, 1868. Including the Debates and Proceedings.* Reported by J. Woodruff, Phonographic Reporter (2 volumes in one; Charleston, S. C., 1868), II, 685–709. Reprinted by Arno Press and the *New York Times* (New York, 1968).

The report was taken up, and the consideration of the fourth section was resumed, the question being on striking out the word "compulsory."

Mr. B. F. RANDOLPH moved to strike out the words "twenty-four" and insert "thirty."[1]

Mr. H. E. HAYNE. I hope the word "compulsory" will not be stricken out. There is every reason why we should have compulsory attendance at school. When we look around and observe the vice and ignorance with which we have to contend, it becomes apparent that force should be exercised to make parents send their children to school. It is contended by some that compulsory attendance will work badly. But the system has worked well in Germany and Massachusetts, and there is no reason why it should not work as well here. I have never yet seen a German without a good education. I hope the section will pass as reported by the Committee.

Mr. B. BYAS. I hope the word "compulsory" will be stricken out. If a father or mother have not interest enough in their children to provide for their education, let the consequences be on their own heads. When such parents are in their graves, their children will rise up and damn them. Let us have a Republican form of government. A man should not be compelled to educate his children, any more than he should be forced to direct them to heaven or hell. Man is a free, moral agent, and he should be left where God put him.

Mr. J. K. JILLSON moved to adjourn, but the motion was not agreed to.

Mr. R. C. DeLARGE. One of the speakers from Marion (Mr. HAYNE) has alluded to the education of the German people, as well as to the practice of the people of Massachusetts. In the language of my friend from Beaufort, yesterday, if Massachusetts chooses to do wrong, it is no reason why South Carolina should follow the example. I claim to be in favor of

---

[1] [The proposed section called for the attendance at some school of every child between six and sixteen for a minimum of twenty-four months.]

Republican institutions, and I desire to see the liberties of the people perpetuated—not restricted, or subject to such encroachments as that which is involved in this remarkable section. . . .

Although laboring under great inconvenience, I shall attempt to defend the amendment proposing to strike out the word "compulsory." In the first place, we have a report which is to become a portion of the Constitution, and that Constitution emphatically declares, in terms that cannot be misunderstood, that "no distinction shall be made on account of race, color, or previous condition." It has been remarked this morning that in the Constitution of Massachusetts, and other Northern States, the same proviso exists. But any one who reflects for a moment upon the condition of the people of Massachusetts, and those of South Carolina, will fully appreciate the great difference between them. As already stated, I object to the word "compulsory," because it is contrary to the spirit and principles of republicanism. Where is the necessity for placing in the Constitution a proviso that can never be enforced. It is just as impossible to put such a section in practical operation, as it would be for a man to fly to the moon. No one will deny that an attempt to enforce it would entail the greatest trouble and expense. Who, I ask, do we propose to set up as a censor of learning? Perhaps the opponents of the measure will say the School Commissioner. I deny that he can do it. He may be the father of half a dozen children. I, too, am the father of children; but will any body tell me that, as a free citizen of South Carolina, I have not the right to choose whether I shall send those children to school or not. Will any one say I shall not teach my child myself? It may be said, such a right is not denied me. Whether it be so or not, I plant myself upon the broad principle of the equality of all men as the basis of true republicanism; and to compel any man to do what this section provides is contrary to this principle.

Again, this clause will lead to difficulties of a serious

character, to which neither you nor myself can blind our eyes. In Massachusetts there is a population cradled in the arms of freedom and liberty, free of all prejudice and devoid of passion, to a great extent. In South Carolina we have an entirely different set of people. We are about to inaugurate great changes, which it is our desire shall be successful.

Mr. C. P. LESLIE. Do I understand you to say that the people of Massachusetts have no prejudices of race?

Mr. F. L. CARDOZO. I would also like to ask the gentleman where he gets his authority for saying that the people of Massachusetts are cradled in the principles of freedom and liberty. Is it so provided in the Constitution of Massachusetts?

Mr. R. C. DeLARGE. I am not well acquainted with all the clauses in the Constitution of Massachusetts, and speak only from my historic knowledge of that people. This section proposes to open these schools to all persons, irrespective of color, to open every seminary of learning to all. Heartily do I endorse the object, but the manner in which it is to be enforced meets my most earnest disapproval. I do not propose to enact in this report a section that may be used by our enemies to appeal to the worst passions of a class of people in this State. The schools may be opened to all, under proper provisions in the Constitution, but to declare that parents "shall" send their children to them whether they are willing or not is, in my judgment, going a step beyond the bounds of prudence. Is there any logic or reason in inserting in the Constitution a provision which cannot be enforced? What do we intend to give the Legislature power to do? In one breath you propose to protect minor children, and in the next to punish their parents by fine and imprisonment if they do not send their children to school. For these reasons I am opposed to the section, and urge that the word "compulsory" shall be stricken out.

Mr. A. J. RANSIER. I am sorry to differ with my colleague from Charleston on this question. I contend that in proportion to the education of the people so is their progress in civilization. Believing this, I believe that the Committee have properly provided for the compulsory education of all the children in this State between the ages named in the section.

I recognize the importance of this measure. There is a seeming objection to the word "compulsory," but I do not think it of grave importance. My friend does not like it, because he says it is contrary to the spirit of republicanism. To be free, however, is not to enjoy unlimited license, or my friend himself might desire to enslave again his fellow men.

Now I propose to support this section fully, and believe that the more it is considered in all its bearings upon the welfare of our people, the greater will be the desire that every parent shall, by some means, be compelled to educate his children and fit them for the responsibilities of life. As to the particular mode of enforcing attendance at school, we leave that an open question. At present we are only asserting the general principle, and the Legislature will provide for its application.

Upon the success of republicanism depends the progress which our people are destined to make. If parents are disposed to clog this progress by neglecting the education of their children, for one, I will not aid and abet them. Hence, this, in my opinion, is an exceedingly wise provision, and I am content to trust to the Legislature to carry out the measures to which it necessarily leads.

Vice and degradation go hand in hand with ignorance. Civilization and enlightenment follow fast upon the footsteps of the schoolmaster; and if education must be enforced to secure these grand results, I say let the compulsory process go on.

Mr. R. C. DeLarge. Can the gentleman demonstrate how the Legislature is to enforce the education of children without punishment of their parents by fine or imprisonment.

Mr. A. J. Ransier. When that question arises in the Legislature, I hope we shall have the benefit of my friend's counsel, and he himself may possibly answer that question. If there is any one thing to which we may attribute the sufferings endured by this people, it is the gross ignorance of the masses. While we propose to avoid all difficulties which may be fraught with evil to the community, we shall, nevertheless, insist upon our right to provide for the exercise of the great moral agencies which education always brings to bear upon public opinion. Had there been such a provision as this in the Constitution of South Carolina heretofore, there is no doubt that many of the evils which at present exist would have been avoided, and the people would have been advanced to a higher stage of civilization and morals, and we would not have been called upon to mourn the loss of the flower of the youth of our country. In conclusion, I favor this section as it stands. I do not think it will militate against the cause of republicanism, but, on the contrary, be of benefit both to it and to the people whom we represent. Feeling that everything depends on the education of the rising generation, I shall give this measure my vote, and use all my exertions to secure its adoption into this Constitution.

Mr. B. F. RANDOLPH. In favoring, as I do, compulsory attendance at school, I cannot for the life of me see in what manner republicanism is at stake. It seems to have been the fashion on this floor to question a man's republicanism because he chooses to differ with others on general principles. Now this is a question which does not concern republicanism at all. It is simply a matter of justice which is due to a people, and it might be just as consistently urged that it is contrary to republican principles to organize the militia, to force every man to enroll his name, and to arm and equip them, as to urge that this provision is anti-republican because it compels parents to see to the education of their children.

Mr. B. O. DUNCAN. Does the gentleman propose to educate children at the point of the bayonet, through the militia?

Mr. B. F. RANDOLPH. If necessary we may call out the militia to enforce the law. Now, the gentlemen on the other side have given no reasons why the word "compulsory" should be stricken out.

Mr. R. C. DELARGE. Can you name any State where the provision exists in its Constitution?

Mr. B. F. RANDOLPH. It exists in Massachusetts.

Mr. R. C. DeLarge. That is not so.[2]

Mr. F. L. CARDOZO. This system has been tested in Germany, and I defy the gentleman from Charleston to deny the fact. It has also been tested in several States of the Union, and I defy the gentleman to show that it has not been a success. It becomes the duty of the opposition if they want this section stricken from the report, to show that where it has been applied it has failed to produce the result desired.

Mr. J. J. WRIGHT. Will you inform us what State in the Union compels parents to send their children to school?

Mr. B. F. RANDOLPH. The State of New Hampshire is one. It may be asked what is the object of law? It is not only for the purpose of restraining men from doing wrong, but for the protection of all the citizens of a State, and the promotion of the general welfare. Blackstone lays it down as one of the objects, the furthering, as far as it can consistently be done, of the general welfare of the people.[3] It is one of the objects of law, as far as practicable, not to restrain wrong by punishing man for violating the right, but also one of its grand objects to build up civilization, and this is the grand object of this provision in the report of the Committee on Education. It proposes to further civilization, and I look upon it as one of the most important results which will follow the defeat of the rebel armies, the establishment among the people who have long been deprived of the privilege of education, a law which will compel parents to send their children to school.

Mr. R. B. ELLIOTT. Is it not regulated by general statutes

----

2 [In 1852 the Massachusetts legislature required school attendance for twelve weeks in the year of all children between the ages of eight and fourteen. Subsequent legislation barred children under ten from working in factories and enforced the educational requirement for those over ten.]

3 [The reference is to Sir William Blackstone's *Commentaries on the Laws of England,* first published during the 1760s, which served as the basic legal text for American lawyers as late as the 1880s.]

in the State of Massachusetts, that parents shall be compelled to send their children to school?

Mr. B. F. RANDOLPH. We propose to do that here. I consider this one of the most important measures which has yet come before this body. I think I can read it in the eyes of the members of this Convention to favor this measure. I feel that every one here believes it to be his duty to the people he represents. I believe every one here is zealous in doing all he can to further civilization, in building up educational institutions in the State, and doing all that is calculated to diffuse intelligence among the people generally. I had the honor of being principal of a free school two years; and, in the midst of one of the most intelligent system[s] of schools, the most trying thing which teachers had to contend with was the want of regular attendance on the part of the children. The most intelligent parents would sometimes neglect to send their children to school. The teachers had to adopt rules closing their doors to those who were irregular in their attendance. This law will assist the teachers and assist our school system. It will prove beneficial to the State not only for the reasons I have given, but for various other reasons. I hope you will all vote for it. I shall vote for it with all my heart, because I believe it to be something beneficial to the welfare of the people of the State.

Mr. A. C. RICHMOND. I desire to say but a few words on this subject. I shall speak principally in reference to our common schools and public funds. We expect to have a public school fund, although it may not be very large. We expect our parishes to be divided into school districts of convenient size. We can erect only a limited number of school houses each year, and it may be five or ten years before school houses are erected in all the districts, and the fund becomes large enough to assist in the education of all the people. If the word "compulsory" remains, it will be impossible to enforce the law for sometime to come. We say the public schools shall be opened to all. Every school district will have its school houses and its teachers. There is to be a particular school fund, school districts, and school houses. It is supposed by legislators and others that it is an excellent thing to have the children to go to school. It opens up a vast field for discussion, and affords a beautiful opportunity for making buncombe speeches. It is admitted by all legislators in every State of the Union, that cheap education is the best defence of the State. There must be schools to which colored children can go; but we wish to look into the propriety of compelling parents to send their children to school. I believe the efforts of the teachers, preachers, and all those interested in the welfare of the State, and the efforts of all those interested in the welfare of the colored people, will bring out nearly all the colored children. I believe nearly all the colored children of the State will go to school. We have societies that will help to furnish the books; we have preachers who are much interested; we have missionaries, all of whom are interested in this class of our people, and who will see to it that the colored children are educated, so that settles that point. The next point is, how are the white children going to school? By means of moral suasion nearly all the colored children will be brought to school; and by means of white schools, nearly all the white children will go to school and be educated. It will regulate itself. The word "compulsory" is used to compel the attendance of children in one or the other class of schools.

Mr. R. C. DeLarge. What does the tenth section of that report say?

Mr. A. C. Richmond. I believe it is the meaning, that if families of white people are not able to send their children to private schools, they shall be obliged to send their children to the public schools, in which all white and colored shall be educated.

Mr. F. L. Cardozo. We only compel parents to send their children to some school, not that they shall send them with the colored children; we simply give those colored children who desire to go to white schools, the privilege to do so.

Mr. A. C. Richmond. By means of moral suasion, I believe nearly all the colored people, as well as a large number of the children of white parents will go to school; such schools as their parents may select. If parents are too proud to take advantage of the means of education afforded, why then I say let their children grow up in ignorance.

Mr. J. A. CHESTNUT [*sic*]. So far as I have been able to see and judge, this report of the Committee is a sensible one, and ought to be adopted as it stands. How it can affect the rights of the people, or interfere with the spirit of republicanism, I am at a loss to discover. On the contrary, from all the experience I have had among the people, I unhesitatingly declare that no measure adopted by this Convention will be more in consonance with their wishes than this, or more productive of material blessings to all classes. Sir, you cannot by any persuasive and reasonable means establish civilization among an ignorant and degraded community, such as we have in our country. Force is necessary, and, for one, I say let force be used. Republicanism has given us freedom, equal rights, and equal laws. Republicanism must also give us education and wisdom.

It seems that the great difficulty in this section is in the fact that difficulty may arise between the two races in the same school, or that the whites will not send their children to the same schools with the colored children. What of that? Has not this Convention a right to establish a free school system for the benefit of the poorer classes? Undoubtedly. Then if there be a hostile disposition among the whites, an unwillingness to send their children to school, the fault is their own, not ours. Look at the idle youths around us. Is the sight not enough to invigorate every man with a desire to do something to remove this vast weight of ignorance that presses the masses down? I have no desire to curtail the privileges of freemen, but when we look at the opportunities neglected, even by the whites of South Carolina, I must confess that I am more than ever disposed to compel parents, especially of my own race, to send their children to school. If the whites object to it, let it be so. The consequences will rest with themselves.

I hope, therefore, that the motion to strike out the word "compulsory" will be laid upon the table.

Mr. R. H. CAIN. It seems to me that we are spending a

great deal of unnecessary time in the discussion of this subject. It is true, the question is one of great interest, and there are few who are not anxious that provisions shall be made by this Convention for the education of all classes in the State. But I am confident that it will not be necessary to use compulsion to effect this object. Hence, I am opposed to the insertion of the obnoxious word. I see no necessity for it. You cannot compel parents to send their children to school; and if you could, it would be unwise, impolitic, and injudicious. Massachusetts is fifty years ahead of South Carolina, and, under the circumstances which exist in that State, I might, if a resident, insist upon a compulsory education; but in South Carolina the case is different. There is a class of persons here whose situation, interests and necessities are varied, and controlled by surroundings which do not exist at the North. And justice is demanded for them. To do justice in this matter of education, compulsion is not required. I am willing to trust the people. They have good sense, and experience itself will be better than all the force you can employ to instill the idea of duty to their children.

Now, as a compromise with the other side, I propose the following amendment, namely that "the General Assembly may require the attendance at either public or private schools," &c.

This is a question that should be left to the Legislature. If the circumstances demand it, compulsion may be used to secure the attendance of pupils; but I do not believe such a contingency ever will occur.

As to the idea that both classes of children will be compelled to go to school together, I do not think it is comprehended in the subject at all. I remember that in my younger days I stumped the State of Iowa for the purpose of having stricken from the Constitution a clause which created distinction of color in the public schools. This was prior to the assembling of the Constitutional Convention. All we claimed was that they should make provision for the education of all the youth. We succeeded, and such a clause was engrafted in the Constitution, and that instrument was ratified by a majority of ten thousand. We said nothing about color. We simply said "youth."

I say to you, therefore, leave this question open. Leave it to the Legislature. I have great faith in humanity. We are in a stage of progress, such as our country never has seen, and while the wheels are rolling on, depend upon it, there are few persons in this country who will not seek to enjoy it by sending their children to school. White or black, all will desire to have their children educated. Let us then make this platform broad enough for all to stand upon without prejudice or objection. The matter will regulate itself, and to the Legislature may safely be confided the task of providing for any emergency which may arise.

Mr. R. G. HOLMES. If there is anything we want in this State, it is some measure to compel the attendance of children between the ages of six and sixteen at some school. If it is left to parents, I believe the great majority will lock up their children at home. I hope, therefore, we shall have a law compelling the attendance of all children at school. It is the statute law in Massachusetts, and I hope we will have the provision inserted in our Constitution. The idea that it is not republican to educate children is supremely ridiculous. Republicanism, as has been well said, is not license. No man has the right, as a republican, to put his hand in my pocket, or steal money from it, because he wishes to do it. I can conceive of a way in which my child may be robbed by that system of republicanism which some members have undertaken to defend. My child may be left an orphan, poor and dependent on the kindness of neighbors or friends. They may think it to the best interest of that child to bind it out as an apprentice to some person. My child may be robbed of an education, because the person to whom it was bound does not think it advisable to send that child to school, as there may happen to be some objectionable children in the school. I have seen white children sitting by the side of colored children in school, and observed that there could not have been better friends. I do not want this privilege of attending schools confined to any exclusive class. We want no laws made here to prevent children from attending school. If any one chooses to educate their children in a private school, this law does not debar them that privilege.

But there are some who oppose all education. I remember the case of an individual who refused to have his children educated because, as he said, he himself had got along well enough without it, and he guessed his children could do the same. There is too much of that spirit in our State, and we want to contrive something to counteract it. In the case to which I have alluded, that individual some fifteen years afterwards, when his children had grown up, regretted his action, and was very much mortified because his children had no education. I hope we will engraft something into the Constitution, making it obligatory upon parents to send their children to school, and with that view, I hope the section will pass as it is.

Mr. R. B. ELLIOTT. I do not rise to make a speech, but simply and briefly to express the hope that the section as reported by the Committee on Education will be adopted. Some gentleman [*sic*] have said it is anti-republican. I deny it. It is in conformity with the ideas of republicanism to punish crime. It is republicanism to reward virtue. It is republicanism to educate the people, without discrimination. That has made New England great, and made her citizens, poor as well as rich, low as well as high, black as well as white, educated and intelligent. The gentleman from Berkley (Mr. Richmond) has said this law is to force the white and colored children into the public schools together. The only question is whether children shall become educated and enlightened, or remain in ignorance. The question is not white or black united or divided, but whether children shall be sent to school or kept at home. If they are compelled to be educated, there will be no danger of the Union, or a second secession of South Carolina from the Union. The masses will be intelligent, and will become the great strength and bulwark of republicanism. If they remain uneducated, they will inevitably remain ignorant, and it is a well known fact, that ignorance is the parent of vice and crime, and was the sustainer of the late gigantic slaveholder's rebellion. If the children remain at home, instead of a harbor of peace and prosperity, we will have a stone blockade.

I have been astonished at many of the grounds taken by many of the gentlemen who have spoken upon this subject. Some have gone into discussion, not on the merits of the fourth section, but either of the eleventh section or some other clause.[4] Many have left that report altogether, and have entered into a statement of what they had the privilege of undergoing already, and what they would like to have the privilege of undergoing in the future. I think if this question was fairly discussed, there would be found but few gentlemen on this floor who was opposed to the report of the Committee. It is not a question of color, but simply as to whether white or black shall keep their children at home uneducated, bringing them up in ignorance, useless to society, or be compelled to send them to school, where they can be made intelligent and useful in the community where they reside. This is the only question to be answered. I appeal to gentlemen of the Convention to know whether they desire to see a state of anarchy, or a state of confusion in South Carolina in the future. I desire to know whether they wish to see an independent people, engaged in industrious pursuits, living happy and contented. The child that remains in ignorance until grown up will never learn the first duty that ought to be learned by every man, which is to love his country and to love his State. If a man is so ignorant as to know nothing of political economy of his State or country, he can never be a good citizen. To be a good citizen every one should know what are the duties of a citizen, and the laws of the State and country in which he resides. He must be able to tell what is a violation of law. We blame a man if he violates the law, though he

---

[4] [The fourth section was under consideration. The eleventh section required publicly assisted schools and colleges to be "open to all the children and youths of the State, without regard to race or color."]

is ignorant. It will not be denied that it is republicanism to punish a man if he commits a crime. If you give a man the privilege of remaining in ignorance, it is anti-republicanism to punish him. You must compel them to learn. Do that and you will have peace in the future. If you neglect to do this, you must expect confusion, vice, and everything of the sort. I hope the section will pass as reported by the Committee.

Mr. J. K. JILLSON. Hitherto I have refrained from entering into the arena of debate, but this subject before us, and the principles involved, are of such vast importance, that I must claim the indulgence of the Convention while I offer a few remarks in regard to the matter. The report received the most careful attention from the Committee, and section four more than any other. We discussed it in all its various points before bringing it before the Convention. The subject of education is one that should command the attention and interest of all nations, all people, and every individual; but in a country or nation where the republican form of government prevails, where the government is of the people, and in, through, and by the people, it is of the most vital importance that the interest of education be cherished and enlarged as second to no other interest. A celebrated modern writer makes the following statement: "It is the clearest duty, prescribed by nature herself, under silent but real and awful penalties, of governing persons in every society, to see that the people, so far as possible, are taught; that wherever a citizen is born, some chance be offered him of becoming a man. This is for ever the duty of governors and persons in authority in human societies," and if we carefully examine the history and status of nations, that the above statement is verified by incontrovertible evidence, and by facts that cannot be gainsayed; for those nations in which the most liberal, careful, and efficient provisions for the education of the people at large are made, stand foremost in the ranks of civilization, progress, humanity, national greatness and glory, and Christianity. But, to come more directly to the question now before us, in my humble opinion, the only rational objection that can be urged against the principles involved in this section, is that they militate against the great and comprehensive principles of republicanism, that they are indicative of an abridgement of, an infringement upon, and a subversion of the rights and liberties of the people, that they assume to dictate as to what a certain class *must* and *shall* do. Mr. President, I am willing to accept, the widest, highest, and most expansive definition of freedom, but I am not disposed to accept the term as synonymous with unbridled license. Sir, while I hold that it is the sacred, solemn, and imperative duty of the State to vouchsafe to all its citizens all their rights, and all their privileges, I also maintain that it is just as much its bounden duty to check and restrain the abuse of those rights and privileges, that the government has the prerogative to assume to act as the regulator, and monitor, as well as the faithful defender and preserver of liberty. No one will deny that individual rights should and ought to be subservient to the great interests of the common weal and prosperity. "No one has a right to do as he pleases, unless he pleases to do right."

In Switzerland, that stronghold of liberty, whose snow clad Alpine crags ring with the bugle notes of freedom, the birth-place of the patriot Tell, a country whose people are noted for their intelligence, morality, patriotism, and piety, the law compels parents to send their children to school six months in each year. In Massachusetts, a State second to none in the Union in regard to the general intelligence, industry, liberality, morality, patriotism, piety, and public enterprise of its people, the pioneer State in the cause of education, there is a law which says parents *must* send their children between certain ages, to either public or private schools, three months in each year; and if the parents are not able to provide the children with the necessary school books, they are furnished by the School Committees. In Massachusetts, only one person in about every three hundred and fifty, is unable to read and write, and I venture the assertion without fear of contradiction, that there is not a single adult person of native parentage, born and raised in the

State, and having ordinary mental capacity, who cannot read, write, and cipher. In South Carolina, where there has never been any system of free public schools, there is one person in every eight who cannot read and write. Here is what a celebrated advocate says of compulsory education in Prussia:

> In the Kingdom of Prussia, every child is compelled to attend some school, whether his parents will or not. The annual report has these words: "There is not a single human being in Prussia who does not receive education, intellectual and moral, sufficient for all the needs of common life." This law of compulsion has been in operation but fourteen years, when pauperism and crime had diminished thirty-eight per cent.
>
> In the present relationships of our mixed population in the United States, this law of compulsion is called for as a defence of our liberties. We have in our country more than a million of children between the ages of five and sixteen who can neither read nor write! Do you ask what we are going to do with them? That is not the question. The question is, what are *they* going to do with *us?* Think of their future power at the ballot-box! We can disarm their animal ferocity and traditional prejudices only by intellectual culture and moral principle; and this preventive process can be effectually applied, in nineteen cases out of twenty, *only* during the period of youth. Society has a right to defend itself against crime, against murder, arson, etc. Has it not an equal and prior right to defend itself against the *cause* of crime, which is ignorance? If you force a young man into prison because he is a thief, we call upon you to force him, while a boy, into a schoolhouse, to prevent his becoming a thief. Here surely "an ounce of prevention is worth a pound of cure."
>
> At this period, when four millions of freedmen are to carry their votes to the ballot-box to help shape the destinies of the republic, what language can overstate the pressing necessity of their being educated to comprehend their new position, exercise their new rights, and obey their new laws? It is the command

of Nature's God, that all children should be educated
in order to answer the purposes of their creation. If a
parent be so weak or wicked as to refuse his child the
daily bread of knowledge, let the Legislature stand in
the place of parent to that child, and do for him what
his nature demands, and the public safety requires.
To enforce the law, let the selectmen of a town be
empowered to impose on that delinquent parent a
fine not less than one dollar, and not more than five
dollars. This fine would not need to be imposed in
any neighborhood more than half a dozen times, because public sentiment would so heartily approve its
benevolent aim, that it would silently change all objections, as it did in Prussia.

I hope we will profit by the experience of others. I am
in favor of the section as it stands, and opposed to any change
being made in the phraseology of it. It is said the word compulsory is harsh. I say it is right. Another point has been made,
that we cannot enforce the law. I hope there will be no occasion for its harsh enforcement. I want to have public opinion
brought to bear upon those parents who keep their children
from school. I hope the section will pass as it is.

Mr. J. J. WRIGHT. Although indisposed and scarcely able
to speak, I feel it my bounden and indispensable duty, as one
deeply interested in this matter and as one who desires to look
after the general welfare of the people, to raise my feeble voice
against the adoption of this clause. I have had seven years experience in teaching school, and I know something about the
influence that should be brought into communities, and the influence that should be brought upon children to cause them to
attend at schools, and I say here that whenever we place in our
Constitution such a clause as this we are trampling upon the
liberties of the people. We are depriving them of those rights,
privileges and immunities which belong to every free people.

Many gentlemen have referred to Massachusetts, New
Hampshire, and several other States, to prove their case; but
they have, so far, failed. They have not shown us that any of

the States referred to have any such law, and we stand upon the defensive and deny that they have. But suppose Massachusetts, New Hampshire, North Carolina, or any other State in the Union, had a law of that kind, it is no reason why we should have it. We occupy an entire different position from what those States do. We have just been born to a new life, and we are not prepared at this stage of our proceedings to enact or enforce any such law, or to incorporate it into the Constitution. Millions of our people now upon the plantations can hardly get bread to satisfy their hunger and to sustain life. It is simply a matter of impossibility for us in the next one, two or even three years, to compel those people to send their children to school. If the young men in Charleston and elsewhere, who are qualified, will go out and organize schools, then we might think about such a measure. But would you put such a clause into your Constitution now, when in many places there are no schools, and children would be compelled, perhaps, to walk ten or twenty miles to reach one. It is absurd. When the time shall come that we have our schools in operation all over the State, and schools enough in every district, then we may enact such a law as to compel the attendance of children at school and enforce it.

I have had some experience among these people, and I know of no class of people upon this earth who desire to abide by the law, when they know what the law is, more than they do. But if we put such a law into the Constitution, it may be five or ten years before we can put that law into execution. Again, how are we going to enforce a law without a penalty. Here are these people that cannot send their children to school. What are you going to do with them? I propose this amendment: "The General Assembly may by law provide for the compulsory attendance at either a public or private school of all children between the ages of six and sixteen."

I simply offer this to meet the exigencies of the case. The General Assembly is elected to provide for the general welfare of the people, not only in respect to schools, but in every respect. If you confer this power upon the General Assembly, then that body, whenever in its judgment it may be deemed prudent and such a law can be enforced, can provide for the compulsory attendance of children at school.

If, at the first session of the Legislature, that body does not make a law that comes up to the provision of this Constitution, the people have a right to complain and murmur, and to say that persons we have elected to the Legislature have not performed their duty. The Legislature is bound to fulfill every requirement of the Constitution we are about to frame. If they do not, they are not faithful servants of the people. I know New England is the glory of the land. She is an example for us. Why? It is not her vast fiscal resources, not her wealth, not her military resources. It is the superior knowledge and zeal which they have given their children. But when you undertake to say there is a law compelling parents to send their children to school, I deny it and challenge the proof. I know that Massachusetts, New Hampshire, and other States have a provision making it obligatory upon every town and every county to have a school for children. If a town or county does not establish a school, then a fine or penalty is imposed upon that county to twice the amount of the cost to establish schools. But I contend that it is incompatable [*sic*] with the general welfare of any people, and even with the Christian religion, to compel men to send their children to school. Mr. WRIGHT then read his amendment.

Mr. B. F. WHITTEMORE. I did not expect it would be necessary for anything to be said in defence of the clause as reported by the Committee on Education. I was perfectly well aware of the ability of the framers of this clause to defend whatsoever they have reported. I am very glad to find that, so far as the discussion has gone, that the general feeling and impression made by the debaters is that it should continue just as reported. I am glad to find so strong a feeling, with regard to the compulsory attendance of children at school. It has been said, with regard to the condition of the people of this State, that it is not to be compared to that of the people of other States; and, secondly, that a provision like this is not adapted to the present condition of the people of South Carolina. I am aware, so far as the children of the State are concerned, it needs no special enactment for the purpose of sending them to school. If we establish school houses at convenient places, I am persuaded that the children themselves will be anxious to go to school. But I am aware that even now, with the scanty provisions made, that in some localities there are parents who endeavor to prevent their children from going to school. I would be in favor of taking away the power from the parent to prevent their children from receiving educational advantages. I believe, if there is a parent so far forgetful of the interests of his child, if there is a guardian, or any one into whose hands a child has been entrusted, so far forgetful of the welfare of that child and of the benefits that attach to educational advantages to prevent it from partaking of those advantages, I hope that that child will be taken out of that parent's or guardian's hands. Show me school houses, show me children going willingly to school, or compelled to go to school, and I will show you a community that has high considerations not only for its own respectability, but a community that will increase and prosper, and whose example is worthy to be followed.

If we provide for the children, we shall provide for the condition of the people. Make children intelligent, give them an opportunity to understand and read their own laws, to understand the constitutional provisions of the law under which they live, let them understand the penalties that attach to a violation of the law, and you protect the children and protect the communities against crime, and in place of a prison, there will be a school house. In other words, let us provide for the diffusion of intelligence, and we keep out of the jails and penitentiaries a large number of people.

It has been said that the punishment inflicted upon the parent, also punishes the children. I wish the ancient Lacedemonian law might be the law which governed us in this State; that the punishment of children found guilty of crimes was visited upon the parents, for it was held that if these children were properly educated they might have grown up good members of society, and have been prevented from committing crime.

The ancient Hebrews had a law among them that a child not taught a trade was, consequently, taught to steal. If it was in my power to make laws for the government of the people, I would not only make it compulsory that the children attend schools a certain number of weeks, or months, but I should make it compulsory that they should have a trade. I would say that no man or woman should be allowed to enter into the solemn relation of marriage until they could read and write, and it is my solemn opinion you would very soon see the people all over the State going to their books.

We simply mean by this section to say that the Legislature, by its enactment, shall provide for the compulsory attendance of all the children in the State at some school. The laws in Connecticut and Massachusetts, which have been cited, make it imperative for children to attend school so many months in the year. Corporations themselves have established schools within their own corporate limits for the purpose of giving education to the children working in their factories, or in their employ. If we had to provide a school house at every cross road in the State, we should provide for the attendance of every child in every section of the State. I am well aware that children walk great distances to go to school. Many little children tramp eight or ten miles to attend school, so earnest are they in their hearts to attain knowledge. Wisdom is above all rubies, above all price. As I look into the faces of the members, I think I can see what the vote will be upon this question. I believe, when we come to declare our verdict, that the large majority will vote for the section as it stands. I trust there will be no half way provision adopted. I trust the cheek will not blanch, nor the lip tremble, when we come to stand upon this question. Let us not say that the General Assembly can, but that it shall, provide for the compulsory attendance at school of all the children within this Commonwealth.

Mr. W. E. JOHNSTON. I do not rise to make a speech. But it has been said by the member from Beaufort (Mr. WRIGHT) that we have just been born. I wish to deny that, and inform the member that we are three years old. Having made such tremendous strides in three years, I think it highly necessary that some method should be adopted by which these three year old children should, instead of running around molasses barrels or stealing cotton, be compelled to go to school. I noticed with regret, on my way here this morning, some eighteen colored children standing before the door of the Guard House of this city. If those little boys and girls were at school they would not have been arrested for stealing. But I think enough has already been said upon this question, and I move an indefinite postponement of all the amendments.

Mr. C. P. LESLIE. If our friends from Massachusetts can be kept quiet a little while, it will gratify me exceedingly to have a little talk with them. When this Convention was first called, some of the delegates in the house, and many of the friends outside, if they met with the slightest possible misfortune, if a man lost his watch, or his pocket book, the first thing he did was to run into the menagerie, when some delegate would immediately offer a resolution that some sort of relief should be extended. After a good deal of nonsense, it was at last thought not really proper to present that style of resolution. Time run on, and the few delegates here in this body from somewhere have seemed so to act, that they were picked out, and told by our enemies to do some pretty thing or things, that would, beyond any question, tend to defeat the adoption of the Constitution we are endeavoring to frame for this State, they could not be doing better than they are now. Sometime ago our friends looked anxiously forward to the various questions that should arise. One important question was that of the judiciary. That, fortunately for all, has been settled in a way that gives satisfaction to every reflecting right-minded man in the State.[5] There were a number of questions that directly affected the fate of the pending Constitution. One important question was the homestead, and our friends again looked forward to see what action the delegates would take in that direction. I know the homestead provision put in our Constitution was one of the very best strokes of policy we have yet made.[6] Right upon the heel of that, and at a time when everything is going on sensibly, so that it is believed no power in the State can by any possibility defeat the adoption of our Constitution, comes a proposition that must be odious to a large class of people in the State. Now, I can live in South Carolina whether the Constitution is adopted or not, and I can vote in this State. I can have every right and privilege that any white voter has; but I say to the colored members of this body if this Constitution is not adopted they cannot do it. I do not suppose, in the present condition of affairs, that we can make a Constitution that is in all respects just exactly what we would have it. There are many good provisions that we may from absolute necessity have to leave out. There are a great many provisions that I myself would be glad to insert in that Constitution, but I will never be guilty of doing an act when my own good sense condemns that act. It is as important to the colored people of the State as to the white; it is important to me, and important to every man in the State, that a fair, liberal, just and generous government should be established. It is important to the rising generation, both white and colored. If you do not happen to get all you

---

[5] [After some discussion, the convention had adopted its judiciary committee's proposal calling for selection of the judges of the state's supreme court by the legislature, but had reversed the committee's recommendations in providing for legislative rather than popular choice of lesser judges.]

[6] [The convention had exempted homesteads of 100 acres from any legal process for the recovery of debt other than taxes or the cost of the homestead and its improvements.]

want; if you do not want to insert a provision which will endanger the result of the vote on the Constitution when it goes
before the people, then for heaven's sake have sense enough to
leave it out. Some people think they can come in here and can
make just such a Constitution as they in their playful judgment
may think proper. They think that a poor miserable South Carolinian can be taken up here and led just where they wish to
take him. Another says he shall have nothing but gingerbread;
and still another comes from Massachusetts, and insists that this
miserable South Carolinian shall eat anything he chooses to
cram him with, and brings in a long doctor's bill. Another from
Massachusetts says he shall not have anything to drink, and so
on until you have enough before you, which, if adopted, will
bring our Constitution beyond any hopes of resurrection.

I appeal to the good sense of the delegates, to reflect that
every time you undertake to force a people to do what you
know they do not want to do, it can never be carried out. I am
to-day a South Carolinian; I am going to live and die a loyal
man; to be loyal to the government, but by the eternal heavens
I will never be forced to do what in my own judgment no one
has the right to force upon me. Who is going to execute this law
if made? That is a direct question, and I want the delegates
from Massachusetts to come up squarely and fairly and answer
it. Our friend from Massachusetts undertakes to tell us the
loyal men are going to do it. Who are they? Are they the black
people in the State? You cannot force them any more than you
can the whites. There is no use making a law unless you can
enforce it; but if you undertake to go on with this wild business, I warn you of the consequences.

Mr. F. L. Cardozo. The gentleman from Barnwell (Mr.
Leslie) has made an appeal to the fear of the colored delegates
on this floor, by holding up before them the bugbear of the
defeat of our Constitution. I would simply say, that I do not
think there is a colored delegate but what knows that we have
carried the Convention against the white people of this State,
and will carry the Constitution also. I will qualify my language,

by saying that we do not fear those whom the gentleman from Barnwell tells us to fear.

Mr. R. J. DONALDSON. Will the gentleman be kind enough to inform the Convention how many native born South Carolinians are upon the Committee on Education?

Mr. F. L. CARDOZO. There is but one Massachusetts man on the Committee.

Mr. C. P. LESLIE. Did any South Carolinian vote for that provision? If so, I would like to know it?

Mr. F. L. CARDOZO. I would say that one style of argument, of appealing to our fears, or cowardice, or our unmanliness, is scarcely worth noticing.

Mr. C. P. LESLIE. The gentleman has asserted or misstated what I said. I did not appeal to the cowardice of the colored delegates; I appealed simply to their good sense.

Mr. F. L. CARDOZO. I still maintain my position, that the style of argument to which I have alluded is low, mean, and unmanly. I desire, in the first place, to divest this question of the false issues which some cunning political demagogues on the floor have connected with it. They have said this section would compel colored and white children to go together in the schools.

Mr. J. J. WRIGHT. I rise to a point of order. I object to the words "political demagogues," used by the gentleman in his argument.

Mr. C. P. LESLIE. He had reference to himself; what do you want to interrupt him for?

Mr. F. L. CARDOZO. I referred to the gentleman from Barnwell.

Mr. C. P. LESLIE. I refer to him.

Mr. F. L. CARDOZO. I will state again, that it is the habit of some members of the Convention, when they want to defeat a measure, to connect false issues with it, and make it appear as odious as possible. I ask members to look at the strategy kept up by members of the opposition. They have said that we compel white and colored to go together in these schools, and by that means they attempt to defeat this section. Their assertion is ungentlemanly, and it is untrue.

The hour of six having arrived, the PRESIDENT announced the Convention adjourned.

Forty-second Day.

WEDNESDAY, March 4, 1868.

. . . The Convention resumed the consideration of the fourth section of the report of the Committee on the Executive part of the Constitution, providing that it shall be the duty of the General Assembly to provide for the compulsory attendance, at either public or private schools, of all children between the ages of six and sixteen years, not physically or mentally disabled, for a term equivalent to at least twenty-four months.

The first question was striking out the word "compulsory."

Mr. F. L. CARDOZO. Before I resume my remarks this morning, I would ask the favor of the Convention, and especially the opposition, to give me their close attention, and I think I can settle this matter perfectly satisfactory to every one in the house.

It was argued by some yesterday, with some considerable weight, that we should do everything in our power to incorporate into the Constitution all possible measures that will conciliate those opposed to us.

No one would go farther in conciliating others than I would. But those whom we desire to conciliate consist of three different classes, and we should be careful, therefore, what we do to conciliate.

In the first place there is an element which is opposed to us, no matter what we do will never be conciliated. It is not that they are opposed so much to the Constitution we may frame, but they are opposed to us sitting in Convention. Their objection is of such a fundamental and radical nature, that any attempt to frame a Constitution to please them would be utterly abortive.

In the next place, there are those who are doubtful, and gentlemen here say if we frame a Constitution to suit these parties they will come over with us. They are only waiting, and I will say these parties do not particularly care what kind of a Constitution you frame, they only want to see whether it is going to be successful, and if it is, they will come any way.

Then there is a third class who honestly question our capacity to frame a Constitution. I respect that class, and believe if we do justice to them, laying our corner stone on the sure foundation of republican government and liberal principles, the intelligence of that class will be conciliated, and they are worthy of conciliation.

Before I proceed to discuss the question, I want to divest it of all false issues, of the imaginary consequences that some gentlemen have illogically thought will result from the adoption of this section with the word compulsory. They affirm that it compels the attendance of both white and colored children in the same schools. There is nothing of the kind in the section. It means nothing of the kind, and no such construction can be legitimately placed upon it. It simply says all the children shall be educated; but how is left with the parents to decide. It is left to the parent to say whether the child shall be sent to a public or private school. The eleventh section has been referred to as bearing upon this section. I will ask attention to this fact. The eleventh section does not say, nor does the report in any part say there shall not be separate schools. There can be separate schools for white and colored. It is simply left so that if any colored child wishes to go to a white school, it shall have the privilege to do so. I have no doubt, in most localities, colored people would prefer separate schools, particularly until some of the present prejudice against their race is removed.

We have not provided that there shall be separate schools; but I do not consider these issues as properly belonging to the question. I shall, therefore, confine myself to the more important matter connected with this subject.

My friend yesterday referred to Prussia and Massachusetts as examples that we should imitate, and I was much surprised to hear some of the members who have spoken, ridicule that argument. It was equivalent to saying we do not want the teachings of history, or the examples of any of those countries foremost in civilization.

It was said that the condition of affairs in Prussia and Massachusetts was entirely different. But they are highly civilized countries, with liberty-loving, industrious citizens, and the highest social order exists there. I want South Carolina to imitate those countries, which require the compulsory attendance of all children of certain ages for fixed periods, at some school. If you deem a certain end worthy of being attained, it must be accompanied by precisely the same means those countries have attained it.

Prussia, in her late victories over Austria, reaped the fruits of the superiority of her school system and the intelligence of her people, and in every conflict with the powers of darkness and error we should imitate just such a country as Prussia.[7] To ignore the example of a country because far from us, would be to ignore all philosophy and history.

It was also remarked that there was no other State that compelled the attendance of their children at schools. Arkansas does it in her Constitution, and notwithstanding assertions to the contrary, I would say that Massachusetts does it in her statutes.

Another argument was that this matter had better be left to the Legislature. I have been charged with appealing to the prejudices and feelings of the colored delegates to this Convention. It is true to a certain extent. I do direct their attention to matters concerning their peculiar interests, but if it is meant to

---

[7] [Prussia had defeated Austria in the "Seven Weeks War" during the summer of 1866.]

charge me with appealing to their passions as against the white people, I respectfully deny the charge, and stamp the assertion as gratuitous. But I do desire we shall use the opportunities we now have to our best advantage, as we may not ever have a more propitious time. We know when the old aristocracy and ruling power of this State get into power, as they undoubtedly will, because intelligence and wealth will win in the long run, they will never pass such a law as this. Why? Because their power is built on and sustained by ignorance. They will take precious good care that the colored people shall never be enlightened.

Again, it has been argued that it was anti-republican, and an infringement of individual rights to pass such a law. Men living in a savage, uncivilized state are perfectly free, and should be untrammeled. But the first thing, when a man goes into society, is to concede certain individual rights necessary for the protection and preservation of society. If you deny this great principle, there can be no law, for every law you propose is an infringement of my individual right. If you tax me for the education of the poor people of the State, I simply say that it shall not be exclusively for the rich to build up their power, but that it is for all the people, the poor as well as the rich.

I hope every gentleman will see that the argument against it is anti-republican and utterly groundless. Some may think that we go too far, and take away too many individual rights. I maintain that in this instance it is only for the benefit of the State, as well as for the benefit of society.

The question is, will you pay the poll tax to educate your children in schools, or support them in penitentiaries? No intelligent person will prefer to support them as criminals.

Some ask how it is to be enforced, and say it is impossible. I will simply say what has been done elsewhere can be done here. Our Legislature will at first, of course, make the penalties very light, will consider all the circumstances by which we are surrounded, and will not make the law onerous. Every law should be considered in a two-fold aspect—in its moral effect and its penalties. The moral power of a law almost always compels obedience. Ninety-nine out of one hundred men who may be indifferent to their children, when they know there is a law compelling them to send their children to school, will make sacrifices in order not to violate that law.

I have had several years experience as a teacher, and I know exactly its effects. I can best satisfy the house by simply describing one out of the one hundred cases that have come under my own observation.

In my school I have the highest class of boys who were kept under my own special care and tuition. Among these boys was one highly gifted, universally loved, and talented. He was not only superior in regard to intellectual qualities, but also in regard to moral qualities. He was a noble boy, truly loveable and talented. I had watched the development of that boy's mind, and took the highest pleasure in assisting that development. I spent much time in assisting the development of that boy's mind, and watched his career with much interest and jealousy. At the commencement of our last session, he came to me with tears in his eyes, and bid me good bye. I asked him, "are you really going to leave school?" "Yes," he answered, "I must go; my parents are going to take me away." "Tell them," I said, "that I will consult with them." The mother, with tears, said she did not want the child to leave, but the father insisted upon it. I talked with him, but with no effect. He was a low, degraded, besotted drunkard. I endeavored by every argument in my power, by praising his boy as he deserved, and by offering to adopt him and take him North to one of the best institutions in the country, to effect my object in giving that boy a thorough education. What do you think was the reply? "No," he said, "I cannot spare him. In the morning he chops the wood, gets the water, and I want him to run on errands." Those errands, I learned, were running to the corner to buy beer and brandy for his father. If by a law of the State we could have taken that boy from his drunken father, and educated him, he would have been an ornament to us and an honor to the State.

As I meet him in the street now, he slinks away from me to go, perhaps, to the corner to get liquor for his father. He told me from the time his father takes a glass in the morning till night he is never sober, and he wished his father was dead.

I am anxious to reconcile all differences on this question, and I move a reconsideration of the previous question, in order to offer an amendment, to the following effect:

> *Provided,* That no law to that effect shall be passed until a system of public schools has been thoroughly and completely organized, and facilities afforded to all the inhabitants of the State for the free education of their children.

The motion to reconsider was agreed to, and the question being taken on the adoption of this amendment, it was agreed to, and the fourth section passed to its third reading.

23.

William T. Harris, "How Far May the State Provide for the Education of Her Children at Public Cost?" 1871

William T. Harris was the preeminent figure in the American educational establishment that came into being during the decades following the Civil War. His hold on his generation's loyalty is somewhat puzzling because (as a dedicated follower of G. W. F. Hegel) he spoke with accents of philosophical statism that conflicted radically with the atomistic individualism of his day. Nevertheless, as this address to the newly formed National Educational Association suggests, his philosophical preoccupations if not his philosophical vocabulary may well have answered to the needs of the academy of educational administrators. On the one hand, he equated education with the highest possible service to civilization and thereby justified its ever-wider diffusion at public expense. At the same time, he upheld essentially traditional ideas of the curriculum, and he treated private property (which he wished to tax for the support of education) as a vehicle of liberation and human self-realization. In addition, while he voiced implicit distaste for the mercenary materialism of his day, he stood back from any political commitment to challenge it in practice. In short, despite its apparent implications, his statism was fundamentally conservative, and it tended to confirm the educators' view that they stood alone in a strategic position between chaos and liberty. It followed that Harris should become United States Commissioner of Education (1889–1906) as well as a major intellectual influence on the first generation of professional school administrators.

Ladies and Gentlemen—Fellow Educators of the United States:

We are assembled at an epoch in which national reconstruction is epidemic. We ourselves have but lately emerged from a convulsion in which grief and desolation came down upon us all; even the bravest among us have been dismayed at the gigantic price of constitutional liberty, a fabulous cost of blood and treasure. Taught circumspection by bitter experience, we look before and after, and ask ourselves, not without misgivings, "What is all this worth?" "Is a government like ours a permanent thing?" "Does it not cost more than it comes to?"

While we are seriously engaged in repairing our damages, and in attempting to provide safeguards for the future, we are startled by earthquake rumblings in the East, beyond the Atlantic. The Prussian and Austrian war begins and ends almost while the on-looking nations of the earth hold their breath in the first suspense. "Is it accident, or self-assured purpose, that performs the new miracle in war?" While the world

From *The Addresses and Journal of Proceedings of the National Educational Association*. Sessions of the year 1871 at St. Louis, Mo. (New York and Washington: James H. Holmes, 1872), pp. 30–37.

is pondering this question, and looking at the threatening aspect of affairs in Southern Europe, France gets impatient, and will probe the mystery for herself. "If the peasant among the Alps shout aloud, or clap his hands, the mountains answer with an avalanche." When Louis Napoleon shook his mailed hand at the new portent beyond the Rhine, united Germany answered with a land-slide of armed men. The end is not yet. France is not yet excavated, like Pompeii, from her ruins. Meanwhile, in the East the holy German empire, long since inurned and its bones canonized, whose ghost only haunted the unquiet dreams of the Frankfort citizens on the Main, has revisited the world of solid reality, and sits under a spiked helmet. Out of the near future, what new phenomenon will arise, or what resurrection of the buried past will come to sight? Shall it be the democracy of Europe, or the firm establishment of monarchy and obligarchy[sic]? Let him who doubts look at the forges and see what manner of weapons are in process of manufacture for the civilization now on its advent: popular education in Italy; popular education and extension of the ballot all over England; popular education the corner-stone of resurgent France; popular education for the past generation throughout Germany now seen to be the bulwark of the invincible might of Prussia![1] The hand on the dial now points to the avatar of democracy, and no one in Europe misreads the time of the night. "Unless we educate the people, and place in their hands the directing power in continually increasing extent, the sceptre drops from our national hand, and we approach the

---

[1] [In 1859 the Kingdom of Sardinia created a national ministry of education with the authority and funds to develop a nationwide system of primary schools. This was subsequently extended to the rest of Italy after its unification with Sardinia. Great Britain extended the suffrage in 1867 and adopted its first comprehensive plan for public education in 1870. In France the Third Republic moved slowly—more slowly than Harris implies—to establish universal elementary education at public expense, more or less on the model of Prussia, victor over the Second Empire in the Franco-Prussian War (1870–1871).]

brink of national death." This is seen alike by the king on the throne and by the people at their daily toil.

It was clear that this conviction gathered strength, and had become organized into the policy of the State, when we read three years ago in the report of the United States Commissioner, Dr. HOYT, of the immense efforts made all over Europe to found a system of industrial education.[2] The democratic idea of civilization sends forward as its advance guard the legions of productive industry, and covers its flanks with all-powerful engines of intercommunication—the railroad, the steamship, the telegraph.

But not by such means can the monarchical idea be preserved and defended much longer. Man will not submit to be educated simply as a director of machines and instrumentalities of industry. He soon aspires to direct himself and be self governed. To be sure there is a long step from the mere hand laborer, the one who turns a crank or carries a hod, the galley-slave who works chained to his oar—there is a long step from the mere physical laborer to the director of a machine: to the engineer, the overseer of a loom, or the manager of a telegraph; the former is all hands; his own brain even is a mere hand governed by the brain of another who directs him. But when directive power develops so far as to direct and govern machine labor, nay, even when it is so far cultured as to reach the principles of natural science and be capable of applying these in mechanic inventions, even then it is not at its summit of realization. It will stop at nothing short of the spiritual culture that makes it alike directive and governing in the sphere of mind, the realm of social, moral and intellectual existence.

----

[2] [John W. Hoyt (1831–1912), a prominent advocate of public higher education and especially of a national university, had been named a United States commissioner to the Paris Exposition of 1867 and had subsequently drafted the commission's *Report on Education* (1870).]

If the monarchies of Europe think to put off the people with mere polytechnic and industrial education they will find that they have fostered a directive power that will grope for and find the helm of the state, and then attempt to direct the administration of government. The mistake will then become visible. For the people must have a universal education, fitting them for the highest as well as the lowest. Human instruments, whether mere hod-carriers or locomotive engineers, will not stay contentedly as *instruments;* they aspire to transcend their hard limits, be they ever so near or never so far off. The higher already, the greater the aspiration. Blind aspiration, from which enlightenment is carefully shut out, leads to July revolutions and reigns of terror; over the ashes of the burnt-out volcano of popular phrensy marches Napoleonic imperialism with cold unsympathetic step toward the return of Bourbonism and absolutism.

Not only mechanical directive power shall be taught in the people's schools, but also spiritual directive power. The London snobbery that patronizingly talks of the education of the lower *"clahsses"* does not know that the industrial civilization it affects to admire is an instrument that only Democracy can wield. Leave out the humanities from that education and you leave out the culture that can guide its course, and communism and socialism and abstract theories will find their way quickly into the heads of the laboring classes. No merely prescriptive education on the part of the church or the school can prevent the people's mind from being fly-blown with crazy political and social theories, destructive to all sound growth. Not merely natural philosophy, chemistry, mathematics and biology must be studies, but likewise the science of society and the state, of art, religion and philosophy, in all their phases. The great educators of the race—Homer, Dante, Shakespeare and Goethe, Plato, Aristotle, Leibnitz and Newton—these must be made accessible to the *people.* Each child must be waited on by the institutions of man and invited to see the spectacle

spread out before him from the lofty summit of human civilization; his human brothers that have added a cubit to the
world's stature by their heroic labors, must be pointed out to
him; the methods and results of the attainment of their ends
must be revealed to him; noblest aspiration and earnest, self-
sacrificing endeavor must be imparted to him as the means of
achieving his individual destiny. The whole world of the past
and present is made, by education, the auxiliary of each man,
woman and child.

From these reflections, for which the aspect of Europe
to-day furnishes the occasion, we turn again to our own condition and the confusion attendant upon our own reconstruction.
While we look abroad, the course may seem clear, and the
way of Providence and the march of events may be made out
with no difficulty. When we look at home the very nearness
of the complicated details prevents us from getting that clear
survey of the whole which is required for the settlement of
practical problems. We may seriously ask ourselves the question; How far may the State provide for the education of her
children at public cost? We may go so far even as to doubt
the right of the State to meddle at all with the subject of education. We may consider it the exclusive business of the family; or of the community; or of the church. Or, granting the
right of the State to legislate on the subject of education, we
may hold that the public should be taxed only for the education
of the poor and indigent. Or, limiting public education in another direction, we may say that it should extend only to the elementary branches, that the State shall not use the wealth of
the people to found institutions of higher education.

Whatever phase of the question we adopt or reject, it is
clear that we can never rest our convictions on a firm basis,
without comprehending thoroughly the nature of the State
and hence its limits and prerogatives; the nature of education
and its relation to the individual at large and to the State.

That man is a two-fold being is obvious to all. He exists

as an immediate individual, in possession of his body and various instrumental faculties. But he has another existence of far greater importance. He has a reflected existence—what he receives back through recognition of his fellow-men. To hold up or support this reflected existence and give it greater reality than the first or immediate existence, man has institutions— society, the State, and others. As a member of society man owns property; he can realize his will in an external thing or chattel, but only by and with the voluntary consent of his fellow-men. Possession does not become property until this recognition of society is obtained; this recognition has made for itself certain prescribed forms. Property is then a form of man's *reflected* existence. Hence we say it is *conventional*.

It is clear, then, that all the bodily wants of man—food, clothing and shelter—depending as they do upon the ownership of property for their satisfaction, are through this means elevated and spiritualized by the institution of society. They are no longer mere immediate attributes, as *animal* wants, but they are coverted into the instruments of realizing man's spiritual or reflected being; he is forced by hunger or cold to combine with his fellow-men and to form a community in which he is to respect their recognition far more than his animal impulses and desires. Thus, too, the institution of the family lifts man above mere sexual passion, and makes him in that respect a *reflected* being, a *rational* being. Civil society is organized for the realization of man's existence as a property owner, so that he shall be a universal or rational essence, and not a mere individual animal, dependent on his mere locality and the season of the year and his unaided might for his physical life. By it each individual commands by his own feeble efforts the resources of the entire globe. The organization of civil society is so perfect that every day's labor of the Missouri wheat-grower affects the price of wheat all over the world. The day-laborer in the streets of this city commands with his meagre wages to that extent a share in the coffee of the distant Indies, the sugar of Louisiana, the tea of China, the drugs of South America, the fruits and grains, the manufactures from all sections of the country.

But the State has a higher function to perform. In it appear other phases of this reflected or spiritual life of man. In fact the generic existence of man comes in the State to independent and actual realization. It does not exist like civil society as a mere instrument for man's voluntary employment, but it stands over and prescribes to the individual his duties and holds him to account by the infliction of penalties. It asserts the rational or generic existence of man as the substantial, and proclaims man's merely animal existence—his life—to be unessential in comparison with it. Directive power shall proceed from it, and not from the mere individual. The State, even in its most despotic form, remains still the realization of man's reflected being, and to it he owes all that is distinctively human.

The lowest nationality realizes for the individual the possibility of his existence in some form of civil society, so that he shall enter into the combination with his fellow-men and reinforce his feeble might by the strength of the race.

But it is a long way from the lowest nationality to the highest. From an Aztec or a Chinese monarchy to a government like that of England or the United States is an immense step. The difference consists wholly in the amount or degree in which the reflected or generic being of man, that the State embodies, is shared consciously by the individual; in short, in how far the directive power of the State exists in and through the conscious will of the individual. In Africa and the islands of the sea there is scarcely any realization of this reflected being of man. In Asia it exists in its isolated substantiality over against man as individual, and in Europe and America we find the various degrees of its mastery and possession by the individual.

It is therefore clear that the goal of nationality is the complete realization *for* man and *through* man of his *reflected, generic,* or rational existence; the development of man as a self-directive or self-determined being. Hence the world-history, is, as the greatest of thinkers states it, the progress of man into the consciousness of freedom.[3]

Now, since man as individual, makes his advent upon this planet as a mere animal, and without the evolution of his second and higher nature, it is clear that he must obtain it by a *process* of growth and culture; this we call education. In this wide compass it is two-fold, and involves, first, practical initiation into the habits and usages and the dexterities of the trades and vocations of life. Secondly, there is theoretical initiation into the consciousness of the directive principles and solvent ideas through which directive power is achieved. It is clear that the final end of all government must be to elevate the individual to this highest participation in his own universal being, and to enable him practically and theoretically to *know himself.*

This idea pervaded men, first as a dim feeling, a prophecy uttered by some poet or saint in a moment of insight; then it got to be a conscious thought, and finally here in America we have set it up as our national idea. We say that we are to be a nation of self-rulers; that our Government is to exist for the individual—all for each and each for all; that the highest possibility of any one of the race shall exist for each of the race, and that accidents of time and place, of birth or wealth, shall not prevail against him. This is our deepest national conviction, and we will all perish sooner than yield this idea.

But then it follows that the naturalness, the accidents of birth and condition, must be made of no avail by means of an education provided for all, and at public expense. The cost to the public is to be recompensed in this wise. Whatever taxation of property is necessary to support a free system of education is a requisition made upon an element or source created by the general recognition of the community. All property is a reflected existence. This taxation for school pur-

---

[3] [The reference, of course, is to Hegel.]

poses is directly applied for the culture of the individual, or, in other words, for his initiation into this very reflected being which creates property. It is, therefore, the application of property for its own production and security. Without any of this recognition which education produces, there could be no security of property, and hence no security of life.

The fact that conscious intelligence—directive power—controls the property of the world, is too obvious to need restatement. Again, the possibility of possession of property by all in this country adds new validity to it here; it is more valuable. That you can alienate your real estate makes it property in a complete sense; if it is entailed it is only part property. The free possession of property without feudal liens and tenures—the dead hands of its past owners still clutching the symbol of their reflected being—comes to existence only when a government of all the people, for all the people, and by all the people, prevails, and when it is rendered possible through universal education. Who would own real estate in Turkey? Who would accept a Russian estate on condition that he must live on it and assume its responsibilities? No one of us, I think. The quality of property—its intrinsic value—depends upon the quality of the community who recognize it. The *status* of the reflected being is the *status* of those who reflect it. Property in a refined and cultivated community is raised to a high *potence* of value; in a barbarous community it is not worth the risks incidental to its possession. In proportion as man is educated he sees the substantial character of reflected existence, and this perception creates continually new kinds of property founded on the new recognition: bodiless possessions, "incorporeal hereditaments," that receive their substance from conventional recognition.

Thus not only does the culture of civilization increase the alienability of property, and hence its value, but it develops into property a vast series of relations of the nature of franchises which, in a rude unpolished age are mere rights of the strongest and non-transferable to the common people. Hence property, in the *highest sense,* cannot exist except it be taxed for universal education.

If we turn, for a moment, to the actual history of nations we shall find public education, in some sort or other, always existing. The only point is to inquire, *in what does the directive power of this people exist?* to find at once where the public money is used for educational purposes. In China, for instance, the schools are supported by the people in their private capacity. But the Government rewards those successfully graduating by its offices. Hence, the money advanced for education is only an investment in public securities.

In *all* countries the military education is at public expense. Where does the support and education of the nobility and royal families come from except from the public? They do no immediate work. *They* are going to *direct* and have *others* obey. But in our country, where each is born to all the rights of mankind without distinction, all must be provided for. Not by *pauper* schools, for that would be to burn into the plastic mind of the youth his misfortune, and he never would outgrow the stigma. Neither is it safe to leave the education of youth to religious zeal or private benevolence; for then inequalities of the most disastrous kind will slip in, and our State find elements heterogeneous to it continually growing up.

The Government of a republic must educate *all* its people, and it must educate them so far that they are able to educate *themselves* in a continued process of culture, extending through life. This implies the existence of *higher institutions of public education.* And these, not so much with the expectation that all will attend them, as that the lower schools, which are more initiatory in their character, and deal with mere elements, depend for their efficiency upon the organization of higher institutions for their direction and control. Without educating in higher institutions the teachers of lower schools, and furthermore without the possibility hovering before the pupils of ascent into the higher schools, there can be no practical effect given to primary schools. The public education must therefore extend through the three grades of culture: 1st, the primary, in which initiation is given into mere elements. 2d, the culture in respect to general relations of the elements; the course of study which involves the digestion and generalization of the isolated facts of primary education. 3d, the university education, wherein elements and relations are subordinated and a knowledge of universals is acquired.

It is, indeed, a great thing to have even one class of society educated. No doubt, all profit by it, even when the education is confined to the few. But in a democracy all must be educated. The interest of property demands it, the interest of the Government demands it. And one generation of well-educated people in a state forces upon all adjacent states the necessity of public education as a mere war measure, as a means of preservation of the state. So also will the existence of one successful democracy force upon the world the adoption of democratic forms of government as the condition of their continued existence. An ignorant people can *be* governed, but only a wise people can *govern itself*.

The question of the morality of popular education demands only a word as we pass on to the close of our discussion.

That education necessarily loosens the hold of mere prescribed rules of morality and religion is true in its negative and elementary aspect. There can be no transition from passive obedience to conscious self-determination except through denial. It is a passing phase, and only a passing phase. But again the state of passive obedience is only a pyramid resting on its apex, and it the most unstable of all rests. The state of conscious insight and conviction is the pyramid on its base, and the most stable of all rests. Passive obedience, mechanical unreason, is utterly non-spiritual existence; a mere windmill with prayers fastened to it, as in Persia, is the symbolic type of it.

When we look closely into this alleged increase of criminality in our day, we find that it rests mainly on the delusive appearence [*sic*] occasioned by the repeating mirror of the press and telegraph. Never before in the history of the world were life and limb so safe as now from the attacks of crime. Crime has indeed ascended from the lower and brutal order—above personal violence in a large measure—and has invaded the realms that belong to man's reflected or second nature. Instead of the violent deed which comes back through the state in sure and swift recoil upon the criminal, we have more and more *intelligent rascality,* to use the words of the distinguished personage who addressed us yesterday. But we must not forget that in the measure of its intelligence, rascality becomes innocuous. Were it perfectly rational, it were no crime. Its circles are much larger than those of brutal violence, and the suffering it inflicts on humanity far less; neither does it stand in the way of the possibilities of the individual to such an extent as brutal violence. It must be confessed, however, that most of the intelligent rescality [*sic*] escapes its deserved retribution. The statistics of penitentiaries show that a very small percentage of well-educated men are incarcerated. The public schools send very few. Out of the 840 criminals in the penitentiary at Jefferson City, over 200 are negroes who have had no education. Of the remaining 600, there are scarcely a dozen who have a thorough public-school education, and most of those did not acquire it in this country. The average statistics of the United States show that out of the small percentage of the people unable to read and write come about one-third of the criminals, and of the remaining two-thirds only one in a hundred had been educated in the higher branches.

   Where all are educated, and directive power exists on every hand, it finds its employment chiefly in building up the wealth of the community. The directive power required every day to manage the large banks of this country, to direct the great railroads, or the manufactories and corporations of various kinds, is infinitely more than that required to direct our Government. The management of the Pacific railroad is as great an affair as the government of a small kingdom. Thus self-directive intelligence makes for itself avenues for employment. Nothing is lost. Directive power finds it easier to secure a competence by industry than by intrigue and rascality.

The discipline of our public schools, wherein punctuality and regularity are enforced and the pupils are continually taught to *suppress mere self-will* and inclination, is the best school of morality. Self-control is the basis of all moral virtues, and industrious and studious habits are the highest qualities we can form in our children.

A free, self-conscious, self-controlled manhood, is to be produced only through universal public education at public cost, and as this is the object of our Government, it is proper for *our* Government to provide this means and at the cost of the people.

24.

George William Curtis, "The Public Duty of Educated Men," 1877

When the editor of *Harper's Weekly* and contributing editor of *Harper's Monthly Magazine* rose to speak at the Union College commencement of 1877, the passage of time had dimmed but not destroyed the vision of democracy as an educational process that Nathan Beman and Henry Ward Beecher had proclaimed. Nevertheless, George William Curtis's oration revealed crosscurrents of doubt and anxiety that could be resolved only by assuming that educated men would succeed in influencing postbellum politics much as they had allegedly influenced the North to repudiate slavery. In this respect, it was typical of the statements of a large number of college men who linked the idea that democracy might be a school of progressive politics with the idea that it should serve as a schoolroom for a self-appointed class of pedagogues, the so-called scholars in politics. In making this connection they harked back to a tradition established early in the nineteenth century by Phi Beta Kappa orators who were fearful of the spread of democracy. They also came dangerously close to arguing that democracy was impossible unless it was led by educated men.

It is with diffidence that I rise to add any words of mine to the music of these younger voices. This day, Gentlemen of the Graduating Class, is especially yours. It is a day of high hope and expectation, and the counsels that fall from older lips should be carefully weighed, lest they chill the ardor of a generous enthusiasm or stay the all-conquering faith of youth that moves the world. To those who, constantly and actively engaged in a thousand pursuits, are still persuaded that educated intelligence moulds states and leads mankind, no day in the year is more significant, more inspiring, than this of the College Commencement. It matters not at what college it may be celebrated. It is the same at all. We stand here indeed beneath these College walls, beautiful for situation, girt at this moment with the perfumed splendor of midsummer, and full of tender memories and joyous associations to those who hear me. But on this day, and on other days, at a hundred other colleges, this summer sun beholds the same spectacle of eager and earnest throngs. The faith that we hold, they also cherish. It is the same God that is worship[p]ed at the different altars. It is the same benediction that descends upon every reverent head and believing heart. In this annual celebration of faith in the power and the responsibility of educated men, all the colleges in the country, in whatever state, of whatever age, of whatever religious sympathy or direction, form but one great Union University.

From *The Public Duty of Educated Men. The Oration of the Honorary Chancellor of Union University, Hon. George William Curtis, LL. D., delivered at the Commencement of Union College, June 27th, 1877* (Albany, N. Y., 1878), pp. 3–12, 17–22.

But the interest of the day is not that of mere study, of sound scholarship as an end, of good books for their own sake, but of education as a power in human affairs, of educated men as an influence in the commonwealth. "Tell me," said an American scholar of Goethe, the many-sided, "what did he ever do for the cause of man?" The scholar, the poet, the philosopher, are men among other men. From these unavoidable social relations spring opportunities and duties. How do they use them? How do they discharge them? Does the scholar show in his daily walk that he has studied the wisdom of ages in vain? Does the poet sing of angelic purity and lead an unclean life? Does the philosopher peer into other worlds, and fail to help this world upon its way? Four years before our civil war, the same scholar—it was Theodore Parker—said sadly: "If our educated men had done their duty, we should not now be in the ghastly condition we bewail." The theme of today seems to me to be prescribed by the occasion. It is the festival of the departure of a body of educated young men into the world. This company of picked recruits marches out with beating drums and flying colors to join the army. We who feel that our fate is gracious which allowed a liberal training, are here to welcome and to advise. On your behalf, Mr. President and Gentlemen, with your authority, and with [a]ll my heart, I shall say a word to them and to you of the public duty of educated men in America.

I shall not assume, Gentlemen Graduates, for I know that it is not so, that what Dr. Johnson says of the teachers of Rasselas and the princess of Abyssinia can be truly said of you in your happy valley: "The sages who instructed them told them of nothing but the miseries of public life, and described all beyond the mountains as regions of calamity where discord was always raging, and where man preyed upon man." The sages who have instructed you are American citizens. They know that patriotism has its glorious opportunities and its sacred duties. They have not shunned the one, and they have well performed the other. In the sharpest stress of our awful conflict, a clear voice of patriotic warning was heard from these peaceful Academic shades, the voice of the venerated teacher whom this University still freshly deplores, drawing from the wisdom of experience stored in his ample learning, a lesson of startling cogency and power from the history of Greece for the welfare of America.[1]

This was the discharge of a public duty by an educated man. It illustrated an indispensable condition of a progressive republic, the active, practical interest in politics of the most intelligent citizens. Civil and religious liberty in this country can be preserved only through the agency of our political institutions. But those institutions alone will not suffice. It is not the ship so much as the skillful sailing that assures the prosperous voyage. American institutions presuppose not only general honesty and intelligence in the people, but their constant and direct application to public affairs. Our system rests upon all the people, not upon a part of them, and the citizen who evades his share of the burden betrays his fellows. Our safety lies not in our institutions but in ourselves. It was under the forms of the republic that Julius Cæsar made himself emperor of Rome. It was professing reverence for the national traditions that James the Second was destroying religious liberty in England. To labor, said the old monks, is to pray. What we earnestly desire we earnestly toil for. That she may be prized more truly, heaven-eyed Justice flies from us, like the Tartar maid from her lovers, and she yields her embrace at last only to the swiftest and most daring of her pursuers.

By the words public duty I do not necessarily mean official duty, although it may include that. I mean simply that constant and active practical participation in the details of politics without which, upon the part of the most intelligent citizens, the conduct of public affairs falls under the control

---

[1] [The reference is to Tayler Lewis, Professor of Oriental Languages and Biblical Literature, whose *State Rights: A Photograph from the Ruins of Ancient Greece* had rallied conservatives to the northern cause in 1864.]

of selfish and ignorant, or crafty and venal men. I mean that personal attention which, as it must be incessant, is often wearisome and even repulsive, to the details of politics, attendance at meetings, service upon committees, care and trouble and expense of many kinds, patient endurance of rebuffs, chagrins, ridicules, disappointments, defeats—in a word, all those duties and services which, when selfishly and meanly performed, stigmatize a man as a mere politician, but whose constant, honorable, intelligent and vigilant performance is the gradual building, stone by stone, and layer by layer, of that great temple of self-restrained liberty which all generous souls mean that our government shall be.

Public duty in this country is not discharged, as is so often supposed by voting. A man may vote regularly, and still fail essentially of his political duty, as the Pharisee who gave tithes of all that he possessed, and fasted three times in the week, yet lacked the very heart of religion. When an American citizen is content with voting merely, he consents to accept what is often a doubtful alternative. His first duty is to help shape the alternative. This, which was formerly less necessary is now indispensable. In a rural community such as this country was a hundred years ago, whoever was nominated for office was known to his neighbors, and the consciousness of that knowledge was a conservative influence in determining nominations. But in the local elections of the great cities of today, elections that control taxation and expenditure, the mass of the voters vote in absolute ignorance of the candidates. The citizen who supposes that he does all his duty when he votes, places a premium upon political knavery. Thieves welcome him to the polls and offer him a choice, which he has done nothing to prevent, between Jeremy Diddler and Dick Turpin. The party cries for which he is responsible are: "Turpin and Honesty," "Diddler and Reform." And within a few years, as a result of this indifference to the details of public duty, the most powerful politician in the empire state of the Union was Jonathan Wild, the Great, the captain of a band of plunderers.[2] I know it is said that the knaves have taken the honest men in a net, and have contrived machinery which will inevitably grind only the grist of rascals. The answer is, that when honest men did once what they ought to do always, the thieves were netted and their machine was broken. To say that in this country the rogues must rule, is to defy history and to despair of the republic. It is to repeat the imbecile executive cry of sixteen years ago, "Oh dear! the states have no right to go; and, Oh dear! the nation has no right to help itself." Let the Union, stronger than ever and unstained with national wrong, teach us the power of patriotic virtue—and Ludlow street jail console those who suppose that American politics must necessarily be a game of thieves and bullies.[3]

If ignorance and corruption and intrigue control the primary meeting, and manage the convention, and dictate the nomination, the fault is in the honest and intelligent workshop and office, in the library and the parlor, in the church and the school. When they are as constant and faithful to their political rights as the slums and the grogshops, the poolrooms and the kennels; when the educated, industrious, temperate, thrifty citizens are as zealous and prompt and unfailing in political activity as the ignorant and venal and mischievous, or when it is plain that they cannot be roused to their duty,

---

[2] [Jonathan Wild was a notorious British robber and informer, hanged at Tyburn in 1725. He is identified here with William M. Tweed of New York, whose political machine had plundered the city of literally millions of dollars.]

[3] [By the time Curtis spoke, Tweed had been tried and convicted in criminal court, only to have his sentence set aside on a technicality. The reformers had then brought civil suit against him and secured his incarceration in the Ludlow Street jail, whence he had "escaped" to Spain only to be returned to the city and the jail nearly a year later. He was to die there in April 1878.]

[In his previous sentence, Curtis refers to President James Buchanan, who thought that secession was unconstitutional but would not act against the southern states when they seceded.]

then, but not until then—if ignorance and corruption always carry the day—there can be no honest question that the republic has failed. But let us not be deceived. While good men sit at home, not knowing that there is anything to be done, nor caring to know; cultivating a feeling that politics are tiresome and dirty, and politicians vulgar bullies and bravoes; half persuaded that a republic is the contemptible rule of a mob, and secretly longing for a splendid and vigorous despotism—then remember it is not a government mastered by ignorance, it is a government betrayed by intelligence; it is not the victory of the slums, it is the surrender of the schools; it is not that bad men are brave, but that good men are infidels and cowards.

But, gentlemen, when you come to address yourselves to these primary public duties, your first surprise and dismay will be the discovery that, in a country where education is declared to be the hope of its institutions, the higher education is often practically held to be almost a disadvantage. You will go from these halls to hear a very common sneer at college-bred men—to encounter a jealously of education as making men visionary and pedantic and impracticable—to confront a belief that there is something enfeebling in the higher education, and that self-made men, as they are called, are the sure stay of the state. But what is really meant by a self-made man? It is a man of native sagacity and strong character, who was taught, it is proudly said, only at the plough or the anvil or the bench. He was schooled by adversity, and was polished by hard attrition with men. He is Benjamin Franklin, the printer's boy, or Abraham Lincoln, the rail-splitter. They never went to college, but nevertheless, like Agamemnon, they were kings of men, and the world blesses their memory.

So it does; but the sophistry here is plain enough, although it is not always detected. Great genius and force of character undoubtedly make their own career. But because Walter Scott was dull at school, is a parent to see with joy

that his son is a dunce? Because Lord Chatham was of a towering conceit, must we infer that pompous vanity portends a
comprehensive statesmanship that will fill the world with
the splendor . . . of its triumphs? Because Sir Robert Walpole
gambled and swore and boozed at Houghton, are we to suppose that gross sensuality and coarse contempt of human
nature are the essential secrets of a power that defend liberty
against tory intrigue and priestly politics? Was it because
Benjamin Franklin was not college-bred that he drew the
lightning from heaven and tore the scepter from the tyrant?
Was it because Abraham Lincoln had little schooling that his
great heart beat true to God and man, lifting him to free a
race and die for his country? Because men naturally great
have done great service in the world without advantages, does
it follow that lack of advantage is the secret of success? Was
Pericles a less sagacious leader of the state, during forty years
of Athenian glory, because he was thoroughly accomplished in
every grace of learning? Or, swiftly passing from the Athenian
agora to the Boston town-meeting, behold Samuel Adams,
tribune of New England against Old England—of America
against Europe—of liberty against despotism. Was his power
enfeebled, his fervor chilled, his patriotism relaxed, by his
college education? No, no; they were strengthened, kindled,
confirmed. Taking his Master's Degree one hundred and
thirty-four years ago, thirty-three years before the declaration
of Independence, Samuel Adams, then twenty-one years old,
declared in a Latin discourse—the first flashes of the fire that
blazed afterward in Faneuil Hall and kindled America—that
it is lawful to resist the supreme magistrate if the commonwealth cannot otherwise be preserved. In the very year that
Jefferson was born, the college boy, Samuel Adams, on a Commencement day like this, on an academical platform like this
on which we stand, struck the key-note of American independence, which still stirs the heart of man with its music.

Or, within our own century, look at the great modern
statesmen who have shaped the politics of the world. They

were educated men; were they therefore visionary, pedantic, impracticable? Cavour, whose monument is United Italy—one from the Alps to Tarentum, from the lagunes [*sic*] of Venice to the gulf of Salerno: Bismarck, who has raised the German empire from a name to a fact: Gladstone, today the incarnate heart and conscience of England: they are the perpetual refutation of the sneer that high education weakens men for practical affairs. Trained themselves, such men know the value of training. All countries, all ages, all men, are their teachers. The broader their education, the wider the horizon of their thought and observation, the more affluent their resources, the more humane their policy. Would Samuel Adams have been a truer popular leader had he been less an educated man? Would Walpole the less truly have served his country had he been, with all his capacities, a man whom England could have revered and loved? Could Gladstone so sway England with his serene eloquence, as the moon the tides, were he a gambling, swearing, boozing squire like Walpole? There is no sophistry more poisonous to the state, no folly more stupendous and demoralizing, than the notion that the purest character and the highest education are incompatible with the most commanding mastery of men and the most efficient administration of affairs.

Undoubtedly a practical and active interest in politics will lead you to party association and co-operation. Great public results—the repeal of the corn-laws in England, the abolition of slavery in America—are due to that organization of effort and concentration of aim which arouse, instruct and inspire the popular heart and will. This is the spring of party, and those who earnestly seek practical results instinctively turn to this agency of united action. But in this tendency, useful in the state as the fire upon the household hearth, lurks, as in that fire, the deadliest peril. Here is our republic—it is a ship with towering canvas spread, sweeping before the prosperous gale over a foaming and sparkling sea: it is a lightning train darting with awful speed along the edge of dizzy abysses and across bridges that quiver over unsounded gulfs. Because we are Americans, we have no peculiar charm, no magic spell, to stay the eternal laws. Our safety lies alone in cool self-possession, directing the forces of wind and wave and fire. If once the madness to which the excitement tends usurps control, the catastrophe is inevitable. And so deep is the conviction that sooner or later this madness must seize every republic, that the most plausible suspicion of the permanence of the American government is founded in the belief that party spirit cannot be restrained. It is indeed a master passion, but its control is the true conservatism of the republic and of happy human progress: and it is men made familiar by education with the history of its ghastly catastrophes, men with the proud courage of independence, who are to temper by lofty action, born of that knowledge, the ferocity of party spirit. . . .

[*In the omitted paragraphs, Curtis elaborates on his criticism of party politics and party loyalty.*]

It is because these consequences are familiar to the knowledge of educated and thoughtful men that such men are constantly to assuage this party fire and to take care that party is always subordinated to patriotism. Perfect party discipline is the most dangerous weapon of party spirit, for it is the abdication of the individual judgment: it is the application to political parties of the Jesuit principle of implicit obedience.

It is for you to help break this withering spell. It is for you to assert the independence and the dignity of the individual citizen, and to prove that party was made for the voter not the voter for party. When you are angrily told that if you erect your personal whim against the regular party behest, you make representative government impossible by refusing to accept its conditions, hold fast by your own conscience and let the party go. There is not an American merchant who would send a ship to sea under the command of Captain Kidd, however skillful a sailor he might be. Why should he vote to send Captain Kidd to the legislature or to put him in command of the ship of state because his party directs? The party which to-day nominates Captain Kidd, will to-morrow nominate Judas Iscariot, and to-morrow, as today, party spirit will spurn you as a traitor for refusing to sell your master. "I tell you," said an ardent and well-meaning partizan, speaking of a closely contested election in another state, "I tell you it is a nasty state, and I hope we have done nasty work enough to carry it." But if your state has been carried by nasty means this year, success will require nastier next year, and the nastiest means will always carry it. The party may win, but the state will have been lost, for there are successes which are failures. When a man is sitting upon the bough of a tree and diligently sawing it off between himself and the trunk, he may succeed, but his success will break his neck.

The remedy for the constant excess of party spirit lies, and lies alone, in the courageous independence of the individual citizen. The only way, for instance, to procure the party nomination of good men, is for every self-respecting voter to refuse to vote for bad men. In the medieval theology the devils feared nothing so much as the drop of holy water and the sign of the cross, by which they were exorcised. The evil spirits of party fear nothing so much as bolting and scratching. *In hoc signo vinces.* If a farmer would reap a good crop, he scratches the weeds out of his field. If we would have good men upon the ticket, we must scratch bad men off. If the scratching breaks down the party, let it break: for the success of the party by such means would break down the country. The evil spirits must be taught by means that they can understand. "Them fellers," said the captain of a canal-boat of his men—"them fellers never think you mean a thing until you kick 'em. They feel that, and understand."

It is especially necessary for us to perceive the vital relation of individual courage and character to the common welfare because ours is a government of public opinion, and public opinion is but the aggregate of individual thought. We have the awful responsibility as a community of doing what we choose; and it is of the last importance that we choose to do what is wise and right. . . . [*An anecdote of the antislavery agitation is omitted.*] Public opinion can do what it has a mind to in this country. If it be debased and demoralized, it is the most odious of tyrants. It is Nero and Caligula multiplied by millions. Can there then be a more stringent public duty for every man—and the greater the intelligence the greater the duty—than to take care, by all the influence he can command, that the country, the majority, public opinion, shall have a mind to do only what is just and pure, and humane?

Gentlemen, leaving this college to take your part in the discharge of the duties of American citizenship, every sign encourages and inspires. The year that is now ending, the year that opens the second century of our history, has furnished the supreme proof that in a country of rigorous party division the purest patriotism exists. That and that only is the pledge of a prosperous future. No mere party fervor, or party fidelity, or party discipline, could fully restore a country torn and distracted by the fierce debate of a century and the convulsions of civil war; nothing less than a patriotism all-embracing as the summer air could heal a wound so wide. I know,—no man better,—how hard it is for earnest men to separate their country from their party, or their religion from their sect. But nevertheless the welfare of the country is dearer than the mere victory of party as truth is more precious than the interest of any sect. You will hear this patriotism scorned as an impracticable theory, as the dream of a cloister, as the whim of a fool. But such was the folly of the Spartan Leonidas, staying with his three hundred the Persian horde and teaching Greece the self-reliance that saved her. Such was the folly of the Swiss Arnold von Winkelried, gathering into his own breast the host of Austrian spears, making his dead body the bridge of victory for his countrymen. Such was the folly of the American Nathan Hale, gladly risking the seeming disgrace of his name, and grieving that he had but one life to give for his country. Such are the beacon-lights of a pure patriotism that burn forever in men's memories and answer each other through the illuminated ages. And of the same grandeur, in less heroic and poetic form, was the patriotism of Sir Robert Peel in recent history. He was the leader of a great party and the prime minister of England. The character and necessity of party were as plain to him as to any man. But when he saw that the national welfare demanded the repeal of the corn-laws which he had always supported, he did not quail. Amply avowing the error of a life and the duty of avowing it—foreseeing the probable overthrow of his party and the bitter execration that must fall upon him, he tranquilly did his duty. With the eyes of England fixed upon him in mingled amazement, admiration and indignation, he rose in the House of Commons to perform as great a service as any English statesman ever performed for his country, and in closing his last speech in favor of the repeal, describing the consequences that its mere prospect had produced, he loftily exclaimed: "Where there was dissatisfaction I see contentment; where there was turbulence, I see there is peace; where there was disloyalty, I see there is loyalty. I see a disposition to confide in you, and not to agitate questions that are the foundations of your institutions." When all was over, when he had left office, when his party was out of power, and the fury of party execration against him was spent, his position was greater and nobler than it had ever been. Cobden said of him, "Sir Robert Peel has lost office, but he has gained a country;" and Lord Dalling said of him, what may truly be said of Washington: "Above all parties, himself a party, he had trained his own mind into a disinterested sympathy with the intelligence of his country."

A public spirit so lofty is not confined to other ages and lands. You are conscious of its stirrings in your souls. It calls you to courageous service, and I am here to bid you obey the call. Such patriotism may be ours. Let it be your parting vow that it shall be yours. Bolingbroke described a patriot king in England; I can imagine a patriot president in America. I can see him indeed the choice of a party, and called to administer the government when sectional jealousy is fiercest and party passion most inflamed. I can imagine him seeing clearly what justice and humanity, the national law and the national welfare require him to do, and resolved to do it. I can imagine him patiently enduring not only the mad cry of party hate, the taunt of "recreant" and "traitor," of "renegade" and "coward," but what is harder to bear, the amazement, the doubt, the grief, the denunciation, of those as sincerely devoted as he to the common welfare. I can imagine him pushing firmly on, trusting the heart, the intelligence, the conscience of his countrymen, healing angry wounds, correcting misunderstandings, planting justice on surer foundations, and, whether his party rise or fall, lifting his country heavenward to a more perfect union, prosperity and peace. This is the spirit of a patriotism that girds the commonwealth with the resistless splendor of the moral law—the invulnerable panoply of states, the celestial secret of a great nation and a happy people.

25.

Proceedings of the National Grange of the Patrons of Husbandry, 1878

American farmers were for a long time skeptical even of elementary schooling, and they were especially critical of higher education at public expense because it increased property taxes without providing tangible benefits for the rural population. However, once it became apparent that education might serve agricultural interests, farmers came to treat it as a right they should share with other elements of the population. The proceedings of the National Grange, the first full-scale farm organization in the United States, exemplify both their dawning interest and the terms in which they stated it.

Whereas leaders of the movement tended to visualize their organization as an informal educational agency that would teach farmers to overcome a wide range of contemporary social and economic evils, the rank and file pressed for limited practical measures such as those outlined in the committee reports below. Particularly, they wanted uniform textbooks because they resented the monopolistic practices of textbook publishers, and they sought elementary education in agricultural science for obvious vocational reasons. They also conceded thereby many of the claims that advocates of universal education had been pressing since the 1830s.

The Committee on Education offered the following reports:

Your committee have also had under consideration the communication of Bro. Wilson, of Florida, recommending such action on the part of this body as will secure uniformity in the choice of school books throughout the country; and have instructed me to report favorably upon the recommendation, and to move the appointment of the committee therein proposed, which shall be instructed to report in writing at the next annual session of the National Grange a plan by which this object, so important to the farmers of the country, may be effected.

The report was received, and on motion, the recommendation for the appointment of a committee adopted.

The committee on Education, to which was referred so much of the addresses of the Worthy Master and Worthy Lecturer as related to the subject of education, have had the same under consideration, and instruct me to make the following report:

From the information we gather from the address and report, we are glad to see that the subject of Grange education is one of growing interest amongst the patrons of the several

From *Journal of Proceedings of the National Grange of the Patrons of Husbandry,* XII (1878), 112–114.

States, and that much earnest thought is being directed towards the perfection of methods which promise the advancement of this important end. The plans of the order for the practical education of its members are simple, efficient and well adapted, and the conclusion of every observing Patron is, that in those Granges in which these plans have been put in practical operation, their members have made the greatest progress in intelligence, prosperity and usefulness. This is justly regarded as one of the most important interests in the Grange and is the basis of its purpose to elevate the farmer and improve his condition by increasing the intelligence which directs him in the pursuit of his vocation, and in the discharge of the duties of good citizenship. In accordance with the demands of the age, it recognizes the necessity for a more specific education for those who are engaged in the various forms of agriculture. Such education as will quicken the intelligence of the farmer, fertilize his fields, diversify his products, and qualify him for enlightened action in all questions of industrial or political interest, which affect his welfare.

Whilst then the demand for industrial and technical education is recognized by every industry, in no department is the necessity for it greater than in the agricultural, and to the Grange belongs the proud distinction of being the pioneer organization in America, in simplifying and popularizing a method by which elementary instruction in agricultural science may be brought within the reach of every farmer and citizen in the land, through the Grange, and the public schools.

Thus while the Order is seeking, through clearly defined methods, to promote the growth of the farmer in practical knowledge, it recognizes in the public schools of the country valuable instrumentalities for advancing this interest upon which alone the Order predicates its hopes of ultimate success, in the grand and progressive purposes which it has declared to the world.

The rapid crystallization of popular sentiment amongst the members of the Order, everywhere, in favor of the only practical method by which this work may be accomplished, is full of encouragement, and is an earnest of the proper appreciation of this valuable auxiliary to the wisely ordered educational plans of the Order. It is one of the most hopeful signs of its future growth and prosperity that those to whom its educational interests are intrusted, are giving more thought to this means of meeting the great want of the age, a system that will reach the masses.

Agricultural Colleges, everywhere established to meet the demand for a higher education for the farm, may afford the highest facilities for education in this direction, but do not supply this growing want, for the masses cannot avail themselves of their benefits, and they are in too many instances languishing because the interest in agricultural education is at so low an ebb in our rural communities. The plan of popularizing such education as is herein proposed, will tend, however, to counteract this indifference, and give an impetus to the growth of such colleges as they are not likely, otherwise, to receive.

In these schools may be imparted an elementary knowledge of the Science of Agriculture, which will not only increase the intelligence that directs our farm management, but will prepare the coming farmer to enter the higher school of the Grange, with a better knowledge of improved methods, a keener zest for the pursuit of practical information, a juster idea of the dignity of labor, and a higher conception of the true aims of life. I am further instructed to offer the following resolution to the Grange, and ask its adoption:

Resolved, That the National Grange recommend to the Patrons of the several States that they demand the introduction of the "study of the elementary principles of agriculture," by legislation, into the public schools of their respective States, and that it further enjoins upon the representatives in this body this especial charge, that they promote by every proper means the furtherance of this end.

The report was received, and, on motion, the resolution was adopted.

26.

James W. Patterson, "National Aid to Education," 1881

One of the by-products of the Civil War was a vain effort to promote elementary education in the South by appropriating the proceeds from the sale of public lands for its common schools. In the years after Reconstruction advocates of national aid to education extended these early plans to embrace the education of children throughout the Union, a step intended both to combat the evils of illiteracy in the North and to offer landless eastern states an incentive to join the cause. One of the prominent spokesmen for the later measure was James W. Patterson of New Hampshire, formerly United States Senator and now State Superintendent of Public Instruction, whose address to the National Educational Association in 1881 is printed here. According to the published proceedings of that body, "animated discussion" followed Patterson's remarks, but none of the bills appropriating federal funds for education passed both houses of Congress despite the grave national emergency that Patterson and others depicted. Even so, his argument remains significant as a relatively moderate statement of the perspectives in which professional educators saw the common schools in a time of growing social disruption caused not only by immigration but also by the industrial development of the country.

The old masters of the world arrogantly assumed that every Roman citizen was born a ruler; and hence the vainest as well as the greatest of Roman orators said, "Any one can make

From United States Bureau of Education, *Circulars of Information*, 1881, Number 3 (Washington, D. C.: Government Printing Office, 1881), pp. 68–78.

himself a jurisconsult in a week, but an orator is the production of a lifetime." Aristotle, more thoughtful and observant of the causes and drift of human affairs, said, "All who have meditated on the art of governing mankind have been convinced that the fate of empires depends on the education of children." The political philosophy of the great Athenian voices the experience of all the ages since his day. It would be easy to fill the time allotted to me with utterances of similar import from publicists and practical statesmen of every period and phase of civil progress.

The conservative forces of government are moral, not physical. It is the intent and spirit of the people which give validity and inviolability to law. Without this it is soulless and impotent. Statutes cannot bring order and prosperity to a state whose citizens are not a law unto themselves. A people who have not an intelligent appreciation of liberty, and do not see the line beyond which it passes into license, will perpetually chafe and rebel against its necessary limitations. They are not safe guardians of civil freedom, if they do not apprehend its nature and the institutions by which it is reduced to a system of practical government. Individuals who, like children and madmen, have not the capacity or disposition to govern themselves in a way to subserve their own or the public interest, cannot claim the right of self government. Equally, a state in which a large majority of the people do not comprehend the nature and genius of free institutions cannot assert the right of popular government, and has no cause to complain of the restraints of a higher power that would suppress the violence or fraud that tends to the overthrow of law and liberty. Should the intelligence of the electorate of any State of our Union decline so low as to render self rule a farce or a peril, unquestionably that article of the Constitution of the General Government which guarantees a republican form to every State comes into action and is paramount to all State authority. The guarantee carries with it an implied power to guard against such a contingency, not necessarily by force, but by demanding or providing in each State the means of popular education. It is idle longer to talk of this as an exclusively local or State question. It involves the welfare and life of the Union, and is therefore a national question. It is true, "the national charter," as Judge Tourgee has said, "is dumb in regard to it;" but it is potentially in it.[1] The conception is as old as the convention of 1787, and destined soon to come to its birth in some living form. As the great war powers slumbered in the Constitution till wakened into activity by the necessities of the Government, so this will be seen to be a legitimate offspring of fundamental law when the instinct of self preservation shall demand it. The Republic carries with it, written or implied, the right to perpetuate itself; and national education being essential to that end, its maintenance will be found necessary to transmute the blind, brutal instincts of ignorant masses into intelligent forces of strength and prosperity. We have not yet realized the full measure of disaster possible to a free state based upon popular ignorance, but the drama is on the stage and may yet become a tragedy of blood.

I will not repeat statistics familiar to the public mind, but must recall for your reflection the painful fact that 45 per cent. of illiteracy in sixteen States of the Union has not only placed all political power, in that section of the country, in the hands of a majority of the remaining 55 per cent. of voters, but, not to mention its weight in the electoral college, has given to one-twelfth of the voting force of the Republic 72 per cent. of power in the lower and 84 per cent. in the upper branch of Congress. The illiterate balance of power, incapable of understanding or too weak to defend their rights, may be excluded

---

[1] [Albion W. Tourgée, author of *A Fool's Errand* (1879), first rose to prominence as a Radical Republican judge of the Superior Court of North Carolina, where he had settled during Reconstruction. He subsequently characterized the attempt to overcome southern aristocratic prejudices as a fool's errand, and therefore he advocated a national system of education.]

or defrauded at the polls, the constitutional guarantee of State republics defied, and the vast interests of the country subjected to a usurped power of legislation.

But history suggests to our apprehension yet graver perils. This blended mass of humanity, which to-day may be the convenient instrument of personal avarice or ambition, awakened in the bitter conflicts of party to a consciousness of its strength, held by no moral restraints, and maddened by some real or fancied social wrong, may at length sweep down, with the resistless power of elemental forces, in the States so cursed, all the forms and landmarks of an inherited liberty, or, like a Parisian mob, stain its altars with the blood of the purest and ablest of the land. Should such an emergency come to us, as it has to other republics, nothing but national power could arrest the desolation; and the Executive, in the discharge of his duty, would be forced to intervene to rescue society from destruction. When we reflect that such possibilities may become an accomplished fact, shall our activity in the cause of popular education be paralyzed by the timid assertion that the work is not national, but one left to the care of the several States? What if the States refuse or neglect to care for this common interest; shall the nation slumber over the restless volcano till it is too late to save our interests, our honor, or our liberties? A people upon whom the responsibilities of the ballot have been cast have a right to demand of the government which conferred it a degree of intellectual training which shall enable them safely to discharge its functions. But we are told we cannot afford to thus secure the future at the cost of sacrificing the fundamental principle of the local distribution of power. Here we are met again by the ever recurring, never ending dogma of State sovereignty, which, without the discrimination of the ghost of Banquo, stalks obtrusively into every subject, seemingly unconscious that it is a ghost. State rights are sacred and impregnable barriers to the usurpations of central power, but are impotent and untimely obstructions in the path of national safety. Will not all State rights perish in the doom that awaits the universal decline of popular intelligence? But will some advocate of local sovereignty tell us how a national supervision of this great department of the common welfare is to imperil State rights more than the regulation of commerce and currency? The exercise of concurrent educational powers in the States is no more dangerous to personal or State rights than the discharge of concurrent judicial functions or the exercise of a concurrent power of taxation. The objection is the spectre of a disordered fancy, and has no real existence. But if it were true, it would be no loss to exchange a paralyzed State function for a national one that would breathe vitality through the whole organism of society. Of what value are rights to a State, if its population cannot discriminate or comprehend them, and have not the ability or spirit to defend them? Abstract political powers are a utopian dream without the intelligence to recognize and embody them in practical laws and institutions. Political power is a dangerous weapon in the hands of a people who have not the wealth, the arts, the utilities, the industries, the altars, and the homes that spring from the schools. Not simply our foreign influence and Federal unity, but the domestic prosperity and security of the States must fall with the decline of local intelligence.

The laws of trade and social economy, the inventive skill, the thrift and enterprise of business, the capacity for industrial production, and the accumulations of wealth, the growth of brain power, and moral stamina which bring influence and character to communities have their birth and nourishment in the schools. All these and the absolute security of States against the encroachments of Federal power will be found in a system of free universal education. The ingenuity and skill of the workshop, the sense and manliness of the farm, the scope and enterprise of commerce, the genius and heroism of arms, the wealth and pathos of literature—all industries and all professions droop and die in the eclipse of popular intelligence.

The question of congressional aid to education is fundamental, and has been forced into the arena of legislation against the wish of parties by vexed problems for which statecraft can find no other solution. The situation is abnormal and disgraceful, and demands the forecast of prudent statesmanship rather than the empiricism of politics. Experience teaches us that this great interest cannot longer be left to the exclusive care of the States.

The census of 1870 revealed the startling fact that more than one-fourth of our whole population above the age of ten years could neither read nor write and more than one-half the population of the late slave States above that age were illiterate. We do not allude to this in a spirit of crimination, but because it is an essential fact in the discussion. The advantage of the North, and especially of New England, in this regard has resulted from the circumstances of settlement and the character of their industries. This difference constitutes no legitimate ground of inaction. We of the North cannot innocently refuse to coöperate in an effort to remedy this great public peril because it is largely local, nor ought we to complain that the funds demanded for its removal, to be effective, will have to be distributed on the basis of illiteracy, and therefore unequally; for, while we may not derive as many advantages, we shall be benefited as essentially as the less favored section and in the only way in which the evil can be reached. We are one people. Our industrial and political interests are bound in a perpetual wedlock, and the whole family of States must rise or fall together. We cannot say one to the other, "I have no need of thee," but the members should have the same care one for another, and whether one member suffer, all the members suffer with it, or one member be honored, all the members rejoice with it.

There is an explicit grant of power in the third section of the fourth article of the Constitution, "to dispose of, and make all needful rules and regulations respecting, the territory or other property belonging to the United States." Basing its action upon this constitutional provision, Congress, in pursuance of a policy adopted anterior to the organic law, has, at successive periods since the administration of Washington, made grants of land for educational purposes, aggregating 95,737,714 acres. It has also made direct appropriations of money for this purpose, which amount to $47,785,197.93.[2] In many of these cases Congress has made, in accordance with the letter of the Constitution, specific regulations for the expenditure of the sums appropriated.

In view of this record, covering the whole period of our history, it is too late to question the power of the General Government to appropriate public funds for educational purposes and to disburse the same directly by its own agents. Such appropriations on the basis of illiteracy are not liable to the charge of an unequal distribution of public funds; for they are not given as donations to States or citizens, but for "the common defence and general welfare." Like forts and lighthouses at ports of entry and military and naval schools, they are not local but general in their purpose and effects. But in what form this national aid can best be applied is a practical question, demanding the most careful consideration. The independent *right* of the General Government to educate its people for the proper discharge of their public functions is incident to its very existence. But as intelligence is an antecedent condition of self government, it must be conceded that the right to educate its

---

[2] [The major grant of federal funds to education had come in the form of the distribution of the surplus revenue in 1837, under the terms of which the federal government "deposited" proportionate shares of its surplus funds with the states for their use in aiding internal improvements and education. In addition, every state entering the Union after 1800 received five percent of the net proceeds of public land sales in the state for these same two purposes. It is not clear what other direct appropriations Patterson may have had in mind, but his figures probably include funds appropriated for the use of the Freedmen's Bureau. The grants of land he refers to included the sections of land regularly reserved for education in organizing new states; additional lands granted most new states either before or after their admission, intended originally to further internal improvements; and still further grants to encourage higher education in state universities and land-grant colleges.]

citizens belongs also to each State; that right, however, cannot *limit* the obligation to the States, for the citizens of the States are citizens of the United States, and therefore the General Government, whose powers are supreme within their range, is bound to secure to all the children of the Republic, directly or through the States, suitable and sufficient opportunities to prepare them to discharge intelligently and safely their political duties. The public welfare is the supreme law of every State, whether founded upon a written or unwritten constitution; but the attempt to supplant State schools by a national system, or to establish a binary system, would be a measure so radical and hazardous that it should only be resorted to as a last expedient against the dissolution of the Republic. On the other hand, the distribution to the States of national funds, to be disbursed by them without supervision or responsibility, would be a failure as a permanent educational policy. Revenues so received would be lost in the scuffle and antagonisms of politics, or, like the old "surplus revenue" of 1836, vanish into thin air through a thousand follies. Should this not happen it would be diverted into special channels by dominant State prejudices or be made to minister to the higher education, while popular ignorance, which it is designed to remove, would be left to increase.

Colleges and universities will spring as a natural growth from public intelligence, but common schools must be planted and fostered by the government. The most urgent demand of the Republic to-day, looking at its political and social necessities, is a system of free primary instruction that shall reach all classes, races, and sects, and be directed and inspired by a supervision at once intelligent and unflagging. Unfortunately, districts the most benighted and deplorable are the last to realize their situation, and others have not the means to better their condition. National aid should be applied to the localities and populations most in want, and by an impartial intelligence that will make no mistakes.

In matters of such moment Congress should be guided by the rules of business which hold between private parties.

Let it be sure that the thing paid for will be received. Security is the law of business between honest men, and surely parties who ignore conscience and repudiate solemn obligations have no reason to complain if held to the same rule.

To devise a wise and practical plan of national aid and supervision of instruction should be the work of an intelligent commission familiar with the wants and conditions of all sections; and even this would have to be perfected by experience, like other permanent institutions.

I would not presume to foreshadow a system in matters so fundamental and organic; but we may venture to suggest that the plan adopted and so successfully administered in the distribution and application of the Peabody fund would be a safe and instructive precedent for statesmen in the disposition of national funds to the same cause.[3] I am disposed to believe that, whether the proposed aid is to come from an invested fund or from annual appropriations, it should be paid directly to districts by educated and responsible agents appointed by the executive, and on such conditions as to improve and lengthen schools already existing and to secure the establishment of others in localities where they are needed. These school agents should act in harmony with local officials as far as possible, but be independent of State control and required to examine by visitation and report in detail the condition and wants of their respective districts to the Commissioner of Education. Such beneficent supervision by the Government if judiciously conducted would be felt to be beneficial to all interests, and would serve to draw the fellowship of the States into a closer union by invisible ties of gratitude and love. Or, if in any case prejudice, pride, or some fancied right should refuse to

---

[3] [In 1867 George Peabody, a wealthy Massachusetts businessman, created a trust fund of $3,000,000 to promote education in the South. His board of trustees used its income to help southern municipalities initiate public schools, to encourage state-wide educational systems, and to train teachers. They did not favor integrated schools, however.]

submit to an inspection designed to increase and perpetuate the blessings of liberty, it would furnish to the Government an opportunity to assert its paramount sovereignty in a case that would command the approval of mankind, which might be an incident little to be feared or regretted. It is best that the lines of power should be sharply drawn, and questions of jurisdiction set at rest by the court. We do not insist on mixed schools nor attempt to lay down the specific conditions on which public moneys shall be distributed for educational purposes; but we insist that it should be in accordance with the constitutional provision that "No State shall make or enforce any law which shall abridge the privileges or immunities of citizens of the United States."

I am not unaware that this scheme of national intervention in the educational interests of the country has been opposed on the plea that we cannot show any express power delegated to Congress to establish a system of schools in the States, and that consequently the power is reserved to and belongs only to the States. Our answer is that the objection is irrelevant, for we are not asking for the overthrow of State systems or the establishment of a national system. We are simply asking that Congress may go into the States and direct the expenditure of funds which, it is admitted, it has a right to appropriate for such purposes.

When Government appropriates public moneys, they should be disbursed by agents responsible to itself; but, if States have exclusive control of education, funds given for its advancement may be so diverted as to defeat the end in view. It has been done, and may be done again, without remedy.

But the right of such *supervision* is denied, on the allegation that it is not in the bond. I admit it is not in the letter; but I claim that it is the intrinsic life of the bond, without which it could not exist. If we are to deny to Congress all powers incidental to those expressed in the Constitution, we must abolish the Department of Agriculture and the Coast Survey, so essential to two of the great industries of the country; shut up our Naval and Military Academies, and fold our arms in war and rebellion, and go to pieces for want of the constitutional power of self defence. Nay, one-third of the legislation of Congress is void, and the very charter of our liberties becomes a procrustean bed upon which the Republic is bound, and beyond which it can never hope to reach in all the progress of the ages.

We are told that "Federal education was not contemplated as necessary to 'establish justice, to insure domestic tranquillity, provide for the common defense, promote the general welfare, and secure the blessings of liberty to the people.'" Such language in our country and at our time is marvellous. Without popular education popular governments have no right of existence and cannot be maintained when established. The Republic has as legitimate a right to protect itself against ignorance as against pestilence and rebellion. Education informs and quickens the inventive powers, by which improved methods and new forces are given to productive industry; it lifts the poor from the ranks of dependent labor into the fields of enterprise and responsibility, and surrounds them with the utilities and beauties of life; it opens to the intellect the realms of thought, and leads it through the galleries of art and science; it gives to the nation wealth for poverty, strength for weakness, and primacy for subordination; but not for one or all of these does the Republic open its treasury for the advancement of knowledge. It is solely as an act of self defence that the Government comes to the rescue of the schools. For this, if the proceeds of the sale of the public lands are insufficient, it has the right to pour out millions and dictate and control the method and the direction of their disbursement.

In this connection we should remember that the strongest defences of nations are not armies and navies, but the affections and patriotism of their citizens. A common pride in the achievements and a common faith in the character and destiny of the government are essential to its peace and perpetuity. Discordant creeds are the precursors of faction and dissolution. The schools are the nurseries of public sentiment, and should have but one curriculum of political philosophy and civil history. The past is admonitory of the future. To remove a cancer and leave its roots is not cure, but relief. The fatal hour is only delayed. In war he conquers whose principle survives the conflict of arms. If history is reversed, if treason and patriotism are transformed, if opposite theories of government are inculcated, and pride and shame interchanged in our sources of national thought, are we acting the part of a prudent regard for the welfare of posterity? Are we not holding a chalice of blood to the lips of our children, and is it playing the rôle of statesmen for our public men to shut their eyes and ignore such facts? Has our government no power to enforce, I do not say a uniformity of text books, but the inculcation of a common national sentiment and political philosophy in the schools?

I realize how difficult and delicate is the subject of which I speak, but it is legitimate to the occasion, and it would be cowardly to blink it out of sight. I cherish no feeling of sectionalism and would utter no word of crimination; but I am sure it is not wisdom to allow great dangers to drift us in silence into irretrievable ruin, when there is no real ground of difference of theory or action, but only pride and prejudice. The irreconcilable antagonism between free and slave labor, from which sprang the divergent theories and sectional bitterness of our old time politics, having perished with the war, there is nothing left but habits of thought and wounded pride to withhold us from mutual regard and a cordial coöperation in all that can advance the prosperity and glory of the country. Neither can deny to the other honesty of convictions or courage in battle, and this rescues the dead of both sections from dishonor. Why contend longer over obstructions and dead issues? Credit and trade, labor and skill, civil power and the social amenities, are all paralyzed by this persistent rancor of sectional jealousy, surviving its causes for a score of years. Our respective industries would be strengthened and made lucrative by mutual confidence and the fraternal emulations of business. Property would appreciate and resources develop, science be quickened and literature enriched, private virtue become more sacred and social happiness more universal, if we should give less time to the differentia of politics and more to the essentials of life. So long as opposing theories as to the nature and later history of the Government shall be taught in the different States, so long there will be bitterness and vituperation in the press, angry debates and disgraceful scenes in Congress, and portents of more direful disasters in the future.

But the cure must come from without. The Ethiopian cannot change his skin, nor an insane man reverse his thoughts. If reason and self interest have lost their control in the States, there must be a supreme power that holds and moves them in their orbits, if we are a nation, that can reach and remove the causes of discontent and peril.

The census reveals the fact that a large percentage of the illiterates of the country are of foreign birth. Emigration has become the policy of European states, as a relief to their institutions from the strain beneath. Our country has been made the field into which the ignorance, poverty, and hate of these revolutionary masses have been poured. Like pent-up gases they become harmless, for the most part, when the pressure is removed; but, crippled in capacity and with nothing to tax, they crowd under the protection of Federal law into the States and fill their school-houses with children. It is but right, therefore, that the enhanced burdens thus thrown upon the property of the States, if they do their duty to the children, and which in the aggregate amount to millions, should be relieved by national aid. There must be a rapid and constant decline in the intelligence, capacity, and character of our population, if these teeming millions are left uneducated and unassimilated.

We do not often stop to consider what changes have taken place since our gates were thrown open to the world. The influx of the overcrowded peoples East and West by the modern facilities of transportation could not be anticipated a century ago. This change necessitates corresponding changes in our internal policy. The schools must be multiplied and improved in methods and force, so as to keep pace with this drifting multitude, whose numbers outrun their means.

The failure to assimilate these millions, and bring them into full sympathy with our institutions and habits of thought, is already felt, especially in those great centres into which they have crowded in the largest numbers. It is not immigration or change we deprecate, but deterioration. The successive invasions of England were terrible visitations, but they poured fresh vigor and broader sentiments into the old Briton, from whose mixed blood has sprung the brawny liberty loving Englishman of history. With them there was a constant growth through their ages of battle. But our pauper immigrants are not Saxon or Norman invaders, and we fear a constant decline through our ages of trade. The children of these strangers within our gates must be made American in thrift and skill and in their political aspirations and pride; they must be lifted by knowledge above the control of party passion and be inspired with a personality that will not suffer them to be the tools of personal ambition; they must be made to apprehend the nature and genius of our institutions and to love the flag of the Republic as the symbol of freedom and power. Does the past justify us in the belief that the States will do all this? The age is characterized by broader views and quickened efforts in the cause of popular education. Governments have at last been forced to adopt it as the policy of success. Its power has been discovered in the productive force imparted to industry, in the triumphs of science, and in the achievements of war. Discoveries and inventions are the footsteps of its progress; it is recognized in the gift of the ballot and the subordination of leaders to the popular will; it is heard, not in the drum roll, but in the music of machinery; its growth is realized in the widened uses of literature and the utilities of art; lightning and steam are the contestants in its Olympiads, and it gathers its battle flags at Sedan.

While the statesmanship of Europe is pouring out millions in the rivalry of her systems of schools, shall we stand still to be swamped in the surf that rolls from her shores? To-day we are hardly abreast with England, France, and Prussia in the character and resources of our schools. And shall we be told that the Government must fold its arms with the shallow pretence of a want of power and leave this work exclusively to the States, which cannot realize or feel the responsibility of this magnificent competition of empires in the march of knowledge and the growth of mental power? The policy will be a cowardly and suicidal acknowledgment of impotency, and, if persisted in, we shall learn to our sorrow that an ignorant people is an inferior people in all the elements of national greatness. If the bill now pending before Congress is too narrow for either aid or incitement, let its gifts be enlarged to the measure of our wants.[4] The nation is not impoverished when it gives to itself. Revenues so bestowed will be a profitable investment. It is but casting bread upon the waters that will be found after many days.

We should be glad to help build the waste places made desolate by war, if only hereafter they may be allowed to blossom with the fruits of an intelligent industry and social peace. The day is not distant, I trust, when both the North and South will learn that the rivalries of labor and trade and the emulations of literature and science are more profitable than the squabbles of politics or the feeding of old fires that ought to be dead. Let us unite in the noble enterprise of making our country foremost in the march of intelligence, foremost in the dignity of power, and foremost in the purity of its civilization.

The national domain is the common property of the Republic, and should be used to promote the general welfare. We can conceive of no employment of the proceeds of its sale of more general and lasting utility, and none more honorable to a free, christian people, than its application to the building up

---

[4] [The Morrill bill appropriated two-thirds of the proceeds of public land sales and certain other federal revenues to common schools according to illiteracy, one-third to land-grant colleges.]

of a permanent system of free schools that shall be adequate to supply the demands of the future. This is an essential condition of national stability and prosperity. No subject of legislation more urgently demands a liberal appropriation than this. It will be an irreparable misfortune if, in a scheme so grand in its nature and so far reaching in its influence, we come to a deadlock over the puerile conceit that any material or moral interest can suffer from a concurrent but carefully defined advisory control of popular education by the General Government. In this the interests of the State and nation are one, and coöperation may bring them more closely together. Nothing is demanded which can limit or subvert any valuable prerogative of State power. Enlarged intelligence imparts a clearer apprehension of rights and an enhanced power to defend them. Armies and navies are defences against foreign aggression, but school-houses are the natural and effective security of governments against the domestic faction and violence that are engendered in the homes of ignorance.

The people are the sovereigns and citizens of both the State and the nation, and can claim the right to be fitted for their political functions from both. When the first is unable to discharge its trust, the latter should come to its aid in a peaceful coöperation. But when a State wilfully neglects to provide the means of knowledge for the poorest and humblest of its children, the supreme power of the nation possesses, beyond a reasonable doubt, the right to intervene in the interest of national intelligence, and provide, in such way and by such agents as Congress may judge best, for the education of the children of its neglected citizens. But we will not dwell upon this, for the question to-day before the American people is rather one of patriotism than one of right. The call is not to the defence of a prerogative, but to the discharge of an imperative duty. National inferiority and ultimate anarchy or despotism are the inevitable fruits of popular ignorance, that cannot discern the real interests or the conditions of safety and prosperity to the country. School-houses have done more for the German Empire than military academies for France or great universities for England. Industrial success, military power, political superiority, intellectual achievements, and national character, all have their springs in high popular intelligence. Our destiny as a republic and our place in the march of civilization are involved in the maintenance or failure of a system of free universal education.

27.

Terence V. Powderly, Letter to a Prominent Democrat, 1883

Not everyone who appealed to popular education to combat the evils of an industrial age was a spokesman for the status quo. Indeed, the Grand Master Workman of the Knights of Labor hoped to redeem the United States from poverty, oppression, and the coercions of the wages system through the creation of a radical politics grounded in labor organization, itself to be grounded in informal deliberation and agitation of contemporary social issues. He elaborated the politics of education in the following letter to the *Pittsburg Times,* and he thought so well of it (as his autobiography points out) that he also incorporated it into his annual address to the national convention of the order in the fall of 1883. The statement makes clear that Powderly shared with George William Curtis and other high-minded publicists the ideal of a politics that would transcend political partisanship; if he recognized the need for labor organization, he visualized it primarily as an agency of impartial discussion and the free dissemination of truth. In the eyes of Powderly and his associates, in other words, the labor movement was only the latest of many "schools" that the American people had been forced to create to maintain their liberties.

A great deal has been said of late concerning the dismemberment of the Knights of Labor, and the forming of a federation of trades. The principal reason given for the proposed action, summed up in a few words is, that each trade or craft, in being organized for itself, can more easily and successfully engage in a strike. There are other arguments made use of to bolster up the "federation" idea, but that appears to be the principal one. At least it is the one to which the most prominence is given in the Eastern press. One thing is certain, the originator of that idea was neither a Knight of Labor, nor a member of a trade union, for members of these associations know that the tendency of the times is to do away with strikes; that remedy has been proved by experience to be a very costly one for employer and employe[e].

The trade union does not favor a strike; it is regarded as a *dernier resort* by every labor association in the land; and as no good can come of the dismemberment of an association which, among other things, aims at the perfecting of a system by which disputes between the laborer and capitalist can be settled without resorting to so costly an experiment as the strike is acknowledged to be, why the Knights of Labor and the various labor associations of the country are in no great danger of being disbanded.

I called the strike an experiment, and I would have every advocate of such a measure note these words. Strikes have been resorted to for centuries, and to-day, after hundreds of trials have been had, men can not embark in a strike with any assurance of success based upon a former precedent. Every one must be decided upon its own merits. I will never advocate a strike unless it be a strike at the ballot-box, or such an one as was proclaimed to the world by the unmistakable sound of the strikers' guns on the field of Lexington. But the necessity for such a strike as the latter does not exist at present. The men who made the name of Lexington famous in

From Terence Powderly, *Thirty Years of Labor, 1859 to 1889* . . . (Columbus, Ohio, 1890), pp. 274–281.

the world's history were forced to adopt the bullet because they did not possess the ballot. We have the latter; and if the money of the monopolist can influence us to deposit our ballots in favor of our enemies; if we can not be depended on to go quietly to the polling booth and summon to our aid moral courage enough to deposit a little piece of paper in our own interest, how can it be expected of us to summon physical courage enough to do battle for our rights as did our fathers at Lexington? and if we do go to the tented field, will not the same agency that induced us to vote against ourselves induce us to thrust our bayonets into the hearts of our friends instead of our foes? I answer yes, for a faithless citizen never made a faithful soldier.

What, then, is the duty of the hour? Men may argue from what I have said that I believe our cause to be hopeless; and did I not have faith in the Knights of Labor I would say, "yes, the cause is lost." Other men entertain different opinions, and positively assert that the panacea for all the ills we suffer will come through the adoption of such advice as they have to offer. For instance, "Democrat" says in his letter of July 4th, that in order to secure the blessings we seek we "have only to merge ourselves into the great Democratic party and help to swell the triumph of the plain people in 1884."[1] I must be pardoned for differing with him. I do not believe that it lies within the province of any party to protect the many against the unjust encroachments of the moneyed few, unless the many are properly instructed in the science of government.

The party is the concrete man. If the individuals comprising the party are ignorant of their rights, and must trust to the wisdom or discretion of party leaders, they either follow

---

[1] ["Democrat" was the Hon. Chauncey Black, son of Jeremiah Black and Lieutenant-Governor of Pennsylvania. His letter appeared in the *Pittsburg Times* on July 4, 1883, and Powderly's reply appeared on July 16. I am indebted to Moreau B. C. Chambers, Archivist of the Catholic University of America, for the identity of "Democrat."]

in the wake of blind leaders, or permit themselves to be blindly led along by their leaders. In either case it will not be the intelligence they display, or the instructions they give, that will urge their leaders forward in an honest groove, and under such circumstances as these the duty of the citizen ceases as soon as he casts his vote.

Will "Democrat" assure us that if each of the associations he names (the Grangers, the Knights of Labor, the Amalgamated Association, and the various trades unions), should cease to work and "merge into the Democratic party," that they would not be obliged to reorganize again in a few years to protect themselves from the Democratic party? Will any Republican assure members of these associations that a general reorganization will not be necessary should they merge into the Republican party? Remember, I am not assailing parties. The party is good or bad, as the majority of its members determine. Who is to blame for the misdeeds of a party? The majority. Who comprise the majorities in the Democratic and Republican parties? Why, "the plain people," of course. I believe that there is no man so good that he will not bear watching.

What is true of man is true of party, and in either case the watchers must be educated; they must be actuated by one common impulse. In other words, they must be organized. That there are men who believe that political parties require both watching and teaching, I am positive. Let me quote the words of a man whose fidelity to the Democratic party can not be questioned, but whose love of justice is stronger than his regard for party. In his letter to the Constitutional Club, of New York, Judge Jeremiah S. Black[2] says:

---

2 [Jeremiah Black, formerly Attorney-General and Secretary of State under James Buchanan, was an eminent constitutional lawyer best known for his efforts to restrain the authority of the federal government in *Ex parte Milligan* and *Ex parte McCardle*. He was also a vigorous advocate of regulating railroads and corporations.]

"What is the remedy? No enforcement of the Constitution and laws, which command what is right and prohibit what is wrong, for that can not be effected without officers that are faithful. As it is our governors do not govern, and legislators laugh in your face when you tell them of their oaths. Shall we turn them out and fill their places with true men? That is easier said than done. Monopoly has methods of debauching party leaders, cheating voters, and deceiving the very elect, which perpetually defeat our hopes of honest government. If the power of the corporations increases a little more, they can put their worst rascal into the highest office as easily as Caligula's horse was elected consul by the people of Rome.

"You will infer from this that I am somewhat discouraged, and it is true that very recent events here in Pennsylvania have much disappointed me. But that is no reason why you should despair. You have what we have not, an organization to make your grievances known, and I hope that from your meeting the truth will go forth to rescue and rouse up like the sound of a trumpet."

It may be inferred from the position I have taken in the foregoing lines, that the mission of the Knights of Labor is to become a political party, and that it is intended to take precedence of the Democratic party. The inference would be wrong. The Knights of Labor is higher and grander than party. There is a nobler future before it than that which clings to its existence amidst partisan rancor and strife. The Knights of Labor is a friend to men of all parties, and believing that the moment it assumes the role of a political party its usefulness will be destroyed, it has refrained and will refrain from doing so. The moment we proclaim to the world that our order is a political party, that moment the lines are drawn, and we receive no more accessions to our ranks from the other existing parties, with the exception of here and there a member who becomes a convert through conviction that we are right.

We have political parties enough. Every one of them in its early days was honest, and gave promise of good results, but the moment that success perched upon its banners, the vultures who feed upon spoils also perched upon its body, and to a certain extent frustrated the designs of its organizers.

The same would be true of the Knights of Labor. If that order is not to become a political party, what good can it accomplish? This brings us to the root of the question, and gives the reason why there can be no dismemberment of the Knights of Labor. One reason why political parties degenerate is because the masses of the common people are not educated. We may be able to read and write, but we are not educated on the economic and social questions with which we are brought in contact every hour. If we were we could more easily discern the difference between good and bad legislation, and we would not be clamoring so often for the repeal of bad laws. The chief aim of the Knights of Labor is to educate, not only men but parties; educate men first that they may educate parties and govern them intelligently and honestly. Ralph Waldo Emerson gave this advice before leaving us. He said:

"Let us make our education brave and preventive. Politics is an after-work, a poor patching. We are always a little late. The evil is done, the law is passed, and we begin the up-hill agitation for repeal of that which we ought to have prevented the enacting. We shall one day learn to supersede politics by education. What we call our root and branch reforms of slavery, war, gambling, intemperance, is only medicating the symptoms. We must begin higher; namely, in education."

"To supersede politics by education," it first becomes necessary to organize the masses into an association where they can be educated. Take fifty men of one calling, and place them in a room organized under the laws of a distinct trade society, and they will discuss nothing but such matters as pertain to their trade. If they do not mingle among those of other trades they will grow indifferent to the wants of others; they will remain in ignorance of their own rights through their ignorance of the rights of others. Selfishness will be the rule, and the "up-hill agitation for a repeal of that which we ought to have prevented the enacting" will stare us constantly in the face.

I am aware that the Knights of Labor meet with opposition from the leaders of some labor organizations. They anticipate that, in the event of their associations becoming a part of the Knights of Labor, their occupation, like Othello's, will be gone; but they entertain groundless fears. We seek the co-operation of every labor society, the dissolution of none. We seek and intend to enlist the services of men of every society, of every party, every religion, and every nation in the crusade which we have inaugurated against these twin monsters, tyranny and monopoly; and in that crusade we have burned the bridges behind us; we have stricken from our vocabulary that word fail; we aim at establishing the complete rights of man throughout the world; we take as our guide no precedent ever set by mortal man unless it be right; we tolerate no dissensions, and will have no disbanding save as ordained by the Great Master Workman when He calls from our ranks each individual member and bids him join that silent majority, whose votes upon the questions of this world find voice only on the pages of the recorded past.

28.

Testimony before the Senate Committee on Education and Labor, 1883

In 1883, stimulated by public controversy over the effects of the tariff, the Senate Committee on Education and Labor devoted a series of public hearings to exploring the condition of labor. Its chairman, Henry W. Blair of New Hampshire (the sponsor of a number of bills calling for national aid to education) made the hearings both a forum for a wide variety of contemporary social commentators and an occasion for testing public sentiment about the needs of the schools. The testimony offered to the Committee by Francis A. Walker and C. H. Johnson exemplifies the tenor of the hearings as well as the value judicious witnesses attached to education.

Walker, the president of M.I.T., was a leading liberal economist. Like many members of his generation, he watched the extension of governmental power with anxiety and maintained a not implausible commitment to the right of the states as against those of the federal government. Yet he also recognized that changing social conditions made political intervention in the economy inevitable and even desirable under certain circumstances, and he felt a genuine sympathy for the plight of the poor. It followed that he would look to education—to improved common schooling and the extension of industrial education—to solve contemporary social problems, and he held out hope that the dissemination of knowledge might diminish the need for other forms of government action.

Johnson appeared as a spokesman for his race. Middle-class Negroes had already appealed to education to improve the lot of their people; Johnson's testimony pointed up the extraordinary burdens working-class Negroes bore, explained their need for power—and maintained the faith that schools would solve the problems of race.

BOSTON, MASS., October 17, 1883.

FRANCIS A. WALKER examined.

By Mr. PUGH:[1]

Question. Have you read the resolution under which we are acting here?—Answer. I have.

From *Report of the Committee of the Senate upon the Relations between Labor and Capital,* 48th Congress, 1st Session (4 volumes; Washington, D. C., 1885), III, 325–332; IV, 635–640.

[1] [James L. Pugh, Democrat, from Alabama.]

Mr. Pugh. Then you understand what sort of information we are seeking on this question of the relations of labor and capital—the condition of the laborer, the share he gets of the product of his work; the subject of labor strikes, and their causes, and all subjects in any way relating to labor. Just in your own way proceed, if you please, to give us such information and opinions as you may have on those subjects.

The Witness. I have stated to the chairman of the committee that I have not prepared any remarks, but I shall be glad to answer any questions that may be asked. The ground which the committee seeks to cover is so large that I thought I could be more useful, if useful at all, by making answers to specific points than by preparing a general address upon the full scope of the committee's inquiry.

I will say in general, that I shall have little of a positive nature to offer, because I believe that all the governmental action which it is desirable to take in the interest of labor is comprised within two heads: Factory acts and sanitary regulations; and governmental action in both those directions, in my judgment, can, under our form of government in the United States, be better done by the legislature or government of each State for itself than by the Government of the United States acting one for all.

I say all the governmental *action*, for I heartily believe in the Government of the United States obtaining and diffusing information in regard to the condition of labor, and in regard, generally, to the industries and the trade of the country to the very largest possible degree. I believe in that, rather, because I think the diffusion of information is the best means of reducing to a minimum governmental action. I believe in general that that government is best which governs least, and that interference with trade or manufactures is very undesirable. Yet I recognize the fact that evils may and do exist which require correction by the force of law. I think government will reduce its function to the desired minimum best by diffusing information and spreading light, rather than by interfering positively by commands and prohibitions. Therefore I believe in governmental collection and diffusion of information in the highest degree, mainly because in that way I believe Government may reduce to the lowest terms its own active interference with trade and industry.

I believe, as I have said, that the action necessary to be taken in regard to the interests of labor, namely, factory acts, in the usual acceptation of that term, and sanitary regulations in the usual interpretation of that term, and perhaps more than the term has heretofore been generally understood to cover— for I believe in the extension of the system of sanitary inspection and control—I believe, I say, that Government action in these directions can be best taken by the governments of the several States, each for itself.

My reasons for holding that opinion are two. The first reason is common to a large class of governmental measures, which base, or should base themselves upon sociological principles, in which class I should include the pauper system of any community, the educational system, treatment of the insane, of the deaf, dumb, and blind, and of prisoners, as well as the factory acts and sanitary regulations of which I speak. All those have this in common, that they should be based upon the results of experience or direct experiment bearing upon the best system to be adopted in one or the other class of public exigencies.

The ground of my belief in thinking that in those cases it is better that each State for itself should determine its policy is, that social science, or sociology, is at present in a very primitive condition. It has made very little progress, and much of the progress which we seem to have made at times we find has not been made. We are not yet advanced in the science of society, especially as concerns the matters I have mentioned— the care of paupers, the deaf, the dumb, the blind, the insane, the idiots, and the criminals, and although we have made some progress in regard to elementary or popular education, we have yet much to learn.

In this matter of factory acts and sanitary regulations, we have still very much to do, and for that purpose our State-rights system is admirably disposed to the development of sociological principles. We have here a great number of States, many of them having populations closely like each other in their character and experience, others very widely unlike. We have these States, each for itself, trying experiments now. That has been so in regard to public elementary education; that is, the system of one State differs more or less from that of every other. Each State is trying a system of poor relief for itself; each is dealing with convicted criminals on a more or less individual system. Those experiments are going on side by side, and as the result of those experiments we shall in time undoubtedly reach a rather positive conclusion that one system is better than others, or than all.

If, therefore, I were asked what was the greatest advantage of our system of government, I should say that it was not the political advantage commonly attributed to the State-rights system, in which I heartily agree, but that it is the sociological advantage—that in a hundred different ways we are trying different experiments in large communities in these various respects. Perhaps twenty years ago publicists and men interested in social science, would have said that we had pretty nearly reached a conclusion in regard to many of the matters I have indicated. To-day we are very much more in doubt and uncertainty than we were then.

To take an illustration from another field: For example, twenty years ago, I suppose there were very few writers on law or governmental policy in this section, at least, of the country, or in New England, who would not have said that it was a settled principle that two legislative houses were better than one; indeed, that you could not have successful popular representative government without an upper and a lower house. To-day the experience of the British colonies in Australia and elsewhere has thrown that matter into doubt. No man would to-day presume to say that it was a certain thing.

The experience of representative governments under very widely differing conditions with a single house is such as to destroy all the confidence which, twenty years ago, the advocate of the bicameral or bifurcated system of legislature would have had; and we now recognize the fact that it is in doubt whether representative government cannot be successfully maintained at least for long periods of time with a legislature which is a unit and not bifurcated.

In the same way, with regard to the elective or appointive system for the selection of judges, the opinion, the *status* of publicists, of men interested in political science and law, has changed not a little in twenty years, where there was formerly, at least here in the East, but one opinion—that they should be appointed.

I mention these matters simply to illustrate the fact that changes are constantly going on. So it is in regard to poorlaw administration; in regard to the treatment of convicted criminals and of the afflicted classes—the deaf, dumb, blind, and insane. We are rapidly unlearning much that we had learned. Therefore I think it exceedingly desirable that the system of experiments under the sanction and authority of the States should go on; and I believe that that argument applies with quite as much force to the system of factory acts and sanitary legislation in the interests of labor as to the other classes of legislative measures I have spoken of.

My second reason for holding the opinion that this sort of governmental action in the direction indicated—factory acts and sanitary regulations—would, with more advantage to the laboring classes and with less danger of injury, or less loss to the community, be taken by the governments of the several States than the Government of the United States, is found in this consideration (to take one of those classes by itself). Factory acts are only needful and not positively harmful in societies which have reached a certain stage of development. For example, in regard to the employment of women and children and the operations of machinery, if such a body of legislation were to be imposed upon a community where manufacturing industry was just making its beginning it not only would do very much less good but infinitely more harm than by being imposed upon a community like Massachusetts or Rhode Island. As to the lack of reason for such regulations being uniform over a country like the United States, if a factory were being set up in a county in Iowa containing a population almost exclusively agricultural of, say, 20,000 people, a factory population of 200 would not require protection by law to anything like the extent that a factory population here in the East would require it, because there there could be recourse to the land; and if the conditions became unfavorable the farming population could absorb the others, who could go on the land. If the factory operatives were ground down by their employers they would resort to the land.

Again, the want of factory legislation comes, in the main, more from the numbers of the factory class at a given time than from the fact that they are a factory population by inheritance or tradition. If you have a factory population in one place for several generations, as they have in the older cities of Europe (and some of our older manufacturing points have industries which are now in the second and even the third generation), they acquire aptitudes that are highly specialized and very minute, which give them great power in production. They acquire certain habits of labor and mental attention which contribute greatly to their success, but also, on the other hand, render them weaker in the general competition for labor than a community of more primitive agricultural condition. A New England farmer can do almost anything. Every one of that class of men is a mechanic; he can turn his hand to almost anything. He has self-assertion, and is accustomed to a great variety of duties. He is a man who can get upon his legs from almost any position. He is a man of a thousand duties. The factory operative, however, especially in the second and third generation, is an artificial creature. What he can do he can do very much better than the farmer or the farmer's son,

but he is not a man of varied experience or acquirements as the
farmer, or country carpenter, or country blacksmith. Hence a
factory population in the second and third generation, particularly, has occasion for protection, in the fact that that population, in becoming highly specialized and adapted in a high
degree to certain operations, has also become, in a degree,
incapable of turning itself readily to other occupations—of
seeking even change of place when that becomes necessary.

That is the reason why, in all the enlightened nations of
the world having large manufacturing interests, there are factory acts, or a body of factory legislation. I do not remember
how it is in Austria or Russia, but I think that, with those two
exceptions, there is no country in Europe without its body of
factory acts. They are very often very minute, and that legislation is approved, with scarcely an exception, by the best political and economic writers of those countries.

But, on the other hand, it would not do to apply such
a body of legislation to a country where manufacturing industry was beginning to spring up, there not being the same occasion for it—perhaps little or no occasion for it in the character
of the population, they not having yet lost their general adapt-
iveness—their power of turning themselves from one thing to
another. Such legislation would be unsuitable there, from the
fact that there would be a large agricultural population that
could absorb them, if that were necessary, and that they could
have resort to the land, if that were necessary, which they
would not have in the neighborhood of Lowell or Manchester.
Not only is there no such occasion for such legislation, but the
positive mischief would be very much greater. Factory legislation is more suitable here. Because here capital is large and
powerful; the conditions of manufacture are well understood;
we have passed the experimental stage; we have achieved
success; have founded great manufacturing establishments,
and great manufacturing cities. I do not say that no factory
legislation that could be passed by the Massachusetts legislature could be so foolish as not to hurt these old communities,

or do any damage. It could. But even if it were not extreme or excessive in any direction, that legislation, applied to a community in which the manufacturers hardly knew what to do, and were trying to start a mill, as in some town of Georgia, Iowa, or some other place where manufacturing had not existed; where they had not trained labor; had not superintendents and overseers thoroughly understanding their business; had very little capital, and with the whole thing in a very tentative, tremulous condition, might put a factory under regulations which would very seriously cripple the enterprise. The old manufacturing communities would not, perhaps, be oppressed or embarrassed at all; they would adapt themselves to it; but where it is difficult to get your manufacturing population anyhow, or your capital anyhow, or to get men fit to conduct such enterprises anyhow—where it is a question whether you have got it or not—these first efforts at manufacturing enterprise over a large space of country, factory legislation prescribed by Congress might totally prohibit.

Therefore while I thoroughly believe in factory acts and in sanitary regulations, I think the action in those directions should be taken by the Government of each State by itself, in view of its own necessities first, as I said, because in the first place we get in that way the very best experience upon the widest possible scale as to different methods and systems of dealing with these social questions; and secondly, because many communities in the United States do not need any such legislation, and it would be positively prejudicial and a hindrance to the development of manufactures if it were undertaken. That is in general the view I take in regard to legislation with reference to labor by the General Government.

By Mr. PUGH:

Q. Have you given any thought to the subject of the power or agency of the Federal or State Governments over the question of wages for skilled labor employed in those manufacturing industries over the mere question of the amount, more or less, of pay? What power or agency can be exercised by the Federal Government or by the State Governments upon that subject? If there is any, what is it—taxational, educational or otherwise?—A. I believe the wages of the laboring class should always be increased with the increase of their intelligence—their general intelligence and their special intelligence. Therefore I believe very heartily in promoting elementary education to secure the general intelligence of the laboring class, and technical and trade education superimposed upon it, to fit them for the industries which they may desire to fill, or which may be especially pursued in the sections where these children are born or brought up.

With reference to the functions of the State or National Government, I should be very sorry to see the Government of the United States interfere in the common-school system of Massachusetts. I believe it is a better system than it would have been if the United States Government had undertaken to direct or establish it in the first instance. As regards communities that find themselves with a vast number of illiterate children—say with millions of illiterates upon their hands, with means more or less crippled, resources destroyed by war or violence—I think it would be perfectly legitimate for the United States Government to intervene, as by the illiteracy act of the last session, in the way of subsidies to the States which are dealing with a mass of illiteracy which makes their cases fairly exceptional and extraordinary.[2] But I think that the scope of such an act should be restricted by a minimum percentage of illiteracy, which would not make it apply to any State that is not in an exceptional or crippled condition. If it were made to apply to 10 or 15 per cent. of illiteracy, then the educational systems of the Northern and Western States, that have already a good school system founded, and which

---

[2] [It is unclear which of several proposed bills Walker has in mind, but in any case no federal bill passed both houses of Congress; hence there was no "act."]

are abundantly able to maintain their school-teachers and house their children well in ample schools—will not be interfered with; and I think the exceptional emergency created by the war in the respect of illiteracy in the Southern States might fairly be met by the intervention of the Federal Government. That state of things was one of the consequences of war, and I see no objection to the Federal Government aiding to remove illiteracy there under the circumstances. At the same time, my opinion is not worthy to be put against the opinions of those who are called to legislate for the people of the United States in such a matter. But I should be very sorry if a system of subsidies in favor of State instruction were to be established which did not have a minimum that would cut out all the communities that are abundantly able to maintain themselves, and which make no such special plea for assistance. I think it would be very unfortunate if the State of Massachusetts were to receive a quarter of a million of dollars for its schools by a contribution from the Federal Treasury. And I think Massachusetts would very much rather let the whole of any sum that may be needed go to communities that are in a condition to need it than to take its share of such money. Because I think the people of this State want to maintain the absolute independence of their own school system, and I do not believe that any good effect, in the long run, could be secured by contribution from the United States Treasury to the schools of Massachusetts. The people of this State are abundantly able to maintain their own schools and they spend every dollar that is needed for the purpose; they only want to know how much is needed for their schools and they supply the money themselves. Educationally and politically it would be setting a bad example to give any such aid to our public schools.

Q. Is there any other governmental power that could be properly and beneficially exercised for the benefit of labor or the improvement of its condition?—A. I think the principle of the English "Truck" acts, as they are called, is perfectly sound, the acts in restraint of "truck," and requiring that the laborers shall be paid "in the coin of the realm," prohibiting, except in agriculture and certain specified forms, the payment of wages at "truck" stores of any kind. That is an instance in which the legislature of Great Britain has intervened by, I think, as many as fifty acts. I do not remember the entire number. Finally, by the act of 1850, I think it altogether prohibited payments in "truck," and I think that that exercise of governmental power is perfectly proper. There is no doubt, I think, in the minds of any who have investigated that subject, that the passage of these "truck" acts prevented the laboring classes from being ground down by various extortions from a greed by which pauperism and crime would be increased. These acts are very numerous and I had those in mind when I spoke of factory acts. "Truck" acts might be made much wider in scope than the ordinary factory acts are.

The State must enforce all contracts for labor as well as other things, therefore it is proper for the State to require that the contract shall be such as to be capable of enforcement. A contract for the payment of wages in kind is not capable of enforcement, as for the payment of wages "in flour," for one kind of flour is worth one sum and another kind of flour another sum. It is perfectly right, therefore, that the State should prescribe that labor shall be paid for in money. "Truck" has not been practiced in this country to a very large extent; it has been to some degree, but is not much resorted to in New England at present. Even the English acts, however, permit "truck" at certain times and places, as where a railroad is building and there may be no shops along its lines, or where mining is going on at any considerable distance from shops, there the master is allowed to furnish supplies to his workmen, but in the majority of cases it is prohibited.

Q. Is there anything else that you think would be of value to suggest upon those questions?—A. I think the Government of the United States may do a great deal of good, as, in my judgment, it has in the past done a great deal of harm, to the working classes of the country, by maintaining a sound currency. There is no evil against which it is so hopeless for the workmen to fight as bad money. As to what is good or bad money: I do not suppose the committee wish me to enter into that much disputed question, as they have doubtless studied it as much as I have, but I think there is nothing that the Government can do for its laboring men that will go so far to protect them against economic evils, and protect them in their work, than to help them by a good, sound currency, in which the wages of labor are to be received and expended.

I believe also in education, as I have said, both technical and general; and I believe that with a mass of illiteracy existing as a result of war, the General Government might properly intervene and apply a remedy. I believe the Government of the United States did well—though I cannot say that it seemed to me the exigency was very great—when it passed the act of 1863, by which the College of Agriculture and the Mechanical Arts was formed, an institution with which I am connected.[3] I think that institutions of that kind have well repaid the effort made for them. It would certainly be ungracious in me to intimate that the bounty was not well bestowed, or that the funds have not been made use of for the general good of the country. I think they have been; but I did not regard the exigency that existed as a very grave one. If there was any constitutional or political objection to it, I do not think the economical or industrial exigency was sufficient to overcome it. But I think the bounty of the Government was well placed and the country benefited by it.

By the CHAIRMAN:
Q. Won't you give the committee your ideas as to the necessity or advantage of technical or trade education to the American people generally—the degree of necessity in which the call for such education now exists, and what, if anything,

---

[3] [The Commonwealth of Massachusetts designated M.I.T. as a land-grant college under the terms of the Morrill Act of 1862.]

is being done to supply it.—A. I think the term "Industrial
education," as it is commonly used in discussions on this
subject, is susceptible of two very different interpretations.
Industrial education may mean elementary high-school education directed to the general accomplishments, equipment,
and training of the person as an industrial agent, without
regard to special trades; or, it may mean trade schools. We
have very few trade schools in this country. I am not certain
that we have yet reached the point where it is desirable to have
them. At any rate, the most important need which the laboring
classes of this country now have, in my judgment, is for giving
direction to elementary education—common-school education,
as we call it in this section of the country—giving it a direction which will better qualify those who leave our schools at
the age of fourteen or sixteen to become industrial agents—
machinists or mechanics—without regard to special trades.
That is the branch of industrial education to which my mind
has been specially turned, and in regard to which I feel altogether the deeper interest.

In Germany, Holland, Switzerland, and other countries
of Europe there are trade schools where young children are
taken and trained thoroughly to learn such occupations as
they are expected to follow in after life.

Sweden, on the other hand, which has a population very
like our own, and systems (except the form of government)
not unlike ours, has a system of education which is not intended to breed artisans, but to make the children of the
ordinary people more apt and intelligent—to give them better
eyes and better hands and minds, trained to work with eye
and hand for the general purposes of an industrial career,
without specialization. And that system of instruction I should
be very glad to see introduced into the schools of the United
States, little by little, tentatively, going down from the high
schools to the lower schools, and from the cities out into the
country, as its success would justify. That is, I believe the
children of the common schools should be trained in the ele-

ments of physics and mechanics, and that they should have a
certain degree of manual training, at the carpenter's bench and
at the lathe, not to make them carpenters or machinists at
all, but to develop, in the first place, the executive faculty
which is likely to be lost in long-continued courses of study;
the disposition to take right hold and *do* a thing; to apply one's
powers promptly, courageously, and effectively. Then for the
development of the perceptive faculties—the training of the
eye and the habit of mind that comes from observing distinctions, as of color, of distance, of faces, of moisture, of
temperature, &c. I believe the perceptive faculties are almost
wholly neglected in our schools, excepting in the kindergarten. The reflective faculties and the memory are developed
at the expense of the executive faculty on the one hand and
perceptive power on the other. And I believe that if the elements of physics and mechanics should be introduced into the
public schools, not for the purpose of training carpenters or
blacksmiths, or training young children to do any one thing
for its own sake, but for the purpose of developing them as
better men and better women, developing them more harmoniously and more fully; developing their constructive powers, instead of developing merely the powers of ratiocination
and memory by an education that seems to me at the present
time wholly one-sided.[4]

---

[4] [In the balance of his testimony, Walker addresses himself to a number of questions urged by Senator Blair. Primarily, he describes in some
detail the manual and mechanical training offered to students at the
Dwight School in Boston and at the state normal schools in Salem and
Bridgewater, as well as the more extensive mechanical training available
at the Worcester Free Institute (now the Worcester Polytechnic Institute)
and M.I.T. He also elaborates on the general educational benefits he
attributes to elementary mechanical training, contrasting it with the
merely bookish knowledge often required by ordinary academic institutions, and he expresses some sympathy with elementary instruction in the
principles of public sanitation as well. Questioned about the condition
of labor in the United States, however, he can only assert that "looking
to one cause or another, I should judge the working classes of this coun-

COLUMBUS, GA., November 20, 1883.

C. H. JOHNSON (colored) sworn and examined.

By the CHAIRMAN:

Question. Where do you live?—Answer. In Columbus.

Q. How long have you resided here?—A. About twenty-six years.

Q. What is your business?—A. I am porter in an auction and commission house.

Q. What pay do you get?—A. About $25 a month.

Q. Have you a family?—A. I have a wife, but no children.

Q. Have you any real estate?—A. No, sir.

Q. Are you able to save anything from your earnings? —A. Yes, sir; I can save a little now and then, but it is very seldom that I see a place to save anything.

Q. Is your wife able to do any work?—A. Yes, sir; she can do some, but she is sickly.

Q. She is not able to help you much, then?—A. No, sir; not much.

Q. Go on, now, and make any statement that you desire to make?—A. Well, I think that the condition of our people, as a general thing, has been stated very fully to you, and I do not see where it is necessary for me to go over the same ground that has been gone over to you.

Q. Do you feel as though your people had had a fair chance to be heard by this committee?—A. I do.

Q. You think there is nothing they want to say to us that they have not had a chance to say?—A. I do not think there is anything. I think they have talked very plain about the condition of the colored race in this city.

---

try, in the past, have received very nearly, if not quite, all that the normal operation of economic laws would bring to them from the products of their industry. That is the only test I could apply."]

Q. And you think they have said all they want to say?—
A. Well, I won't say that they did that. There are some things, probably, that they wanted to say that they did not say.

Q. Why didn't they say them?—A. Well, it is just like as it was in time of slavery. There was a great many things that they would have liked to have done, but for fear, and they have got that same feeling now, a great many of them have, and they want to say things, but they are afraid of the white people; afraid that the white people will say to them afterwards, "Look here, John, you remember the sort of remarks you made before that committee. I am done with you now." That is the case with some of the colored folks; they are afraid to say what they want to say; but I aint of that sort. Whatever I want to say I am going to say it. Unfortunately I am not an educated man, but I think, in my own judgment, I would have been a help to my people if I had been educated, because I see a great many things going on among them that I think they ought to be advised about that they need advice about, and I do not think anybody else but a colored man could take hold of it and work it like it ought to be worked to their interests, because every man, and every nation, and every race, is bound to look out for their own people. A white man is a white man, I don't care where he is. If it is in a manger a white man looks for a colored man to look up to him as a white man and to respect him as a white man.

Now, speaking of education, I have heard a good deal about it here, enough about it. If you could give it to us all together to get us all up as high as you all are, that would be best. But then, of course, that is a long way off. But speaking of education, I think the first thing our race ought to consider, and the first thing they ought to learn, is to respect themselves, and then when they do that they will certainly command respect from everybody else. That is the way I look at it. Now, as a general thing, our people do not do that, not in Columbus here, and the reason why they do not do it is that they are so poor and get such little wages for their work, that they are ready any time to be bought up by dimes and quarters and fifty cents, or by a five-mile ride, with whisky thrown in, at any election. They allow themselves to be bought up in just that way. Now, there is where I think the colored man ought to come in and give us advice about such matters as that, for I don't believe that any man that would do that would ever be respected by a white man, or by any colored man either, that respects himself. I do not think that any man that does things like that demands respect or ought to have it. I have been living in Columbus now for about twenty-six years. My native home was in Atlanta. I have not got the time to tell you all that I would like to say about some things, but will make it short, and I will say this: As far as the feelings that have been existing here among the colored people and the whites, I think we have got a very good feeling among us. I have not seen any signs of bad feeling among the whites and the colored people. It is true that a great many thinks they are not treated right in some things. I think I am right about that. I may be wrong, though, but I do not think I am.

The great trouble with us poor colored people is that we need more power. Where are we going to get it? That is the question, as I look at it. We need more power, and if we have not got the power, there is no use to talk about negroes sitting on juries, and all that sort of thing. If we do not have the power to put them there, we cannot do it; that is all about it. There is no use to go asking a man for a thing that he don't want to give you, for he aint going to give it to you unless he is obliged to do it. I don't say that the negro would give his fellow-man any more justice than the white people give us. I do not believe he would give him justice any more than the white jury would—that is, than some white juries would—for I believe there is some people here that would give a colored man just as much justice as a colored jury would, and may be a little more, because I tell you right now there is feelings that has always existed among the colored people to pull down amongst them that is higher than others. That is the great trouble with them, and I believe that white juries would give a colored man as much justice, but I think that if you mix them up on the juries, and had one for white and the other for colored, a colored man that was in trouble would think that he got justice from that kind of a jury whether he did get it or not, and I believe the races would think so as a general thing. That is the reason why they would like to have it, and I don't know but they would be right.

It is true that we do not have any strikes among us here. We have been getting along peaceably. We have not had such a thing as a strike here for a long time. There is no spirit among the people to get up such a thing. We have got along very quietly, I believe, as a general thing.

I was speaking about the respect that the colored people ought to have for themselves, and I may say that I think the white people, some of them, love the colored folks most too much down here, anyhow. I am afraid it will get so after awhile that there aint going to be any colored race, and then the white man and the black man will get too close altogether. I believe I have about as many white friends as any colored man here. I have never had any one deny me a favor that I asked of him—that is, any one that was able to grant it— and I believe I am about as well known in this city and in the country here as any man around Columbus. I have been staying at a public house so long that both white and black people, men, women, and children, all know me. I have got a good many that come to me for advice as to what is best for them to do, and so on, and I do not know anything that would do any more good than to get that power that I was speaking about. But then where are we going to get it? They have been talking a good deal here about money to educate the children—the young generation. I think myself that the first thing we have got to do is to go to work to get up the money and to get power to do what is right. That is the way I look at it.

Q. What form of power do you mean?—A. I don't want

anybody to understand me to say that I am advocating the
cause that has been existing for some time around over the
country about the civil rights bill.[5] I don't see that we are just
exactly prepared to stand the pressure that the civil rights bill
would put upon the colored people if they had it in existence.
That is the way I am thinking about it. I think this, that we
want the power of having social equality amongst us, as a
general thing, in the city and in the country around, and there
is a great many things that ought to be looked after that cannot be—that there can't be nothing got done about except we
have the power to do it.

By Mr. Pugh:
Q. What do you mean by social equality?—A. I mean
that when we go into places that a man has a right to go into,
we want to be treated right. Suppose I get on the cars, for instance; I want to be treated fairly. As I said about the civil
rights bill, if I get on the cars to ride from here to Montgomery,
or to Atlanta, although I pay the same fare that you pay—they
make me do that—I do not have the same accommodations.
Now, I think that if I have to pay the same fare that you pay
I ought to have a right to ride in the same car that you ride in.
Q. Suppose you have one just like it, won't that do?—
A. Well, if it is just like it; still, it may not be the car that I
want to ride in, because I ought to have a chance to ride in
any one I wanted to. I think if they are going to make a law
not to allow a colored man to ride in a first-class car they have
no right to make him pay first-class fare. That is the trouble
between the colored man and the whites about this civil rights

---

[5] [Apparently Johnson refers to civil rights legislation intended to protect the equal rights of Negroes in public accommodations like railroads
and hotels, which the United States Supreme Court had just nullified
in the *Civil Rights Cases* (109 U.S. 3) on the grounds that the Fourteenth
Amendment could not be extended to individual citizens acting in their
private capacities as railroad managers and hotel keepers.]

bill. I myself do not care anything about the civil rights bill; but then, as I said about social equality, I think we ought to demand our rights in that respect.

By the CHAIRMAN:

Q. Suppose you have a car just as good as the one the white folks have, but are not allowed to go into their car, will that be satisfactory?—A. But that is not going to be done. They are not going to make a law of that kind.

Q. But if that was done, would it satisfy you?—A. Of course, I do not want to mix up with white people, because I do not really think it would be right.

Q. If they have a right to mix with you, you have a right to mix with them, haven't you?—A. That's it.

Q. But suppose the matter were fixed in such a way that you could not mix with each other?—A. If you owned this house here, and a man rented this room from you, and paid you $10 a month for it, and then if I came to get a room, and you said to me, "I am going to put you down in the kitchen, and I will make you pay me $10 a month," I would know that that was not right.

Q. That would be a different case. I am supposing a case where the accommodations provided for the two races are just the same, and neither has the right to go into the car devoted to the other.—A. Well, if you give me just as good a room right next door as the other man, and to pay only the same rent, I would be satisfied. But don't allow a man to come in over my wife, or any other lady that respects herself as a lady, swearing and spitting and cursing around. That is not allowed you in white cars, and I do not blame them for not allowing it. But if a man don't contend for his rights he will never get them. That is how I look at it. When I pay for anything I like to get it. When I go uptown and buy a woolen blanket, and when some other man goes uptown to buy a woolen blanket, and the storekeeper sells him a cotton blanket, because he is ignorant, and makes him pay the same price I

pay for mine, that is not treating him right. All I want is just
what I pay for, just what is right, and I do not want to kick up
a fuss with any one, or with the white people about getting
in amongst them, or being with them, because I do not believe it is right that we should be mixed up and always be
together in every place, and such things as that; but I think
that if a colored man is paying the same fare on the railroad
that a white man pays, he has just as much right as the white
man has to proper accommodations. I do not care whether it
is on a railroad or on a boat. I think about it in this way, that
if a man is in a hotel and a colored man comes along and pays
the same fare that the white man pays, he has the same rights
as the white man. Of course, they might go to work and do as
they said of the Republican party, disfranchise the colored man
from voting because he is not able to read and write. They
might go to work and fix up something like that, but I do not
expect to see any such thing.

Q. Have you any other ideas to suggest?—A. Yes, sir;
there is one thing that I would be glad to speak of. As I came
up in this world as a motherless child (and probably that is
the reason that I am not educated), I feel an interest in all
children situated that way, because you know the old saying
that "a burned child dreads the fire." Now we talk a great deal
about education and all that, but there is a great many motherless children around Columbus and in the county that is not
looked after by nobody. Everybody picks them up and they
are treated very badly by some of the people that picks them
up, and there is nobody to lay claim to them because they are
scattered around alike and somebody just goes to work and
picks them up and takes them. A great many people have the
feelings to treat them proper, but a great many of them is
treated mighty bad, and I think there ought to be some means
appropriated to attend to that sort of thing.

Q. What has become of the parents of those children?—
A. There is a good many children in this town and in the country around, where the parents has died out entirely, and they

have no relations, and they get to strolling around and they get into other people's hands that treats them bad, and I think somebody ought to look after them—somebody ought to be empowered to do that.

Q. What becomes of those children under present circumstances?—A. They just drift along with the people, a heap of them does, and some people, both white and colored, will take them home with them and raise them and do the best they can for them—some that has feelings for such things, but a great many of them just goes to the bad; they are not treated better in some cases than a dog, because I know a great many men that thinks a heap of their dogs. I think that ought to be looked after.

By Mr. Pugh:
Q. Who are the people that treat them in that way?—A. Well, a great many of the people that picks them out.

By the Chairman:
Q. How do they treat them? Do they abuse them?—A. Lashing them and dogging them about as if they were nothing at all; nothing more than a brute, not a human at all. I think that if persons are not able to take care of a child as a human they have not any business with them.

By Mr. Pugh:
Q. Are they white people or black people that pick those children up?—A. The white people pick them up sometimes and so do colored people sometimes. There is a good many colored ones that get hold of them that way and treat them just as badly as any of the whites, and worse too, and I think there ought to be some way fixed to stop it, and I hope there will be.

Q. Does nobody complain?—A. I had several complain to me of these things no longer ago than last Sunday. I did not see it with my own eyes, but I had men that stated the truth to me about it.

Q. Is there not a grand jury in this city?—A. Yes, sir; but if a man goes before the grand jury and takes up a thing, he has got to fight it himself. Of course, you know there is very few men going to take up a thing of that kind unless they have got an interest in it.

Q. If you would send the names of those people to the city solicitor I presume he would present the matter to the grand jury?—A. Well, I have said about all I care to say on that. As my friends, who testified before me have stated, we need more education and more money. I have no children myself, but I would be glad to see other people's children have a chance to be educated and elevated, and, also, I would like to have a chance myself, but I don't know that I shall ever have the chance of it now.

By the CHAIRMAN:

Q. Would you attend to school if you had the opportunity?—A. Well, the way it is with me I have not a chance to go to school in the day-time, and at nights I am too tired to go. That has been the trouble with me all the while. Being brought up as a motherless child, I had no chance to go in the day-time, and at nights I was too tired.

Q. What work have you been doing in the day-time?—A. For about twenty-six years I have been porter in an auction and commission store, but, of course, that is day and night work. At the present time, I have day-work and night-work too. I have got the contract of lighting the city, and I do that of nights, so that helps me out right smart, but I have to lose right smart of sleep to attend to it as it should be done.

Q. What is your age?—A. I am thirty-seven years old. I registered my name as thirty-six, but since then I have come to be thirty-seven years of age.

29.

Laurence Gronlund, *The Cooperative Commonwealth*, 1884

While most native Americans of the postbellum generation probably subscribed to a view of society not very different from Francis A. Walker's modified liberalism, a few turned to radical ideologies—imported for the most part from Europe—to explain contemporary social evils and to solve contemporary social problems. One of the best-known writers in this vein was Laurence Gronlund, a Danish immigrant become attorney and publicist who applied a tempered version of Marxian sociology to the American scene. Like other radicals, he challenged the prevailing American belief that education could overcome evils that were grounded in the very structure of the American economy and society; but like them too he also looked to the reform of education itself to flow from a valid social order. A chapter of his book *The Cooperative Commonwealth* elaborates his hopes in this area.

[*The chapter opens with quotations from contemporary clergymen who deplore extended popular education at public expense because it interferes with the divine economy that visits the sins of fathers on their children. It continues by mocking the liberal pretension that public schooling is warranted by its influence in diminishing crime. Rather, Gronlund argues, it is indispensable because the socialist state is upon us.*]

From Laurence Gronlund, *The Co-operative Commonwealth in its Outlines . . .* (Boston, 1884), pp. 220–233.

. . . A book, called "Dynamic Sociology" by Lester F. Ward was published a short time ago by the Appletons.[1] It would be a most instructive book if it were not so voluminous, and so terribly learned—and yet we cannot agree to its two principal propositions. These are: Happiness is the end of human life—which seems at least doubtful to us—and Education is the initial means to that end. Let the State only give a scientifically perfect education to all and the whole problem is solved, according to Ward. Education is, so to speak, a crank which, when properly applied, will, with comparatively little effort, turn the otherwise so unwieldy social machine.

So it will. Education indeed, can accomplish wonders; no thick volumes and pretence of much learning are necessary to prove that.

But how get the State to take the initiative? Who shall decide what is the scientifically perfect education? How get the parents to cooperate with the State? And what is the use, anyway to try to educate children who are poorly fed, poorly clad and poorly housed?

All these first steps are taken when we get the Cooperative Commonwealth.

We have seen that Social Cooperation demands first, and last, and at all time *Competence.* In order to get the greatest ability in every branch of affairs and in every post of duty: in order to sift out the most competent for the direction of affairs, and in order to make the citizens pass with ease from one employment to another, when required, all citizens will have to be trained all-sidedly and to the highest point. Monotonous toil now crushes out millions of potential luminaries of Society; if the true merits of mankind are to be brought out, it must be done by equalizing the opportunities for all.

And "minimum" education will not do at all. Simply to

---

[1] [Lester F. Ward (1841–1913) was the main early proponent of what Eric Goldman has described as "Reform Darwinism"–the belief that social evolution could be and must be controlled by mankind. Cronlund's summary of Ward's *magnum opus* is apt if unsympathetic.]

teach children to read and write is the same as to teach them the use of knife and fork without giving them a particle of meat; or as to furnish them the key to a larder, containing poisons as well as victuals, without telling them which is food, and which poisons. In fact, children are more likely to choose the poisons than the food: witness their voracious consumption of trashy novels and other vicious literature. The highest grade of education will be the best possible investment for the future Commonwealth.

Again, the Interdependent Commonwealth will take care that all children *do* get roast beef and plum pudding and that they, besides, have warm clothes to their backs, clean linen to their bodies, and comfortable shoes to their feet, and warmth and light at home, and these goodies will be provided before their education is thought of.

Again, the Interdependent Commonwealth will relieve children from the task of being bread-winners. The 182,000 children who according to the Census of 1880 were employed in manufactures in our country were not thus robbed of the bright days of childhood solely because employers could coin money out of them. The horrible fact is that their parents cannot make both ends meet without the labor of their children, and that in Massachusetts where a few weeks schooling yearly is required by law of children between 10 and 15, many parents feel themselves tempted to evade that law by false swearing in regard to the age of their children. It is an infamous system that bears such fruits. And yet there are political economists whose hearts are so seared and whose understanding is so obscured by being trained in that system that they glory in the fact that children can be utilized in augmenting the wealth of the country! These hundred thousands of children, as well as the urchins who gain their own precarious existence and partly that of their parents as newsboys, bootblacks, cash-boys, will have the most important period of their lives—that in which *character* is formed—saved to them, as soon as their parents are secured a decent living.

But that is by no means all. This that not only the

children but that the parents also will have roast beef and plum pudding is of vast importance to the cause of education. For it will relieve the fathers and mothers of the body-and soul-devouring *care* which is the special curse of our age; it will give these fathers and mothers, to whom now even reflection is forbidden, LEISURE, and thus make them effective allies of the Commonwealth, because leisure is the incentive to all progress.

The bread-and-butter-question is therefore the fundamental question. We see here again how Socialism, by revolutionizing the economic relation of Society, will revolutionize all other relations.

Education, then, will be the second important branch of the activity of the New Commonwealth. Let us now consider what organ is likely to be intrusted with the function of education.

In the discourse above referred to our Episcopal Mentor also laid it down:

"God has instituted three coordinate authorities: the Family, the Church and the State. The Family is *imperium in imperio*—a dominion within the dominion;—the parent is exclusive master within that dominion."

Well, we can pretty safely assert to the contrary that the Coming Commonwealth will not acknowledge the Church as a coordinate "authority."

There was a time when the two were coordinate authorities. At that time it was still doubtful which of them was destined to be the embodiment of the social organism. Out of that struggle the State has already virtually issued as the victor: the "Church" is in all civilized countries already virtually nothing but a voluntary association. "God" thus has already decided against the pretensions of the Church; and this, as we already noticed in the fifth chapter, is the most important step, perhaps, in the movement of the State toward Socialism.

And we can also be assured that the Church will not be made the organ of the State for education purposes.

There is one all-sufficient reason: *the Church is not competent.*

Circumstances for centuries gave education into the hands of the Church, and she then perhaps performed that function as well as could be done. Let us grant that much. But we are not living in the Middle Ages. So far from being in our age an institution of enlightenment, the Church is now looked upon by all well-informed people as an institution to darken men's minds. We simply state facts. The men of science assume the falsity of all theological dogmas. The Church is incompetent, because she knows nothing worth knowing—we are again simply stating facts. The Church has still some influence, partly on account of our hypocrisy, and hypocrisy is prevailing as it is, just because this is a transition age; but the Coming Democracy will want to *know* and will wage an unrelenting war against all shams.

We, furthermore, maintain that neither will the *Family* be acknowledged a coordinate authority.

This, however, is a much more important assertion than the former, and is not quite as evident, though on reflection it will be found just as true. But we cannot fail in passing to remark that it is amusing to see the solicitude the Church has for the authority of the Family now, when her own importance is on the wane. When she had supreme power, she certainly did not consider the Family coordinate with herself.

The first evidence we shall adduce to show that the Coming Commonwealth will assert supremacy as against the Family is that which we everywhere throughout this book place at the head: the logic of events. *Just in the same proportion the State has aggrandized itself, the Family has dwindled in importance.* The State commenced to repudiate the "dominion" of the Family the moment it forbade parents to destroy their children; it absolutely rejected that "dominion" the moment it, the State, fixed the age of majority, when the child is entirely emancipated from parental control.

Why! the system where authority is vested in the Family, as distinguished from the State, is that patriarchal, bar-

baric, system from which we are more and more retreating. Proudhon is decidedly right when he says: "It is on the model of the Family that all feudal and antique societies have organized themselves, *and it is precisely against this old patriarchal constitution that modern democracy revolts and protests.*" It is yet sometime said that "blood is thicker than water," but that is not often the case now; and this fact that the Individual has become almost independent of the Family is merely the preparatory step to the supremacy of the State.

Next, in the very nature of things, Family-Supremacy will be absolutely incompatible with an *Interdependent,* a solidaric, Commonwealth, for in such a State the first object of education must be to establish in the minds of the children an indissoluble association between their individual happiness and the good of all. To that end family exclusiveness must be broken down, first of all. A public spirit, *i. e.* the spirit of all being members of one social organism, must be substituted for family-spirit. Now please do not misunderstand the Socialist position in this respect! We do not make war on the *family;* on the contrary, our aim is to enable every healthy man and woman to form a family. But we *do* make war on family-*exclusiveness*—perhaps a better word than "selfishness" —on family-*prejudices* and family-*narrowness* and we are glad to be able to say that our common schools are doing very much to break down that spirit.

To hear some fathers talk of what is commonly called "compulsory" education, one should suppose that a man's children were literally a part of himself. When they are not allowed to be masters over their offspring, to choose what is wrong for their children—and we know that as to education the greater the need the greater is the dislike—they call that an infringement of their "liberty;" the fact is, they do not value *liberty,* but irresponsible *power.*

Children do not belong to their parents; they belong to Society. The observation of Franklin, that, if we go back but a few generations, we necessarily come to common ancestors expresses the truth, that we are more the children of Society than of our several families. Again, the education of children is of far more importance to the State than to parents, since the effects of it will be felt by Society, and principally *after* these parents are dead and gone. It is because through it Society accomplishes the end of its being, that all education is a public *trust*.

Just as little as parents will the many denominational and private schools and colleges which we now have do. Even granted that the education in, say, the Quaker college of Swarthmore is fully up to the standard of any public college, the New Order cannot get along with such one-sided, awry, cramped men and women as necessarily must issue from such a one-sided school.

Lastly, the same objection applies to the Family as to the Church: *it is incompetent to teach*. That is the main objection against Herbert Spencer's justly popular book on "Education."[2] He assumes throughout his treatise (which might better have been called "Home Training") that parents are competent to teach their children. Why! the fact is, that even now most children of the age of twelve are more fit to teach their parents in all more important branches than the reverse. If any man might be supposed qualified to teach his son, it was James Mill, and yet we know from the pen of John Mill that he would have been of greater service to the world, if he had been trained in a public school. Now it is true, that in the New Commonwealth mothers will be far better qualified to assist in the development of their infants than now, yet their general incompetency will still remain, on account of the higher grade of education which will obtain. At all events, a sufficient objection is and will remain that

---

[2] [Herbert Spencer (1820–1903) was an intransigent English liberal who became the preeminent spokesman on both sides of the Atlantic for "Conservative Darwinism," a position that owed more to Malthus and laissez-faire economics than to the author of *The Origin of Species*.]

seeming paradox, that parents know none so poorly as their own children; they prate of qualities which no impartial person can discover.

The Coming Commonwealth must radically do away with all and any form of quackery and amateurship, in educational matters especially. Education is essentially scientific labor. A competent and qualified body of educators must therefore be raised up to whom the whole function of education can be intrusted.

Teaching is now a "business" and a temporary one at that. To teach in order to get pocket-money, or wait for a chance to get into some other "business," or for a chance to marry, if the teacher is a woman as generally is the case, does not qualify for the grand art. The time teachers in our country practice their profession is simply their own training period. We cannot have that genuine education which the new Commonwealth will demand, before we have teachers who have themselves been genuinely educated, next, thoroughly trained as teachers and who then will devote themselves with their whole soul to their profession.

Here again, and more clearly than at any other point, we see how all-important, how indispensable the economic side of the New Order is to all other progress. For these teachers will not be raised up, before we have given them a dignified position economically. Teaching is now a temporary "business," because it is one of the most unprofitable positions, and because the teacher occupies a very low round in the social ladder. In the New Social Order he will be rewarded proportionately to his important function and need take no thought for his advancing age. Furthermore, he will be a member of a corporation of the highest dignity in the State; a corporation embracing the teachers in the most elementary schools, as well as the professors in the various universities— genuine universities for untrammelled scientific investigation in all departments—and whose directors, superiors and representatives in the National Board of Administration we shall suppose elected and dismissed exactly as they will be in the other departments.

This corps of educators will have in their exclusive charge the whole education from top to bottom and all scientific investigations. They will be perfectly untrammelled, for such a system will enable them to say to all charlatans in their department as the bakers, artisans and agriculturists can say in theirs: "mind your own business, sir! You are not competent to say aught in this matter."

There is not the smallest reason to fear that this will result in any spiritual tyranny, for the influence of this theoretic body of men is sure to be counteracted by that Public Opinion of the practical majority which we saw will be of extraordinary force in the Coming Commonwealth. We ought rather to hail such a strong and independent organization of a class, devoted to the cultivation of knowledge, as a healthy counterpoise to that Public Opinion. We may also suggest that the present tendency of founding universities in every section and almost every State of our country (though so far it has generally only resulted in founding university *buildings*) may be the sowing of germs of many different centres of science under the New Order, and thus contribute, as it has in Germany, to intellectual freedom and all-sidedness.

Then, and not till then, we can begin to have anything that deserves the name of education. Then, as we have noticed several times, we shall have arrived at the true starting point of the Cooperative Commonwealth. It will thus be seen that, even if all the conditions were ripe tomorrow for the inauguration of the New Order, we could not hope to do anything more in the generation, then living, than lay the foundation, deeply and firmly, for its upbuilding; among other things by training capable persons belonging to the second generation to be the educators of the third—to have charge of this third generation *from its earliest infancy till it reaches the adult age.*

Consider how many, many children are now sent into the world at an age, when those of wealthy parents are still in the nursery; consider that the average time children attend school is in our cities but *five*, and outside our cities but *three* years; consider that such an "enlightened" state as Massachusetts requires only a yearly school-attendance of *twenty-weeks* of her children under fifteen years; consider that in spite of this law 25,000 of her children *never* have seen the inside of a school-room; consider that 10,000 infants *under ten years* are working in the factories of that same *enlightened* State;* consider that all over our country, with *all* our children, schooling stops when the thinking process really first commences, and is it any wonder that our educational results are wretched?

Why! the sixteenth, seventeenth and eighteenth years constitute the most critical period of a boy's life, and left to himself he is, during those years and until he become restrained by experience, really one of the most dangerous members of Society. That these boys turn out to be as noble men as many of them do is a sufficient proof of the inherent goodness of human nature. But when the New Order has arrived, we shall be unanimous in acknowledging that restraint is just needed as a sort of astringent, to give maximum of power. We shall have learned that a young man who is kept under close and continued discipline of proper persons till twenty-one is sure to have a more vigorous and original character than one left to its own devices at an age when mind is yet unformed. And as far as our girls are concerned we shall yet sooner have learned a similar lesson.

You will very likely doubt that such a radical change will take place here where, preeminently, it is the practice to leave the young men and women to shift for themselves. In the same way many doubts might have been raised as to the success of the common school system, judging from the opposition to it from so many quarters at its introduction. Yet nearly all parents now avail themselves of it, driven by an uncon-

---

* For these facts see an article on "Children's Labor" in *Atlantic Monthly,* December, 1880.

scious impulse. And so, when the Great Change occurs, novelties will soon become familiar.

But the greatest novelty will be the new *ideal* of education.

That is the only matter left us to consider. We have nothing to do with what will be taught or how to teach it. That we for our part shall leave to the competent; already too many amateurs have had their say on that subject. But even those now most qualified would be incompetent to frame a curriculum for our future schools, for the ideal of education now will by no means be the ideal of the Coming Commonwealth.

The ideal, the end sought to be attained, now of education is to enable the individual to achieve *success in life, to get the better of their fellowmen* in the struggle for the good things of this world. That is the meaning of Individualism. No matter that in the nature of things but few can achieve that success, and that those who do succeed generally at the end of their career consider their success not worth the trouble, *that* teacher is considered the best who best knows how to qualify his pupils for the battle of life. That is why teachers stimulate the "ambition" of their scholars with prizes, marks, relative places in the school-room &c. That is also why they cram their pupils with facts and common-places of received opinions and persist in teaching them Latin and Greek so that they may afterward quote classical extracts for the sake of effect.

The end to be attained by education in the Coming Commonwealth will be a very different one. It likewise will be to qualify the pupils for the battle of life, but *against nature* and *in accord with their fellows*. That is the meaning of Social Cooperation.

In that Commonwealth prizes will not be used, because they only excite a few while leaving the mass phlegmatic; they will be condemned as *anti-social*. Perhaps in their place the educators will have recourse to Bentham's suggestion of a

scholar-jury, scholar-suffrage, leaving it to the scholars themselves to determine by their votes the relative position of each
other in the school-room. That will be a proper extension of
the suffrage and will bring home to the minds of the pupils,
that all suffrage is a trust.

Conformably to that new ideal the scholars will be impressed with gratitude for the blessings which all past generations have conferred upon them, and it will be urged upon
them that they owe *all* to Society.

They will be taught how to utilize all the sources of
happiness which Nature and the Commonwealth supply, for
the New Order will want them to have many tastes and needs.

But especially will they be taught to perform well their
functions in Society.

It will by that time be fully known, that a man trained
for one subject only never becomes a good judge in that one,
even, whereas enlightenment and enlargement of his circle
gives him increased power and knowledge in a rapidly increased ratio. Therefore a harmonious and balanced cultivation of all the faculties will be the first object. The pupils will
be taught all that is known, and though that field seems immense they will easily master it, for they will be led to the
bottom of things and learn the fundamental laws and the
connection of phenomena. They will be profound and complete
human beings, all of them. We are tending more and more in
that direction; that is why such *incomplete* men and women,
as Puritans and Quakers, have hardly any of their old-time
influence left.

Again, a great deal will be done in order to find out the
peculiar fitness of every child. Now next to nothing is done to
discover the natural aptitude of children, or to substitute
choice for chance in the allotment of the various social functions. And so it may be said that *the* mistake which all teachers
make is to teach the same lesson in the same way to all.

But Goethe suggests in the second volume of his *Wil-
helm Meister,* that every human being is born into the world

with a particular talent of some kind or other. In his opinion, it is only requisite to recognize that particular talent in the child, and foster it, in order to develop all its other faculties, and that, if that talent be not found out and developed, it is the fault of the educator. He grounds this suggestion of his on the well-known pedagogic experience, that a teacher can succeed with even the dullest child, as soon as he manages to win its interest for some object, whatever it may be; in other words as soon as he succeeds in discovering *the drift of that inborn talent in the child.* As soon, then, as a scholar is incited to voluntary activity and finds out that he is able to accomplish something in *some one* direction, it would be comparatively easy to awaken his self-confidence, so that he will succeed in other respects. This special talent thus insures the possibility *that every healthy child,* male and female, may have all its human faculties harmoniously developed.

Now we do not say, that it is remarkable that educators have hitherto been entirely deaf to this important hint—for it is not, considering the present ideal of education—but we cannot help here to notice that an obscure teacher in Hoboken, N. J., Dr. *Adolph Douai,* who, were the New Commonwealth now in existence, would undoubtedly be found in the front rank of its leading minds, has been the first and only professional educator who publicly has called attention to this suggestion.[3] We may be sure that the Coming Commonwealth, which can only furnish the necessary favorable conditions for the verification of this thought, will not be slow to utilize it.

---

3 [Karl Daniel Adolf Douai (1819–1888), a German-born refugee from the Revolution of 1848, introduced the kindergarten to Boston before being compelled to move to Hoboken because of his insistent atheism. Once located near New York he kept school, published a kindergarten manual and a series of "rational readers" for children, and edited labor newspapers. In 1883 he appeared before the Senate Committee on Education and Labor as a spokesman for the Socialist Labor Party. He also used the occasion to elaborate the theory of democratic education Gronlund summarizes here.]

The institutions that have already shown themselves specially adapted to the discovery and unfolding of these latent talents in children, are the *Kindergartens*. Though as yet but comparatively few of them exist in our country or elsewhere, those who teach in them have been able to discern in many children geometrical talent and aptitude for the study of natural sciences in whom otherwise nobody would probably ever have suspected them. These Kindergartens the Cooperative Commonwealth will in all probability establish in all the nooks and corners of the country, not to say in every family, as the first and most important link in the chain of its educational institutions.

Mr. Bain[4] in his treatise on Education makes an important observation which is pertinent here: "If from the beginning one can interpolate five shades of discrimination of color where another can feel but one transition, the careers of the two can be foreshadowed as widely apart. To observe this native inequality is important in predestining the child to this or that line of special training."

This observation and predestination will be made in the Kindergartens, where also a *taste* for manual work will be imbibed at a very early age. Thereafter we suppose general education and special training will accompany each other, under the eye of the teacher, till the child reaches adult age. We judge so, not merely from considering the natural requirements of the Commonwealth, but from observing the various attempts that now are being made to find a substitute for that slavish and wasteful apprentice-system which happily is a thing of the past, by founding industrial schools, so-called "developing schools," and trying to make them a part of our common-school system.

---

[4] [The reference is to Alexander Bain (1818–1903), a friend to John Stuart Mill and author of many important works in psychology, logic, and rhetoric. *Education as a Science* (1879) applied his psychological theories, which were based indirectly upon Utilitarianism, to pedagogy.]

We do not know whether this hypothesis of Goethe, that all normal men are capable of being educated up to the same level of intelligence and knowledge, is true or not. We know of no fact that militates against it, but think there are many facts that confirm it. At all events, only the Interdependent Commonwealth can furnish the necessary conditions for its verification. Should it be found true, it is easy to see that it will prove of transcendant significance as it will lay the foundation for that perfect, absolute *equality* which is the ideal of Socialism—and yet, mark what an *unlikeness,* what a *variety* there will be!

As the boys will be really educated, so the girls will be. In the New Commonwealth they will no longer be trained to please the man-fool, or acquire only accomplishments which give fullest scope to vanity, luxury and passion. No, they will be equally fitted for *their* appropriate functions as members of society, as wives and mothers, *in institutions adapted for them.* The latter qualification is important, for the motto which is the prominent characteristic of the modern American school-system, that "boys' and girls' schools should be one, and that one the boys'[,"] will surely be rejected by the Coming Commonwealth, as one against which physiology protests. But the future woman will, by methods and regimen adapted to her sex, reach the same plane of knowledge and intelligence as man and in that way become his *equal* and true *companion.* We shall then surely have *complete men and complete women.*

But how can the State, when once it has taken charge of education, draw a line where education ends and moral indifference begins?

The great need of the age is to organize, diffuse and assimilate that which is known. Humanity, indeed, does not now so much need more isolated facts, as to understand how all these facts are related to each other, and most of all, it needs to have that deeper, real knowledge made common property. Then first we can enjoy all the fruits of the tree of knowledge. Then, more particularly, we shall again reach a substantial agreement of opinion as to this Uuiverse [sic] in which we live, what it means and what therefore is the part we ought to play in it. The anarchy of opinion of this transitory age is an enormous evil. Unity of belief is the normal condition of the human intellect; it is just as natural for healthy men to think and believe alike, as it is for healthy men to see alike.

When one harmonious sentiment thrills through the whole of Society, we may expect a revival of the aesthetic sense of ancient Greece. This Gilded Age with its so-called "promoters of the arts" create[s] prostitutes of art, who exercise it, not for love of it, but to "make" money by it. Imagine if you can, a Raphael painting a Madonna, or Phidias sculpturing an Aphrodite for—profit! Art always is prostituted, when it only serves the vanity of the rich. In the present age poets do not sing for the masses, artists do not fashion their masterpieces for the masses as during the Christian Middle Ages or in classical Greece and Rome.

In Athens the whole people in the amphitheatre witnessed the spectacles, here—how different it is! We have expensive theatres where our comfortable classes can idle away their time, but, as Beecher says, they are not for the poor. The theatre to which the poor have entrance is perhaps the most vitiating of all social institutions. If there is anything that needs the helping, the reforming hand of the Commonwealth we should say it is the stage. It can be made the mightiest educational instrument. In particular, manners and address can be learned to perfection in the theatre, and only there.

Matthew Arnold says, pointedly: "A handful of Athenians of two thousand years ago are more interesting than millions of our contemporary nations—because they present us the spectacle of a cultured *people*. It was the many in the highest development of their humanity; the *many* who relished these arts and were satisfied with nothing less than those monuments."

So in the Cooperative Commonwealth where *care* is forever banished art will once more belong in the midst of the people, because of its eminently educational importance. He who has learned to appreciate the Beautiful will never after have a taste for the Low. Art will re-enter into the open arena of life.

But the greatest effect of this common education and common opinion will be the feeling of a *common duty.*

30.

Washington Gladden, "The Wage-Workers and the Churches," 1886

Still another response to the problems of an industrial society was articulated by a handful of troubled clergymen who sought to ameliorate contemporary evils without turning either to class conflict or to coercive social legislation to accomplish their ends. Their political orientations ranged from profit sharing and employer paternalism to a vaguely defined "Christian socialism," but they had in common a belief that the Protestant churches might teach men to overcome social injustice by linking the teaching of social ethics to the study of actual social conditions. In many cases, their anxiety over contemporary labor conditions originated in their observation that industrial workers no longer attended church, and except in rare instances their evangelical background predisposed them to visualize social amelioration in terms of combating the false creed of political economy, but despite these limitations they succeeded in extending both the scope and the functions of education conceived as a vehicle for middle-class values. Washington Gladden was one of their first and most important leaders, and this lecture to his congregation in Springfield, Ohio, exemplifies both the concerns and the educational commitments of the "social gospel."

[*The first half of the essay is devoted to a discussion of evidences that industrial workers are alienated from the Protestant churches.*]

. . . It is evident that the wage-workers, as a class, are discontented. They feel that they are not getting their fair share of the gains of advancing civilization.

It is evident that they are becoming more and more widely separated from their employers in the social scale.

It is evident that the old relations of friendliness between the two classes are giving place to alienation and enmity.

It is evident that the working people have the impression that the churches are mainly under the control of the capitalists and of those in sympathy with them.

If all these things are so, the reasons why the working people are inclined to withdraw from the churches ought also to be plain.

The fact of a great and growing discontent among the working classes, the fact of the increasing separation and alienation between wage-workers and their employers, are facts that cannot be disputed by any intelligent person. It may be doubted whether existing circumstances are bearing as severely upon the laborer as he imagines; it may be that he is better off than he thinks he is. But the question with which we are now concerned is, What does he think about it? He may be wrong in cherishing such unfriendly and resentful feelings toward his employer; but does he cherish them? He may be in error in thinking that the capitalist classes exercise a preponderating influence in the churches; but does he think so? If his state of mind is what it is assumed to be in this discussion, you have a reason for church neglect which is widespread and deep-seated; you have a disorder to cure which is

From Washington Gladden, *Applied Christianity: Moral Aspects of Social Questions* (Boston, 1886), pp. 162–179.

constitutional and obstinate, and which will never be removed by the sprinkling of rosewater; you have a problem on your hands which calls for clear thinking and heroic endeavor.

The "masses" of our cities that we are trying to reach are composed, to a large extent, of these wage-workers, and we shall never reach them over this barrier. The sooner the churches recognize this fact and adjust their theories and their methods to it, the sooner they will begin to see daylight shine through this dark problem of church neglect. So long as we ignore this fundamental difficulty, all our efforts to allure these neglecters will be in vain. A few of them will come in now and then in response to our urgent invitations; some of them, less thoughtful, or more hopeful, or more long-suffering than the rest, will continue to worship with us, finding in the promise of the life to come some help to bear the hardships of the life that now is; but the great multitude will turn upon us suspiciously or resentfully when they hear our invitations, saying: We want none of your free seats, we can do without your fine music and your pious commonplaces, we do not greatly care for your hand-shaking in the house of God and the perfunctory calls of your visitors at our houses. All we ask is justice. We want a chance to earn a decent living. We want a fair share of the wealth that our labor is helping to produce. We do not want to be left far behind when our neighbors, the employers, the traders, the professional people, are pushing on to plenty and prosperity. In the midst of all this overflowing bounty, we want something more than meagre subsistence. We are not quite sure whether you people of the churches want us to have it or not. Many of you, as we are bitterly aware, act as though you did not greatly care what became of us; and we hear from many of you hard and heartless comments on every effort we make to fight the fates that are bearing us down. It looks to us as though your sympathies were chiefly given to the people who are getting rich at our expense. Until our minds are clearer on this score, we shall never be drawn to your churches, charm you never so wisely.

What are you going to do with people who talk in this way? That is the one tremendous question which the Church of God is called to answer to-day.

Suppose you say that these people are all wrong in these theories, and all astray in their censure. Suppose you insist that they are getting their full share of the gains of this advancing civilization, or, if they are failing to do so, that it is wholly their own fault. Then it is your business to convince them of this by patient and thorough discussion. You cannot remove their misconceptions by denouncing them, or contemptuously ignoring them. You cannot disabuse them by abusing them. If they are wholly in error with respect to this matter, their error is most deplorable and hurtful to them, and to society at large; and the Church has no more urgent duty than that of convincing them that they are wrong.

Suppose that they are all wrong in their impression that the sympathies of the churches are on the side of the classes with which they are in conflict. The impression is there, and no headway can be made in bringing them into the churches until it is somehow eradicated.

"The only cure of all this trouble," some one will confidently answer, "is the gospel. Preach the gospel faithfully, and it will make an end of all this strife." This answer assumes that the fault all lies with the people now in the churches. What effect can the faithful preaching of the gospel have upon those who do not and will not hear it? If the gospel thus preached reaches these neglecting multitudes, it can only be through those who now listen to it. And the very trouble we are considering is that those who now frequent the churches find it difficult, and almost impossible, to put themselves into friendly relations with the neglecting multitudes.

What is meant by those who use this language is simply this: that the strife between labor and capital arises from the natural depravity of the human heart; and that, if men were soundly converted, all these grounds of contention would be removed. Unfortunately, this reasoning overlooks some important facts. The gospel, considered simply as an evangelistic or converting agency, will never put an end to this trouble. There are plenty of people in our churches to-day, who give every evidence of having been soundly converted, but who are conducting themselves continually in such a manner as to cause this trouble, instead of curing it. When a man is converted, he has a purpose to do right; and if you choose to go a little farther and say that he has the disposition to do right, I will not stop to dispute you. But he may have very crude ideas as to what right is; his heart may be regenerated, but his head may still be sadly muddled. And there are thousands of people in all our churches who mean to do right by their working people, but whose ideas have been so perverted by a false political economy that they are continually doing them grievous wrong. If a man has been taught the wage-fund theory,[1] or if he has got into his head the idea that *laissez faire* is the chief duty of man, the gospel, in the ordinary acceptation of that term, will not correct the defects in his conduct towards his work people. He may believe that he is a sinner, that he cannot save himself, that he must be saved from his sins by faith in Christ; and he may humbly confess his conscious faults, and trust in Christ for forgiveness and salvation. But his habit of taking the law of supply and demand as his sole guide in dealing with his working people is not a conscious fault. He has been diligently taught that labor is simply a commodity; that what Carlyle calls the "cash-nexus" is the only bond between himself and his employees.[2] As Toynbee puts it, Political Economy has steadily said to him, whenever

---

[1] [The wage-fund theory holds that at any given time wages and profits are derived from a fixed quantity of capital, and that efforts to increase the laborers' share can only destroy profits, discourage saving, and diminish available capital.]

[2] [Thomas Carlyle (1795–1881), the famous Scottish essayist, historian, and philosopher, was an outstanding early critic of laissez-faire individualism and industrialism.]

he has thought of governing himself, in his relations with his work people, by Christian principles,—"You are doing a very foolish thing. You might as well try to make iron swim as to alter the rate of wages by your individual will. The rate of wages, like the succession of night and day, is independent of the will of either employer or employed. Neither workmen nor employers can change the rate determined by competition at any particular time."[3] Fortified by this philosophy, the converted employer feels that any attempt to give his men a larger share of his gains would be superfluous, if not mischievous; that the fates will have it all their own way in spite of him; that all he can do is to buy his labor in the cheapest market, and sell his wares in the dearest. In other words, he has been taught, and he believes, that the industrial world is a world in which the Christian laws of conduct have no sway; in which sympathy is fallacious, and good-will foolishness. What can preaching the gospel, in the ordinary sense of the word, do for such a man? His purpose is right, his heart is right, but his theories are all wrong. Some people say that it makes no difference what a man believes if his heart is right. It makes a tremendous difference!

The gospel, then, as the simple evangel, will not cure this evil. But Christianity will cure it. Christianity is something more than a gospel. Christianity is a law, as well as a gospel. And the Christian law, faithfully preached, as the foundation of the gospel, will put an end to all this trouble. We sometimes hear it said that the pulpit of the present day is derelict, because there is not enough preaching of the law. It is true. What the Church needs is a great deal more enforcement of law—not necessarily more threatening of penalty, but more preaching of law—of the law of Christ, in its application to the relations of men in their every-day life. By the law is the

---

[3] [Arnold Toynbee (1852–1883) was an English social philosopher and reformer whose work among the poor of London's East End stimulated the settlement-house movement.]

knowledge of sin. Many of the Christian people in our churches have not been convicted of their sins, because the law has not been laid down to them. This Christian law, when it is faithfully preached, will make short work with the theories of materialistic political economy. It will cause the employers to understand that their wills do affect the condition of their work people; that they are bound to consider the interests of those by whose labor they make their gains—actually to love them as themselves; to use the power which capital and intelligence give them, not merely in seeking their own prosperity, but in ministering to the welfare of those nearest them. It will enforce the doctrine that wealth is a trust, and that business capacity is a trust; that both are to be used with a solemn sense of responsibility to God; and that the first obligation of the employer binds him to the people in his employ. What he can do to increase their welfare, to make their homes happier, to encourage provident habits among them, to open a door of hope to them, to increase their self-respect, and develop their manliness, he is bound to do. They are not his natural foes, to be battled with and beaten down, under the stern law of competition; they are his allies, his associates, the helpers of his prosperity, to be cherished and befriended, and bound to him with hooks of steel. In deed and in truth, they are his business partners; and it is only right that he should so consider them, and therefore identify them with himself in his enterprise, letting them share in his profits, and making their reward depend, in part, upon the abundance of his gains.

All good Christians believe, of course, that they ought to love their neighbors as themselves; but there are many among them who need help in answering the question, "Who is my neighbor?" The idea that the operatives in his factory, the brakemen on his freight trains, the miners in his coal mines are his neighbors, is an idea that does not come home to many a good Christian. He has been told that the law that governs his relations with them—the only law that can usefully govern his relations with them—is the law of competition, the law of supply and demand. In all this vast industrial realm, as he has been taught, self-interest is the only motive power. In the family, in social life, to a certain extent also in civil life, the force of good-will must be combined with the force of self-love; altruism must be coördinated with egoism; but in the industrial world, in the relations of employer and employed, this benevolent impulse must be suppressed. In this kingdom of industry they say that altruism is an interloper. In the family, in the neighborhood, in the state, if men were governed only by self-interest, we should have endless strife; in the industrial world, if we are governed by self-interest alone, we shall have peace and plenty. So he has been instructed. Over the entrance to the thronging avenues and the humming workshops of the industrial realm, an unmoral science has written, in iron letters: "ALL LOVE ABANDON, YE WHO ENTER HERE!" If beyond those portals is pandemonium, who can wonder? The first business of the Church of God is to preach that legend down, and to put in place of it: "YOUR WAGE-WORKER IS YOUR NEAREST NEIGHBOR."

In many respects the old relation of lord and villain, of master and slave, was a better relation than that now subsisting between the employer and the workman. There was many a master who tried to obey the Christian law; who remembered those in bonds as bound with them; who identified himself with his bondmen, loved them, cared for them, ministered unto them, and who was loved by them in return. We used to preach to the masters that their slaves were their brethren; and it was the right doctrine to preach. In one respect the Christian master did infringe upon the Christian law of brotherhood; he deprived his slave of his liberty. That was a great injury. We did right to upbraid him because of it. Doubtless the denial of liberty is a grave wrong—the gravest, perhaps, of wrongs—because liberty is the very condition of character. But while the Christian master deprived his slave of liberty, he gave him love. And now, when the slave gains his liberty, and becomes the hired man of his former master, is there no more love due from the one to the other? Is the "cash nexus" the only bond between them now? Is there no responsibility of the stronger for the welfare of the weaker? When we pass from status to contract,[4] do we leave Christ's law behind? Is the relation between the capitalist and the laborer either love without liberty, or liberty without love? Nay, but it is liberty and love,—the good fellowship of brethren, whose rights are equal, whose duties are reciprocal, whose interests are identical.

This is what the Church of God has to say about this business; and it is high time that the Church of God were saying it from hearts of flame with tongues of fire. We must make men believe that Christianity has a right to rule this kingdom of industry, as well as all the other kingdoms of this world; that her law is the only law on which any kind of society will rest in security and peace; that ways must be found of incorporating good-will as a regulative principle, as an integral element, into the very structure of industrial society.

You must not understand me as denying that there have been and are many Christian employers who recognize this truth, and try to make it practical in their relations with their workmen. And there are many others who, although they always deal with their workmen *as* workmen on "strictly business" principles—always paying the lowest wages for which they can get the work done; discharging men with families when they can get from boys or girls the same service for less money, without troubling themselves to ask what will become of the families; striving to attract into the neighborhood of their industries great numbers of surplus workmen, that in the keen competition between these they may reduce the price of labor; reckoning labor always only as a commodity, and always studying how they can get it at the lowest figure—are yet

---

[4] [Gladden refers to the theory, popularized by Herbert Spencer, that society had progressed from a stage of servile dependence to one of individual autonomy, and would in time move on to altruism.]

quite generous in the use of their money for benevolent purposes; giving it liberally for the support of churches and missions, for the endowment of libraries and colleges, even for the
support as paupers or dependents of the people who have been
reduced to penury by their own masterful combinations in the
labor market. A great deal of the money that is given in charity is thus gained by the exploitation of labor. And not seldom
it happens that families pauperized on starvation wages, are
fed with alms taken from the fortunes that their labor has
helped to heap up. With one hand capital thrusts labor down
toward mendicancy by the stern law of competition; with the
other hand it flings to these mendicants it has made the dole
that confirms them in their life of degradation. It is hard to
tell by which method we have made the most paupers, whether
by our heartless political economy, or by our sentimental
charity.

　　It should not be wondered at if the workmen de-
nounce the bounty thus wrung from their labor, as the alms
of hypocrites; if they have bitter words to speak of the men
whose princely gifts come from wealth produced by their
own poorly requited toil. But I do not think this judgment
just. I do not think that it is, in all cases—I doubt if it is in
the most cases—conscious hypocrisy or wanton selfishness.
These men have made their money by the operation of laws
which they have been taught to believe are beneficent; their
generosity to the churches, the schools, the heathen, is not
always ostentation; it is often genuine good-will; they give
of their increase, because the impulse to do good is in their
hearts; they would have shared their fortunes, just as cheerfully, with the people who have helped them make their
fortunes, if they had not been so sedulously instructed that
it was foolish for them to do it; that a benevolent purpose
could find no standing room in the realm where workman
and employer make their contract. Of course there is selfishness on both sides of this quarrel; there are selfish employers
and selfish workmen; but the majority of the masters that

are in our churches are not brutes nor tyrants; they would
have done justice to their men if they had not been misled
by a false philosophy. That philosophy must be killed; no
other dragon is devouring so many precious lives; and it is
the first business of the Christian Church to kill it. We want
no other weapon than the sword of the Spirit, which is the
Word of God. Christ's law, faithfully applied to the relations
of workman and employer, will settle the whole question.
With Christ's law in our minds, instead of the laws of
Ricardo and Bastiat[5]—and with Christ's grace in our hearts,
we shall very quickly get the barrier out of the way which
keeps the working people out of the churches.

Just a word or two more by way of specific practical
suggestion.

1. It goes without saying that we must manage in
some way to convince the wage-workers that the churches
are not on the side of capital in the struggle now going on.
It may not be necessary that the Church should take either
side in this battle. She ought to rebuke the selfishness and
rapacity of both sides; certainly she ought not to take the
side of the stronger against the weaker, nor ought it to be
possible for any fair-minded man to believe that this is her
attitude.

2. The Church ought not to censure, but rather to
approve and encourage, the combination of laborers for the
protection of their own interests. The acts of violence and
oppression perpetrated by these unions are, of course, to be
denounced; but the unions themselves are lawful and necessary. I know of no reputable political economist of any school
who does not now approve of the organization of labor.

---

[5] [David Ricardo (1772-1823) was the leading economist of the Utilitarian school; his *Principles of Political Economy* (1817) was for many
years the Bible of classical economics. Frédéric Bastiat (1801–1850), a
French economist, was a major advocate of international free trade and
a prominent liberal critic of early European socialism.]

Capital combines to control the price of labor; and labor is helpless to protect itself without organization.

3. Compact labor unions can secure arbitration of labor disputes. Under the present industrial system this is the best way of avoiding strife and securing justice. The influence of the churches ought to be thrown energetically and constantly in favor of arbitration. Most labor troubles are now peacefully arbitrated in England; they ought to be and can be arbitrated in this country.

4. It is not, perhaps, necessary for the pulpit to discuss the methods by which the Christian law can be applied to the relation between workmen and employer, but if any minister will make himself familiar with the facts about the working, in France and in Germany, and to some extent also in this country, of the system of industrial partnership or profit-sharing, and will bring these facts in a lecture clearly before the minds of the employers in his congregation, he may render them a great service. Profit-sharing is simply the incorporation of good-will into the industrial system as a working force; and the scores of great companies on the continent of Europe that have won magnificent success upon this basis prove it to be no visionary scheme, but one of the solidest of accomplished facts. Christianity is not a chimera; it will work. Try it! Get your capitalists to try it! Jesus Christ knew a great deal more about organizing society than David Ricardo ever dreamed of knowing, and the application of his law to industrial society will be found to work surprisingly well.

The appearance within a few months past in several quarters of a disposition to venture upon experiments of this sort shows that a better conception of their calling is beginning to gain possession of the minds of employers. I can take you to more than one manufacturing village in New England, where the capitalists, though not yet adopting the method of profit-sharing, have flung *laissez faire* to the winds, and have begun to study their workmen's welfare—villages that blossom as the rose under the breath of this benign influence.

I cannot help hoping and believing that the worst of the warfare between capital and labor is now past in this country, and that the day of peace is even now dawning.

> A terrible interval of suffering there was [says Arnold Toynbee], when the workman, flung off by his master, had not yet found his feet; but that is passing away, and the separation is recognized as a necessary moment in that industrial progress which enabled the workman to take a new step in advance. . . . If, however, history teaches us that separation is necessary, it also teaches us that permanent separation is impossible. The law of progress is that men separate, but they separate in order to unite. The old union vanishes, but a new union springs up in its place. The old union, founded on the dependence of the workman, disappears—a new union arises, based on the workman's independence. And the new union is deeper and wider than the old.

God grant it! God hasten it! And let the Church of God, from all her steeples, with the chiming of ten thousand Christmas bells,
"Ring out the old, ring in the new!"

31.

Bishop John H. Vincent,
The Chautauqua Movement, 1886

One of the characteristic American institutions of the late nineteenth century was the Chautauqua, a sort of latter-day version of the lyceum that sought to bring culture to a people who had generally been too busy or too poor to acquire it in college. Not surprisingly, the movement built upon a tradition of self-improvement and self-culture that stemmed at least from the 1830s, and it was infused with a religious spirit that reflected its immediate origins in a summer institute devoted to Bible study and the training of Sunday-school teachers. But it also addressed itself to contemporary social questions, which its authors surveyed in a series of adult text-books intended to explain sociology and economics to a puzzled middle class whose preindustrial values did not equip them to understand the society in which they now lived. The first chapter of the history of the movement written by one of its founders depicts both the religious importance and the democratic hopes it attached to informal education beyond the public school.

> *"If a man write a book, let him set down*
> *only what he knows."*—GOETHE.

The task I have taken upon myself is to tell, in a simple way, the story of Chautauqua,—a story of to-day; without romantic, heroic, or tragic element; a story of the people; a story in which the scholars will be interested, because the scholars are a part of the people; a story in which the rich and the refined will be interested,—the rich who are truly refined, and the refined whether rich or poor,—because they believe in the brotherhood of the race and in its high destiny, and are proud to account themselves a part of it.

I shall make no effort to excite the pity of the wealthy and the learned for the poor and the illiterate,—class for class, upper for lower. Chautauqua is not one of the "associated charities," nor is it a department of "home missions." It comes alike to the door of want and of wealth, with proffered blessings for both, and is as likely to gain entrance at one door as at the other. It deals with matters which, by the order of an impartial Providence, belong to "all classes and

---

From John H. Vincent, *The Chautauqua Movement* (Boston, 1886), pp. 1–15.

conditions of men." The full-orbed "Chautauqua idea" must awaken in all genuine souls a fresh enthusiasm in true living, and bring rich and poor, learned and unlearned, into neighborship and comradeship, helpful and honorable to both.

Education, once the peculiar privilege of the few, must in our best earthly estate become the valued possession of the many. It is a natural and inalienable right of human souls. The gift of imagination, of memory, of reason, of invention, of constructive and executive power, carries with it both prerogative and obligation. No man dare with impunity surrender, as to himself, this endowment, nor deny to his neighbor the right and obligation which it involves. Given, intellectual potentiality; required, intellectual discipline and power. The law holds among leaders of thought, teachers and law-makers; among nobles and the favorites of fortune. It holds no less among the lowly,—the plebeians and the peasants of society.

Diversity in the direction of talent, and difference in degree, together with inequalities of social condition, may modify the demand upon the individual for culture and service; but the utter neglect of intellectual capacity is criminal, whether it be by menial or millionnaire. It involves a wrong to self, to the family, to the state: to self, since it leaves him blind whom God created to enjoy the light; to the family since it turns him into a physical or commercial machine whom God appointed to be companion and comforter; to the state, since it makes him a mere figure-head—whether of clay or gold—whom God intended to be a counsellor and helper, and to "have dominion" according to the measure of his power. No man has a right to neglect his personal education, whether he be prince or ploughboy, broker or hod-carrier. He needs knowledge, and the wisdom which makes knowledge available. Where the power lies, there rests responsibility for its use. Circumstances seem to favor the prince, and to be against the ploughboy; but, after all, the latter, overcoming adverse conditions, may acquire an education worth a great deal more to the world than that of the prince with his opportunities. Struggle against what men call fate brings power. One hour of study every day, with heroic purpose, may prove more valuable to the student than five hours a day of easy memorizing and reciting. The prince may complete his course in a few years, and, having "finished," graduate. The ploughboy, moving slowly, may require four times the number of years to cover the same ground; but that length of time may be an advantage to the humble student. It may require greater concentration when he does study; and the long hours of manual labor may be enriched by thought, and thus may knowledge gain a firmer hold, and its vitalizing power be increased.

Chautauqua has a work to do for college graduates. It enters protest against the suspension of intellectual effort when the compulsory *régime* of the recitation-room has been remitted,—a fault so common and so pernicious that college men themselves frequently bring into disrepute the college system. Intellectual activity must be continuous in order to promote intellectual health and efficiency. College life is the vestibule to a great temple. He who crosses its pavement, and reads the inscriptions on its doors, but goes no farther, might as well never have entered the campus at all. Too many suspend literary pursuit when the diploma is won, and the world of business opens before them. Chautauqua provides, for such as these, incentives to a personal review of the entire college curriculum in a series of English readings. It urges them to prosecute advanced courses of study, and suggests a plan by which college prestige and power may be used in helping less favored neighbors who desire education. This last class is large. It is made up of eager minds who need direction and encouragement. They would ask questions, and gratefully accept assistance, if college graduates would simply place themselves within reach.

Chautauqua has therefore a message and a mission for the times. It exalts education,—the mental, social, moral, and religious culture of all who have mental, social, moral, and religious faculties; of all, everywhere, without exception. It aims to promote a combination of the old domestic, religious, educational, and industrial agencies; to take people on all sides of their natures, and cultivate them symmetrically, making men, women, and children everywhere more affectionate and sympathetic as members of a family; more conscientious and reverent, as worshippers together of the true God; more intelligent and thoughtful as students in a universe of ideas; and more industrious, economical, just, and generous, as members of society in a work-a-day world. The theory of Chautauqua is that life is one, and that religion belongs everywhere. Our people, young and old, should consider educational advantages as so many religious opportunities. Every day should be sacred. The schoolhouse should be God's house. There should be no break between sabbaths. The cable of divine motive should stretch through seven days, touching with its sanctifying power every hour of every day.

Kitchen work, farm work, shop work, as well as school work, are divine. They hide rare pearls in their rough shells. They are means of discipline in the highest qualities of character, and through them come some of the greatest and mightiest energies from the heavens. People should be guarded against that baleful heresy, that, when they leave the hour of song, prayer, and revival power, and go to homely service in shop or field, they are imperilling spiritual life, as though only so-called sacred services could conserve it.

We need an alliance and a hearty co-operation of Home, Pulpit, School, and Shop,—an alliance consecrated to universal culture for young and old; for all the days and weeks of all the years; for all the varied faculties of the soul, and in all the possible relations of life.

Chautauqua teaches that each of these institutions embodies and represents an idea, and that every man needs in his own life these representative ideas,—the home idea of mutual love and tenderness; the church idea of reverence and conscientiousness; the school idea of personal culture; and the shop idea of diligence, economy, and mutual help. The young and the old need these things. The rich and the poor need them. Capital and labor need them. The educated and the illiterate need them. Chautauqua says therefore: Give them to the people. Hold up high standards of attainment. Show the learned their limitations, and the illiterate their possibilities. Chautauqua pleads for a universal education; for plans of reading and study; for all legitimate enticements and incitements to ambition; for all necessary adaptations as to time and topics; for ideal associations which shall at once excite the imagination, and set the heart aglow. Chautauqua stretches over the land a magnificent temple, broad as the continent, lofty as the heavens, into which homes, churches, schools, and shops may build themselves as parts of a splendid university in which people of all ages and conditions may be enrolled as students. It says: Unify such eager and various multitudes. Let them read the same books, think along the same lines, sing the same songs, observe the same sacred days,—days consecrated to the delights of a lofty intellectual and spiritual life. Let the course of prescribed reading be broad and comprehensive; limited in its first general survey of the wide world of knowledge; opening out into special courses, according to the reader's development, taste, and opportunity. Show people out of school what wonders people out of school may accomplish. Show people no longer young, that the mind reaches its maturity long after the school-days end, and that some of the best intellectual and literary labor is performed in and beyond middle life. College halls are not the only places for prosecuting courses of study. College facilities are not the only opportunities for securing an education. A college is possible in everyday life if one choose to use it; a college in house, shop, street, farm, market, for rich and poor, the curriculum of which runs through the whole of life; a college that trains men and women everywhere to read and think and talk and do; and to read, think, talk, and do, with a purpose; and that purpose, that they may *be:* a college that trains indolent people to work with their own hands; that trains people who work with their hands, to work also with their brains,—to think in their work, to think for their work, and to make other people work and think.

A plan of this kind, simple in its provisions, limited in its requirements, accepted by adults, prosecuted with firm purpose, appealing to the imagination and to the conscience, must work miracles, intellectual, social, and religious, in household, neighborhood, and nation. And this is the "Chautauqua Idea;" and the idea in active operation is the CHAUTAUQUA of which I write.

Its benefits are manifold and obvious. It brings parents into fuller sympathy with their children, at the time when sympathy is most needed,—sympathy with them in their educational aims, sympathy with them in lines of reading and study.

It helps parents to help the teachers of their children, preparing infants under school age to make a good beginning; inciting and assisting the children who have entered school, to do good work in preparation and recitation; protecting them against the peculiar temptations of playground and class-room; holding them to the end of the high-school course; inspiring them to seek the higher education of the college, or to pursue after-school courses of reading and study at home.

So general a scheme of education must increase the refining and ennobling influence of home life, promoting self-control and dignity of deportment, mutual respect and affection, a laudable family pride, and true social ambition; giving the whole house an air of refinement; touching with artistic skill floors, walls, and windows; finding the right place and the right light for the right picture; putting the right book on shelf and table; furnishing a wider range of topics for home conversation; crowding out frivolity and gossip; removing sources of unrest and discontent at home; making evenings there more agreeable than life on the street; creating a real independence of the outside world, and making one's own house the centre of the whole world of science, literature, art, and society. Windows open out through every wall; and beyond vines, trees, and garden, the inmates see the old world of history, the new world of science, the rich world of literature, the royal world of art. And through sky-lights they look up and see the world of God,—his love and holiness, and the boundless life to which he invites us. And thus they all in that household learn, that, seen aright, all realms of knowledge, both past and present, are flooded with the light of God.

Popular education through the Chautauqua scheme increases the value of the pulpit by putting more knowledge, thoughtfulness, and appreciation into the pew, and encouraging the preacher to give his best thought in his best way.

It must put more good sense into popular religious utterances, so that the talk of the prayer-meeting will be sobered by wisdom and directed by tact, thus gaining in its influence over cultivated people, and especially over the young people of high-school and lecture-hall. It must enable everybody more accurately to measure the worth and the limitations of science, and must cause them to fear far less the dogmatism of pseudo-scientists concerning religious facts and doctrines.[1]

Such popular education must increase the power of the people in politics, augmenting the independent vote

---

[1] [Vincent's exhortation reflects the experience of several decades of controversy between the advocates of religious faith and those of natural science, whose criticisms of each other had been markedly heightened by the appearance of Charles Darwin's *The Origin of Species* (1859).]

which makes party leaders cautious where lack of conscience would make them careless concerning truth and honesty.

It must tend to a better understanding between the classes of society, causing the poor to honor wealth won by honest ways of work, by skill and economy; to despise wealth and winners of wealth, when greed and trickery gather the gold; to honor knowledge and a taste for knowledge, whether it be found clad in fine linen or in linsey-woolsey; to hate with resolute and righteous hatred all sham and shoddy, all arrogance and pretentiousness; to avoid struggles between capital and labor, and to promote, in all possible ways, the glorious brotherhood of honesty, sympathy and culture,—a culture that addresses itself to all sides of a man's nature.

Under the auspices of this great Chautauqua "every-day college," you may imagine the soliloquy of a woman more than forty-five years of age. She says,—

"I am busy with many duties,—household cares or shop work. I have something to do all the time. There seems no end to calls, toils, worry, and weariness. In kitchen, parlor, farm, or factory, something is to be done.

"I am old,—that is, older than I once was. Don't let us talk about that. Gray hairs? No, you cannot find any gray hairs in my head—or, can you? Never mind. The heart's young, and it's nobody's business how old the bones are.

"I am going to college! Never mind about thirty years, or fifty, or seventy: I am going to college. Harvard? No, nor Yale, nor Boston, nor Middletown, nor Evanston, nor Welles-ley. I don't want to mix with a lot of reckless boys, or ambitious girls, just now. I have enough of them at home or in the neighborhood. I am going to college, my own college, in my own house, taking my own time; turning the years into a college term; turning my kitchen, sitting-room, and parlor into college-halls, recitation-rooms, and laboratory. What a *campus* I have! green fields and forests, streams and mountain ranges, stretching out to the sunset. What a dome surmounts my college! vast space, blue background, billowy clouds, resplendent stars! What professors I have, in books! immortal books of history and science and art, books of poetry, fiction, and fact.

"In my college are enrolled the names of glorious men and women who never enjoyed any other college,—Shakspere [*sic*], Benjamin Franklin, Washington Irving, John G. Whittier, Horace Greeley, Abraham Lincoln, and hosts of others who went to their own college, and wrought out their own education, as I will do in 'my college.' I can never be what they were; but I can be something, and can make the world better, and children happier, and life nobler, because of the feeble efforts I put forth to get a better education.

"I am going to college! I want to improve all my talents. I have intellect. I intend to develop and enrich it. I must know more. I must love to know. I must know more, for the sake of larger influence over others for their good,— children, servants, neighbors, church associates. God has given me at least one talent. I ought to improve it. I will improve it.

"I am going to college! I am a 'child of a King,' and have a right to my inheritance. 'All things are yours.' Well, I want to take up my property in stars and flowers, and in the knowledge men have gathered about my royal Father's kingdom. Astronomers, bring me what you have discovered in the outlying domains of my Father's universe! Geologists, tell me the story you have learned from the rocky pages of the earth, concerning the beginnings and the development of the planet I live on. Thus I intend to lay hold of all the treasure-seekers and teachers and high priests of nature and literature and art, and bid them bring the truth they hold, my Father's truth, *my* truth, and place the goodly inheritance at my feet. 'Whatsoever things are true, . . . think on these things.' I am going to college!

" 'Where am I going? I shall stay at home, and construct a college there. My house—small, poorly furnished

(never mind)—is my college centre. My neighbors, the rich-
est of them and the poorest, the most humble and ignorant,
and the most scholarly, shall be my professors. I will ask
questions about every thing, and of everybody, till I find out
what I want to know. Some of the stupidest people can tell
me something, and when I draw them out I do them good.
Getting, I can give.

"And don't talk to me about age. Let the poet answer
your raven cry:—

> 'But why, you ask me, shall this tale be told
> To men grown old or who are growing old?
> It is too late! Ah! nothing is too late
> Till the tired heart shall cease to palpitate.
> Cato learned Greek at eighty; Sophocles
> Wrote his grand "Œdipus," and Simonides
> Bore off the prize of verse from his compeers,
> When each had numbered more than fourscore years;
> And Theophrastus at fourscore and ten
> Had but begun his "Characters of Men;"
> Chaucer, at Woodstock with the nightingales,
> At sixty wrote the "Canterbury Tales;"
> Goethe at Weimar, toiling to the last,
> Completed "Faust" when eighty years were past.
> These are, indeed, exceptions; but they show
> How far the gulf-stream of our youth may flow
> Into the arctic regions of our lives,
> When little else than life itself survives.
> Shall we, then, idly sit us down and say:—
> The night hath come: it is no longer day?
> The night hath not yet come: we are not quite
> Cut off from labor by the failing light.
> Something remains for us to do or dare;
> Even the oldest tree some fruit may bear;
> For age is opportunity no less
> Than youth, though in another dress;
> And as the evening twilight fades away,
> The sky is filled with stars invisible by day.' "[2]

---

[2] [The lines are from Longfellow's *Morituri Salutamos*.]

The entire Chautauqua movement is based upon the following propositions:—

1. The whole of life is a school, with educating agencies and influences all the while at work, from the earliest moment to the day of death. These agencies and influences should be wisely and continuously applied by and in behalf of each individual, through life, according to circumstances, capacities, and conditions.

2. The true basis of education is religious. The fear of the Lord is the beginning of wisdom,—the recognition of the Divine existence, and of his claims upon us as moral beings; the unity and brotherhood of the race, with all that brotherhood involves; harmony with the Divine character as the ideal of life for time and eternity; and the pursuit and use of all science in personal culture, the increase of reverent love for God, and of affectionate self-sacrifice and labor for the well-being of man.

3. All knowledge, religious or secular, is sacred to him who reverently surrenders himself to God, that he may become like God, according to the divinely appointed processes for building character. And he has a right to all attainments and enjoyments in the realm of knowledge, for the possession of which he has capacity and opportunity. Science, travel, literature, the works of art, the glories of nature,—all things are his who is one with God. This law applies to the poor and lowly, as well as to the rich and so-called "favored classes" of society. It gives lofty ideals to lowly life, and transforms humble homes into places of aspiration and blessedness.

4. In mature life, beyond the limits of the usual school period, the intellect is at its best for purposes of reading, reflection, and production. While the training of the schools may discipline the juvenile mind, and thus give it an advantage as its powers mature, the discipline of every-day life, in solving problems of existence, support, and business, gives a certain advantage to the so-called uneducated mind during the middle period of life. Between the ages of twenty and eighty lie a

person's best intellectual and educational opportunities; and he needs direction, encouragement, and assistance, in order to use them most effectively.

5. Early lack of culture, felt by full-grown people, begets a certain exaltation of its value and desirability, and a craving for its possession. This craving creates intellectual susceptibility and receptivity, and renders the more easy the acquisition of knowledge. Mere verbal memory may be less efficient in these adult years; but the power of reasoning, and of utilizing knowledge for practical results, is much greater than in the early years.

6. The necessity for wise direction, assistance, and encouragement of this mature intellectual power and desire is as great as in the period of youth and of school life. Therefore grown people need courses of study outlined, books for reading indicated, questions answered, associations formed, and all the conditions guaranteed which tend to promote hope, confidence, ambition, and strong purpose.

7. Where a mature mind desires to use its energies and opportunities to the maximum of its possibility, and to do thorough intellectual work of the most exacting sort, the influence of the best teachers may be brought to bear upon him by frequent correspondence, including questions, answers, praxes, theses, and final written examinations of the most exhaustive and crucial character. To such persistent purpose and faithful effort, after rigid testing, there should come the testimonials and honors in diploma and degree, to which any student anywhere else, or at any other period of his life, would be entitled.

8. The advantage of mental attrition by personal recitation and conversation is a large factor in the schools. This advantage may be enjoyed by voluntary associations, local circles, contact with resident scholars, occasional attendance upon special lectures, and class recitations in local high-schools, seminaries and colleges, and at summer schools and assemblies.

These are some of the fundamental thoughts on which

the Chautauqua movement is based. It is a school for people out of school who can no longer attend school,—a college for one's own home; and leads to the dedication of every-day life to educational purposes. . . .

32.

Controversy over the Bennett Law in Wisconsin, 1889

During the nineteenth century Americans generally subordinated their religious and cultural differences to the needs of the common school, but their efforts to extend public education often rankled in the breasts of those of their fellow citizens who put religious orthodoxy or cultural idiosyncrasy before the claims of government. This was nowhere more apparent than in Wisconsin, where a seemingly harmless enactment requiring elementary instruction, in the English language, of every child in the state created a furor among German-speaking Lutherans and Catholics who had already been aroused by contemporary nativist agitation. The Bennett law neither precluded instruction in the German language nor affected the right of parents to send their children to parochial schools, but it proved to be the temporary undoing of the Republican party, which had sponsored it and which lost the governorship in 1890 and the state's presidential vote in 1892 because of that fact.

The following extracts from contemporary newspapers illustrate both the passions the law elicited and the uncomprehending assurance with which its English-speaking advocates upheld its provisions. The first is a letter by Governor William Hoard published in the *Wisconsin State Journal* (Madison) in a vain attempt to discourage partisan agitation of the issue. The second, from the *Milwaukee Sentinel*, reports a speech in opposition to the law delivered by Colonel Conrad Krenz, one of its leading critics. The

Sentinel filled out its column on the subject with editorial extracts, also printed here, from other newspapers that supported the law.

A Letter from Governor William Hoard

MADISON, Nov. 11, 1889.

My Dear Mr. Luchsinger:

I am not seeking to make the Bennett law an issue in the next campaign. If it becomes the issue it will be through the opponents of the law, a portion of them, by manifesto, having already declared their hostility to any one who favored the measure.

I have, I believe, as friendly a feeling towards our German-American population as any man in this country; and if I did not believe that the Bennett law would assist in the advancement of their youth, I would certainly oppose its continuance on the statute books. I want the little German boy and girl, the little Norwegian, the little Bohemian and little Pole, the children of all foreign-born parents, to have the same chance in life as my children. Without a knowledge of the English language they cannot have this chance. This is a very plain proposition, with which I know you will agree. I plead for these children of foreign-born parents for the reason that I personally know many who were born in this country who are handicapped by ignorance of the language of the country. Should not something be done to give these bright young people an opportunity to rise according to the ability God has given them? Advancement in life for them is out of the question without a knowledge of the language of the country.

I am confident that when the Lutheran people come to look at the Bennett law in its right light, and study its provi-

---

From the *Wisconsin State Journal*, November 30, 1889.

sions, they will fail to see in it any menace to their rights or tenets. It seeks to interfere with no religion. It simply requires that for a certain number of weeks in each year children must attend some school where a certain amount of English instruction is given. It does not seek to abolish the parochial school, or interfere with the teaching o[f] German.

Let the opponents of the Bennett law take a case that recently came under my observation. A short time since, Hon. R. M. La Follette caused a competative [*sic*] examination to be held for cadet at West Point. A number of candidates entered for the place, some of whom had graduated at the University of Wisconsin. An impartial committee awarded the prize, after a severe and critical examination, to a German lad in Grant county, whose education had been obtained in the common schools, if I am not mistaken. The boy had an equal chance with the American boy, and he won. No one rejoices more at his success than his American friends. If he had been deprived of the English language, this opportunity would have been lost to him.

I cannot believe that it would be doing justice to the little boy of the present, born of foreign parents, to deprive him of all opportunities to become the peer of the native born boy, by postponing this question for a score of years; nor can I believe his father or mother will think so when they come to know just what the Bennett law means. Of course they love their children, and they cannot wish to keep them down as underlings by the side of the Yankee boy. "Knowledge is power." Knowledge of the English language will give the German boy and girl the power of equality that nothing else will. It cannot be that any German father or mother can oppose a law which is enacted for the sake of their children.

I would not ask the good old German to abandon the use [of] the language of the fatherland, or to cease to look upon that language as the best in use. I would only ask him one question: "Do you want your sons and daughters to have the same opportunities for advancement as the Yankee boy and girl?" If he will reflect a moment, and consider his responsibility for his children's existence in this country, he will answer "Yes." I do not believe that the German parent loves his child less than the native born loves his.

Assuring you that the Bennett law will not be made a campaign issue, unless it be by those who are opposed to giving the children of foreign born parents a fair show, I remain
Sincerely your friend,

WILLIAM D. HOARD.

A Speech by Colonel Conrad Krenz

The Herold in its Sunday edition publishes what it claims to be the complete minutes of the meeting of representatives of the several Lutheran congregations, which was held at the residence of the Rev. Mr. Bading, on Friday night. Col. Krez [*sic*], who was present at this meeting, made the first speech, which, as translated from The Herold's report, was as follows:

"I have lived in this country many years. From the beginning of our republic until now quiet has always prevailed; we Germans have lived in peace with the whole world, and now, all at once, the cry is raised that the Germans are dangerous people. In Russia, America, everywhere this claim is being made. But, now, are we opposed to the English? By no means. But the state has no right to prescribe to a father as to how he should raise his children. Is a superintendent more interested in the welfare of the child than a father? Why then this hue and cry? The German children of the parochial schools are better raised (erzogen) than the German children in the public schools. Where do the loafers on the street come from?

From the *Milwaukee Sentinel*, December 30, 1889.

"We want to live in peace with the English people. I acknowledge that they also do some good, and among them we will also find good friends for our cause; among the Germans, too, there are some traitors. Only one English-American born in this state has succeeded in gaining for himself fame in this country as well as in Germany, and he was once a pupil of a German parochial school in Sheboygan. I refer to Mr. Heinrich Nehrling.[1] What is necessary now is that the 'Pommeranians advance.' If the state has the right to decree for twelve weeks, then also for forty-eight weeks; then also a total suppression of the parochial schools.

"The law is tyrannical! A father dare not send his child to Germany to be educated, lest he make himself liable to punishment! A teacher dare not instruct his own child lest he violates the state law! We want to be understood that we are the state! We pay the officials, the governor, the legislature.

"But, again, the law is tyrannical in this respect: A little boy who plays truant a few times can be taken away from his father and sent to the Reform school. What father would submit to this? If a citizen of Holland promenading on the dyke notices a mouse-hole therein, then he knows that there is danger that the country may be inundated. This law is such a mouse-hole through which danger threatens, and it is therefore necessary to take precautionary steps in time.

"The Germans only want their rights as they have had them heretofore; if they suffer them to be taken away from them, then they are not worthy to speak the language of Luther, not worthy to be the brothers of those Germans who fought at Mars-la-Tour.[2] But they will only be heeded if they

---

[1] [Henry Nehrling (1853–1929) was an internationally recognized horticulturist and ornithologist. Both of his parents came of German families, and he was educated initially at home and in a Lutheran parochial school.]

[2] [Mars-la-Tour was the site of a battle during the Franco-Prussian War in which the Prussian Third Corps outfought and outwitted a defending French force three times its size.]

are feared! Hence they must close their ranks and must be able to say: So and so many votes are ours.

"As I understand it, the law has many defects; every violation must be taken to the courts, and an appeal from the decision may be taken to the Supreme court. It has decided in one case that a father may determine what branches his children shall not study and, if the state adheres to this, then things are as they ought to be. A child must be allowed to study English in his mother tongue. I never attended an English school, but notwithstanding I have always been able to get along with every Englishman."

Editorials from Wisconsin Newspapers

FOR THE GENERAL GOOD.

Waupun Leader: The Bennett law contemplates only a limited education in the English language for every child in the state. This language is *the* language of the United States. As a rule no man can be posted in the affairs of the government who cannot read and write the English language. The man who is thus ignorant is not qualified to vote intelligently on public questions. It is not a question of compelling an element of citizens to do something which is against their interest, but is simply to fit the rising generation for intelligent citizenship.

THE LAW A WHOLESOME ONE.

Marinette Eagle: Strenuous efforts are being made by opponents of the Bennett school law to force the same upon the people as a partisan political issue. The opponents of the

From the *Milwaukee Sentinel,* December 30, 1889.

law are placing themselves squarely upon the record as opposed to the instruction of the common branches taught in
our schools, in the language of the country. The law is a
wholesome one, and those who are opposed to its enforcement are actively misrepresenting its provisions, hoping
thereby to arouse religious prejudices. They will miserably
fail. The patriotism of the citizens of this country, whether
native or foreign born, is too pure and too strong to allow the
language of the country to be supplanted, either directly or
indirectly, by that of any foreign state. It is not a question of
either politics or religion, but a question of the protection
of the rights of the state by extending such protection to the
children who are to make its future citizens. If the issue must
come, let it come. The youth of our land will be protected in
acquiring a knowledge of the language of the country.

BUT IT GENERALLY BLUNDERS.

Stevens Point Journal: Since the publication of Gov.
Hoard's letter in regard to the Bennett law, he has received
letters from a number of prominent Democrats in the state,
strongly endorsing his position on that measure and pledging
their support should it be made an issue against him next fall.
The Democratic party of Wisconsin may make mistakes, but it
surely will not commit the colossal blunder that the forcing
of an issue of that kind would be. Any party that would go
before the people of Wisconsin with a plank in its platform
opposed to educating the children of the state, for at least
twelve weeks of the year, in the rudiments of the English
language, would be buried under a very heavy majority. With
that as the issue, the Republican party in favor and the Democratic party opposed, thousands of Democrats would vote with
the Republicans.

33.

The *National Economist*, 1889 and 1891

When the amorphous social protest of the 1880s finally took shape in the Populist movement, it embraced both the ideal of social change and the confidence in educational processes that two generations of American social critics had expressed. Like the Granges, the Farmers' Alliances of the 1880s hoped to secure amelioration of the farmers' lot through the dissemination of vocational information, but they also held out ever greater hopes for achieving a social revolution through the systematic dissemination of democratic principles of economic and politics. Die-hard members of the Southern Alliance tended (like Terence Powderly) to look to "education" to serve the ends even of political organization; their views were epitomized in an editorial that introduced the weekly *National Economist*, official organ of the Southern Alliance. On the other hand, northern agitators were more likely to espouse a third party, as Thomas J. Davis of Indiana did in the first issue of its fifth volume. Nevertheless, southerners and northerners alike portrayed a country that would be converted to social justice by the force of factual argument. The possibility that we may discount their "education" as "propaganda" does not diminish the significance of their commitment to it.

Introductory Editorial, 1889

The National Economist takes its position in the field of journalism with no flourish of trumpets or ostentatious display of pyrotechnics. It is not, nor will it ever attempt to be,

From the *National Economist*, I, 1 (March 14, 1889), 1–2.

a showy publication that catches the eye, tickles the senses, or panders to popular tastes and prejudices. Neither will it strive to supply its readers with the current news of the day. That is a distinct branch of work and now so thoroughly performed by an immense number of daily and weekly papers that the public is offered almost every hour large sheets of from eight to forty pages closely printed in small type at an expense of two or three cents each, thus leaving nothing to be desired in that line. But, as the name and avowed objects of this journal indicate, its aspiration will be to appeal to the reason and judgment of its readers and to educate in the principles of society, finance, and government rather than to relate the visible effects of the violation of such principles. To perform this work it will of necessity be a plain, sober, solid home journal, dealing with the serious and vital problems of the age and submitting measures and policies to the crucial test of analytical dissection under the calcium light of historical experience, statistical deduction, and logical reasoning. Under the confederated form of republican government, recognizing the voice of the people as the supreme law, nothing short of such critical analysis and affirmative and intelligent indorsement can justify the individual in favoring any policy. An object very much to be desired is that the masses of the people should think more for themselves and not, as is now too often the case, accept the declarations and conclusions of leading journals or men without analyzing and understanding them. Questions of public policy are not too complicated for the average common mind if properly presented and examined according to the plain rules of common sense. But a popular belief that they are too complicated, coupled with a lack of the means and opportunity to so examine them on the part of many, has led to this now too common and much to be deplored custom of accepting platforms and political creeds at second hand from those who arrogate to themselves the wisdom and sagacity to act as oracles. This tendency, if persisted in and allowed to increase, must in time prove fatal to the present system of government, because popular self-government can only continue while the people possess sufficient intelligence to govern themselves, and whenever they accept their doctrines and policies second hand it becomes autocratic and not intelligent, and as such is subject to all the evils and abuses that selfishness may dicate, which can have but one result, and that incompatible with a just and equitable system of popular self-government. If, then, the very existence of the present form of government depends on the intelligence of the people, it is no stretch of analogy to assume that its prosperity, advancement, and efficiency will be greatly aided and assisted by a more thorough knowledge and understanding on the part of the people of every principle involved in the laws of the government and of every policy pursued or sought to be pursued by those entrusted with the power to administer the affairs of state and of those who aspire to such power. The crying necessity of the hour is for the people to think for themselves, and the danger to the Government is that it will get too far from the people and that they will not understand its workings and watch its every act. There are vast enterprises interested in complicating government matters so as to blind the vision of the tax-payer, which desire to see him despair of ever being able to understand such matters, give up trying, and settle down to delve out his life like the patient donkey and yield all the gain accruing from his labors to those who have the cunning to secure government aid to assist them in appropriating it. It will be a part of the mission of this paper to simplify and express in plain and easily understood language the present and proposed methods and policies of this government and compare them to historical precedents when possible and show the teachings of political economy on the same subjects. The feature of this effort, most valuable to a large class of readers who do not have access to extensive libraries, will be that it offers them in a condensed and simple form the conclusions of all the greatest authors as well as the experiences of all nations so compiled and arranged as to be useful in understanding and solving correctly the problems of the present.

For the purpose of investigation the population of the country may well be divided into two classes, the producers and the non-producers, and a comparison made as to the relative numerical strength and importance of each. It will also be of interest to note the incomes of each and from whence derived, also the use and benefit that each class seems to be, in the true economic conditions of life. From such investigation will come correct conclusions as to whether either class should be increased or diminished, and whether either is entitled to governmental interposition to check its growth and aggrandizement or to foster and protect it. Such investigation will also probably demonstrate whether America is rapidly building up an aristocracy or not, and, if it is, whether there is any necessity for such a class. An examination of the drones, their habits, customs, and profits, will be interesting and beneficial. The producers are usually divided by economists into three classes, the agricultural, the manufacturing, and the commercial (which includes transportation); and in regarding the relative importance of each by the light of the statistics of this country for the last thirty years, the loyal citizen must be alarmed at the rapid decline of wealth and importance shown in the class of agricultural producers. Can this condition of affairs continue? Is not the country in a critical condition in consequence and rapidly approaching a crisis? Evidently energy could not be expended in a better cause than an effort to correctly evolve methods calculated to check such disastrous results. Agriculture must ever be the basis of all true prosperity in this country, and any apparent flush of prosperity enjoyed by any class, if it be at the expense of the true interests of agriculture, must of necessity be short lived and attended with a corresponding degree of depressing reaction. That is to say, if unjust conditions have prevailed whereby other classes have, through the power of governmental support, been made prosperous at the expense of agriculture, such classes have been sapping the life-blood of their own tenure of existence; and while it may have made them abnormally fat, it is because they in their greed were not content with good rich milk from the cow, but have been feasting on her flesh also, and will soon have the bones picked clean, when they will get neither meat nor milk and starvation must stare them in the face. The perpetuation of such unjust conditions must be equally as fatal to all other classes as to the agriculturist.

A correct solution of the great problems of the present by any person or publication will be productive of no good unless it meets with a responsive approval from the people, and that is impossible without thorough enlightenment on the part of the people in regard to all the particulars and principles. This demonstrates the necessity for the publication of this journal as a means of producing such enlightenment, and should it succeed in any degree in achieving that result it will have been a blessing to mankind.

In taking the exalted position that only such principles and policies will be advocated and contended for as can be sustained by experience and precedent or by sound logical reasoning, it will be necessary on the part of readers and journal to avoid the common error of jumping at conclusions and then seeking evidence to sustain them. If the premises are sound and correct a true conclusion will follow. While these investigations will be conducted on general principles of justice and equity, they will at present be carried on with a special tendency to an examination and solution of the now most prominent features of the situation—that is, finance, transportation, and land. There is much confusion in regard to each of these subjects, and if it be possible to lead the million farmers who read *The National Economist* through the same course of plain, simple, and irrefutable reasoning from actual cause to inevitable effect in each one of these important branches, it will bring order out of chaos and result in great good. This is striking at the very foundation of the superstructure, because the agriculturist is the great conservative and thinking element of the nation—the ballast, as it were. He it is who holds the volatile elements of society from running into excesses, and he it is who must step forward and insist upon reforms. City life is conducive to polish and show, but country life to depth of thought and research. In presenting the solid food for thought to the agriculturists of the country it is done with implicit confidence in their judgment to receive and indorse the same, and a firm belief that when they indorse the measure their honesty and integrity will compel them to advocate such measures until they prevail.

Letter to the *National Economist*, 1891

The first purpose, principles and aims of the Alliance and all other industrial organizations are education. The second purpose is the action, the good, the benefit we may obtain as a result of such education. The public press of to-day controls and leads public opinion. If we read capitalistic papers, we'll get capitalistic news; if we read old party papers and advocates, we'll get old party news; if we read Alliance papers and reform literature, we'll get Alliance news, and that is what we want if we are true Alliance men. I want to offer my sincere thanks and say God bless *The Economist* for its article, "The Mississippian," of March 8. We don't want to play second fiddle or be tacked on to the tail end of any old corrupt political organizations that have brought us into the deplorable condition we are in to-day.

One of the most important questions, and one that interests us more, perhaps, at the present time, is the Alliance in politics. Is it necessary that we should take a hand in politics, which is the science of government[?] All true thinking men will agree with me that, if we ever expect to get out of this

---

From the *National Economist*, V, 1 (March 21, 1891), 7.

depressed condition we are in now, we must take a hand in legislation. If we are satisfied that we have equal chances and advantages with other classes of men engaged in other pursuits, then perhaps it would be unwise to enter politics. The time was when a man, by his personal magnetism, powerful intellect, and individual wisdom, could lead men in any direction, into any reform he chose. That time is past. All true reforms must come through the people themselves hereafter.

The Alliance is purely educational, but is surely political. It brings the laborers and wealth producers together and encourages them to study, to think; to investigate the gigantic evils which surround mankind, and impresses upon our mind, the duty, the responsibility that rests upon us as American citizens. It wakes us laboring people up to a realization of the fact that we are surrounded by corporations, monopolies, trusts and combines, and teaches us that we can never successfully compete with such combinations unless we come together, lay aside our selfishness and prejudice, talk together, think together, act together, and vote together.

The question we Alliance men must settle agreeably is this, will we take part in the two old monopoly-ridden parties, or form a new distinct party of our own? That which will benefit a Democratic laborer will benefit a Republican laborer. We can never draw the Republicans into the Democratic party, [any] more than we can draw the Democrats into the Republican party. We Alliance men would rather not be drawn into either old party, for both are owned, controlled, and run in the interests of the millionaires, the greedy capitalistic thieves that are sapping the life blood out of the working people all over this great country of ours. We can never join hands with either of the two leading parties because we must necessarily be divided. Either old party will use every means fair and foul to beat the other party. We can never succeed in our reform movement so long as half of our brothers are fighting the other half.

We admire Brother Clarke Lewis' statement when he says he stands "flat-footed on the platform of the National

Farmers Alliance and Industrial Union," but we don't know
if he is in earnest or not; we think not, if he still persists in
being a Democrat. Come, my worthy brothers of the South,
and join forces with us laboring people of the North, and let us
start this great reform movement on the road to victory before
it is everlastingly too late. Brother Lewis' plan might work in
the South, where the majority of the Order are Democrats;
but it won't work here in the North where the brothers are
so evenly divided between the two leading parties[.] [W]e
know; for we've tried it. We know if we join hands with either of
the two old parties, we simply place a club in the hands of monopolies with which they may beat out our own brains. The
brothers of the North and West, and I believe a great portion of
our southern brothers, are willing to bury the bloody shirt, lay
aside our prejudices, and forever extinguish the fires of sectional
hate that have been burning and keeping the toiling, slaving
masses divided so long; and join hands in this, the greatest, the
grandest struggle for freedom that has ever swept over this fair
land of ours. We do not oppose a man so much for acquiring an
immense fortune if he does it honestly and fairly, but we do condemn a system of government that allows millionaires and corporations to spring up and grow on one hand, and tramps and
toiling, starving masses of working men and women on the other
hand. Will we come together and try to suppress these growing
evils or will we let "Shylock take the last pound of flesh?" We
point with pride to the finger board on *The Economist's* editorial page, N. R. P. A.,[1] and wonder if all the brothers know
what that means, and we imagine they do, and we can't refrain
from saying, Amen! and shouting, Glory! Glory!! May God
speed the day when the labor and wealth-producing masses
will rise up and declare and show by their action that they are

---

[1] [This finger board first appeared in the issue of December 20, 1890,
following the Ocala (Florida) meeting of the Supreme Council of the
Southern Alliance. The pages of the journal devoted to that meeting do
not indicate what the letters meant, but presumably they epitomized the
commitment that the gathering had made to the plan for an agricultural
subtreasury.]

independent, freethinking men, who will strive to secure the "greatest good to the greatest number."

Come, you brothers of undeniable and unquestionable faith in our platform of principles, and, as Brother Cockrell says. "Meet us half way" in independent action. We've got the principles, let's have the party; not an Alliance party, but a people's party. And as proof of our position, we will take for example Georgia and Kansas. Which one has proved the most successful in the last election? The answer comes rolling back: Georgia will forever remain in the shodow [*sic*] of doubt, while Kansas stands first and foremost in the sunlight of victory, the bulwark of American patriotism, and the leader of the grandest and greatest reform movement that has ever been known to the civilized world.[2]

34.

Charles W. Eliot, "One Remedy for Municipal Misgovernment," 1891

Most nineteenth-century commentators who sympathized with democracy also sympathized with popular education, understood as the ever-wider diffusion of knowledge and technical skills. One of them was Charles W. Eliot, president of Harvard University, prominent educational reformer, and sponsor of the "five-foot shelf"

---

[2] [In the elections of 1890, the People's party had gained control of the lower house of the Kansas state legislature as well as the state's congressional delegation. Hence they were able to secure the choice of one of their number, William A. Peffer, as United States senator. In Georgia, on the other hand, comparable electoral successes were tainted by the fact that they had come through Alliance members' control of the Democratic party machinery, which prevented their candidates from exercising the same degree of autonomy as the third-party candidates in Kansas.]

of great books. Confronted with mounting social problems, however, far-sighted men like Eliot began to sense that even with the best of intentions ordinary men were not capable of managing the society in which they lived. To some extent, their skepticism derived from and reinforced an elitist educational tradition that scholars in politics and other patrician writers had frequently expressed, but it also stood as a consideration that convinced democrats would increasingly have to examine on its merits. It received one of its clearest expressions in an essay Eliot contributed to the *Forum* in 1891, in which he praised democracy but documented its shortcomings and pointed to the need for experts in city management to deal with modern urban problems. In doing so, he took a major step toward redefining democracy in the United States.

In these days, when so many sanguine philanthropists are advocating large extensions of governmental activity, and indeed are hoping for a beneficent re-organization of society, in which popular governments shall plan, order, make, store, and distribute every thing,—all without unduly abridging individual liberty,—it may be wholesome to discuss sometimes the practical shortcomings of democratic government within its present rather limited field. Before we take courage to believe that governmental management would be successful in many new fields and on a much larger scale, we ought to be satisfied with the results of that management within its actual province. It is more instructive to discuss shortcomings close at hand than those remote, evils right under the eyes of the people than those they can hardly discern. To discuss the evils which attend municipal government is, therefore, more edifying than to consider the evils of the national and state administrations.

In peaceful times the national government is remote from the daily life of the average citizen. Its wastefulness does not come home to him. Its corrupting patronage and jobbery are unperceived by him. Errors in the financial policy of the government become plain to him, only when he experiences their ill effects. The post-office is the only function of the national government which concerns him intimately, and that function is really a simple business, and has always been a government monopoly; so that the average citizen who gets his mail with tolerable regularity, and has no experience of any other method of sending letters and newspapers generally, thinks that the post-office business is as well done by government as it could be by any agency. Municipal functions, on the other hand, touch the average citizen very nearly. It makes a great difference to him whether the city keeps good schools or bad, and clean streets or dirty, supplies him with good water or bad, and taxes him fairly or unfairly. Moreover, all critics of the working of the institutions of the United States during the last fifty years—whether friendly or hostile, whether foreign or native—agree that municipal government has been the field in which the least efficiency for good has been exhibited and the greatest positive evils have been developed. To what causes the existing evils of municipal government in the United States are to be ascribed, and in what direction the remedies are to be sought, are, therefore, questions of the profoundest interest for the average citizen, as well as for the social philosopher.

It is easy to attribute these evils to the inherent viciousness and recklessness of the urban population,—wickedness and folly which are more and more effective for evil as the proportion of urban to rural population rises. It is easy for people whose forefathers came to this western world one or more generations ago to believe that the people who have just come are the source of all municipal woes. But neither of these explanations can be accepted as probable or reasonable. When we examine the working of the American democracy on the greatest state questions,—such as independence of Great Britain, the federation of the States, and the indissoluble union of the States,—we find that the democracy has dealt wisely with these great questions, and just as wisely in the generation of

1860–90 as in the generations of Revolutionary times. We observe, that, in the management of a great national debt, our democracy has exhibited better judgment, and, on the whole, juster sentiments, than any oligarchy or tyranny has ever exhibited. We see that private property is more secure under the democractic form of government than under any other form. We find that there has been an unequalled amount of diffused intellectual and moral energy among the mass of the people during the last forty years; and we are sure that the democratic form of government, working in combination with democratic social mobility, is eminently favorable to religious, social, and industrial progress. Into the immense material development of the period since the civil war there has gone a deal of sound moral force as well as of mental and physical activity. The census teaches us that the proportion of the urban to the rural population has rapidly increased during the last thirty years; but these new city people have all come in from the country. During this same period, rural town governments have fully maintained their excellence, and have in many States exhibited a new efficiency and enterprise; as, for example, in the development of primary and secondary education, the maintenance of free libraries, the restriction of the liquor traffic, and the improvement of bridges and highways. I submit, therefore, that there is no good reason to believe in any widespread and progressive demoralization of the mass of the population, whether urban or rural. I would not be understood, however, to maintain that there have not been particular spots or particular occasions, some of them conspicuous, where failure and disgrace have resulted from moral causes; such as indifference on the part of voters to the bad character of the men they voted for; the corrupt procuring of votes in return for appointments, licenses, or tariffs; or the importation into municipal affairs of passions aroused in national party strife. My contention is, that, in spite of these manifestations, there is no good reason to believe that American constituencies, whether large or small, have frequently been dishonest or corrupt at heart, although they have sometimes chosen dishonest or corrupt agents.

The theory that the immigration of a few millions of foreigners within thirty years is the true cause of municipal evils in the United States must also be rejected, although the too quick admission to the suffrage of men who have had no acquaintance with free institutions has doubtless increased the evils of city government in a few localities. The great majority of the immigrants have been serviceable people; and of late years many of them—particularly the Germans, English, Scotch, Scandinavians, and Swiss—have had a better education than the average rural American can obtain. The experienced voters of the country cannot shelter themselves behind the comparatively small contingent of the inexperienced, particularly when the former are wholly responsible for admitting the latter to the suffrage.

I venture to suggest in this paper another explanation (a partial one, to be sure) of the comparative failure of municipal government in the United States,—an explanation which points to a remedy.

It is observable that the failures of the democratic form of government have occurred chiefly in those matters of municipal administration which present many novelties, and belong to the domain of applied science: such as the levying of taxes; the management of water-supplies and drainage systems; the paving, lighting, and cleaning of highways; the control of companies which sell in city streets light, heat, power, transportation for persons, and communication by electricity; the care of the public health; and the provision of proper means of public enjoyment, such as open squares, gardens, and parks. All these matters require for their comprehension and proper management a high degree of scientific training, and all of them require the continuous execution, through many years, of far-reaching plans. I proceed to consider each of the topics I have mentioned, with the intention of showing that antiquated methods of municipal administration, and particularly short and insecure tenures for the heads of departments, are responsible for the greater part of the municipal evils which are bringing discredit on free institutions, and that the altered nature and conditions of municipal business require that these old methods, which answered very well in earlier times, be fundamentally reformed.

In the course of this rapid sketch it will appear at various points that the monarchical and aristocratic governments of Europe have grappled with modern municipal problems much more successfully than our democratic government. The discussion will, I think, suggest that explanations of this result, so unsatisfactory to lovers of liberty, are to be found in the slowness of a democracy to change governmental methods, and in the comparatively small and temporary influence of political and administrative leaders under a form of government which makes frequent appeal to universal suffrage.

I. I begin with the levying of municipal taxes. One of the greatest mischiefs in American municipal government is the system of local taxation; for this system is, in many places, an effective school in evasion and perjury, and, as a rule, an agency of stinging injustice. The trouble is twofold.

In the first place, the incidence of taxes is one of the most difficult subjects in political economy, and very few American legislators know any thing about it. More than that, very few Americans in any profession or walk of life know any thing about it. The colleges and universities of the country are greatly to blame for this condition of things. They never began to teach political science in any serious way till about twenty years ago. The generation of men now in their prime either never studied any political economy at all, or studied it in one small textbook for a few hours a week for perhaps half a year at school or college, or they picked up a few notions about it in the intervals of professional or business occupation after they had entered upon their life-work. The number of living Americans who have any thorough and systematic knowledge of the principles of political economy, including the incidence of taxes, is absolutely insignificant; and these few are mostly either professors, or business-men who have been also life-long students. The average business-man and the average professional man have never given any attention to the science, except perhaps to some little scrap of it, like the doctrine of protection, which has temporarily had some political interest.

Secondly, the forms of property have changed so prodigiously within forty years, that a theory of assessment which worked reasonably well before 1850 has become thoroughly mischievous in 1890. The old theory of taxation was, that every man should be assessed at his home on all his property. It was all there, or it returned thither periodically, like his ox-cart or his vessel. If, by rare chance, a man had property out of the town where he lived, it was a piece of real estate which was to be assessed for taxes in the town where it lay, and there only. Nowadays in cities this is all changed. In the country and in remote communities by the sea, the lakes, and the rivers, the old forms of property—namely, lands, buildings, implements, livestock, carriages, and vessels—remain the same that they were fifty years ago, and in such communities there is no difficulty about the assessment and incidence of taxes; but in all the urban populations there are innumerable forms of property which are of very recent creation. The various bonds of railroad, telegraph, telephone, land, and bridge companies —which are a kind of preferred stock without any liability or any voting power—have been almost entirely created within thirty years. The English statute which provides for incorporation with limited liability dates only from the year 1855. The innumerable stocks of transportation, financial, and manufacturing companies, have almost all been created since the present type of American municipality was established. The history of Harvard University, like that of any old institution, illustrates the newness of these forms of property which have become so common. In 1860 only two per cent of the quick capital of Harvard University was in railroad stocks and bonds; now fifty per cent is so invested. If we go back in the history of the university thirty years more, to the year 1830, we find that the university owned neither stock nor bond, except fifty-two shares in a Boston bank, one share in a local canal, and certain interests in three wooden bridges leading out of Boston. Legislators, assessors, and voters have been quite unable to grasp the new situation so suddenly created. They have been unable to master quickly enough the new conditions. The conservatism of a democracy is intense, partly because the average voter is afraid of administrative novelties, and partly because inexperienced officials necessarily follow precedent. The more rapid the change of officials, the more surely will this unreasoning following of precedent prevail. A new official is afraid to depart from custom, lest he fall into some dangerous or absurd difficulty. Yet to follow precedent when conditions have changed is the surest way to fall into both absurdity and danger. Clinging to the old theory that a man was to be taxed at the place of his residence on all of his property,—a perfectly good theory under former conditions, and, indeed, under present conditions among a rural population,—American legislators and assessors have endeavored to tax at the place of residence property which did not lie there, never returned thither, and was wholly invisible there. Hence all the inquisitorial methods of assessment which disgrace the American cities.

At present, in many States of the Union the attempt is made to tax the house and the mortgage on it, the merchant's stock and the note he gave for the money with which he bought it, a railroad and the bonds which built it. So far as this method is successful, it falsifies the total valuation of the country, and produces inequality and injustice in the distribution of the public burdens. So far as it is unsuccessful, it causes another kind of injustice, excites suspicions and enmities among neighbors, and dulls the public conscience. These grave evils take effect, for the most part, in urban communities, and there work their most serious mischiefs. Yet they result from popular persistence in a theory which was perfectly good no long time ago, and from the inability of ill-trained and often changed officials to adapt public policy quickly to new conditions of finance and trade very suddenly created. To deal wisely with public taxation in the face of rapid and progressive changes in business and social conditions requires on the part of the tax officials exact knowledge, sound judgment, wide experience, and continuous service: in short, it requires highly trained experts, serving the public on independent tenures, for long terms.

II. The management of water-supplies and drainage systems is another municipal function which is of recent growth and of a highly scientific character. As a regular part of city business it has all been created within fifty years. I was brought up in one of the best built houses in Boston, situated near the top of Beacon Hill. The house drainage was discharged into a cesspool in the rear of the lot, and the whole family drank the water from a deep well which was not more than fifty feet from the cesspool. Moreover, five private stables stood near the rear of the lot, all of them but a short distance from the well, and the natural slope of the land was from the stables and the cesspool toward the well. There was at that time no sewerage system in the city of Boston and no public water-supply.

The mayor of Boston is elected to-day in the same way and for the same term as in those not remote times; but his function and the whole municipal business which he superintends have utterly changed. I need not say that the provision of adequate supplies of wholesome water in a large city is a work of great and increasing difficulty, which can be successfully managed only by men who have received an elaborate training, and who have labored for years continuously in that one field. The difficult subjects of average annual precipitation, natural water-sheds, prevention of pollution, and effective distribution, will always task the full powers of gifted men who have received the best possible training. Continuity of policy is of great importance in regard to the water-supply of any large population. The same may be said of the related problem of sewerage. The disposition of the fluid and semi-fluid refuse of cities is an engineering problem which presents great variety in different localities, and almost always great difficulty. In our expanding cities the moment one difficulty or danger is overcome, another presents itself. The planning of sewerage works pre-eminently requires foresight; and durability is always a primary merit in their construction. That the water-works and sewer system of a great municipality should be under the charge of constantly shifting officials is irrational to the last degree. The forms and methods of our city governments were determined when no such problems were to be solved by city agents.

    III. I turn next to the care of highways, including paving, lighting, and cleaning. It is unnecessary to dilate upon the intelligence and skill which are needed in modern cities for the right conduct of this department of the public work. The services of engineers of the highest intelligence and skill, and of the highest professional honor and business capacity, are constantly requisite. In the great European capitals, these departments of municipal service are admirably managed by men trained, in schools long famous, expressly for the planning and direction of such public works, and kept in service, like officers of the army and navy, during good behavior and efficiency. There is not a great capital in Europe. I had almost said there is not even a small city, which does not immeasurably excel in the care of its highways the best governed of American cities. The monarchical and bureaucratic governments of Europe see to it that city streets and country highways are smooth, hard, and clean. The streets of European capitals, and their public squares, are incessantly swept and washed, and all rubbish, manure, and offal are promptly removed; but in most American cities the manure of animals, the sputa of human beings, and much other vegetable and animal refuse, are suffered to dry up, and blow about as dust. The footways in American cities are as inferior to those of foreign cities as the carriage-ways, in respect to convenience and cleanliness, except, indeed, that there are some portions of the oldest European cities in which originally no footways were provided. Spain is not considered a particularly clean country; but I remember sitting down in a small public square in Seville to eat an orange, and so absolutely tidy was the enclosure that I could see no place where it was possible to leave the skin of the orange, and I had to carry it away with me. The inferiority of American cities in this respect is not due to lack of sufficient expenditure on the highways: it is due primarily to the fact that competent experts are not steadily employed to direct this important branch of municipal business, and, secondarily, to a flood of abuses which become possible in the absence of competent and honest supervision. There is no point at which municipal government in the United States has been so complete a failure as here. It has disastrously failed to provide for the convenience and comfort of the people in a matter which seriously affects the daily well-being of every inhabitant.

IV. I speak next of an important municipal function which is of very recent origin, which, indeed, has hardly as yet been developed at all; namely, the control in the public interest of the companies which sell light, heat, power, transportation, and telegraphic or telephonic communication. The value of these franchises has only recently been demonstrated; and the many ways in which these companies may affect the business interests and the comfort, health, and pleasure of a compact community, are not yet fully developed. The introduction of electricity for all these purposes, except heating, has very recently greatly modified the methods of the purveying corporations. Not a single American city has succeeded in dealing with these serviceable monopolies justly and at the same time to the public advantage; and, so long as the present modes of electing and organizing a municipal government continue in this country, we may well despair of seeing any effective control over these corporations exercised in the public interest. They are controlled in Europe by skilful engineers whose duty is to the public, and whose authority is exercised steadily and independently. This grave municipal problem is, however, very new.

It is only about forty years ago that the first street-railways were built in the United States; the telephone seems to many of us a thing of yesterday; and the introduction of electric lights and electric cars is quite within the memory of children still in school. Within five years a wholly new class of municipal difficulties has arisen from the multiplication of overhead wires, for all sorts of purposes, along and across the public highways. How absurd it is to expect an effective discharge of supervisory functions over these novel and enterprising corporations, which are eagerly pursuing their private interests, from city officials who are elected by universal suffrage once a year or once in two years, or who depend for their positions on the single will of an official so elected!

V. One would imagine, *a priori*, that "government by the people, for the people," would always have been careful of the people's health; but here we come upon one of the most conspicuous failures of free institutions in urban populations. Democratic government is at present at a serious disadvantage, in comparison with aristocratic and monarchical governments, as regards the care of the public health. The evidence of that disadvantage is of two sorts. In the first place, there are several cities in the United States which already, in spite of their comparative newness, have a death-rate absolutely higher than that of the best conducted cities of Europe. London, with its six millions of people, has habitually a lower death-rate than Boston, New York, Brooklyn, or Chicago. A few facts must suffice to illustrate this point. In the third quarter of 1889, the summer quarter, Chicago, Boston, and New York had a higher death-rate than Rome, Milan, and Turin, in hot Italy. In the fourth quarter, Chicago had a higher death-rate than Copenhagen, Christiania, Prague, Hamburg, Bremen, Cologne, Dresden, Leipsic, Berlin, Lyons, Amsterdam, Edinburgh, Sheffield, Birmingham, Liverpool, or London. In the first quarter of 1890, the death-rate in New York was a little higher than the mean rate in the twenty-eight great English towns, including London, some of those great towns being confessedly in habitually bad sanitary condition. The population of New York is about equal to that of Berlin. In the first quarter of 1890, the deaths in New York were at the annual rate of 28.8 persons in every 1,000, against 23.3 in Berlin; a fact which means that in those three months 2,600 more persons died in New York than in Berlin, although New York has great advantages over Berlin as regards both climate and situation. In the fourth quarter of 1890, the death-rate in New York and Brooklyn was higher than in Berlin by more than 3 in 1,000. In the second place, in those American cities which have made some effort to preserve the public health and to lower the death-rate, no such success has rewarded the effort as in many European cities, although the newness of most American cities should give them great advantage over the European. London, which is supposed to contain in East London the largest mass of human misery in the civilized world, is the best example in the world of sanitary success. Berlin is another striking example of sanitary success under extremely unfavorable conditions. Before 1871 the annual death-rate in Berlin had for thirty years been from 37 to 39 per 1,000. Of late years, 21 to 23 per 1,000 have been common rates,—an immense annual saving of life, which is chiefly due to the construction of a good water-supply and a good sewerage system. The worst district of Glasgow—No. 14, a physical and moral plague-spot—had in 1871 a population of 14,000 and a death-rate of 42.3 per 1,000; in 1881 a population of about 8,000 and a death-rate of 38.3; in 1888 a population of about 7,000 and a death-rate of 32.45. No American city has obtained sanitary successes like these. Boston among cities, and Massachusetts among states, have taken as much pains in sanitary matters as any American communities, yet the death-rate has not been reduced during the past twenty-five years, either in the city or in the state at large. How much saving of life is possible under favorable conditions may be inferred from two comparisons. In the year 1888, the death-rate in Boston was 24.57 per 1,000: in the adjoining, or rather interjected, town of Brookline, it was 11.43. In urban England, the death-rate during the last quarter of 1890 was 21.2 per 1,000: among the remaining population, it was 17.5 per 1,000.

What are the reasons of the comparative inefficiency of democratic government in the care of the public health? I maintain that they are not vice and criminal negligence, but ignorance and unwisdom. Is it not obvious that the care of the public health requires a high degree of intelligence and of scientific training in the officers who have charge of it? and that our system of municipal administration almost precludes the employment of such competent officers? Preventive medicine is a comparatively new science, and it has been more effectively cultivated in Europe than in this country, partly because the methods of municipal administration which there prevail give a chance for putting its principles into practice which American methods have not given. In its respect for personal liberty and the rights of the individual, democracy lets ignorance and selfishness poison water-supplies with fecal matter, distribute milk infected with diphtheria, scarlet-fever, or tuberculosis, and spread contagious diseases by omitting the precautions of isolation and disinfection. Clearly, this feebleness of democracy is largely due to ignorance. Aristocratic and autocratic governments have learned quicker than democracies the economic and humane value of sanitary science, and have applied that science more promptly and efficiently. If the sufferings inflicted on the poorer and less intelligent portions of the community, and the economic losses inflicted on the whole community, by incompetent practitioners of medicine and surgery, could be brought home to American legislators, the quacks and charlatans would have short shrift, in spite of the inevitable interference with so-called private rights. Registration acts for practitioners of medicine would be promptly passed, and vigorously enforced. In like manner, if a democracy were only persuaded that contagious diseases—like yellow-fever, small-pox, and diphtheria—might be closely limited by isolation, the present careless methods of dealing with these scourges would soon be as obsolete as surgery and midwifery without antiseptics. The multitude does not know how typhoid-fever lurks in contaminated water; it does not comprehend either the suffering or the economic loss which inevitably falls on any population breathing polluted air, or drinking polluted water; it does not realize that public health is only the sum total of the individual healths, and that every avoidable injury to the public health means individual sufferings and losses which need not have been incurred. A few American states and cities have made some progress in the care of the public health; but the good work has been done chiefly by educated physicians and engineers serving gratuitously on boards of health. Such an organization is vastly better than none; but, as the results show, it is less efficient than the steady, paid service of such competent health-officers as all large European communities nowadays employ. Again we see that this recently created but important municipal function requires experts for its satisfactory performance.

VI. Another matter in which democratic government manifests, in comparison with aristocratic and autocratic governments, a curious neglect of the interests of the masses, is the provision, or rather lack of provision, of parks, gardens, open-air parlors, and forests for the enjoyment of the populace. This subject is closely connected with the last to which I referred,—the public health. One would have supposed, that, before the urban populations began to feel keenly their deprivation of fresh air and rural beauty, liberal reservations of unoccupied land would have been made in our country for the use of the public. The fact is, however, that European towns and cities, both large and small, are much better provided with parks, gardens, small squares, and popular open-air resorts of all kinds, than American towns and cities. The gardens, parks, and game-preserves of royalty and nobility have there been converted, in many cases, to popular uses with the happiest results. The largest and densest European cities—London, Vienna, Berlin, and Paris—are greatly better off in this respect than any

American city. Even the least progressive parts of Europe, like Spain and Sicily, surpass the United States in making provision for the out-of-door enjoyments of crowded populations. All about our large cities and towns the building-up of neighborhoods once rural is going on with marvellous rapidity, and the city population is progressively excluded from private properties long unoccupied, but now converted into brick blocks and wooden villages, mostly unsightly. Meantime the municipalities take no measures to provide either small squares or broad areas for the future use of the people. Some of the smaller New England cities have actually hesitated to accept, or have even declined, the gift of valuable tracts which public-spirited citizens have offered them. A notion has been spread abroad by assessors and frugal citizens who prefer industrial or commercial values to spiritual and æsthetic or joy-giving values, that any area exempt from taxation is an incubus on the community; the fact being that the exempted areas in most towns and cities represent, as a rule, just those things which make a dense community worth having at all, namely, the churches, museums, libraries, hospitals, colleges, schools, parks, squares, and commons. One would infer from democratic practice, that in democratic theory public parks and gardens were made for the rich or the idle, whereas they are most needed by the laborious and the poor. The richer classes can provide their own enjoyments; they can go to the country or the sea when they please: it is the laboring masses that need the open-air parlor, the city boulevard, and the country park. The urban population in the United States has not yet grasped these principles; and herein lies one great difficulty in regard to good municipal administration in this matter. But there is another serious difficulty: the satisfactory construction and maintenance of public works of this nature require many years of steady work upon one plan, and they require both artistic and engineering skill in the officials who devise, execute, and maintain such works. Again we see that good municipal administration must, in this department also, be in the hands of competent experts, and that not for a year at a time, but for long periods.

I have now touched, I believe, on the chief municipal functions which have a distinctly scientific quality. There remain the administration of justice, the protection of the city against fire, disorder, and crime, and the conduct of the public schools. Experience has abundantly proved that independent and permanent tenures, after proper periods of probationary or subordinate service, are indispensable for the heads of all these departments of municipal administration; but these functions are less novel than those with which I have chiefly dealt, although even in these departments many new questions present themselves nowadays which never troubled at all the men of the last generation.

Of the judicial and legal departments of a great municipality it is perhaps unnecessary to say more than this,—that their efficiency depends on the steady employment of learned, independent, and honorable lawyers and judges. Of the education department I can say with confidence, that the welfare of the schools will always be best promoted by superintendents and teachers who have been selected by a professional appointing body, proved in actual service under the observation of competent inspectors, and then appointed to permanent places. Academies, endowed schools, and colleges often have better modes of selecting teachers than the public schools, and more secure tenures of office. Hence, in part, the greater comparative success of these institutions, their relative resources being considered. It is interesting to notice, that, under stress of great disasters, the fire department has become the best-managed public organization in an American city. In that department are often found all the features of an efficient service,—careful selection of the members of the force, steady employment, advancement for merit, compensation for injury, and a pension on retirement after faithful service.

I believe it is no exaggeration to say that good municipal administration has now become absolutely impossible without the employment, on permanent tenures, of a large number of highly trained and highly paid experts in various arts and sciences as directors of the chief city departments, and that the whole question of municipal reform is covered by the inquiry, How can a city government be organized so as to secure the services of these experts? Without attempting to go into the details of municipal organization, I venture to indicate the direction in which reform must be sought. Of late years the direction of reform movements has been towards increasing the responsibility of the mayor, by freeing him from the control of municipal elective bodies, and giving him larger rights of appointing and dismissing his subordinates. This method will succeed only so far as it procures for the city independent and highly trained expert service. I do not see that it tends to secure such service, unless the tenure of the mayoralty itself is prolonged and the heads of departments are made safe from arbitrary dismissal. On the whole, there is but slight tendency in the American cities to prolong the period of service of mayors. To give the mayor, who is himself a short-term official, larger powers of appointment and dismissal, does not tend to secure to the heads of departments long terms of service. Competent men will not leave their own business or the service of the numerous corporations which give useful men secure positions, to accept municipal positions the tenure of which is no longer, to say the least, than the tenure of the mayor. The inevitable result will be that the city will secure only second-, third-, or fourth-rate servants. As a rule, only incompetent people, or people out of work, or adventurers, will accept casual employment. I believe that all reform efforts ought to be primarily directed to the means of procuring under democratic government, as under aristocratic and autocratic governments, honest, highly trained, and well-paid permanent officials. The intelligent American closely resembles the intelligent European in preferring an independent and permanent position. He will always accept lower pay for a steady job. He will always prefer, when he has passed the speculative and adventurous age, a moderately paid position with which go public consideration and a prospect of steady usefulness, to higher paid but insecure positions. The method of employing competent persons in permanent positions is also more economical than any other: it procures more service, and more faithful and interested service, than any other method. The experience of many American corporations illustrates this fact. In the service of banks, trust companies, insurance companies, railroads, factories, shops, colleges, and hospitals, it is the almost universal practice to retain as long as possible well-proved managers, trained clerks, and skilful workmen. This policy is, indeed, the only profitable policy. In many towns and counties, also, the tenure of elective officers is practically a tenure during efficiency. For a cure of the evils which now attend democratic government in cities, it is of the utmost consequence that the methods of municipal service should be assimilated to the methods of the great private and corporate services which require intelligence, high training, and long experience. The doctrine of rotation in office when applied to such functions as I have been describing is simply silly.

I adverted at the opening of this paper to the fact that town governments in the United States have remained good, down to the present day, through all the deterioration of city governments. The principal reason for this fact seems to be that the best men in a rural town can undertake the service of the town without interfering with their regular occupation or business, and may derive from that service a convenient addition to their ordinary earnings. A selectman, road commissioner, or school commissioner in a New England town, has a position of respectability and local influence, with perhaps some small emolument; and he holds it without suffering any loss in his private business. In large cities, on the other hand, it is quite impossible for the chief officials to attend to their private business and at the same time to fulfil their municipal functions. Moreover, city men of capacity and character are sure to be absorbed in their own affairs so completely that they give but a reluctant and spasmodic attention to the business of the public. Democratic freedom inevitably tends to produce this devotion to their own affairs on the part of intelligent and industrious citizens. An able professional man, merchant, or manufacturer, cannot abandon his regular vocation to take municipal service, until his success in his profession or business has been so great that he can afford to impair, or dispense with, his ordinary annual earnings. Aside from persons of fortune and leisure, there are but two classes of competent and desirable men in this country who can, as a rule, enter the public service at all without sacrificing their individual and family interests. These two classes are lawyers, and business-men whose business is already so well organized that they can temporarily abandon it without incurring any loss which they care about. Of the Fifty-first Congress of the United States, nearly three-quarters are lawyers—fully three-quarters of the Senate, and nearly three-quarters of the House. Of the other quarter, the majority are business-men of the kind I have described. A lawyer returning from public service to his profession generally finds, if he is a man of ability, that his private practice has been increased. A manufacturer or merchant who is already rich can of course run the risks of the public service. If the voters abandon him, or his superior discharge him, he returns to his private business. As a rule, no other persons in the American community can really afford to enter the public service, either municipal or national, as it is at present conducted.

Before municipal government can be set right in the United States, municipal service must be made a life-career for intelligent and self-respecting young Americans; that is, it must be attractive to well-trained young men to enter it,— as they enter any other profession or business,—meaning to stay in it, learn it thoroughly, and win advancement in it by fidelity and ability. To enforce this principle, to indicate this one necessary direction of all reform movements, has been my modest object in this paper. To say that this reform is impracticable is equivalent to saying that American cities cannot be well conducted; and that, again, is equivalent to saying that the democratic form of government is going to be a failure for more than half of the total population. Free institutions themselves are valuable only as a means of public well-being. They will ultimately be judged by their fruits; and therefore they must be made to minister fairly well to the public comfort, health, and pleasure, and to conform in their administrative methods to the standards of intelligence and morality which are maintained by other trustees and large business agencies in the same communities.

35.

"What Hinders and What Helps to Build a Parochial School," *American Ecclesiastical Review*, 1891

During the 1840s and 1850s Roman Catholics sought to acquire public funds for parochial schools on the grounds that neither a nondenominational Protestant education nor a completely secular alternative was acceptable to devout Catholics. Their campaigns met with but slight success, and they turned reluctantly to financing their own schools out of their own funds. By 1884 it was apparent that few American Catholics actually sent their children to their church's schools; accordingly, its Third Plenary Council (which convened in Baltimore in that year) instructed them to do so except under extraordinary circumstances. This action, subsequently confirmed by the Vatican, prompted the creation of a full-fledged system of parish schools paralleling the public system.

Even so, parochial schools spread relatively slowly. As an anonymous author indicated in the *American Ecclesiastical Review* in 1891, they were handicapped by exaggerated versions of many of the same difficulties that had beset the common schools during the 1830s—the dispersion of eligible population, the practice of child labor, popular resistance to additional financial burdens. He also pointed out the grounds that Catholic clergymen must occupy in order to persuade Catholic laymen to play their part in the creation of a school system—not only an appeal to conscience, but an appeal to religious pride with an overtone of pride in being outsiders. To this extent, he anticipated a pluralistic view of education in American society that would continue to be influential in the twentieth century.

The Decrees of the late Plenary Council were ratified in 1885. They were promulgated and declared as in force at the beginning of 1886.

According to section 199 (Tit. VI), every parish was to begin the erection of a Parish-school within two years from the date of publication of the Decrees. Where serious difficulties demanded a longer term the Ordinary was to extend the time, whilst, in cases of evident neglect on the part of a pastor, the Bishop was authorized to remove him from his rectorship without other cause.

Since the year 1888 schools have sprung up everywhere. In many cases they are models of building, appointment and scholastic management. Those who looked simply on have marvelled how it was possible, and the fears of those who considered the united move of the Catholic Hierarchy in this matter as a mere outburst of religious zeal which would die as soon as brought face to face with the difficulties involved in carrying out the project, have been disappointed. Pastors who have vigorously entered upon the design of erecting their own school will tell you in most cases that it has not only not hampered them in carrying on their parochial work without embarrass-

From the *American Ecclesiastical Review*, V, 5 (November 1891), 334–341.

ment in a financial point of view, but that it has actually infused new blood and fresh energy into their parishes. Young
men's societies are almost in every instance a natural outcome
of the school, which furnishes both accommodation and promises a permanent nucleus of active members. Other advantages
which foster union and live activity in the parish are self-
evident results of a well-managed school.

Nevertheless there are still many parishes which have
no schools and which, except under a partial view of the necessity of such an annex to the Church, could have them.

Many a pastor feels the difficulties which are ahead and
which he may not be able to analyze in detail or account for
to another. If he begins the work he must complete it; he is
pledged to sustain it permanently and, what is more, he must
as far as possible make it reach the level of his neighbors, the
state-schools.

There are, however, causes which seem to argue not
only against the prudence but also against the necessity of
building a parish school. Let us take some instances.

Suppose the district is one where the children frequent
school, if at all, only for a very short time. They are sent to
pick slate in the coal-mines, or they do light work in the mills
when they are still very young, in order that they may swell
the moderate earnings of their parents. The number of children therefore who go to school is disproportionately small.
If they remain for a couple of years or three in the public
school, they learn what their elders consider enough for their
state of life. The old folks having the faith which is the inheritance of persecution, deep in their hearts, consider that an
hour's Sunday-school will supply the religious needs of their
children. The same may be said of Catholics in the rural districts where the youngest boy or girl is often required to help
in the field and garden during the spring and harvest seasons.

Another objection of no slight account in the matter of
erecting a school is the fact that in the country districts many
of the children live scattered. They cannot attend a school

which is at a distance, especially during the inclement seasons of the year.

Again a pastor who with considerable sacrifice would find it possible to build or equip a school, is deterred by the thought that he must secure religious teachers in order to bring it up to a good standard. The maintenance of a teaching community implies in almost every case the support of at least three teachers who have to have their separate lodgings and cannot shift as a lay teacher might do. This is a serious difficulty which will persuade many a well-intentioned priest to defer the work to a more auspicious time rather than inaugurate an ultimate failure.

Last and not least is the number of pastors who believe that the building of a separate Parish-school is unadvisable, because the Public schools of this district satisfy all the present demands of Catholics inasmuch as the teachers like the majority of their pupils are Catholics and that a Catholic atmosphere actually reigns in the schoolroom whilst the people are not burdened with extra taxes to support an establishment which could scarcely differ in anything from the state school. What adds to the weight of this as to that of all the foregoing objections against the erection of a parish-school is the attitude of the Catholic people themselves who are opposed to making a sacrifice of money where the demand seems founded only on a needless and unreasonable interpretation of ecclesiastical laws.

We have stated these objections to the erection of a parish school in particular localities, principally to show that we do not ignore or undervalue them, when we undertake to show that theoretically they are of no weight whatever and that practically they can be overcome in most cases, provided we look beyond the first steps and calculate our gains as a good business-man does who first advertises his goods and is willing to lose something in the beginning that he may attract his future customers to prove his purpose of fair dealing in reliable material.

It is needless to say, in addition to what is being constantly broached in the sound Catholic press, that Catholics cannot be properly educated except in distinctly Catholic schools and by other than merely nominally Catholic teachers. Neither the smallness of numbers, nor the poverty of our people can really prevent us from fitting up a school which would answer to the need of our congregation. It must not be forgotten that a really and thoroughly Catholic school, whatever degree of intellectual attainment it may reach or fail to reach, is in every case superior to the best School of sciences where the training of the heart, that is to say of morality or religion as a constantly accompanying element is neglected. Intellectual training and wordly culture, while it frequently commands success, does not prevent a child from becoming thoroughly bad, immoral and a pest to society and the state. But true religion, such as is imparted in a good Catholic school will always make the child better, more virtuous if less learned, and a more trustworthy citizen even if a less cultivated society man.

If a Catholic child attends a Catholic school even for a short time, it will be the better for him during life and for his fellow-citizens likewise, provided that Catholic school is rightly looked after, which requires less money and less learning than it requires true zeal which does not shirk labor and sacrifice and which easily finds means to give a thoroughly sound if only elementary education. What hinders a prosperous commonwealth is public corruption and immorality in spite of a high standard of school teaching. Honesty and peaceful industry are the outcome of religious influences which to be effective must be constant.

The most real difficulty in the case of Catholic school building arises probably from the scattered condition of the children in certain districts. But then this fact almost always implies that the priest is not harassed with constant parish duties like the parochial Clergy of large cities and towns, and that therefore he has sufficient time to supply the need of a school in some measure at least by arranging that the children should assemble at certain convenient centres and be systematically taught by some competent person of the district. It must be a poor fold indeed wherein some willing member, more intelligent than the rest could not be trained into such service as would prove a benefit to the little ones of the neighborhood. Nor is such work one from which a pastor need shrink himself. Some of our early missionaries, right royal intellects and men of solid culture, have given us the example of how good and able citizens may be trained in a log-cabin or under the straw roof of a plantation shed. There are indeed at this instant numerous parishes where the pastor himself teaches and where non-Catholics prefer to send their children because the priest teaches them not only knowledge but virtue also.

As for those public schools which employ Catholic teachers and where Catholic children are perchance in the majority, they certainly furnish not sufficient solid reason for neglecting to attempt the building of a distinct parish-school. The public school-management depends in many places, on the bias of political jobbers. We have seen the tide suddenly turn through the influence of a single moneyed man, who had Catholic teachers replaced by those who had no religion or, what is worse, who were prejudiced against the "Romanists" or the "Irish." The children are thus at once placed at the mercy of a politician's caprice, and have no alternative between leaving the school or being subjected to insult for their religion's sake.

But besides this a Catholic teacher, no matter how exemplary, is violating the contract under which he is ordinarily employed, if he attempts to bring his religion in any positive way into the class room of the public school. And if it is a mere negative influence which he exercises, it is of no practical worth in the education of the child. We say nothing about the text-books which are usually chosen by a school-board and which, though they frequently contain uncatholic and false notions concerning important facts, are placed in the hands of the pupils. If on the other hand the authorities for the time being connive at the practice of Catholic teachers who make their religion felt in a school to which non-Catholics also send their children because it is supposed to be unsectarian and supported by the state, then we have no right to complain of teachers who make their sectarian prejudices felt in schools frequented by Catholic children. However favorable our conditions in this respect might be for the time being, and in certain localities it is simply improvidence to depend on the contingency of political influence for the right training of our children which can hardly in any of these cases be said to be truly Catholic, that is such as supplies the religious wants of the children.

Yet what are we to do when the fact remains that in many cases our people are not willing to make the united sacrifice required for the erection of a Parish school?

We answer, that, if Catholics are unwilling to take up the burden of erecting and supporting a parish school it is solely because they do not realize that any harm is done to their children or themselves through the absence of such schools, especially if the public school is wholly unsectarian and there is a good Sunday-school in the parish. Even among priests, few would care to undertake the work of erecting a school if they were not convinced of the immense importance of distinctly Catholic education in our day.

The first step therefore in securing the good will and coöperation of our people is to make them view the question from an intelligent standpoint. This requires more than one or two sermons preparatory to a collection when the project of building has already been settled upon. Catholics must feel and be thoroughly convinced that their best interests are jeopardized through the want of a Catholic school. The very same reasons which induce them to seek the positive teaching of the Catholic Church rather than the vague religiousness of protestantism or agnosticism, hold good for selecting a school in which their children are taught that religion together with other useful knowledge. The ordinary man or woman do[es] not reflect upon how much of the happiness of their children depends on the direction given to their minds and hearts in early youth. It must be brought home to them by consistent illustration in the pulpit and in private instructions. People are easily convinced by any earnest appeal for a good end if it is intelligently put before them and there is nothing in the world that we can have justly more at heart than the bringing up fervent and practical Catholics the young of our flock.

However to bring home to Catholics the necessity of a thoroughly Catholic school training for their children is only one of the things which will guarantee a vigorous coöperation on their part. To show the way to the actual fulfilment of this necessity is another and an important factor in the work of erecting a school.

To this purpose it will be well to show our people the workings of such a school as we propose for them according to the means placed within our reach. Enthusiasm for any cause is developed by the raising of ideals. Great things are accomplished only by those who have high and noble ideals before them. Draw then a picture of Catholic education in the past and at present in other places. Give the people an insight into the activity of the religious teaching orders, how they live, how the effects of their teaching is seen in the conduct of the children and acts upon the whole community. Show them how industry, sobriety, obedience, peace and general prosperity are the natural and legitimate result of a good and thorough Catholic training. In short make them long for such a state of things in their midst as you know for certain can be brought about by a really efficient parish-school. If opportunity offer take some intelligent layman from your parish to a model Catholic school. Let him see the workings of it, and how the same may be done at home even if on a smaller scale. That man if he understands the work will be a host of arguments in favor of the school. People like to have a part in the work and feel honored to have one or more of their own number consulted in this way.

And if we begin need it be less energetically because it is to be less pretentious than in places where the parishioners are more wealthy? Our coat need only fit us; and if it suits our circumstances it is always an excellent coat, much more so indeed then if it passed that limit. We shall have to labor and watch and above all to instruct rather than compel by mere appeals for money or threats of exclusion from the privileges of our holy religion. In some instances the Church authorities have indeed found it necessary to use harsh measures against those who keep unreasonably aloof from supporting Catholic schools. We can only suppose that in such cases the apathy on the part of Catholics is really equivalent to opposition and that the Catholic schools are in such condition that no one can validly object to send his children to them except he wholly undervalue his religion. As to these measures which are in their nature censures, their application belongs to the proper judicial tribunals under whose care religious schools are established. We are not competent to pronounce on their value unless in a given case. But their very use shows how closely the school is bound up with the most important interests of religion.

What may be done to increase our schools in constant efficiency when we have them once in running order, we shall leave to another writer for a future article.

36.

Andrew D. White, "Some Practical Lessons of the Recent Campaign," 1896

The political and economic enthusiasms of the 1880s and 1890s stimulated a sharp negative reaction, which reached a climax during the presidential campaign of 1896. Looking back on the Republican victory in November, the former president of Cornell University took it as a victory for popular education, but he also pressed the idea that colleges and universities must be strengthened to combat political heresy and to deal adequately with contemporary problems. In doing so he expressed a distinctly conservative version of Eliot's principle of expert management and discounted (if he did not repudiate) processes of informal education that had for many decades seemed the bulwark of democracy.

Every man who thinks to any purpose on public affairs must see that our country has escaped a great peril, the greatest perhaps that it has encountered thus far; the second of a series,—the "Greenback craze" being the first.

Decisive as the victory is, it is after all a somewhat more narrow escape than many wished and than some expected; yet it may well be that this less triumphant vindication of right reason brings blessings of its own. It is easily conceivable that a more sweeping victory over the Chicago candidate and platform might have led to over-confidence, easy-going optimism, and neglect to provide adequately for the future; and that instead of an evolution of right reason there might have finally resulted reaction and revolution. As it is there is increased reason for high hope and strenuous endeavor. Once more the American people have redeemed their character and vindicated their theory of government. Once more they stand before the world as fit for free institutions; as they did when they grappled first with slavery, next with disunion, and next with the national debt.

But this new victory brings new duties. Upon leaders it enforces faith in justice and right reason, with more courage in unholding this faith. Never has it been more clearly shown that an intelligent democracy does not in any great crisis look for the final and decisive word to mere tonguey demagogues, but that it seeks real leaders.

Among the many lessons taught by the recent contest I shall, then, emphasize mainly this one,—the need of leadership and some ways of securing it.

From the *Forum*, XXII, 4 (December 1896), 414–422.

And first, of leadership among the great body of citizens. To say nothing at present of Republicans we find the most striking object-lesson as regards this need in the Democratic party. If we look at the writings of Jefferson and the men best known in the party down to the development of secession doctrines we find everywhere evidences that their leadership was something very real and effective. Their correspondence shows them constantly discussing political doctrines and policies with each other, and having thus satisfied themselves as to what was right and advisable they promulgated it among the people.

In the recent campaign these earlier leaders have as their worthy successors in journalism and in public life a long list of publicists and statesmen who have shown themselves, by fearlessness in defence of Democratic principles, worthy of the best period of their party. These did not wait to find out what grotesque conclusions in political economy or in social science had been reached by this demagogue or that clique, but they showed themselves statesmen: and they gave the main proof of statesmanship—they *led*. Casting to the winds all low prudence they broke from the Chicago platform makers and marshalled a movement—all the more honorable because sure of defeat. Thereby they have added a noble chapter to the history of their country, and, if any salvation be possible to the old Democratic party, they have saved it. Contrast with this the flabby utterance and sickly attitude of men entrusted with high office who allowed anti-Democratic and anti-social doctrines to develop rankly in their respective States, who made no effective effort to withstand ideas which they must have loathed, and who finally abdicated the leadership which the party had assigned to them, turned it over to the Tillmans, Altgelds, Waites, Peffers, Stewarts, and to Mrs. Lease, and submitted to their bidding.[1] No more pitiful sight has been seen

---

[1] [These names represent leading figures in the protest movement of the 1890s. Ben Tillman, Democratic Senator from South Carolina, was notoriously able to rouse his state's rural voters against his state's establish-

in political history, and the future historian will award a most unenviable place to the men who, having thus allowed the foe to steal upon them, surrendered their positions at the first onslaught and finally went over to the enemy.

One grand exception has redeemed Southern statesmanship—the course of Mr. Carlisle.[2] From the beginning of the recent contest he has been a leader. At an earlier period, before responsibility and a close examination of the great questions at issue had settled his convictions, he had perhaps wavered, but now there was no uncertain sound. His speech to the workingmen of Chicago set the true key-note of the campaign in its economical aspect. Calm, clear, convincing, weighty, that was great; but something far greater followed. His campaign in Kentucky, in which he braved the hostility of old friends, wild abuse, and even personal insult, is one of the nobler things in American history. The greatest man of his great commonwealth since Henry Clay, he has restored Kentucky to her proud position of old;—as a State toward which the Union may look for counsel and leadership. Compare his

---

ment. John P. Altgeld, the Democratic governor of Illinois, had outraged middle-class opinion by pardoning some of the convicted Haymarket rioters and by opposing President Cleveland's use of federal troops to put down the Pullman strike. (He was defeated for reelection in 1896.) Davis "Bloody Bridles" Waite had played a similar role as Populist governor of Colorado; he was also a fanatic on the silver question. William A. Peffer was a relatively moderate Populist best known for his tract *The Farmer's Side: His Troubles and Their Remedy* (1891) and for the fact that the Kansas legislature had sent him to the Senate in 1890. William M. Stewart, Senator from Nevada since 1887, had bolted the Republican party in 1893 to run (and win) as an apostle of free silver. Mary Elizabeth Lease, who called herself Mary Ellen and who was called "Mary Yellin" by her critics, was an outspoken Populist agitator best known for her injunction to Kansas farmers to "Raise less corn and more hell."]

[2] [John G. Carlisle of Kentucky, Speaker of the House from 1883 to 1889 and Senator from 1890 to 1893, had at one time advocated the unlimited coinage of silver. As Secretary of the Treasury under Cleveland, however, he had been a leading advocate of "sound money," and he supported the Gold Democrats in 1896.]

position before the country, before the world at large, before history, with that of the vast majority of Southern men in high office, and especially of the Senator from his State whom the recent result leaves so utterly discredited.[3]

Several years ago, visiting the House of Representatives and sitting at the side of one of the strongest Republicans in that body—a man who has since represented the State of New York in the national Senate—I asked him what he thought of Mr. Carlisle, at that time Speaker of the House. His answer greatly impressed me. It was simply this: "As you know, he is a life-long Democrat from the South, I a life-long Republican from the North. Politically he is opposed to me at every point, and yet by the utmost stretch of my imagination I cannot imagine him as doing anything unjust or in any way violating his real convictions." This judgment recent events have verified.

A great lesson, then, in this campaign is afforded by the contrast between Mr. Carlisle and other men who ought to have been the leaders of Southern Democracy but were not. Had Mr. Mills in Texas shown anything like Mr. Carlisle's faith in truth, he would have gained not only a national but a world-wide reputation; had Mr. Morgan in Alabama possessed Mr. Carlisle's courage, he would have risen to the reputation which he was once expected to attain; could Mr. Daniel of Virginia have shown but a tithe of that courage, taking the lead in that grand old commonwealth which only needed such direction to have brought her into a leading place among the States standing for real democracy, his place in history would have been far different.[4]

---

[3] [The reference is to Senator Joseph C. S. Blackburn, defeated for reelection in 1896.]

[4] [The references are to Roger Q. Mills, Senator from Texas (1892–1899); John T. Morgan, Senator from Alabama (1877–1907); and John W. Daniel, Senator from Virginia (1887–1900). Daniel played a major role in causing the Democratic national convention to nominate Bryan.]

While such is the main lesson as regards leadership in the country at large, there is a lesson of no less importance as to leadership in the national councils.

Never since the civil war has there been an Administration or a Congress called to more severe thought and earnest work. The problems are vast and complicated. What is demanded is not declamation but statesmanship—the statesmanship which shall devise measures to remedy real evils, to explode imaginary evils and to restore prosperity. We need a larger number of quiet, strong, thoughtful men to open paths for the energy of our people and a smaller number of declaimers to delight the galleries; more men like Governor Dingley, fewer men like Mr. Bryan. We want men in support of the new Administration, who, when Mr. McKinley, Mr. Reed, Mr. Sherman, Mr. Allison, and Mr. Dingley lead, shall be wise enough and strong enough to act effectively with them.[5]

The metropolitan press, which has almost universally rendered noble service in the recent contest, may continue that service and gain a new hold upon the people by henceforth giving less prominence to Congressional oratory and more to real leadership and effective public service. Let these journals give us, not "The Profound Logical Reasoning" of the

---

[5] [These men were already well known as conservative Republican heroes. William McKinley, the President-elect, had always been a vigorous advocate of protection and had long since repudiated his early report of free silver. Thomas B. Reed of Maine, Speaker of the House when it was controlled by the Republicans, was noted for his support of the tariff, the navy, and veterans' pensions, as well as his masterly management of the House of Representatives. John Sherman, Senator from Ohio, was the leading Republican expert on currency and the primary author, as Secretary of the Treasury under Hayes, of the arrangements for resuming specie payments. William B. Allison of Iowa had made a name for himself in the Senate as an opponent of the silver bloc. Nelson Dingley, Representative from Maine and recently Chairman of the Ways and Means Committee, was a prominent tariff advocate and would soon be identified with the Tariff of 1897.]

Hon. Mr. A. on some vanishing point in political metaphysics; not "The Greatest Effort of His Life" by the Hon. Mr. D. in his diatribe against the Administration regarding a post-office; but let us have the best arguments and the best work of men who show themselves real leaders in solving the problems now confronting us.

There is ample opportunity here for leadership in many directions. The great leaders above named will need strong men to coöperate with them. Leadership in the devising of an effective financial and industrial policy is naturally the first demand, but there is another great work to be done. Much of the outcry regarding the encroachments of corporations, trusts, and monopolies is doubtless unjust and "for buncombe"; but no one can doubt the necessity of wise and vigorous regulation of these combinations. Leaders are wanted in Congress, not to set the key-note for new howls at all men engaged in great industrial enterprises, but to pave the way for such enterprises and to devise wise and just measures for controlling them. Four years hence the leaders on the stump must be able to show not only that the new Administration has promoted prosperity but that it has done so within the limits of justice.

Much has been said, and justly said, during the recent campaign, to expose the cant that the rich are growing richer and the poor poorer; that poor men's sons are robbed of their chances; that our leading statesmen in Congress have for years past been devoting their main energies to committing a series of monstrous crimes against the men of small means; that capitalists are enemies of the human race; and it has been amply demonstrated that the position of the farmer and workingman is better in this than in any other country. But it may be a costly mistake to suppose that this is enough. Men "hunger and thirst after righteousness,"—which is *rightness*. Leaders are needed to introduce more and more justice into legislation, to make law more and more the evident incarnation of right, and to teach the people what right and justice are. Mere prosperity fails to satisfy; it must be prosperity with justice. Men can bear poverty, but not poverty which they believe the result of injustice.

It used to be supposed, especially by those who had read Arthur Young's "Travels in France," or even Alison's "History," that the fearful excesses, atrocities, ruin, and despotism of the French Revolution had their origin in the fact that the French peasantry were poverty-stricken above all others.[6] To any man who has arrived at this old stock conclusion of ill-read historians there comes a great awakening when he reads Goethe's account of the French peasantry as he found them. Goethe was in the invading German army and he tells us that on arriving on French soil he was surprised to find evidences of much more comfort and prosperity among the French peasantry than he had known among the German tillers of the soil. DeTocqueville has shown that the French agriculturists as a whole were, at the beginning of the Revolution, more prosperous than they had been for a long time previously, and that this better condition was one important cause of their terrific uprising. In other countries those who tilled the soil were so thoroughly crushed and besotted that they could only lie quiet beneath the encroachments of justice. In France the mere fact that the rural population were better off than other peasants were, or than they themselves had formerly been, was one of the main reasons for their insurrection. The deepest cause of the French Revolution among the tillers of the soil was not their poverty but their wide-spread sense of injustice. The vague sense of injustice, wrong-headed as most of it is, has been the most troublesome thing that the advocates of right reason have had to meet during the recent campaign. It was

---

[6] [Arthur Young (1741–1820) was an eminent English agriculturist and writer on agricultural questions. His *Travels in France during the Years 1787, 1788, and 1789* appeared in 1794. Sir Archibald Alison (1792–1867), a lawyer, government official, and amateur historian, was author of a widely read *History of Europe* (10 volumes, 1833–1842).]

the chief string on which our mob orators played their varia-
tions. In future the first thing necessary is to make every effort
that legislation be just, and the next thing is that leaders and
the press show the people how and why it is just. This will
interest the people far more than accounts of what Senator A.
eats, what Representative B. drinks, and what the wives of
cabinet ministers wear.

But leadership is needed not only in general political
effort but in administrative work and in continuing the "campaign of education." This "campaign," of which we have heard
so much, is to go on, and out of many means of continuing it
I will here mention one.

No thinking man can have failed to notice that the recent victory was given us by the States in which education is
best developed and most widely diffused. Every proper measure should be taken to spread and strengthen this popular
education which has thus so signally justified its existence.
Four years may thus add to the grand phalanx favoring sound
money and good government at least such States as Virginia,
Georgia, Missouri, Tennessee, Nebraska, and Washington. For
this progress in public education, as given in the public
schools, we must mainly rely upon the people at large acting
through their legislatures; but for another part of this progress,
which is especially important because nearer the centres and
sources of educational thought, we must largely rely on men
who unite patriotism with wealth.

Never in the history of mankind have there been such
admirable examples of the patriotic use of great fortunes as in
our own country. A long line of our most prosperous fellow-
citizens have clearly seen that while in Great Britain and various other countries rich men may found families to carry the
family name down through many generations, this in our country is impossible, and that a legitimate ambition to be borne
in honorable remembrance after death can be satisfied only by
doing something for the public good. The opportunities for
thus rendering public service are so vast that there is no space

for giving anything like a complete list of them in a single article; but one thing should be borne in mind by all rich men, and this is that revolution can be prevented only by evolution, —the evolution of right reason in obedience to the best knowledge and thought thus far attained by men. Out of the multitude of agencies which should be immediately strengthened in the interests of this evolution of forces which shall keep this republic in the right path, I therefore confine myself to one— that of our leading institutions for advanced instruction.

Never was there a time when our great universities and colleges were exercising so strong and healthful an influence upon the country, and especially upon public life, as now. In the middle years of this century a comparatively small proportion of the men entering public service came from these institutions; now the proportion is much greater and it is steadily increasing. In those years two or three hundred students constituted a very large institution of learning; now several of our universities have ten times these numbers, and each year sees an ever increasing body of active-minded young men seeking their advantages. In the contest just ended they have done nobly. Their faculties almost unanimously and their students by vast majorities have been on the side of right reason and well regulated liberty. Among hardly any other bodies of men has there been such earnest unanimity. These, then, are fortresses to be strengthened.

Twenty years ago I urged the necessity of creating departments of history and political and social science in all such institutions in order to fit young men for public life in general and especially to enable them to grapple with the more and more complicated social and political problems rising before us.* By several of our universities this has been done, and

---

* This was especially done in my report as Commissioner at the Paris Exposition of 1878 on "Education in History and Political Science, at the European Universities" and in addresses at the Johns Hopkins, Michigan, and Cornell Universities on the general subject of such education.

every close observer must have noticed, during the recent struggle, that with hardly an exception every such institution has been a centre of the best influences; that from each has radiated light upon the great questions at issue, and that from their training have gone forth men who as a rule have done admirable work through the press and upon the platform.

Here is a hint to men who are both rich and patriotic. Our leading colleges and universities should be strengthened more and more as fortresses against future outbursts of demagoguism and Jack-Cadeism.[7] Such institutions as the University of Virginia, that of North Carolina, and Tulane University, in the South, and a multitude of universities in our Northern States might well be thus strengthened. New departments of history, of economical, political, and social science, of comparative legislation, and of international law should be created, and old ones strengthened. There are endowments possible to all fortunes. Professorships, lectureships, fellowships, scholarships, travelling bachelorships, and funds for buying books should be established or increased: thus shall future leaders be supplied and equipped—leaders in public life and in the press to marshal and guide the forces of right reason in the future developments of the present struggle and in other struggles. And not only this: from such central institutions sound doctrine will filter down through various channels into the popular mind. The clergy, teachers, and broad-minded men of business will thus be equipped as missionaries of sound ideas, social and political. Not one of our universities, North, South, East, or West, is equipped in this respect as it should be: not one is there that cannot be made, with such aid, far more effective in the present struggle and in other conflicts before us.

---

[7] [Jack Cade led the people of Kent when they rose in 1450 against the exactions of King Henry VI's ministers. His motley army fought its way into London, where it released a number of prisoners, executed two especially hated royal officials, and engaged in some desultory looting before being driven out.]

Down to a recent period their graduates have been somewhat handicapped. The college-bred man, trained in Greek, Latin, Mathematics, and Metaphysics, has had generally a good training of his mental powers, and thus has often given us valuable public service; but too often such ingenuous youth have been abashed and reduced to silence in the public councils by plain men of business whose training in public affairs has been gained in State legislatures or even in county boards.

The training of our best and brightest young men in political history, comparative legislation, and in the group of studies comprehended under the term "social and political science," promises to be of vast use to our country. Such training is a crying need, not only for the national legislature but for the State, county, city, and village legislatures. Studies in finance, in general administration, in comparative legislation, in international law, in the best methods of public instruction and the most approved dealings with pauperism, insanity, inebriety, crime, and the like,—all these come within the scope of such departments as should be fully established and equipped in our universities and colleges. Let wealthy and patriotic men consider this. How can they better hand down an honorable name to posterity? How can they better serve the country which they love?

The time is coming when, in the increasing complications of public affairs, public men will take more and more the character of experts. In order to deal successfully with most public questions there will be needed the preparation which comes only from thorough acquaintance with the best thinking upon such questions, and from careful study of the best methods and results in our own and other times and in our own and other countries. Such training and knowledge will not supersede practical facility gained in public life itself, but it will fit men for entering public life; just as training in the best methods in law, medicine, or engineering is a preliminary to practical experience in those professions. The critic may say, "This will produce doctrinaires." Even if so, doctrinaires are vastly better than destructives. But there is no real danger of doctrinairism in a country where all theories are so constantly subjected to practical tests as in ours. One of the needs of the country which cannot be too strongly urged is the need of enlisting our best, strongest, and brightest young men in public life. Here is the opportunity for far-sighted men of wealth to promote this enlistment.

Every great republic the world has yet seen has failed. Nearly every one has gone down in blood or in despotism brought on by the clamor of demagogues working upon an unenlightened populace;—exciting their distrust, stimulating their hate, luring their greed, inflating their vanity. An unenlightened democracy is a mere mob, even though it be spread over a whole continent. The first necessity of a great republic is education; an education which shall make much of religion in its higher sense, of morals, of honor, and which shall give the best teachings of history and the wisest conclusions of human thought. How does our Republic differ from others that have sunk beneath the waves of demagoguism and despotism? Simply in being the first in which liberty has been largely united with education.

The recent campaign, among its most practical lessons, teaches most clearly that the enlightenment of the citizens is the most important of public duties and the main condition of continued freedom. All should, so far as possible, contribute to that education which extends the area, not of the license urged on by anarchists and the utopias pictured by socialists, but of liberty as developed healthfully and steadily in obedience to the lessons of history and constructive thought.

It must be confessed that during recent years there have been some conduct of rich men and several careers of rich men's sons fit to breed nihilism and anarchy. Many wild doctrines among the poor may be traced back to senseless ostentation among the rich. Glorifications in our press of this woman's "tiara" and that woman's wardrobe; of this young millionaire's genius in driving a four-in-hand and that young millionaire's talent in cooking terrapin; of some Crœsus buying or begging his way into the society of London or Paris; of social or financial infamy condoned by foreign matrimonial alliances; —what wonder that men out of work in tenement houses or struggling with past-due mortgages on the prairies should be led by such examples to look at all property as robbery? Let patriotic men of wealth efface such impressions by continuing the better American traditions; by recognizing the duties as well as claiming the privileges of wealth. To say nothing of great benefactors still living, let such exemplars as Peter Cooper, Cornell, Johns Hopkins, Stanford, Peabody, Vassar, Tulane, Stevens, Case, Pratt, Rose, Drexel, and their like be held in honored remembrance. Let a new and greater growth of munificence come in with the approaching growth of prosperity. Thus shall wealth justify its existence: thus shall the outcries against the selfishness of the rich be proved slanderous: thus shall the liberty of our more enlightened States be increased and the foundations of rational liberty be imbedded deeply in the popular gratitude and in the universal sense of justice. No answer to nihilist or anarchist, in the press or upon the platform, is so effective as the mention of Americans who, having gained wealth in developing the great enterprises of their country, have used it largely in promoting the public good. Let this patriotic list be now extended in every field, and especially for the enlightenment of our people and the strengthening of our free institutions.

37.

Edward Bellamy, *Equality*, 1897

In *Equality*, Edward Bellamy gave voice to precisely the radical humanitarian ideals that so troubled Andrew D. White and other conservative commentators. From their point of view, the sequel to *Looking Backward* was utopian in every bad sense of the term: revolutionary in its criticisms of American social values, foolhardy in its economic theory, appallingly naive in its vision of erecting a new social order on the ruins of the old. Looked at more nearly in its own terms, however, the novel was a climactic version of nineteenth-century hopes made radical by contingencies an earlier generation had never dreamed of. Nowhere was it more characteristic of its century than in the extraordinary value it placed upon education; in effect, Bellamy solved all the problems of achieving social justice by referring them to a process of popular education, gradual at first but gaining in intensity, that would achieve the objectives of revolution without causing its bloodshed. In 1897, as half a century before, the education of the people connoted a combination of religious effort and political deliberation to secure the good society.

Chapter XXXIV

WHAT STARTED THE REVOLUTION

. . . "Beginnings are always misty," he said,[1] when I straight-way opened at him with the question when the great Revolution began. "Perhaps St. John disposed of that point in the simplest way when he said that 'in the beginning was God.' To come down nearer, it might be said that Jesus Christ stated the doctrinal basis and practical purpose of the great Revolution when he declared that the golden rule of equal[ity] and the best treatment for all was the only right principle on which people could live together. To speak, however, in the language of historians, the great Revolution, like all important events, had two sets of causes—first, the general, necessary, and funda-

---

From Edward Bellamy, *Equality* (New York, 1897), pp. 304–308, 322–324, 328–330, 336–341, 342–347.

[1] [The hero of the novel is being instructed by his host of the year 2000, Dr. Leete.]

mental cause which must have brought it about in the end, whatever the minor circumstances had been; and, second, the proximate or provoking causes which, within certain limits, determined when it actually did take place, together with the incidental features. These immediate or provoking causes were, of course, different in different countries, but the general, necessary, and fundamental cause was the same in all countries, the great Revolution being, as you know, world-wide and nearly simultaneous, as regards the more advanced nations.

"That cause, as I have often intimated in our talks, was the growth of intelligence and diffusion of knowledge among the masses, which, beginning with the introduction of printing, spread slowly through the sixteenth, seventeenth, and eighteenth centuries, and much more rapidly during the nineteenth, when, in the more favored countries, it began to be something like general. Previous to the beginning of this process of enlightenment the condition of the mass of mankind as to intelligence, from the most ancient times, had been practically stationary at a point little above the level of the brutes. With no more thought or will of their own than clay in the hands of the potter, they were unresistingly molded to the uses of the more intelligent and powerful individuals and groups of their kind. So it went on for innumerable ages, and nobody dreamed of anything else until at last the conditions were ripe for the inbreathing of an intellectual life into these inert and senseless clods. The process by which this awakening took place was silent, gradual, imperceptible, but no previous event or series of events in the history of the race had been comparable to it in the effect it was to have upon human destiny. It meant that the interest of the many instead of the few, the welfare of the whole instead of that of a part, were henceforth to be the paramount purpose of the social order and the goal of its evolution.

"Dimly your nineteenth-century philosophers seem to have perceived that the general diffusion of intelligence was a new and large fact, and that it introduced a very important force into the social evolution, but they were wall-eyed in their failure to see the certainty with which it foreshadowed a complete revolution of the economic basis of society in the interest of the whole body of the people as opposed to class interest or partial interest of every sort. Its first effect was the democratic movement by which personal and class rule in political matters was overthrown in the name of the supreme interest and authority of the people. It is astonishing that there should have been any intelligent persons among you who did not perceive that political democracy was but the pioneer corps and advance guard of economic democracy, clearing the way and providing the instrumentality for the substantial part of the programme—namely, the equalization of the distribution of work and wealth. So much for the main, general, and necessary cause and explanation of the great Revolution—namely, the progressive diffusion of intelligence among the masses from the sixteenth to the end of the nineteenth centuries. Given this force in operation, and the revolution of the economic basis of society must sooner or later have been its outcome everywhere: whether a little sooner or later and in just what way and with just what circumstances, the differing conditions of different countries determined.

"In the case of America, the period of revolutionary agitation which resulted in the establishment of the present order began almost at once upon the close of the civil war. Some historians date the beginning of the Revolution from 1873."

"Eighteen seventy-three!" I exclaimed; "why, that was more than a dozen years before I fell asleep! It seems, then, that I was a contemporary and witness of at least a part of the Revolution, and yet I saw no Revolution. It is true that we recognized the highly serious condition of industrial confusion and popular discontent, but we did not realize that a Revolution was on."

"It was to have been expected that you would not," replied the doctor. "It is very rarely that the contemporaries of great revolutionary movements have understood their nature until they have nearly run their course. Following generations always think that they would have been wiser in reading the signs of the times, but that is not likely."

"But what was there," I said, "about 1873 which has led historians to take it as the date from which to reckon the beginning of the Revolution?"

"Simply the fact that it marked in a rather distinct way the beginning of a period of economic distress among the American people, which continued, with temporary and partial alleviations, until the overthrow of private capitalism. The popular discontent resulting from this experience was the provoking cause of the Revolution. It awoke Americans from their self-complacent dream that the social problem had been solved or could be solved by a system of democracy limited to merely political forms, and set them to seeking the true solution.

"The economic distress beginning at the last third of the century, which was the direct provocation of the Revolution, was very slight compared with that which had been the constant lot and ancient heritage of other nations. It represented merely the first turn or two of the screw by which capitalism in due time squeezed dry the masses always and everywhere. The unexampled space and richness of their new land had given Americans a century's respite from the universal fate. Those advantages had passed, the respite was ended, and the time had come when the people must adapt their necks to the yoke all peoples before had worn. But having grown high-spirited from so long an experience of comparative welfare, the Americans resisted the imposition, and, finding mere resistance vain, ended by making a revolution. That in brief is the whole story of the way the great Revolution came on in America. But while this might satisfy a languid twentieth-century curiosity as to a matter so remote in time, you will naturally want a little more detail. There is a particular chapter in Storiot's History of the Revolution explaining just how and why the growth of the power of capital provoked the great uprising, which deeply impressed me in my school days, and I don't think I can make a better use of a part of our short time than by reading a few paragraphs from it." . . .

[*These paragraphs, omitted here, recount in consid-erable detail the progress of plutocracy between the 1830s and the 1890s. They emphasize the development of permanent class divisions, the erosion of democratic government, and the im-mense disparities between rich and poor that were already recognized in serious economic studies published before 1897.*]

Chapter XXXV

WHY THE REVOLUTION WENT SLOW AT FIRST BUT FAST AT LAST

"So much for the causes of the Revolution in America, both the general fundamental cause, consisting in the factor newly introduced into social evolution by the enlightenment of the masses and irresistibly tending to equality, and the im-mediate local causes peculiar to America, which account for the Revolution having come at the particular time it did and for its taking the particular course it did. Now, briefly as to that course:

"The pinching of the economic shoe resulting from the concentration of wealth was naturally first felt by the class with least reserves, the wage-earners, and the Revolution may be said to have begun with their revolt. In 1869 the first great labor organization in America was formed to resist the power of capital. Previous to the war the number of strikes that had taken place in the country could be counted on the fingers. Before the sixties were out they were counted by hundreds, during the seventies by thousands, and during the eighties the labor reports enumerate nearly ten thousand, involving two or three million workers. Many of these strikes were of continental scope, shaking the whole commercial fabric and causing general panics.

"Close after the revolt of the wage earners came that of the farmers—less turbulent in methods but more serious and abiding in results. This took the form of secret leagues and open political parties devoted to resisting what was called the money power. Already in the seventies these organizations threw State and national politics into confusion, and later became the nucleus of the revolutionary party.

"Your contemporaries of the thinking classes can not be taxed with indifference to these signs and portents. The public discussion and literature of the time reflect the confusion and anxiety with which the unprecedented manifestations of popular discontent had affected all serious persons. The old-fashioned Fourth-of-July boastings had ceased to be heard in the land. All agreed that somehow republican forms of government had not fulfilled their promise as guarantees of the popular welfare, but were showing themselves impotent to prevent the recrudescence in the New World of all the Old World's evils, especially those of class and caste, which it had been supposed could never exist in the atmosphere of a republic. It was recognized on all sides that the old order was changing for the worse, and that the republic and all it had been thought to stand for was in danger. It was the universal cry that something must be done to check the ruinous tendency. Reform was the word in everybody's mouth, and the rallying cry, whether in sincerity or pretense, of every party. But indeed, Julian, I need waste no time describing this state of affairs to you, for you were a witness of it till 1887."

"It was all quite as you describe it, the industrial and political warfare and turmoil, the general sense that the country was going wrong, and the universal cry for some sort of reform. But, as I said before, the agitation, while alarming enough, was too confused and purposeless to seem revolutionary. All agreed that something ailed the country, but no two agreed what it was or how to cure it."

"Just so," said the doctor. "Our historians divide the entire revolutionary epoch—from the close of the war, or the beginning of the seventies, to the establishment of the present order early in the twentieth century—into two periods, the incoherent and the rational. The first of these is the period of which we have been talking, and with which Storiot deals . . . in the paragraphs I have read—the period with which you were, for the most part, contemporary. As we have seen, and you know better than we can, it was a time of terror and tumult, of confused and purposeless agitation, and a Babel of contradictory clamor. The people were blindly kicking in the dark against the pricks of capitalism, without any clear idea of what they were kicking against. . . .

[*At this point Dr. Leete presents a brief critique of late nineteenth-century nostrums and reforms, none of which was sufficiently fundamental to be relevant, and all of which were ineffectual against the power of organized wealth.*]

"Of the vast, anxious, and anguished volume of public discussion as to what should be done, what after twenty-five years had been the practical outcome? Absolutely nothing. If here and there petty reforms had been introduced, on the whole the power of the evils against which those reforms were directed had vastly increased. If the power of the plutocracy in 1873 had been as the little finger of a man, in 1895 it was thicker than his loins. Certainly, so far as superficial and material indications went, it looked as if the battle had been going thus far steadily, swiftly, and hopelessly against the people, and that the American capitalists who expended their millions in buying titles of nobility for their children were wiser in their generation than the children of light and better judges of the future.

"Nevertheless, no conclusion could possibly have been more mistaken. During these decades of apparently unvaried failure and disaster the revolutionary movement for the complete overthrow of private capitalism had made a progress which to rational minds should have presaged its complete triumph in the near future."

"Where had the progress been?" I said; "I dont see any."

"In the development among the masses of the people of the necessary revolutionary temper," replied the doctor; "in the preparation of the popular mind by the only process that could have prepared it, to accept the programme of a radical reorganization of the economic system from the ground up. A great revolution, you must remember, which is to profoundly change a form of society, must accumulate a tremendous moral force, an overwhelming weight of justification, so to speak, behind it before it can start. The processes by which and the period during which this accumulation of impulse is effected are by no means so spectacular as the events of the subsequent period when the revolutionary movement, having obtained an irresistible momentum, sweeps away like straws the obstacles that so long held it back only to swell its force and volume at last. But to the student the period of preparation is the more truly interesting and critical field of study. It was absolutely necessary that the American people, before they would seriously think of undertaking so tremendous a reformation as was implied in the substitution of public for private capitalism, should be fully convinced not by argument only, but by abundant bitter experience and convincing object lessons, that no remedy for the evils of the time less complete or radical would suffice. They must become convinced by numerous experiments that private capitalism had evolved to a point where it was impossible to amend it before they would listen to the proposition to end it. This painful but necessary experience the people were gaining during the earlier decades of the struggle. In this way the innumerable defeats, disappointments, and fiascoes which met their every effort at curbing and reforming the money power during the seventies, eighties, and early nineties, contributed far more than as many victories would have done to the magnitude and completeness of the final triumph of the people. It was indeed necessary that all these things should come to pass to make the Revolution possible. It was necessary that the system of private and class tyranny called private capitalism should fill up the measure of its iniquities and reveal all it was capable of, as the irreconcilable enemy of democracy, the foe of life and liberty and human happiness, in order to insure that degree of momentum to the coming uprising against it which was necessary to guarantee its complete and final overthrow. Revolutions which start too soon stop too soon, and the welfare of the race demanded that this revolution should not cease, nor pause, until the last vestige of the system by which men usurped power over the lives and liberties of their fellows through economic means was destroyed. Therefore not one outrage, not one act of oppression, not one exhibition of conscienceless rapacity, not one prostitution of power on the part of Executive, Legislature, or judiciary, not one tear of patriotic shame over the degradation of the national name, not one blow of the policeman's bludgeon, not a single bullet or bayonet thrust of the soldiery, could have been spared. Nothing but just this discipline of failure, disappointment, and defeat on the part of the earlier reformers could have educated the people to the necessity of attacking the system of private capitalism in its existence instead of merely in its particular manifestations.

"We reckon the beginning of the second part of the revolutionary movement to which we give the name of the coherent or rational phase, from the time when there became apparent a clear conception, on the part of at least a considerable body of the people, of the true nature of the issue as one between the rights of man and the principle of irresponsible power embodied in private capitalism, and the realization that its outcome, if the people were to triumph, must be the establishment of a wholly new economic system which should be based upon the public control in the public interest of the system of production and distribution hitherto left to private management." . . .

[*Here Dr. Leete elaborates the new social vision that controlled the development of the second revolution.*]

"If the reformers had been put in possession of press, pulpit, and university, which the capitalists controlled, whereby to set home their doctrine to the heart and mind and conscience of the nation, they would have converted and carried the country in a month.

"Feeling how quickly the day would be theirs if they could but reach the people, it was natural that they should chafe bitterly at the delay, confronted as they were by the spectacle of humanity daily crucified afresh and enduring an illimitable anguish which they knew was needless. Who indeed would not have been impatient in their place, and cried as they did, 'How long, O Lord, how long?' To men so situated, each day's postponement of the great deliverance might well have seemed like a century. Involved as they were in the din and dust of innumerable petty combats, it was as difficult for them as for soldiers in the midst of a battle to obtain an idea of the general course of the conflict and the operation of the forces which would determine its issue. To us, however, as we look back, the rapidity of the process by which during the nineties the American people were won over to the revolutionary programme seems almost miraculous, while as to the ultimate result there was, of course, at no time the slightest ground of question.

"From about the beginning of the second phase of the revolutionary movement, the literature of the times begins to reflect in the most extraordinary manner a wholly new spirit of radical protest against the injustices of the social order. Not only in the serious journals and books of public discussion, but in fiction and in belles-lettres, the subject of social reform becomes prominent and almost commanding. The figures that

have come down to us of the amazing circulation of some of
the books devoted to the advocacy of a radical social reorganization are almost enough in themselves to explain the revolution. The antislavery movement had one Uncle Tom's Cabin;
the anticapitalist movement had many.

"A particularly significant fact was the extraordinary
unanimity and enthusiasm with which the purely agricultural
communities of the far West welcomed the new gospel of a
new and equal economic system. In the past, governments had
always been prepared for revolutionary agitation among the
proletarian wage-earners of the cities, and had always counted
on the stolid conservatism of the agricultural class for the force
to keep the inflammable artisans down. But in this revolution
it was the agriculturists who were in the van. This fact alone
should have sufficiently foreshadowed the swift course and
certain issue of the struggle. At the beginning of the battle the
capitalists had lost their reserves.

"At about the beginning of the nineties the revolutionary
movement first prominently appears in the political field. For
twenty years after the close of the civil war the surviving animosities between North and South mainly determined party
lines, and this fact, together with the lack of agreement on a
definite policy, had hitherto prevented the forces of industrial
discontent from making any striking political demonstration.
But toward the close of the eighties the diminished bitterness
of feeling between North and South left the people free to
align themselves on the new issue, which had been steadily
looming up ever since the war, as the irrepressible conflict of
the near future—the struggle to the death between democracy
and plutocracy, between the rights of man and the tyranny of
capital in irresponsible hands.

"Although the idea of the public conduct of economic
enterprises by public agencies had never previously attracted
attention or favor in America, yet already in 1890, almost as
soon as it began to be talked about, political parties favoring
its application to important branches of business had polled

heavy votes. In 1892 a party, organized in nearly every State in the Union, cast a million votes in favor of nationalizing at least the railroads, telegraphs, banking system, and other monopolized businesses. Two years later the same party showed large gains, and in 1896 its platform was substantially adopted by one of the great historic parties of the country, and the nation divided nearly equally on the issue.

"The terror which this demonstration of the strength of the party of social discontent caused among the possessing class seems at this distance rather remarkable, seeing that its demands, while attacking many important capitalist abuses, did not as yet directly assail the principle of the private control of capital as the root of the whole social evil. No doubt, what alarmed the capitalists even more than the specific propositions of the social insurgents were the signs of a settled popular exasperation against them and all their works, which indicated that what was now called for was but the beginning of what would be demanded later. The antislavery party had not begun with demanding the abolition of slavery, but merely its limitation. The slaveholders were not, however, deceived as to the significance of the new political portent, and the capitalists would have been less wise in their generation than their predecessors had they not seen in the political situation the beginning of a confrontation of the people and the capitalists—the masses and the classes, as the expression of the day was—which threatened an economic and social revolution in the near future."

"It seems to me," I said, "that by this stage of the revolutionary movement American capitalists capable of a dispassionate view of the situation ought to have seen the necessity of making concessions if they were to preserve any part of their advantages."

"If they had," replied the doctor, "they would have been the first beneficiaries of a tyranny who in presence of a rising flood of revolution ever realized its force or thought of making concessions until it was hopelessly too late. You see, tyrants are always materialists, while the forces behind great revolutions are moral. That is why the tyrants never foresee their fate till it is too late to avert it."

"We ought to be in our chairs pretty soon," said Edith. "I don't want Julian to miss the opening scene."

"There are a few minutes yet," said the doctor, "and seeing that I have been rather unintentionally led into giving this sort of outline sketch of the course of the Revolution, I want to say a word about the extraordinary access of popular enthusiasm which made a short story of its later stages, especially as it is that period with which the play deals that we are to attend.

"There had been many, you must know, Julian, who, while admitting that a system of co-operation must eventually take the place of private capitalism in America and everywhere, had expected that the process would be a slow and gradual one, extending over several decades, perhaps half a century, or even more. Probably that was the more general opinion. But those who held it failed to take account of the popular enthusiasm which would certainly take possession of the movement and drive it irresistibly forward from the moment that the prospect of its success became fairly clear to the masses. Undoubtedly, when the plan of a nationalized industrial system, and an equal sharing of results, with its promise of the abolition of poverty and the reign of universal comfort, was first presented to the people, the very greatness of the salvation it offered operated to hinder its acceptance. It seemed too good to be true. With difficulty the masses, sodden in misery and inured to hopelessness, had been able to believe that in heaven there would be no poor, but that it was possible here and now in this everyday America to establish such an earthly paradise was too much to believe.

"But gradually, as the revolutionary propaganda diffused a knowledge of the clear and unquestionable grounds on which this great assurance rested, and as the growing majorities of the revolutionary party convinced the most doubtful that the hour of its triumph was at hand, the hope of the multitude grew into confidence, and confidence flamed into a resistless enthusiasm. By the very magnitude of the promise which at first appalled them they were now transported. An impassioned eagerness seized upon them to enter into the delectable land, so that they found every day's, every hour's delay intolerable. The young said, 'Let us make haste, and go in to the promised land while we are young, that we may know what living is'; and the old said, 'Let us go in ere we die, that we may close our eyes in peace, knowing that it will be well with our children after us.' The leaders and pioneers of the Revolution, after having for so many years exhorted and appealed to a people for the most part indifferent or incredulous, now found themselves caught up and borne onward by a mighty wave of enthusiasm which it was impossible for them to check, and difficult for them to guide, had not the way been so plain.

"Then, to cap the climax, as if the popular mind were not already in a sufficiently exalted frame, came 'The Great Revival,' touching this enthusiasm with religious emotion."

"We used to have what were called revivals of religion in my day," I said, "sometimes quite extensive ones. Was this of the same nature?"

"Scarcely," replied the doctor. "The Great Revival was a tide of enthusiasm for the social, not the personal, salvation, and for the establishment in brotherly love of the kingdom of God on earth which Christ bade men hope and work for. It was the general awakening of the people of America in the closing years of the last century to the profoundly ethical and truly religious character and claims of the movement for an industrial system which should guarantee the economic equality of all the people.

"Nothing, surely, could be more self-evident than the strictly Christian inspiration of the idea of this guarantee. It contemplated nothing less than a literal fulfillment, on a complete social scale, of Christ's inculcation that all should feel the same solicitude and make the same effort for the welfare of others as for their own. The first effect of such a solicitude must needs be to prompt effort to bring about an equal material provision for all, as the primary condition of welfare. One would certainly think that a nominally Christian people having some familiarity with the New Testament would have needed no one to tell them these things, but that they would have recognized on its first statement that the programme of the revolutionists was simply a paraphrase of the golden rule expressed in economic and political terms. One would have said that whatever other members of the community might do, the Christian believers would at once have flocked to the support of such a movement with their whole heart, soul, mind, and might. That they were so slow to do so must be ascribed to the wrong teaching and non-teaching of a class of persons whose express duty, above all other persons and classes, was to prompt them to that action—namely, the Christian clergy. . . .

[*A disquisition follows describing the failure of the churches and of most clergymen to recognize how changing circumstances necessitated the development of a new social ethic.*]

"The reformers of that time were most bitter against the clergy for their double treason to humanity and Christianity, in opposing instead of supporting the Revolution; but time has tempered harsh judgments of every sort, and it is rather with deep pity than with indignation that we look back on these unfortunate men, who will ever retain the tragic distinction of having missed the grandest opportunity of leadership ever offered to men. Why add reproach to the burden of such a failure as that?

"While the influence of ecclesiastical authority in America, on account of the growth of intelligence, had at this time greatly shrunken from former proportions, the generally unfavorable or negative attitude of the churches toward the programme of equality had told heavily to hold back the popular support which the movement might reasonably have expected from professedly Christian people. It was, however, only a question of time, and the educating influence of public discussion, when the people would become acquainted for themselves with the merits of the subject. 'The Great Revival' followed, when, in the course of this process of education, the masses of the nation reached the conviction that the revolution against which the clergy had warned them as unchristian was, in fact, the most essentially and intensely Christian movement that had ever appealed to men since Christ called his disciples, and as such imperatively commanded the strongest support of every believer or admirer of Christ's doctrine.

"The American people appear to have been, on the whole, the most intelligently religious of the large populations of the world—as religion was understood at that time—and the most generally influenced by the sentiment of Christianity. When the people came to recognize that the ideal of a world of equal welfare, which had been represented to them by the clergy as a dangerous delusion, was no other than the very dream of Christ; when they realized that the hope which led on the advocates of the new order was no baleful *ignis fatuus*, as the churches had taught, but nothing less nor other than the Star of Bethlehem, it is not to be wondered at that the impulse which the revolutionary movement received should have been overwhelming. From that time on it assumes more and more the character of a crusade, the first of the many so-called crusades of history which had a valid and adequate title to that name and right to make the cross its emblem. As the conviction took hold on the always religious masses that the plan of an equalized human welfare was nothing less than the divine design, and that in seeking their own·highest happiness by its adoption they were also fulfilling God's purpose for the race, the spirit of the Revolution became a religious enthusiasm. As to the preaching of Peter the Hermit, so now once more the masses responded to the preaching of the reformers with the exultant cry, 'God wills it!' and none doubted any longer that the vision would come to pass. So it was that the Revolution, which had begun its course under the ban of the churches, was carried to its consummation upon a wave of moral and religious emotion."

"But what became of the churches and the clergy when the people found out what blind guides they had been?" I asked.

"No doubt," replied the doctor, "it must have seemed to them something like the Judgment Day when their flocks challenged them with open Bibles and demanded why they had hid the Gospel all these ages and falsified the oracles of God which they had claimed to interpret. But so far as appears, the joyous exultation of the people over the great discovery that liberty, equality, and fraternity were nothing less than the practical meaning and content of Christ's religion seems to have left no room in their heart for bitterness toward any class. The world had received a crowning demonstration that was to remain conclusive to all time of the untrustworthiness of ecclesiastical guidance; that was all. The clergy who had failed in their office of guides had not done so, it is needless to say, because they were not as good as other men, but on account of the hopeless falsity of their position as the economic dependents of those they assumed to lead. As soon as the great revival had fairly begun they threw themselves into it as eagerly as any of the people, but not now with any pretensions of leadership. They followed the people whom they might have led.

"From the great revival we date the beginning of the era of modern religion—a religion which has dispensed with the rites and ceremonies, creeds and dogmas, and banished from this life fear and concern for the meaner self; a religion of life and conduct dominated by an impassioned sense of the solidarity of humanity and of man with God; the religion of a race that knows itself divine and fears no evil, either now or hereafter."

"I need not ask," I said, "as to any subsequent stages

of the Revolution, for I fancy its consummation did not tarry long after 'The Great Revival.' "

"That was indeed the culminating impulse," replied the doctor; "but while it lent a momentum to the movement for the immediate realization of an equality of welfare which no obstacle could have resisted, it did its work, in fact, not so much by breaking down opposition as by melting it away. The capitalists, as you who were one of them scarcely need to be told, were not persons of a more depraved disposition than other people, but merely, like other classes, what the economic system had made them. Having like passions and sensibilities with other men, they were as incapable of standing out against the contagion of the enthusiasm of humanity, the passion of pity, and the compulsion of humane tenderness which The Great Revival had aroused, as any other class of people. From the time that the sense of the people came generally to recognize that the fight of the existing order to prevent the new order was nothing more nor less than a controversy between the almighty dollar and the Almighty God, there was substantially but one side to it. A bitter minority of the capitalist party and its supporters seems indeed to have continued its outcry against the Revolution till the end, but it was of little importance. The greater and all the better part of the capitalists joined with the people in completing the installation of the new order which all had now come to see was to redound to the benefit of all alike."

"And there was no war?"

"War! Of course not. Who was there to fight on the other side? It is odd how many of the early reformers seem to have anticipated a war before private capitalism could be overthrown. They were constantly referring to the civil war in the United States and to the French Revolution as precedents which justified their fear, but really those were not analogous cases. In the controversy over slavery, two geographical sections, mutually impenetrable to each other's ideas were opposed and war was inevitable. In the French Revolu-

tion there would have been no bloodshed in France but for
the interference of the neighboring nations with their brutal
kings and brutish populations. The peaceful outcome of the
great Revolution in America was, moreover, potently favored
by the lack as yet of deep class distinctions, and consequently
of rooted class hatred. Their growth was indeed beginning to
proceed at an alarming rate, but the process had not yet gone
far or deep and was ineffectual to resist the glow of social
enthusiasm which in the culminating years of the Revolution
blended the whole nation in a common faith and purpose.

"You must not fail to bear in mind that the great Revolution, as it came in America, was not a revolution at all in
the political sense in which all former revolutions in the popular interest had been. In all these instances the people, after
making up their minds what they wanted changed, had to
overthrow the Government and seize the power in order to
change it. But in a democratic state like America the Revolution was practically done when the people had made up their
minds that it was for their interest. There was no one to dispute their power and right to do their will when once resolved
on it. The Revolution as regards America and in other countries,
in proportion as their governments were popular, was more
like the trial of a case in court than a revolution of the traditional blood-and-thunder sort. The court was the people, and
the only way that either contestant could win was by convi[n]c-
ing the court, from which there was no appeal.

"So far as the stage properties of the traditional revolution were concerned, plots, conspiracies, powder-smoke, blood
and thunder, any one of the ten thousand squabbles in the
mediæval, Italian, and Flemish towns, furnishes far more material to the romancer or playwright than did the great Revolution in America."

"Am I to understand that there was actually no violent
doings in connection with this great transformation?"

"There were a great number of minor disturbances and
collisions, involving in the aggregate a considerable amount of

violence and bloodshed, but there was nothing like the war with pitched lines which the early reformers looked for. Many a petty dispute, causeless and resultless, between nameless kings in the past, too small for historical mention, has cost far more violence and bloodshed than, so far as America is concerned, did the greatest of all revolutions."

"And did the European nations fare as well when they passed through the same crisis?"

"The conditions of none of them were so favorable to peaceful social revolution as were those of the United States, and the experience of most was longer and harder, but it may be said that in the case of none of the European peoples were the direful apprehensions of blood and slaughter justified which the earlier reformers seem to have entertained. All over the world the Revolution was, as to its main factors, a triumph of moral forces."

Index*

*Page numbers in parentheses are citations to notes by the editor.

THE AMERICAN HERITAGE SERIES

THE YOUNG NATION

Hamilton, Alexander *Papers on Public Credit, Commerce, and Finance* AHS 18 Samuel McKee, Jr., J. Harvie Williams

Jefferson, Thomas *The Political Writings of Thomas Jefferson: Representative Selections* AHS 9 Edward Dumbauld

Madison, James *The Political Thought of James Madison* AHS 39 Marvin Meyers

Gallatin, Albert *Selected Writings of Albert Gallatin* AHS 40 E. James Ferguson

The Government and the Economy, 1783–1861 AHS 65 Carter Goodrich

Marshall, John *John Marshall: Major Opinions and Other Writings* AHS 42 John P. Roche

Democracy, Liberty, and Property: The State Constitutional Conventions of the 1820's AHS 43 Merrill D. Peterson

THE MIDDLE PERIOD

Social Theories of Jacksonian Democracy: Representative Writings of the Period 1825–1850 AHS 1 Joseph L. Blau

Jacksonian Civilization: A Documentary History AHS 85 Edward Pessen

Channing, William Ellery *Unitarian Christianity and Other Essays* AHS 21 Irving H. Bartlett

The Writings of Justice Joseph Story AHS 45 Henry Steele Commager

Manifest Destiny AHS 48 Norman A. Graebner

Slavery in America AHS 66 Willie Lee Rose

The Antislavery Argument AHS 44 Jane and William Pease

Calhoun, John C. *A Disquisition on Government and Selections from the Discourse* AHS 10 C. Gordon Post

Lincoln, Abraham *The Political Thought of Abraham Lincoln* AHS 46 Richard Current

The Radical Republicans and Reconstruction, 1861–1870 AHS 47 Harold Hyman

THE LATE NINETEENTH CENTURY

Late Nineteenth Century American Liberalism AHS 26 Louis Filler

The Forging of American Socialism: Origins of the Modern Movement AHS 24 Howard H. Quint